W9-APL-637

PREVIEWS

SENIOR AUTHOR

Leo Fay

AUTHORS

Barbara D. Stoodt
Dorothy Grant Hennings
Joan M. Baker
Myron L. Coulter

Bilingual Materials
George A. González

The Riverside Publishing Company

Chicago ● Chamblee, Georgia ● Dallas, Texas ● Glendale, California ● Lawrenceville, New Jersey

Acknowledgments: We wish to thank the following publishers, authors, photographers, illustrators and agents for permission to use and adapt copyrighted materials.

"Adventures of a Boy in Vietnam" is abridged and adapted from pp. ix-xi, 43–51 in THE LAND I LOST: Adventures of a Boy in Vietnam by Huynh Quang Nhuong. Pictures by Vo-Dinh Mai. Illustrations p. 4, 44, opp. title page, 4 color cover art, logos, pp. 27, p. 10, p. 43. Text copyright ©1982 by Huynh Quang Nhuong. Illustrations copyright ©1982 by Vo-Dinh Mai. By permission of Harper & Row, Publishers, Inc.

"Alesia" is an adapted excerpt and eight photos from ALESIA by Eloise Greenfield and Alesia Revis, photos by Sandra Turner. Text copyright ©1981 by Eloise Greenfield and Alesia Revis. Photographs Copyright ©1981 by Sandra Turner Bond. Reprinted by permission of Philomel Books. Also by permission of Curtis Brown Ltd.

"Alice Yazzie's Year" and four illustrations from ALICE YAZZIE'S YEAR by Ramona Maher, illustrations by Stephen Gammell. Text copyright ©1977 by Ramona Maher. Excerpt and adaptation of Carl N. Gorman's notes by permission of Ramona Maher Weeks. Illustrations by permission of Coward, McCann & Geoghegan.

"All Things Wise and Wonderful" is from ALL THINGS WISE AND WONDERFUL by James Herriot. Copyright ©1976, 1977 by James Herriot. Reprinted by permission of the publisher, St. Martin's Press, Inc., Harold Ober Associates Inc. and David Higham Associates, Ltd.

"All You've Ever Wanted" from SMOKE FROM CROMWELL'S TIME AND OTHER STORIES by Joan Aiken. Copyright ©1970 by Joan Aiken. Reprinted by permission of Brandt and Brandt, the author, and Jonathan Cape Ltd.

"Analysis of Baseball" from NEW AND SELECTED THINGS TAKING PLACE by May Swenson. Copyright ©1971 by May Swenson. By permission of Little, Brown and Company in association with the Atlantic Monthly Press.

"And What Do You Do?" is adapted from AND WHAT DO YOU DO? text and photographs by George Ancona. Copyright ©1976 by George Ancona. Reprinted by permission of the publisher, E. P. Dutton, Inc.

"As still as a flower" is from MY OWN RHYTHM by Ann Atwood. Copyright ©1973 by Ann Atwood. Reprinted by permission of the author.

"The Beastly Creature and the Magical Flower" is adapted from the story of that name in MEXICAN FOLK TALES by Juliet Piggott. Copyright ©1973 Juliet Piggott. Reprinted with the permission of Charles Scribner's Sons and Frederick Muller, Ltd.

"Behind the Scenes at the Amusement Park" is adapted from BEHIND THE SCENES AT THE AMUSEMENT PARK (text only) by Elizabeth Van Steenwyk. Copyright ©1983 by Elizabeth Van Steenwyk. Adapted by permission of Albert Whitman & Company.

"Bet You Can't! Science Impossibilities to Fool You" is an adaptation of pp. 9–10, 13–15, 19, 21, 27, 32–34, and 40–41 in BET YOU CAN'T! SCIENCE IMPOSSIBILITIES TO FOOL YOU by Vicki Cobb and Kathy Darling. Copyright ©1980 by Vicki Cobb and Kathy Darling. By permission of Lothrop, Lee & Shepard Books (A Division of William Morrow & Co.)

"The Black Stallion" is from THE BLACK STALLION by Walter Farley. Copyright ©1941 and renewed 1969 by Walter Farley. Reprinted by permission of Random House, Inc. and ICM.

"Catalog" by Rosalie Moore from *The New Yorker*, May 25, 1940. Copyright ©1940, 1968 The New Yorker Magazine, Inc. Reprinted by permission.

"A Colorful Symphony" and "Dischord and Dynne" are adapted from THE PHANTOM TOLLBOOTH by Norton Juster. Copyright ©1961 by Norton Juster. Adapted by permission of Random House, Inc. and Collins Publishers, London.

"Courage Isn't Something You're Born With" is adapted from SKITTERBRAIN by Irene Bennett Brown. Copyright ©1978 by Irene Bennett Brown. Reprinted by permission of the publisher, E. P. Dutton, Inc.

"Daedalus and Icarus" is adapted from THE GOLDEN TREASURY OF MYTHS AND LEGENDS by Anne Terry White. Copyright ©1959 by Western Publishing Company, Inc. Reprinted by permission.

"Daydreamers" is from DAYDREAMERS by Eloise Greenfield and Tom Feelings. Text copyright ©1981 by Eloise Greenfield; illustrations copyright ©1981 by Tom Feelings. Reprinted by permission of the publishers, Dial Books for Young Readers, a Division of E. P. Dutton, Inc. and Curtis Brown, Ltd.

"Desert Person" from DESERT VOICES by Byrd Baylor and Peter Parnall. Text copyright ©1981 by Byrd Baylor; illustrations copyright ©1981 by Peter Parnall. Reprinted with the permission of Charles Scribner's Sons.

CONTENTS

THIS GROWING TIME 103

"A Dream About the Man in the Moon" is from "A Dream About the Man in the Moon" from YOU READ TO ME, I'LL READ TO YOU by John Ciardi (J. B. Lippincott Co.) Copyright ©1962 by John Ciardi. By permission of Harper & Row, Publishers, Inc.

"Earl" is from WON'T KNOW TILL I GET THERE by Walter Dean Myers. Copyright ©1982 by Walter Dean Myers. Adapted by permission of Viking Penguin Inc. and Harriet Wasserman Literary Agency.

"Finn Magic" is from THE MAID OF THE NORTH by Ethel Johnston Phelps. Copyright ©1981 by Ethel Johnston Phelps. Reprinted by permission of Holt, Rinehart and Winston, Publishers.

"Georgia O'Keeffe: An Artist Looks at Nature" is from CONTRIBUTIONS OF WOMEN: ART by Carol Fowler. Dillon Press, Inc., Minneapolis, MN 55415. Reprinted by permission of the publisher.

"The Glad Man" is adapted from THE GLAD MAN by Gloria Gonzalez. Copyright ©1975 by Gloria Gonzalez. Adpated by permission of Alfred A. Knopf, Inc.

"The Grand Tour of the Planets" is adapted from "The Grand Tour of the Planets" from SKY ABOVE AND WORLDS BEYOND. Copyright ©1983 Judith Herbst. Reprinted with the permission of Atheneum Publishers and Bertha Klausner International Literary Agency, Inc.

"The Great Brain and the Dude" is adapted from THE GREAT BRAIN DOES IT AGAIN by John D. Fitzgerald. Copyright ©1975 by John D. Fitzgerald. Reprinted by permission of the publisher, Dial Books for Young Readers, a Division of E. P. Dutton, Inc. and Ann Elmo Agency.

"The Great Persian Horse Race" by Ruth Hume is reprinted by permission of Paul Hume. This appeared originally in *Cricket*, July 1982.

"Harry's Joke" is adapted from APPLE IS MY SIGN by Mary Riskind. Copyright ©1981 by Mary Riskind. Reprinted by permission of Houghton Mifflin Company.

"Hidden Heroines: Women of the West" is from HIDDEN HEROINES: WOMEN IN AMERICAN HISTORY by Elaine Landau. Copyright ©1975 by Elaine Landau. Reprinted by permission of Julian Messner, a division of Simon & Schuster, Inc.

"How to Tell a Joke" is adapted from HOW TO BE FUNNY by Jovial Bob Stine. Copyright ©1978 by Jovial Bob Stine. Reprinted by permission of the publisher, E. P. Dutton, Inc.

"The Hunter Who Wanted Air" is from VOICES IN THE WIND by Alex Whitney. Copyright ©1976 by Alex Whitney. Published by David McKay Company, Inc. and reprinted with their permission.

"The Incredible Shrinking Moon" by Richard Berry and Robert Burnham is from *Odyssey Magazine*, May 1983. Copyright ©1983 by Astro Media Corp. and reprinted with their permission.

"The Keynote Clue" by Kristen Randlev Morsy is from CHILD LIFE magazine. Copyright ©1977 by The Saturday Evening Post Company, Indianapolis, Indiana. Adapted by permission of the publisher.

"Lady Merida" is from STORIES FROM THE BLUE ROAD by Emily Crofford. Copyright ©1982 by Emily Crofford. Published by Carolrhoda Books, Inc., Minneapolis, and used with their permission.

"Lenny Kandell, Smart Aleck" is from LENNY KANDELL, SMART ALECK by Ellen Conford. Copyright ©1983 by Ellen Conford. By permission of Little, Brown and Company and McIntosh and Otis, Inc.

"Lineage" is from FOR MY PEOPLE by Margaret Walker. Published by Yale University Press, 1942. Copyright by Margaret Walker and reprinted by permission of the author.

"The Long Hungry Night" is an excerpt from THE LONG HUNGRY NIGHT by E. C. Foster & Slim Williams. Copyright ©1973 by E. C. Foster and Slim Williams. Reprinted with the permission of Atheneum Publishers.

"Magdalena" is adapted from MAGDALENA by Louisa R. Shotwell. Copyright ©1971 by Louisa R. Shotwell. Reprinted by permission of Viking Penguin Inc. and Lester Lewis Associates.

"Magic and the Night River" is an abridgement of the text of MAGIC AND THE NIGHT RIVER by Eve Bunting and also includes illustrations by Allen Say from the book. Text copyright ©1978 by Eve Bunting. Illustrations copyright ©1978 by Allen Say. Illustrations from pp. 6, 19, 27, 35. By permission of Harper & Row, Publishers, Inc.

"The Man Who Loved to Laugh" is adapted from PLAYS FROM AFRICAN FOLKTALES by Carol Korty. Copyright ©1969, 1975 Carol Korty. Reprinted with the permission of Charles Scribner's Sons. By permission also of Alice Bach.

"Maybe Next Year . . . " is adapted from MAYBE NEXT YEAR . . . by Amy Hest. Copyright ©1982 by Amy Hest. Reprinted by permission of Ticknor & Fields/Clarion Books, a Houghton Mifflin Company.

"Moon Trivia" is an adaptation of "Moon Trivia" from SKY ABOVE AND WORLDS BEYOND by Judith Herbst. Copyright ©1983 Judith Herbst. Reprinted with the permission of Atheneum Publishers. Also by permission of Bertha Klausner International Literary Agency, Inc.

"The Mother's Song" is from THE BOOK OF ESKIMOS by Peter Freuchen. Copyright ©1961 by Peter Freuchen. Reprinted by permission of Harold Matson Company, Inc.

"Mrs. Frisby and the Rats of NIMH" is from MRS. FRISBY AND THE RATS OF NIMH by Robert C. O'Brien. Copyright ©1971 by Robert C. O'Brien. With permission of John Schaffner Associates, Inc.

"Nature's Champions" is adapted from NATURE'S CHAMPIONS by Alvin and Virginia Silverstein. Copyright ©1980 by Alvin and Virginia Silverstein. Adapted by permission of Random House, Inc.

"The Night of the Leonids" is from ALTOGETHER, ONE AT A TIME by E. L. Konigsburg. Copyright ©1971 by E. L. Konigsburg. Reprinted with the permission of Atheneum Publishers.

"The Nit Nowns" is adapted from THE GIFT-GIVER by Joyce Hansen. Copyright ©1980 by Joyce Hansen. Reprinted by permission of Ticknor & Fields/Clarion Books, a Houghton Mifflin Company.

"Pair Skating" is adapted from THE WORLD BOOK ENCYCLOPEDIA. Copyright ©1984 by World Book, Inc. By permission of World Book, Inc.

"Pluto" is from TEMPLE INTO TIME by Sansoucy North. Copyright ©1977 by Sansoucy North. Published by Commoner's Books and reprinted with their permission.

"Quiet cardinal . . . " is from FAT POLKA-DOT CAT AND OTHER HAIKU by Betsy Maestro. Copyright ©1976 by Betsy Maestro. Reprinted by permission of the publisher, E. P. Dutton, Inc.

Illustration: GINGER BROWN 374 RICHARD BROWN 384-391 PENNY CARTER 420, 421, 423, 425, 428-432 DAVID CELSI 129, 130, 132-135, 139, 141, 142, 480-484 BRADLEY CLARK 378, 380, 381 FLOYD COOPER 31, 32, 34-41, 249, 250, 252, 257 CAROLYN CROLL 554-576 HELEN DAVIE 184, 185, 189, 190, 192 LINDA DeVITO 300, 303, 305-307, 311, 312, 314, 453-455, 457, 460, 461 NANCY DIDION 51, 52, 54-57, 59-69, 511-513, 515, 518, 521, 522, 524, 525 JULIE EVANS 319, 322, 326, 327, 494, 526 SHELLY FRESHMAN 62-67, 69-71 JEREMY GUITAR 209-211, 260, 261, 268 MIA IACONI 495, 497, 500, 502, 505, 510 JAN NAIMO JONES 400, 402, 406, 408, 411, 413, 416, 419 CHRISTA KIEFFER 392-394, 396-398 ELLIOT KRELOFF 30, 154-157, 441, 443-451 RON LIEBERMAN 13, 287 ANITA LOVITT 43-45, 119, 125-127, 236, 237, 240, 241, 243, 246, 247 MICHELE NOISET 73-76, 78-80, 82, 85 BEVERLY PARDEE 145, 148, 149, 151 JIM PEARSON 86-101 TOM POWERS 47, 291 JOHN RICE 223, 225, 228, 231, 232 ROGER ROTH 105, 106, 109, 112, 116, 118 CLAUDIA KARABAIC SARGENT 197, 270-273, 284, 462, 463, 465 ROD SHOPIS 46, 328-330, 332, 333, 336, 337, 340, 341 MARTI SHOHET 258, 259 LAURA SMITH 103, 383 SANDRA SPEIDEL 159, 160, 162, 163, 165, 167, 360, 361, 364, 368, 371, 372 KRYSTYNA STASIAK 435-437, 439, 440 ARVIS STEWART 344, 345, 348, 351, 356-358 MOU SIEN TENG 466-478, 470, 472, 475, 476, 578 GEORGE ULRICH 289, 293, 296

Photography: ANIMALS ANIMALS 210 BLACK STAR ED LALLO 126 BRUCE COLEMAN HANS REINHARD 214 BOTH DUOMO DAN HELMS 527 EARTH SCENES JOHN GERARD 216 STOUFFER PRODUCTIONS 219 L.L.T. RHODES 217 COURTESY HIRSCH AND ADLER GALLERIES 263 TOP RIGHT THE GRANGER COLLECTION 294 PHILIPPE HALSMAN, *LIFE* MAGAZINE, 1949 265 THE METROPOLITAN MUSEUM OF ART, GIFT OF DAVID A SCHULTE, 1928 263 TOP LEFT NASA 15-27, 29 NEBRASKA STATE HISTORICAL SOCIETY, THE SOLOMON E. BUTCHER COLLECTION 491 PHOTO RESEARCHERS RUSSE KINNE 212 UPI/BETTMAN NEWSPHOTOS 263 BOTTOM, 265 BOTTOM RIGHT, 390, 533 WOODFIN CAMP AND ASSOCIATES DAN BUDNICK 268 YERKES OBSERVATORY 28

Cover Art: Tom Powers / Mulvey Associates

Printed in the U.S.A.

ISBN: 0-8292-4106-X

CDEFG-VH-89876

LIVING WITH NATURE 197

CONNECTIONS 287

SET IN MOTION 383

How to Learn New Words

1. Look at the letters in the word.

2. Think of the sound clues.

3. Use the sentence clues.

4. Read the word.

How to Read for Meaning

1. Set a purpose for reading.

2. Think about what you already know.

3. Read the selection.

4. Answer the purpose question.

5. Apply the information.

UNIT 1

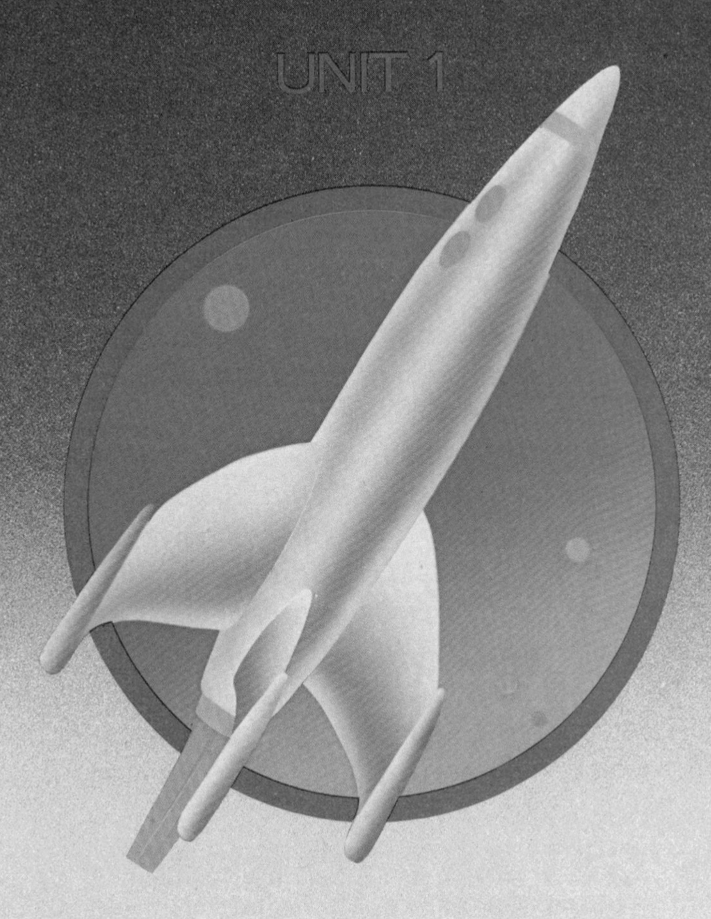

Out of This World

LEARN NEW WORDS

1. Scientists who study the stars and the planets are called **astronomers.**
2. The earth spins on its **axis**, an imaginary line running through the North and South poles.
3. The science fiction story described **cosmic** explosions taking place far beyond our solar system.
4. In the past, meteors have hit the surface of the moon, leaving deep, hollow **craters** behind.
5. We found the **diameter** of the circle by placing a ruler across the center of the circle and measuring from one side to the other.
6. The imaginary line that goes around the middle of the earth is called the **equator**.
7. My cousin says last summer was hot enough to make all the water in the pond **evaporate**.
8. The heat from the fire was so **intense** that the iron railings on the steps melted.
9. Rock or metal in a hot, liquid state is said to be **molten**.
10. Scientists have sent space **probes** to most of the planets to take photographs and gather information.

GET SET TO READ

What would a voyage to the planets be like? What would you see and learn on such a trip?

Listen as your guide takes you on a grand tour of the planets. Find out why there's no place quite like home.

The Grand Tour of the Planets

by JUDITH HERBST

Welcome to the vacation trip of your life. In the next several pages you will be visiting our spectacular solar system. Unpack your imagination, stretch your mind, and sit back and enjoy the flight.

Mercury—The First Stop

It is almost morning, but here the sky is still cold and black. The surface temperature is −280°F and would flash-freeze a person in less than a second. The gray, powdery soil is bone-dry. Deep craters scar the surface.

This is Mercury, a tiny planet sitting dangerously close to the fiery jaws of the sun. Mercury is a world that might have been dreamed up during a nightmare. Every three Earth months, it is alternately baked and frozen.

Mariner 10 took this photo of Mercury's surface. Like our moon, Mercury has many craters believed to have been caused by meteor strikes in the planet's distant past.

Mercury flies around the sun in just under eighty-eight Earth days, yet it takes fifty-nine days to make one turn on its axis. These two odd movements combine in an unusual way to give Mercury a day that lasts almost as long as its year. Its day is a very strange one, too, as we shall soon see.

Sunrise is now upon us. Suddenly, the monster sun awakes and lifts its enormous head. It fills the sky, turning the blackness to orange. The temperature starts to climb—50° . . . 100° . . . 500°F. It is hot enough on Mercury to bake pizza. Just as the sun clears the tops of the crater walls, it stops suddenly and hangs motionless in the sky. Then, as if it has changed its mind, it begins to sink below the horizon. There is another sunset, and the temperature thunders downward.

We hold our breaths. Night is returning! But no, the sun rises again, and this time it is for real, growing larger with every hour. At midday, Mercury is 800°F, baking in the sizzling sun.

No moon has ever been found for Mercury. And as far as we from Earth can tell, there is no life there either. Scientists believe that for life to develop there must be water. There is no water anywhere on Mercury—just the dead volcanoes that once spilled out liquid rock and poisonous gases.

Venus—Beneath the Veil

When I see Venus against the lavender horizon of morning, I cannot believe my eyes. But what I see, what we all see, is just a heavy veil that Venus hides behind. This planet leads a secret life far below the layers of poisonous clouds.

Our ship is now sixty miles above the surface and falling fast. From here, Venus looks like a yellow fuzzy ball.

At fifty-seven miles we drop through a strange fog, the highest level of the clouds. Then we drop suddenly, engines-first, into the swirling clouds below, knowing that the mounting heat and pressures could squeeze our ship into a molten mass.

At the thirty-eight-mile level the clouds have become frighteningly thick. They are deadly poison, made up mostly of sulfuric

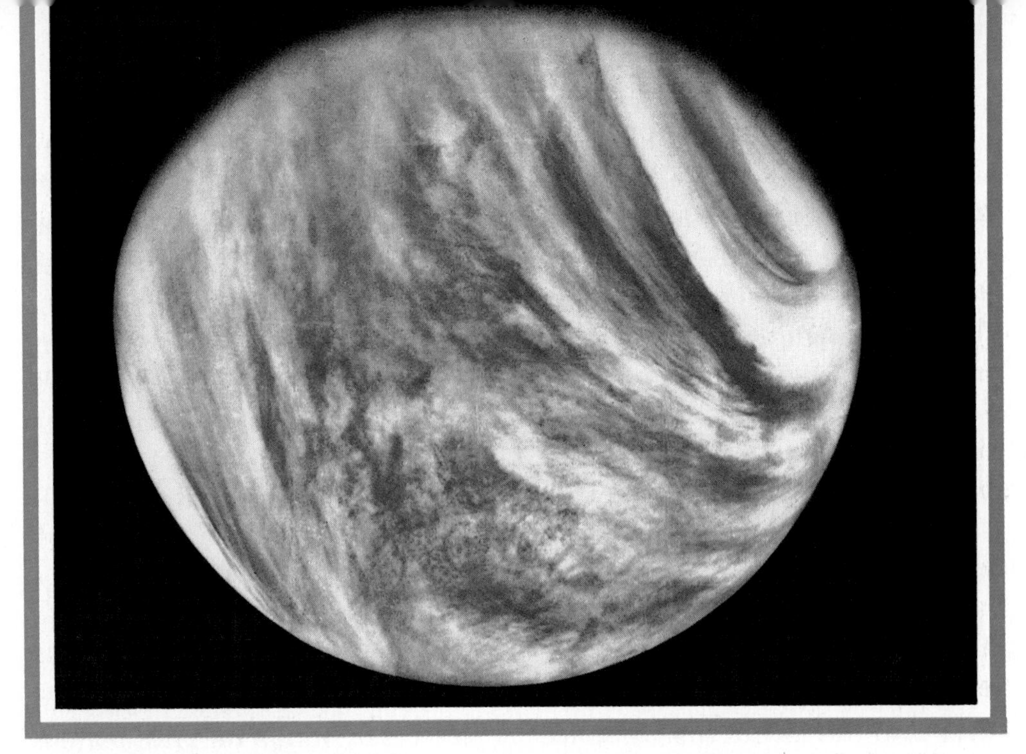

Clouds cover most of Venus. The dark swirls show their speedy rotation.

acid. The temperature is well over 300°F and rises as we sink deeper into the gas soup.

Now the acid forms drops, and they begin to stream down like rain. The rain continues for many miles before the heat becomes so intense that the drops evaporate.

At thirty miles the clouds thin out and we enter Venus's true atmosphere. No person can breathe this mixture of gases, which is mostly made up of carbon dioxide. The temperature is 400°F and still climbing.

At twelve miles we see a strange glow, and at six miles we are blinded by lightning flashes. The temperature is now nearly 900°F, and the pressure is ninety times that felt on Earth.

We touch down on the surface and feel a gentle breeze. It is the movement of carbon dioxide. It sweeps along at just four feet a second, so it is not strong enough to wear away rocks the way Earth winds do. Instead, surface features on Venus are eaten away by acids in the atmosphere.

Only through magic are we able to step out of our ship and walk across the landscape, but without radar eyes we can see very little. The heavy clouds block out nearly all the sun's light, and we find ourselves standing in the middle of a thick fog. Even though we can't see very far on Venus, we know that there are mountains, valleys, and great sunken areas that look like waterless oceans.

Venus has no moons and so travels its orbit alone. It is just over two-thirds Earth's distance from the sun. Since it is closer than Earth, it takes less time to make one complete orbit—about 225 days. This is Venus's year.

Venus rotates once on its axis in 243 Earth days, which makes its day longer than its year. Even crazier, instead of turning counterclockwise, the usual direction, the planet turns clockwise so that the sun appears to rise in the west and set in the east!

Venus specializes in being mysterious. It allows us a few pictures and a few answers. No matter how hard we try, many secrets of Venus remain, jealously guarded by the planet beneath the veil.

Most space probes burn up before they can land on Venus. One probe, however, lasted long enough to send back this photo of its rocky landing site.

Earth—From Sea to Shining Sea

"Giant marble rising on right side! Prepare to cut engines on three. One . . . two . . . three, shutdown!"

We drift silently over a white whirlpool forming in the North Pacific Ocean. Between patches of white we can see vast blue, green, and brown areas. This heavenly marble is planet Earth, and its colors set it apart from every other known world. They are the colors of water, the liquid of life.

Here is Earth as it looked to the Apollo 17 astronauts. Antarctica is at the bottom, and you can trace parts of the coastline of Africa.

The earth has freestanding water because of the planet's special place in the solar system. At 93 million miles from its parent star, Earth receives just the right amount of heat and light. If it had been a little bit closer, all the oceans would have evaporated, leaving behind a hot, airless desert. A few million miles further from the sun and Earth's water would be frozen solid. Instead, Earth held onto this precious fluid, and from the seas and creeks and streams and ponds came the ingredients that maintain life.

"Prepare to break from Earth orbit. Course correction fire at zero nine hundred. Fifty-eight . . . fifty-nine . . . and go! We have a clean engine burn. Nice work everyone. Thanks for your help. Next stop, Mars."

Mars—Red, Dusty, and Fascinating

Mars is by far the most fascinating of all the planets. Only Mars changes colors from season to season, just as Earth does. At the poles there are two obvious ice caps that grow during the Martian winter and shrink during the Martian summer. Its day is about forty minutes longer than ours, and in midsummer Mars registers the same temperature as Caribou, Maine. Here is a planet that is so much like Earth, we cannot help wondering why there are no Martians.

We land on the Martian surface with ease. There is no heavy atmosphere to crush us, no sizzling temperature to fry us. Mars's atmosphere is very thin and made up mostly of carbon dioxide. During the day, Mars is a comfortable 50°F at the equator and a rather chilly −110°F at the poles, but this second reading is still within life range. The lowest temperature ever recorded on Earth was −126°F in Antarctica. Mars at night is quite another story, however. Its weak atmosphere is not able to hold the sun's heat, and Mars gets unbearably cold. Even though our spacesuits keep us warm, we hurry to the protection of the Mars Lodge.

The Lodge has windows on all sides so we can see the Martian moons. The moons are little more than chunks of rock, pitted with craters and shaped strangely like potatoes.

At dawn we awake to the wild beauty that is Mars. We look out the windows at a salmon-pink sky and rusty red landscape. The sun is much smaller than it would be when seen from Earth, but it is still large enough to cast long shadows. We put on our air packs and head out across the Martian desert.

Like Mercury and the moon, Mars has craters, vast plains, basins, and volcanoes. The largest volcano is Olympus Mons. It is so big that it makes Earth's Hawaiian Islands look like anthills. The base of Olympus Mons goes on and on for 370 miles.

The volcanoes are dead now but once, long, long ago, they were very much alive. They spilled their flaming lava until an exhausted Mars finally fell silent. Now the great champion Olympus Mons is just a shell.

Small amounts of water have been found in the atmosphere of Mars and on its surface. The polar caps, for instance, are mostly water ice. The rocks show

Mars at last! It's so much like an Earth desert, you almost expect to see a couple of backpackers hiking up over the horizon.

signs of wearing away that would be produced by running water. We also have strong evidence that even more water is trapped underground. And there is always snow for the Martian Christmas. In winter, a thick layer of frost blankets the ground.

Is it possible that long ago the dry Martian dust was wet, glistening mud? Perhaps all the water has turned to ice, trapped in the jaws of an ice age. Perhaps Mars is only waiting for the past warmth to return.

Jupiter—Hydrogen Monster

We are 480 million miles from the sun, and there is a monster outside our starship. The monster's faintly glowing body bathes the cabin in a ghostly orange light. We drift south, and a huge red eye slowly rises over the edge of the window. The eye stares blindly at us. Its threatening white lid churns in knots and eddies. There is no mistaking this frightening planet. It is the hydrogen monster Jupiter. With a diameter of more than 88,000 miles, it is by far the largest of the nine planets.

Don't expect to land and step out onto a rocky surface. Here all is swirling gas and raging storms above an ocean of liquid hydrogen 18,000 miles deep. We could try to look into Jupiter's heart, but it would do no good. The temperature and pressure of the wild atmosphere would destroy our equipment long before it could radio back information. Instead, we have to guess that thousands of miles down lies a molten core of rock.

I have shifted our ship into satellite drive so we can circle Jupiter like a moon. If you look out the window on your left, you will see something that nobody has ever seen before—Jupiter's upper atmosphere. This is weather gone crazy. The colorful winds and graceful eddies are really mad storms. Some are large enough to swallow the Earth whole. The average wind speed is 330 miles an hour. Back home we would call that a tornado.

But the thing that grabs our attention most is the Great Red Spot. Its shape is a flowing oval

This picture of Jupiter was taken from four million miles up. The small curls are windstorms, and the swirl on the right is the famous red spot.

about 25,000 miles in length. (That's three Earth diameters!) Its color is most often screaming orange, but the spot has been seen to pale until it is almost invisible. What is this creepy eye on the face of the hydrogen monster?

Our best guess is that the Great Red Spot is a stormy whirlpool. For some reason, material in the deeper layers is swirling upward. Why this should happen in only one place on Jupiter is a mystery. In fact, scientists are trying to figure out why it is happening at all.

Maybe it's too eerie to look out the left window, but you won't find it much better on the other side. The scene there is total chaos. Jupiter is circled by a thin ring of thousands and thousands of fine particles. This ring is believed to stretch all the way to the planet, so we are in the thick of what seems like a hailstorm.

A little farther out lie Jupiter's weird family of moons. At last count there were sixteen, but keep your eyes peeled. You may spot others. We must leave Jupiter now, but we'll return sometime in the near future. If you think Jupiter has given up all its secrets, you're dead wrong.

Saturn—Cosmic Speedway

This planet needs no introduction. It's the one that brings oohs and ahs when viewed through a telescope. From a million miles away, Saturn is beautiful—pale, glorious, and ringed by a halo of gold. But up close, Saturn with its rings is a wild cosmic speedway. Come on. I'll show you.

Saturn is made up of most of the same gases as Jupiter. The upper atmosphere is an unbelievably cold −285°F but the temperature and pressure rise quickly the deeper you go. Thousands of miles in, the gas becomes a molten, sticky goo.

Saturn looks like a yellow ball of fuzz through the telescope. As we draw nearer, however, the fuzz turns out to be a kind of fog fifty miles thick. Beneath the fog are clouds that are churned by gases rising from deep inside. To make the nightmare even worse, Saturn's winds are four times as fast as Jupiter's. They whip around the planet at over 1100 miles an hour!

But we are only on the outskirts of the speedway. It gets

The rings of Saturn cast a shadow on the planet's cloudy surface. Also shown in this artist's view are six of Saturn's known satellites.

wilder and much more crowded the farther away from Saturn we go. Saturn's rings number in the hundreds. Each one is actually billions of ice chunks, and all the chunks race around Saturn in their own private orbits. Saturn also has at least seventeen moons. Most of them are under 300 miles in diameter, and five circle very close to the rings.

In airless space there are no sounds, no roar of engines, no squeal of brakes. The Saturn racers fly on silently, as we move on our way.

Uranus—Rings and Bull's Eye

We have been wandering in the desert of space for ten years. That's roughly how long it takes us to go from Saturn to Uranus. Our speed is 10,000 miles an hour. Since escaping Saturn, our journey has been a lonely one. But now we are one billion miles out, and at last our goal is in view. We drift closer. Slowly Uranus grows in size until it has become an emerald-green globe.

There is a lot of excitement aboard. Any minute we expect to enter the mysterious Uranian rings. Some say there are nine very thin rings orbiting the planet. They would be mostly dust grains and tiny chips of ice. Others believe the rings are not solid particles at all. Uranus may be circled by bracelets of gas!

We're coming at Uranus from the same direction as we approached all the other planets. And yet, Uranus shows us the top of its head instead of its waist. Our ship is heading directly for Uranus's north pole, right through the middle of the ring band! *What's going on here?*

Uranus is truly unique. All the other planets spin on their axes very much like dancers twirling. But Uranus's axis is so tilted that the planet spins on its side, as though it's rolling over in its sleep. Astronomers don't know if Uranus was always that way or if something happened to knock it off its feet.

Uranus is an ugly mess of a planet. It is smaller than its cousins Jupiter and Saturn, but

An artist drew this picture of what Uranus looks like with its north pole facing the sun. The rings of Uranus and its moons all circle around the planet's equator.

it's the same frozen combination of gases. The temperature in the upper clouds is about −340°F. The core is molten hot and probably rocky. So after all these years of traveling, there is still no place to land our ship.

The first of Uranus's family of five moons is about 81,000 miles out. From its surface, Uranus is enormous, and at full planetrise, Uranus fills the entire sky. The sun, nearly two billion miles away, looks about as bright as Venus does from Earth.

All the moons and rings orbit Uranus in the same plane. If you picture the system as a bow-and-arrow target, Uranus is the bull's eye. Its rings are the twenty-five-point circle. The first moon's orbit is the next circle, and so on. The orbit of the furthest is the outermost circle. Uranus's tilted orbit even means that the target is standing upright.

Without more information about Uranus, there's no reason to linger. We have at least a ten-year trip ahead of us, so we really ought to be on our way.

Neptune and Pluto—In and Out

There is a cosmic wrestling match going on some three billion miles from the sun. The contestants are not evenly paired at all, so one of them has taken to cheating. In Ring Eight is Neptune, a planet nearly four times Earth's size. In Ring Nine is the challenger Pluto, a small rocky world not even 5000 miles in diameter.

Every 164 Earth years, Neptune makes one long, slow orbit around the sun. Pluto takes even more time, 248 years. Understandably, Pluto is jealous of Neptune's inner position, and so it has come up with a sneaky plan whereby it can become the eighth planet. Cleverly, Pluto wrestles Neptune into the ninth position and forces it to remain there for twenty years. But Pluto has to cheat in order to carry this off. Here's how Pluto does it.

Imagine all the planets unwinding golden strings as they orbit the sun. What you see are eight ovals of about the same shape, one inside the other. Pluto, however, does not form a ninth oval. Pluto's orbit is slanted with respect to the others.

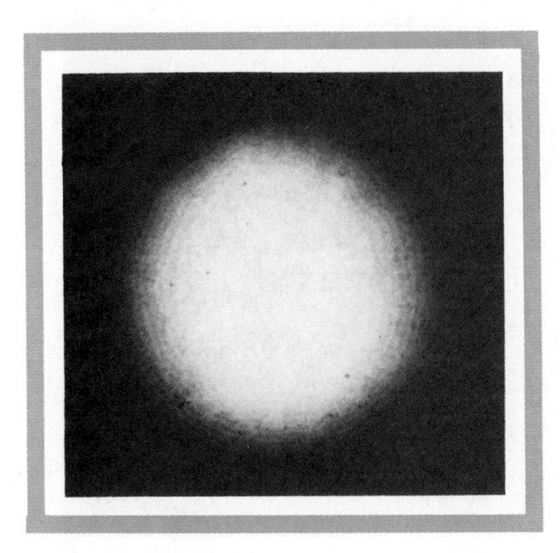

Here's what Neptune looks like through a large telescope.

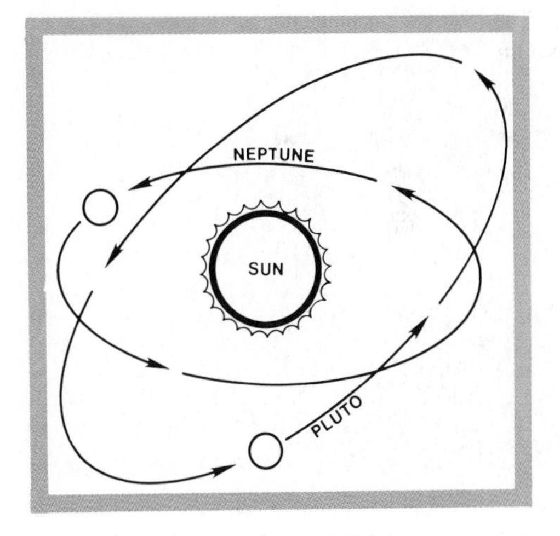

Pluto crosses Neptune's orbit twice, becoming the eighth planet of the solar system for about twenty Earth years.

Because of this tilt, Pluto's orbit is able to cross Neptune's orbit. Pluto can move inside the orbit of Neptune and wind up closer to the sun. Pluto stays inside for twenty years and then crosses back outside to become the ninth planet again.

Neptune, of course, is helpless to do anything about Pluto's cheating. In fact, Neptune may have caused Pluto to cheat in the first place. Some astronomers believe that Pluto was once a moon of Neptune.

Neptune is much like its three neighbors—Jupiter, Saturn, and Uranus. Following the pattern, Pluto should be like them, too. But it is very much smaller and more like the four inner planets. What, then, is it doing here?

Neptune has two known moons, a large one and a small one. Pluto looks a lot like them. Also, consider how weird Pluto's orbit is. No other planet moves like Pluto. Perhaps Pluto once circled Neptune as a small and distant moon. Then a close pass with another object knocked Pluto free of Neptune's gravity and sent it into its strange orbit.

Pluto is so far away that even through a large telescope, it looks like just another star.

Our long and wondrous trip is at an end. Magically, we return to Earth and set down among the fields, the plains, the mountains, and the meadows. The moon is full and welcomes us back home.

We slowly file out of our starship, talking in hushed whispers. We have been moved by the mysteries of the solar system. As we walk home in the starlit darkness, we know we will never be the same again. So when your friends and neighbors ask you where you've been all these years, you'll say, "I've been on the Grand Tour!" And you'll really mean it.

The bright central area above is a nebula, a cloud of dust and gas in space.

Think About It

1. Why is Mercury's day almost as long as its year?
2. In what way is Mars like Earth?
3. What special things make Earth different from all the other planets?
4. Why do some astronomers think that Pluto was once a moon of Neptune?
5. Do you think that in the future you'll be able to take a tour of the planets in the same way that today you can take a tour of a country? Why or why not?
6. Write a description of your favorite planet as if you were trying to get people to vacation there.

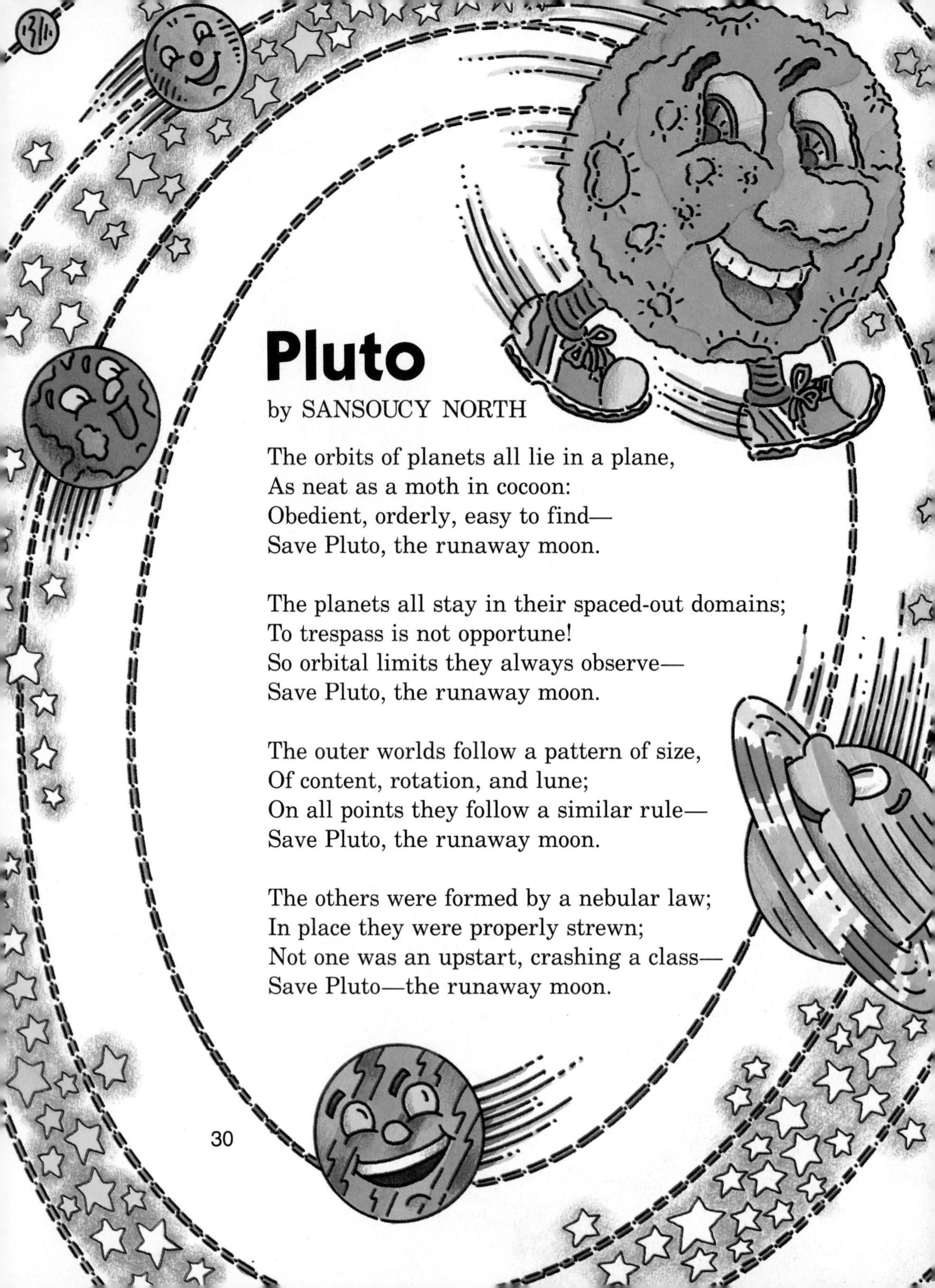

Pluto

by SANSOUCY NORTH

The orbits of planets all lie in a plane,
As neat as a moth in cocoon:
Obedient, orderly, easy to find—
Save Pluto, the runaway moon.

The planets all stay in their spaced-out domains;
To trespass is not opportune!
So orbital limits they always observe—
Save Pluto, the runaway moon.

The outer worlds follow a pattern of size,
Of content, rotation, and lune;
On all points they follow a similar rule—
Save Pluto, the runaway moon.

The others were formed by a nebular law;
In place they were properly strewn;
Not one was an upstart, crashing a class—
Save Pluto—the runaway moon.

LEARN NEW WORDS

1. Their trip **abroad** took them to Spain, France, and England.
2. Shooting stars are really parts of **comets** that burn up when they enter the earth's atmosphere.
3. The night was especially clear, and I could see the Big Dipper as well as the **constellation** Leo.
4. Camels are very suited to a desert **environment**, because they don't need much water and their thick hides protect them from the heat.
5. I wasn't sure she heard me the first time, so I **inquired** again when the fireworks would start.
6. There was a long **pause** before anyone spoke again.
7. The astronauts' **reentry** into the earth's atmosphere went as smoothly as planned.

GET SET TO READ

Seeing a comet or an eclipse can be a once-in-a-lifetime event. What would you do if you had the opportunity to see something really out of this world?

Read to see what happens when Lewis and his grandmother have an opportunity to see a shower of stars.

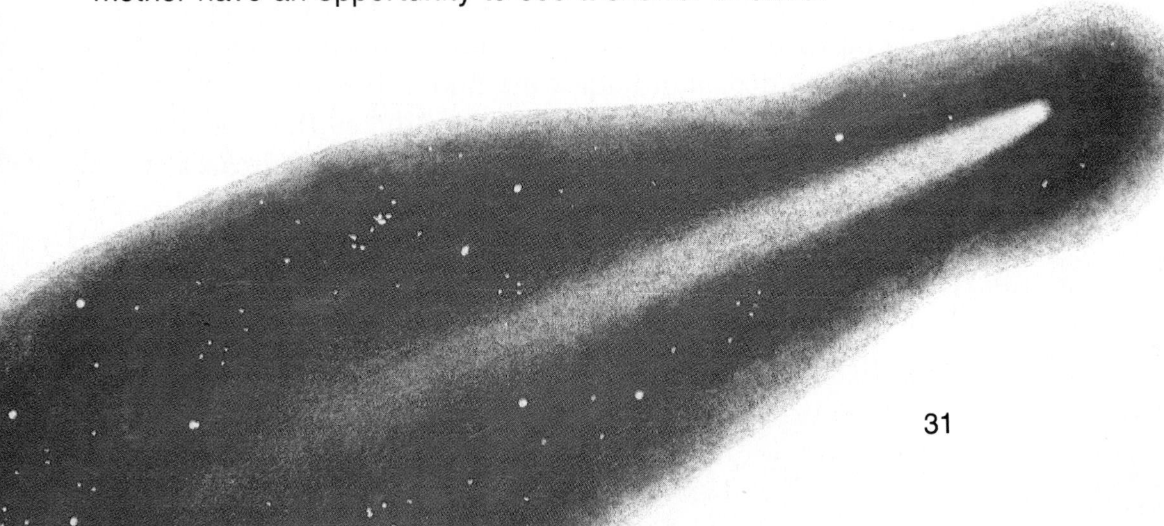

THE NIGHT of the LEONIDS

by E.L. KONIGSBURG

The Leonids are a particularly bright shower of shooting stars that lights up the sky once about every thirty-three years. They are called Leonids after Leo, the constellation from which they appear to fall. Shooting stars, whether in a shower or alone, are not really stars at all. They are parts of comets that burn up in the earth's atmosphere, as Lewis unexpectedly finds out one day.

I arrived at Grandmother's house in a taxi. I had my usual three suitcases, one for my pillow and my coin collection. The doorman helped me take the suitcases up, and I helped him. I held the elevator button so that the door wouldn't close on him while he loaded the suitcases on and off. Grandmother's new maid let me in. She was younger and fatter than the new maid was the last time. She told me that I should unpack and that Grandmother would be home shortly.

Grandmother doesn't take me everywhere she goes and I don't take her everywhere I go; but we get along pretty well, Grandmother and I.

She doesn't have any pets, and I don't have any other grandmothers, so I stay with her whenever my mother and father go abroad; they send me postcards.

My friend Clarence has the opposite: three Eiffels and two Coliseums. My mother and my father are very touched that I save their postcards. I also think that it is very nice of me.

I had finished unpacking, and I was wondering why Grandmother didn't wait for me. After all, I am her only grandchild, and I am named Lewis. Lewis was the name of one of her husbands, the one who was my grandfather. Grandmother came home as I was on my way to the kitchen to see if the new maid believed in eating between meals better than the last new maid did.

"Hello, Lewis," Grandmother said.

"Hello, Grandmother," I replied. Sometimes we talk like that, plain talk. Grandmother leaned over for me to kiss her cheek. Neither one of us adores slobbering, or even likes it.

"Are you ready?" I asked.

"Just as soon as I get out of this girdle and these high heels," she answered.

"Take off your hat, too, while you're at it," I suggested. "I'll set things up awhile."

Grandmother joined me in the library. I have taught her double solitaire, fish, cheat, and casino. She has taught me gin rummy; we mostly play gin rummy.

The maid served us supper on trays in the library so that we could watch the news on color TV. Grandmother has only one color TV set, so we watch her programs on Mondays,

Wednesdays, Fridays and every other Sunday; we watch mine on Tuesdays, Thursdays, Saturdays and the leftover Sundays. I thought that she could have given me *every* Sunday since I am her only grandchild and I am named Lewis, but Grandmother said, "Share and share alike." And we do. And we get along pretty well, Grandmother and I.

After the news and after supper Grandmother decided to read the newspaper; it is delivered before breakfast but she only reads the ads then. Grandmother sat on the sofa and held the newspaper at the end of her arms; then she squinted, and then she tilted her head back and farther back so that all you could see were nostrils, and then she called, "Lewis, Lewis, please bring me my glasses."

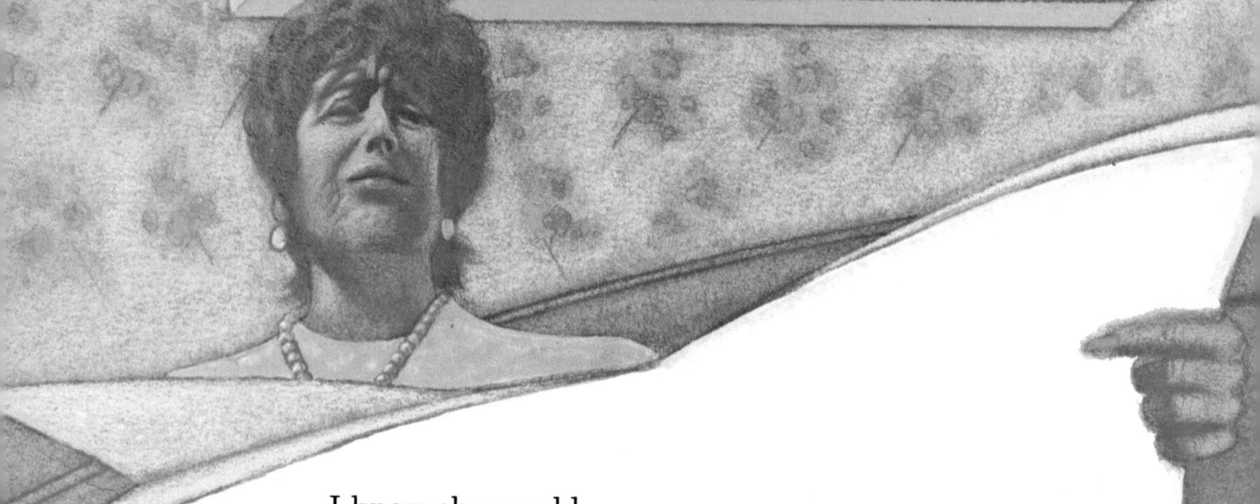

I knew she would.

I had to look for them. I always have to look for them. They have pale blue frames and are shaped like sideways commas, and they are never where she thinks they are or where I think they should be: *on the nose of her head.* You should see her trying to dial the telephone without her glasses. She practically stands in the next room and points her finger, and she still gets wrong numbers. I only know that in case of fire, I'll make the call.

I found her glasses. Grandmother began reading messages from the paper as if she were sending telegrams. It is one of her habits I wonder about; I wonder if she does it even when I'm not there. "Commissioner of Parks invites everyone to Central Park tonight," she read.

"What for?" I asked. "A mass mugging?"

"No. Something special."

"What else?"

"Something special."

I waited for what was a good pause before I asked, "What special?"

Grandmother waited for a good pause before she answered, "Something spectacular," not even bothering to look up from the newspaper.

I paused. Grandmother paused. I paused. Grandmother paused. I paused, I paused, I paused, and I won. Grandmother spoke first. "A spectacular show of stars," she said.

"Movie stars or rock and roll?" I inquired politely.

"Star stars," she answered.

"You mean like the sky is full of?"

"Yes, I mean like the sky is full of."

"You mean that the Commissioner of Parks has invited everyone out just to enjoy the night environment?" We were studying environment in our school.

"Not any night environment. Tonight there will be a shower of stars."

"Like a rain shower?" I asked.

"More like a thunderstorm."

"Stars falling like rain can be very dangerous and pollute our environment besides." We were also studying pollution of the environment in our school.

"No, they won't pollute our environment," Grandmother said.

"How do you know?" I asked.

"Because they will burn up before they fall all the way down. Surely you must realize that," she added.

I didn't answer.

"You must realize that they always protect astronauts from burning up on their reentry into the earth's atmosphere."

I didn't answer.

"They give the astronauts a heat shield. Otherwise they'd burn up."

I didn't answer.

"The stars don't have one. A heat shield, that is."

I didn't answer.

"That's why the stars burn up. They don't have a shield. Of course, they aren't really stars, either. They are Leonids."

Then I answered.

"Why don't you tell me about the shower of stars that isn't really a shower and isn't really stars?" She wanted to explain about them. I could tell. That's why I asked.

Grandmother likes to be listened to. That's one reason why she explains things. She prefers being listened to when she *tells* things: like get my elbow off the table and pick up my feet when I walk. She would tell me things like that all day if I would listen all day. When she *explains*, I listen. I sit close and listen close, and that makes her feel like a regular grandmother. She likes that, and sometimes so do I. That's one reason why we get along pretty well.

Grandmother explained about the Leonids.

The Leonids are trash that falls from the comet called Tempel-Tuttle. Comets go around the sun just as the planet Earth does. But not quite just like the planet Earth. Comets don't make regular circles around the sun. They loop around the sun, and they leak. Loop and leak. Loop and leak. The parts that leak are called the tail. The path that Earth takes around the sun and the path that Tempel-Tuttle takes around the sun were about to cross each other. Parts of the tail would get caught in the earth's atmosphere and light up as they burn up as they fall down. Little bits at a time. A hundred little bits at a time. A thousand little bits at a time. A million bits.

The parts that burn up look like falling stars. That is why Grandmother and the Commissioner of Parks called it a Shower of Stars. The falling stars from Tempel-Tuttle are called the Leonids. Leonids happen only once every thirty-three and one-third years. The whole sky over the city would light up with them. The reason that everyone was invited to the park was so that we city people could see a big piece of sky instead of just a hallway of sky between the buildings.

It would be an upside-down Grand Canyon of fireworks.

I decided that we ought to go. Grandmother felt the same way I did. Maybe even more so.

Right after we decided to go, Grandmother made me go to bed. She said that I should be rested and that she would wake me in plenty of time to get dressed and walk to Central Park. She promised to wake me at eleven o'clock.

And I believed her.

I believed her.

I really did believe her.

Grandmother said to me, "Do you think that I want to miss something that happens only three times in one century?"

"Didn't you see it last time?" I asked. After all, there was a shower of Leonids thirty-three and one-third years ago when she was only thirty, and I'll bet there was no one making her go to bed.

"No, I didn't see it last time," she said.

"What was the matter? Didn't the Commissioner of Parks invite you?"

"No, that was not the matter."

"Why didn't you see it then?"

"Because," she explained.

"Because you forgot your glasses and you didn't have Lewis, Lewis to get them for you?"

"I didn't even wear glasses when I was thirty."

"Then why didn't you see it?"

"Because," she said, "because I didn't bother to find out about it, and I lost my chance."

I said, "Oh." I went to bed. I knew about lost chances.

Grandmother woke me. She made me bundle up. She was bundled, too. She looked sixty-three years lumpy. I knew that she wouldn't like it if I expressed an opinion, so I didn't. Somehow.

We left the apartment.

We found a place in the park. The only part that wasn't crowded was up. Which was all right because that was where the action would be.

The shower of stars was to begin in forty-five minutes.

We waited.

And waited.

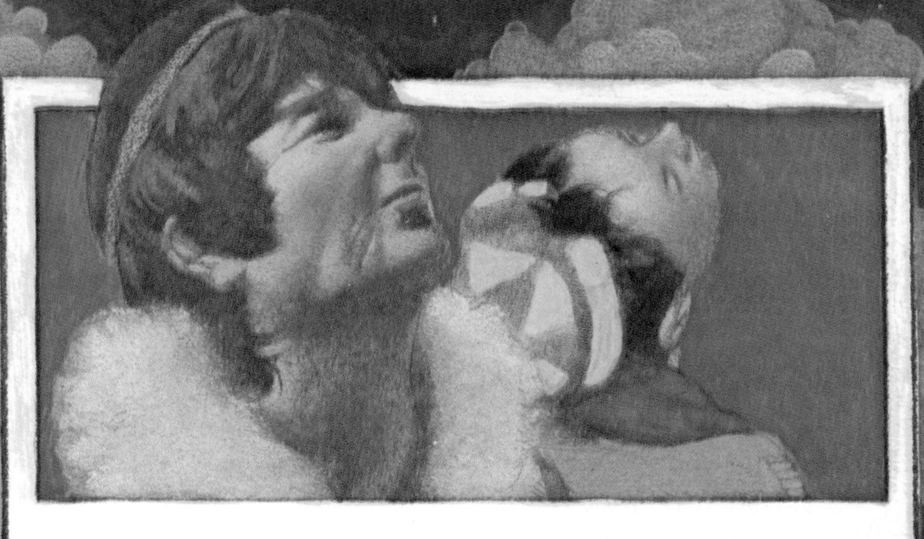

And saw.

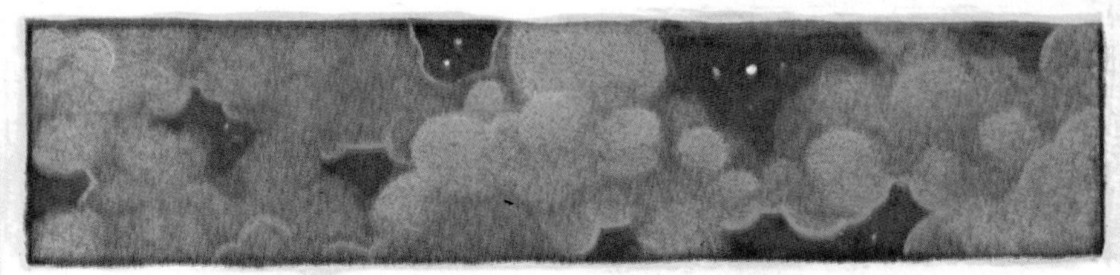

"What are you crying about?" Grandmother asked. Not kindly.

"I have to wait thirty-three and one-third years before I can see a big spectacular Shower of Stars. I'll be forty-three before I can ever see a Leonid."

"Oh, shut up!" Grandmother said. Not kindly.

"I'll be *middle-aged*."

"What was that for?" I asked. "What did I do?" I asked. "What did I do?" I asked again. I had always thought that we got along pretty well, my grandmother and I.

"You add it up," Grandmother said. Not kindly.

So I did. I added it up. Sixty-three and thirty-three don't add up to another chance.

I held Grandmother's hand on the way back to her apartment. She let me even though neither one of us adores hand holding. I held the hand that hit me.

Think About It

1. Why hadn't Lewis's grandmother seen the Leonids thirty-three years before?
2. What kept Lewis and his grandmother from seeing the Leonids on that night in Central Park?
3. Why was Lewis's grandmother angry with him?
4. Why did Lewis and his grandmother hold hands at the end?
5. Why do you think Lewis and his grandmother get along well together?
6. The last Leonid shower took place in 1966, so the next one will be in 1999. Write about what might happen to you when you have the opportunity to see the Leonids.

LEARN NEW WORDS

1. Use a calculator to add the figures if you want to be sure the total is **accurate**.
2. As she helped the dazed man to his feet, she said, "**Apparently** you've just fallen down the stairs."
3. I hardly recognized my teacher at the theater, because in my mind he is always **associated** with school.
4. The astronaut sat in a small space **capsule** on top of a huge rocket.
5. According to the travel plans, Chicago is our first stop and Seattle is our final **destination**.
6. The weather conditions were perfect, so the rocket was **launched** on schedule.
7. The child tried first crying and then screaming to get his way; neither of these **methods** worked, however.
8. While one astronaut prepared the command **module** for reentry, the other two stayed behind at the space station.
9. His winning a prize in the baking contest was **startling** news because he has always been such a bad cook.
10. Not only could she tell him who pitched the most no-hit games, but she surprised him with other baseball **trivia** that even he didn't know.

GET SET TO READ

What do you think of when you look at the moon?

Read to find out how people can look at the moon and see different things.

Moon Illusions

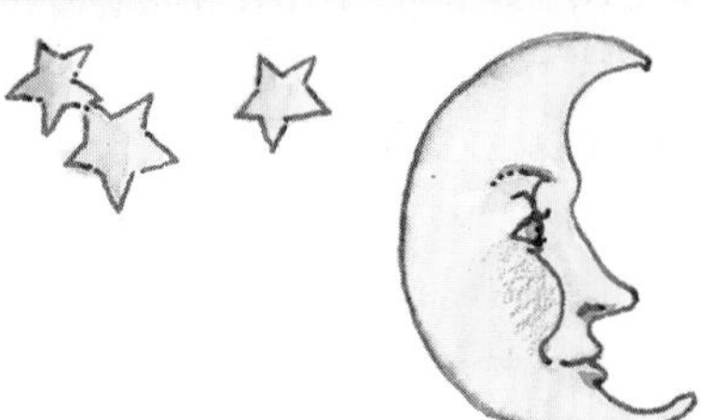

The Incredible Shrinking Moon

by RICHARD BERRY and ROBERT BURNHAM

There are many mysteries associated with the moon. Here's one for you: When is the moon bigger in the sky—when it's close to the horizon or when it's overhead? Most people would say that the moon is larger when it's low in the sky. But is it really? Try this experiment and find out!

First, you will need to make a moon ruler like the one on this page. Draw your moon ruler on cardboard, making sure that your moon units measure about the same as the ones in the book. Next, cut out your moon ruler.

Full moon is the best time to do this experiment. You can also do it a few days before or after a full moon.

Go outside around sunset (earlier before full moon; later after full moon). The moon will be rising in the east.

Hold your moon ruler at arm's length. Close one eye and measure the diameter of the moon in moon units. Be as accurate as you can. Write down your results.

Repeat your measurement a few hours later, when the moon is high in the sky. Again hold

the moon ruler at arm's length. Although the moon now looks smaller, you'll find that its diameter is exactly the same!

A full moon close to the horizon looks enormous—two or three times larger than a full moon seen in the sky. This is called the *moon illusion*. Actually, the moon is always the same size, no matter where it is in the sky.

What's the explanation? Nobody really knows. Apparently, the moon looks "closer" when it is low in the sky because we judge its size against buildings and trees on the horizon. When the moon is overhead, it seems farther away and so we "see" it as smaller. If you remove the horizon, the illusion is spoiled.

To show the same thing, try another experiment when the moon is close to the horizon. Close one eye and look at the moon through the cardboard tube from a roll of paper towels. Then take the tube away and open both eyes. What startling discovery do you make?

Moon Trivia

by JUDITH HERBST

- One day of every week belonged to the moon. In English the moon's day became Monday. In Spanish the word for moon is *luna* and Monday is *lunes*. In French it is *lune* and the day is *lundi*.
- A full moon was said to stir the emotions. People who caught moon madness were called "lunatics."
- Because of its color and shine, silver was the metal associated with the moon. At the first sighting of a new moon, it was the custom to turn over a silver coin in your purse or pocket.
- The illusion of the "man in the moon" is created by the moon's craters. Some societies saw a woman's face, which just goes to show you that equal rights is not a new idea.
- In the seventeenth century Sir Paul Neale made the startling announcement that he had

seen an elephant on the moon. His methods of observing left something to be desired, though. Apparently, what Neale saw was a mouse that had crawled into his telescope!

- In 1835 the *New York Sun* carried a story that a large human population had been discovered on the moon. Thousands of people actually believed the report to be accurate. This proves that you really can fool some of the people some of the time.
- In 1865 French author Jules Verne wrote a book called *From the Earth to the Moon.* In it Verne described a voyage to the moon. The space capsule, named Columbiad, was launched somewhere in Florida. It carried three men and took four days to reach its destination.

A little more than one hundred years later, Apollo 11 lifted off for the moon. The capsule was launched from Cape Canaveral, Florida, carried three men, and spent four days in flight. The command module was called Columbia.

Think About It

1. Give one explanation why the moon looks bigger when it's close to the horizon than when it's overhead.
2. Give one explanation why the moon looks smaller when viewed through a cardboard tube.
3. How did we get the term "lunatic"?
4. Why do you think people in the past believed so many stories about the moon?
5. Do you think the moon continues to puzzle us today? Why or why not?
6. Pretend that you'll be going to the moon. Write about an amazing discovery you make there.

from
A Dream About the Man in the Moon

by JOHN CIARDI

I ran till noon
And found the moon
Asleep in the top of a tree.
"What! Sleep all day?"
I stopped to say,
"Why don't you shine?" Said he:

"I shine for the owl. I shine for the bat.
I shine for the fox. I shine for the cat.
I shine for the rabbits that dance in the dew.
What makes you think I should shine for you?

I shine for the sea, I shine for the land.
I shine for the frogs when they strike up the band
As they sit in the water all in a line.
Now you tell me—for whom do *you* shine?

I shine when the night-things come out of their den.
I shine for the fire-flies. I shine then
For the dog in the yard and mice in the hall.
When do *you* shine—if you shine at all?"

MOON

by EMILY DICKINSON

The moon was but a chin of gold
A night or two ago,
And now she turns her perfect face
Upon the world below.

Word Pictures Using Metaphors and Similes

Emily Dickinson is known for writing short poems that say a lot. In the poem you just read, "Moon," she creates a word picture of the moon by using a *metaphor*—a comparison in which one thing is called by the name of another. In her metaphor, Dickinson compares the phases of the moon to different views of a woman's face. She calls the crescent moon a "chin of gold." The full moon is a full view of a woman's "perfect face."

A writer cannot use colors or shapes as a painter can. But by creating unusual metaphors, a writer can call up colors and shapes in the mind of the reader or listener. All writers use metaphors. But the poet especially tries to create clear word pictures by putting together unusual comparisons.

Haiku is a Japanese form of poetry that contains a single word picture. A haiku poem is unrhymed and has only three lines. It generally has five syllables in the first line, seven syllables in the second, and five syllables in the third. Not all haiku poets follow this exact syllable count, however. Nature, especially the seasons of the year, is often the subject matter of haiku.

To keep their haiku short and simple, poets often make unusual comparisons to create a clear word picture. What picture do you imagine as you read this haiku?

Quiet cardinal
Is like a bright red ribbon
In the snowy tree.
—Betsy Maestro

To what does the poet compare the cardinal? What is the season of the year in the poem? What holiday do these two details make you think of? The comparison in this poem is called a *simile*. A simile usually begins with either *like* or *as*.

Read the following haiku. Notice the way it is laid out on the paper. Also notice the poet's use of a colon to set off the metaphor. Then answer the questions below.

In a cloudy sky
the pale winter sun peeks through:
a pearl wreathed in smoke.
—Judy Rosenbaum

1. What picture does the poet paint with words?
2. What two things does the poet compare?
3. Is this comparison a metaphor or a simile? How do you know?
4. How does the way this haiku is laid out on the paper differ from the way the first haiku is laid out?

Now read this haiku and answer the questions below it.

As still as a flower,
yet unlike the flower: the cat
thinking his own thoughts.
—Ann Atwood

1. What makes this poem a haiku?
2. What comparison does the poet make?
3. In what way does the poem say the cat is like a flower?
4. In what way does the poem say the cat is unlike a flower?

LEARN NEW WORDS

1. Lunch today **consisted** of soup, milk, and fruit.
2. We tried comforting the child and making him laugh, but neither of these methods **consoled** him.
3. We were very **distressed** to hear about the accident.
4. The dog that ran barking through the store caused quite a **disturbance**.
5. Too tired to walk up the stairs, we rode the **escalator** to the second floor.
6. The time they chose to visit was **inconvenient**, because I was busy washing my dog.
7. All the astronauts aboard the space module were so **overwhelmed** by the view that they were speechless.
8. Our destination was the North Pole, a lonely place of **perpetual** ice and snow.
9. She gave her boss a letter of **resignation** two weeks before she left her job.
10. Whenever he was nervous, he **stammered** so badly you could hardly understand him.
11. The **vegetation** around her house was mostly ivy and bushes, with a few flowers.

GET SET TO READ

What's the best kind of birthday present?

Read this story to find out how Matilda's birthday present from her aunt creates a terrible problem.

All You've Ever Wanted

by JOAN AIKEN

Matilda, you will agree, was a most unfortunate child. Not only had she three names, each worse than the others—Matilda, Eliza, and Agatha—but her father and mother died shortly after she was born, and she was brought up by her six aunts. These were all active women. So on Monday Matilda was taught algebra and arithmetic by her Aunt Aggie, and on Tuesday biology by her Aunt Beattie. On Wednesday she was taught classics by her Aunt Cissie, and on Thursday dancing and deportment by her Aunt Dorrie. On Friday she was taught essentials by her Aunt Effie, and on Saturday French by her Aunt Florrie. Friday was the most alarming day, because Matilda never knew beforehand what Aunt Effie would decide on as the day's essentials—sometimes it was cooking, or target practice, or washing, or boiler fixing ("For you never know what a girl may need nowadays," as Aunt Effie rightly observed).

So that by Sunday, Matilda was often worn out. She thanked her stars that her seventh aunt, Gertie, had left for foreign parts many years before, and never threatened to come back and teach her geology or grammar on the only day when she could do as she liked.

However, poor Matilda was not entirely free from her Aunt Gertie. On her seventh birthday, and each one after it, Matilda received a little poem wishing her well, written on pink paper, decorated with silver flowers, and signed like this:

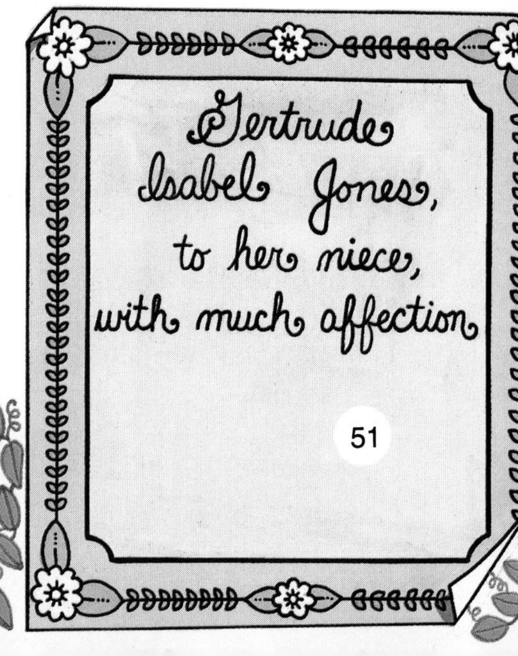

And the terrible disadvantage of the poems, pretty though they were, was that the wishes in them always came true. For example, the one on her eighth birthday read:

Now you are eight, Matilda dear,
May shining gifts your place adorn
And each day through the coming year
Awake you with a rosy morn.

The shining gifts were all very well. They consisted of a flashlight, a luminous watch, pins, needles, a steel soapbox, and a useful little silver pin which said "Matilda" in case she ever forgot her name. But her rosy morns were a great mistake. As you know, a red sky in the morning is the shepherd's warning, and the terrible result of Aunt Gertie's well-meaning verse was that it rained every day for the entire year.

Another poem read:

Each morning make another friend
Who'll be with you till light doth end,
Cheery and frolicsome and gay,
To pass the sunny hours away.

For the rest of her life Matilda was overwhelmed by the number of friends she made in the course of that year—365 of them. Every morning she found another of them, anxious to cheer her and play with her. The aunts complained that her lessons were being constantly interrupted. The worst of it was that she did not really like all the friends. Some of them were so *very* cheery and playful and insisted on pillow-fights when she had a toothache. Or sometimes twenty-one of them would get together and make her play hockey, which she hated.

She was not even consoled by the fact that all her hours were sunny, because she was so busy in passing them away that she had no time to enjoy them.

Long miles and weary though you stray
Your friends are never far away,
And every day though you may roam,
Yet night will find you back at home

was another inconvenient wish. Matilda found herself forced to go for long, tiresome walks in all weathers. She was not consoled by the fact that her friends were never far away, either, for although they often passed her on bicycles or in cars, they never gave her lifts.

However, as she grew older, the poems became less troublesome, and she began to enjoy bluebirds twittering in the garden and endless vases of roses on her windowsill. Nobody knew where Aunt Gertie lived, and she never put in an address with her birthday greetings. It was therefore impossible to write and thank her for her many forms of good wishes, or hint that they might have been more carefully worded. But Matilda looked forward to meeting her one day, and thought that she must be a most interesting person.

"You never knew what Gertrude would be up to next," said Aunt Cissie. "She was a thoughtless girl, and got into endless scrapes. But I will say for her, she was very good-hearted."

When Matilda was nineteen, she took a job in a government office where, instead of typewriter ribbon, they used red tape. There was a large laundry basket near the main entrance labeled *The Usual Channels* where all the letters were put which people did not want to answer themselves. Once every three months the letters were re-sorted and dealt out afresh to different people.

Matilda got on very well here and was perfectly happy. She went to see her six aunts on Sundays, and had almost forgotten the seventh by the time that her twentieth birthday had arrived. Her aunt, however, had not forgotten.

On the morning of her birthday, Matilda woke very late and had to rush off to work, stuffing her letters unopened into her pocket to read later on in the morning. She had no time to read them until ten minutes to eleven, but that, she told herself, was as it should be, since, as she had been born at eleven in the morning, her birthday did not really begin till then.

Most of the letters were from her 365 perpetual friends, but the usual pink and silver envelope was there, and she opened it with the usual feeling of slight uncertainty.

May all your leisure hours be blest,
Your work prove full of interest,
Your life hold many happy hours
And all your way be strewn with flowers

said the pink and silver slip in her fingers. "From your affectionate Aunt Gertrude."

Matilda was still thinking about this when a gong sounded in the passage outside. This was the signal for everyone to leave their work and dash down the passage to a cart which sold them buns and juice. Matilda left her letters and dashed with the rest. Sipping her orange juice and chatting with her friends, she had forgotten the poem when the boss's voice came down the passage.

"What is all this? What does this mean?" he was saying.

The group round the cart turned to see what he was talking about. And then Matilda flushed scarlet and spilled some of her orange juice on the floor. For all along the respectable brown carpeting of the passage were growing flowers in the most outrageous amounts—

daisies, crocuses, mimosa, foxgloves, tulips, and lotuses. In some places the passage looked more like a jungle than anything else. Out of this jungle the little red-faced figure of the boss fought his way.

"Who did it?" he said. But nobody answered.

Matilda went quietly away from the chattering group and pushed through the vegetation to her room, leaving a trail of buttercups and rhododendrons across the floor to her desk.

"I can't keep this quiet," she thought desperately. And she was quite right. Mr. Willoughby, who headed her department, noticed almost immediately that when Matilda came into his room there was something unusual about her.

"Miss Jones," he said, "I don't like to be personal, but have you noticed that wherever you go, you leave a trail of mixed flowers?"

Poor Matilda burst into tears.

"I know. I don't know what I shall do about it," she sobbed.

Mr. Willoughby was not used to office workers who left lobelias, primroses, and the rarer forms of cactus behind them when they entered a room.

"It's very pretty," he said. "But not very practical. Already it's almost impossible to get along the passage. I shudder to think what this room will be like when these have grown a bit

higher. I really don't think you can go on with it, Miss Jones."

"You don't think I do it on purpose, do you?" said Matilda, sniffing into her handkerchief. "I can't stop it. They just keep on coming."

"In that case, I am afraid," replied Mr. Willoughby, "that you will not be able to keep on coming. We really cannot have the office overgrown in this way. I shall be very sorry to lose you, Miss Jones. What caused this unfortunate condition, may I ask?"

"It's a kind of spell," Matilda said, shaking the damp out of her handkerchief onto a fine polyanthus.

"But my dear Miss Jones," Mr. Willoughby exclaimed crossly, "you have a National Magic Insurance card, haven't you? Why don't you go to the Public Magician?"

"I never thought of that," she confessed. "I'll go at lunchtime."

Fortunately for Matilda the Public Magician's office was just across the square from where she worked so that she did not cause too much disturbance. But the Borough Council could never account for the rare and exotic flowers which suddenly sprang up in the middle of their dusty lawns.

The Public Magician received her quickly and asked her to state her problem.

"It's a spell," said Matilda, looking down at a pink Christmas rose growing unseasonably beside her chair.

"In that case we can soon help you. Fill in that form, *if* you please." He pushed a printed slip at her across the table.

It said: "To be filled in by persons suffering from spells."

Matilda filled in name and address of patient, nature of spell, and date, but when she came to name and address of person by whom spell was cast, she paused.

"I don't know her address," she said.

"Then I'm afraid you'll have to find it. Can't do anything without an address," the Public Magician replied.

Matilda went out into the street very distressed. The Public Magician could do nothing better than advise her to put an advertisement into *The Times*

and the *International Sorcerers' Bulletin,* which she accordingly did.

AUNT GERTRUDE PLEASE COMMUNICATE. MATILDA MUCH DISTRESSED BY LAST POEM.

While she was in the Post Office sending off her advertisements (and causing much disturbance by the number of forget-me-nots she left about), she wrote and sent her resignation to Mr. Willoughby. She then went sadly to the nearest subway station.

"Haven't you left something behind?" a man said to her at the top of the escalator. She looked back to the trail of daffodils across the station entrance and hurried anxiously down the stairs. As she ran round a corner at the bottom, angry shouts told her that lilies had worked their way into the machinery and caused the escalator to stop.

She tried to hide in the gloom at the far end of the platform, but a furious station official found her.

"What do you mean by it?" he said, shaking her elbow. "It'll take three days to put the station right, and look at my platform!"

The stone slabs were split and pushed aside by vast peonies, which kept growing and threatened to block the line.

"It isn't my fault—really it isn't," Matilda stammered.

"The company can sue you for this, you know," he began, when a train came in. Pushing past him, she squeezed into the nearest door.

She began to thank her stars for the escape, but it was too soon. A powerful and penetrating smell rose round her feet where the white flowers of wild garlic had sprung.

When Aunt Gertie finally read the advertisement in a ten-months' old copy of the *International Sorcerers' Bulletin,* she packed her luggage and took the next plane back home. For she was still just as Aunt Cissie had described her—thoughtless, but good-hearted.

"Where is the poor child?" she asked Aunt Aggie.

"I should say she was poor," her sister replied sharply. "It's a pity you didn't come home before, instead of making her life a misery for twelve years. You'll find her out in the summer-house."

Matilda had been living out there ever since she left her job. Her aunts kindly but firmly, and quite reasonably, said they could not have the house overwhelmed by vegetation.

She had an ax, with which she cut down the worst growths every evening, and for the rest of the time she kept as still as she could and earned some money by doing odd jobs of typing and sewing.

"My poor dear child," Aunt Gertie said breathlessly. "I had no idea that my little verses would have this sort of effect. Whatever shall we do?"

"Please do something," Matilda begged her, sniffing. This time it was not tears but a cold she caught from living in perpetual drafts.

"My dear, there isn't anything I can do. It's bound to last

till the end of the year. That sort of spell cannot be changed at all."

"Well, at least can you stop sending me the verses?" asked Matilda. "I don't want to sound ungrateful. . . ."

"Even that I can't do," her aunt said gloomily. "It's a banker's order at the Magician's Bank. One a year from seven to twenty-one. Oh, dear, and I thought it would be such *fun* for you. At least you only have one more, though."

"Yes, but heaven knows what that'll be." Matilda sneezed sadly and put another sheet of paper into her typewriter.

There seemed to be nothing to do but wait. However, they did decide that it might be a good thing to go see the Public Magician on the morning of Matilda's twenty-first birthday.

Aunt Gertie paid the taxi driver and tipped him heavily not to grumble about the mass of delphiniums sprouting out of the mat of his cab.

"Good heavens, if it isn't Gertrude Jones!" the Public Magician exclaimed. "Haven't seen you since we were in college together. How are you? Same old irresponsible Gertie? Remember when you gave that hospital those endless beds and the trouble it caused?"

When the situation was explained to him, he laughed heartily.

"Just like you, Gertie. Well-meaning isn't the word."

At eleven promptly, Matilda opened her pink envelope.

Matilda, now you're twenty-one,
May you have every sort of fun;
May you have all you've ever wanted,
And every future wish be granted.

"Every future wish be granted," Matilda repeated. "Then I wish Aunt Gertie would lose her power of wishing," she cried; and immediately Aunt Gertie did.

But as Aunt Gertie with her usual thoughtlessness had said, "May you have all you've *ever wanted,*" Matilda had quite a lot of rather inconvenient things to get rid of, including a lion cub and a baby hippopotamus.

Think About It

1. What problems did Aunt Gertie's birthday poems cause Matilda?
2. Why did Matilda have to give Mr. Willoughby her resignation?
3. In what way was Aunt Gertie "thoughtless but good-hearted"?
4. How did Aunt Gertie finally solve Matilda's problem?
5. When did you first know that this story is a fantasy?
6. Write a story about what might happen to you if you got "all you've ever wanted."

LEARN NEW WORDS

1. The rainbow made a colorful **arc** in the sky.
2. He was a pale, **gaunt** man who looked as though he hadn't eaten in a week.
3. "What causes a rainbow in the sky?" the child asked **inquisitively**.
4. The ballet dancer **pirouetted** so many times that I got dizzy just looking at her.
5. The speaker stood on the **podium** so that all members of the audience could see her.
6. We were surrounded by a **profusion** of brightly colored flowers.
7. To show her love for the young man, the young woman softly sang him a **serenade**.
8. We saw only one person that day; in the late evening a **solitary** traveler passed by.
9. The cloudy, rainy weather gave a **somber** tone to the day.
10. The display of colors in the arc of a rainbow is called a **spectrum**.
11. The orchestra will be playing a **symphony** this evening.
12. To make his painting bright, he chose red and yellow, the most **vivid** colors of the spectrum.

GET SET TO READ

What can happen if you try to do something you don't really know how to do?

Read to see what happens when Milo takes on more than he can handle.

A Colorful Symphony

by NORTON JUSTER

The following story is taken from The Phantom Tollbooth. *The book tells of the magical adventures of a boy named Milo who drives his toy car through a mysterious tollbooth into The Lands Beyond. Milo meets many characters along the way. One of them is a watchdog named Tock who has the body of a noisy alarm clock, although everything else about him—head, feet, tail—is quite normal. Then there is Alec, a boy Milo's age who stands about three feet off the ground. Alec explains to Milo that everyone in his family is born in the air and grows down instead of up.*

Join Milo and his friends as they attend an unusual evening concert.

The sun was dropping slowly from sight. The stripes of purple and orange and red and gold piled themselves on top of the distant hills. The last shafts of light waited patiently for a flight of birds to find their way home. And a group of anxious stars had already taken their places.

"Here we are!" cried Alec, and, with a sweep of his arm, he pointed toward a very large symphony orchestra. "Isn't it a grand sight?"

There were at least a thousand musicians ranged in a great arc before them. To the left and right were the violins and cellos, whose bows moved in great waves.

Behind them in numberless profusion the piccolos, flutes, clarinets, oboes, bassoons, horns, trumpets, trombones, and tubas were all playing at once. At the very rear, so far away that they could hardly be seen, were the percussion instruments. Lastly, in a long line up one side of a steep slope, were the somber bass fiddles.

On a high podium in front stood the conductor, a tall, gaunt man with dark, deep-set eyes and a thin mouth placed carelessly between his long pointed nose and his long pointed chin. He used no baton but conducted with large, sweeping movements which seemed to start at his toes and work slowly up through his body and along his slender arms and end finally at the tips of his graceful fingers.

"I don't hear any music," said Milo.

"That's right," said Alec. "You don't listen to this concert—you watch it. Now pay attention."

As the conductor waved his arms, he molded the air like handfuls of soft clay. The musicians carefully followed his every direction.

"What are they playing?" asked Tock, looking up inquisitively at Alec.

"The sunset, of course. They play it every evening, about this time."

"They do?" asked Milo quizzically.

"Naturally," answered Alec. "And they also play morning, noon, and night, when, of course, it's morning, noon, or night. Why, there wouldn't be any color in the world unless they played it. Each instrument plays a different one," he explained. "Depending, of course, on what season it is and how the weather's to be, the conductor chooses his score and directs the day. But watch: the sun has almost set, and in a moment you can ask Chroma himself."

The last colors slowly faded from the western sky. As they did, one by one the instruments stopped until only the bass fiddles, in their somber, slow movement, were left to play the night and a single set of silver bells brightened the constellations. The conductor let his arms fall limply at his sides and stood quite still as darkness claimed the forest.

"That was a very beautiful sunset," said Milo, walking to the podium.

"It should be," was the reply. "We've been practicing since the world began." And, reaching down, the speaker picked Milo off the ground and set him on the music stand. "I am Chroma the Great," he continued, gesturing broadly with his hands, "conductor of color, maestro of pigment, and director of the entire spectrum."

"Do you play all day long?" asked Milo when he had introduced himself.

"Ah yes, all day, every day," he sang out, then pirouetted gracefully around the platform. "I rest only at night, and even then *they* play on."

"What would happen if you stopped?" asked Milo, who didn't quite believe that color happened that way.

"See for yourself," roared Chroma, and he raised both hands high over his head. Immediately the instruments that were playing stopped, and at once all color vanished. The world looked like an enormous coloring book that had never been used. Everything appeared in simple black outlines. It looked as if someone with a set of paints the size of a house and a brush as wide could stay happily occupied for years.

Then Chroma lowered his arms. The instruments began again and the color returned.

"You see what a dull place the world would be without color?" he said, bowing until his chin almost touched the ground. "But what pleasure to lead my violins in a serenade of spring green or hear my trumpets blare out the blue sea and then watch the oboes tint it all in warm yellow sunshine. And rainbows are best of all—and blazing neon signs, and taxicabs with stripes, and the soft tones of a foggy day. We play them all."

As Chroma spoke, Milo sat with his eyes open wide, while Alec and Tock looked on in wonder.

"Now I really must get some sleep." Chroma yawned. "We've had lightning, fireworks, and parades for the last few nights, and I've had to be up to conduct them. But tonight is sure to be quiet." Then, putting his large hand on Milo's shoulder, he said, "Be a good fellow and watch my orchestra till morning, will you? And be sure to wake me at 5:23 for the sunrise. Good night, good night, good night."

With that, he leaped lightly from the podium and, in three long steps, vanished into the forest.

"That's a good idea," said Tock, making himself comfortable in the grass. Alec stretched out in midair.

And Milo, full of thoughts and questions, curled up on the pages of tomorrow's music and eagerly awaited the dawn.

One by one, the hours passed, and at exactly 5:22 (by Tock's very accurate clock) Milo carefully opened one eye and, in a moment, the other. Everything was still purple, dark blue, and black, yet scarcely a minute remained to the long, quiet night.

He stretched lazily, rubbed his eyelids, scratched his head, and shivered once as a greeting to the early-morning mist.

"I must wake Chroma for the sunrise," he said softly. Then he suddenly wondered what it would be like to lead the orchestra and to color the whole world himself.

The idea whirled through his thoughts until he quickly decided that since it couldn't be very difficult, and since they probably all knew what to do by themselves anyway, and since it did seem a shame to wake anyone so early, and since it might be his only chance to try, and since the musicians were already poised and ready, he would . . . but just for a little while.

And so, as everyone slept peacefully on, Milo stood on tiptoes, raised his arms slowly in front of him, and made the slightest movement possible with the index finger of his right hand. It was 5:23 A.M.

As if understanding his signal perfectly, a single piccolo played a single note and off in the east a solitary shaft of cool lemon light flicked across the sky. Milo smiled happily and then cautiously crooked his finger again. This time two more piccolos and a flute joined in and three more rays of light danced lightly into view. Then with both hands he made a great circular sweep in the air and watched with delight as all the musicians began to play at once.

The cellos made the hills glow red. The leaves and grass were tipped with a soft pale green as the violins began their song. Only the bass fiddles rested as the entire orchestra washed the forest in color.

Milo was overjoyed because they were all playing for him, and just the way they should.

"Won't Chroma be surprised?" he thought, signaling the musicians to stop. "I'll wake him now."

But, instead of stopping, they continued to play even louder than before, until each color became more brilliant than he thought possible. Milo shielded his eyes with one hand and waved the other desperately, but the colors continued to grow brighter and brighter and brighter, until an even more curious thing began to happen.

As Milo frantically conducted, the sky changed slowly from blue to tan and then to a rich magenta red. Flurries of light green snow began to fall, and the leaves on the trees and bushes turned a vivid orange.

All the flowers suddenly appeared black. The gray rocks became a lovely soft chartreuse. Even peacefully sleeping Tock changed from brown to a magnificent ultramarine. Nothing was the color it should have been, and yet, the more he tried to straighten things out, the worse they became.

"I wish I hadn't started," he thought unhappily as a pale blue blackbird flew by. "There doesn't seem to be any way to stop them."

He tried very hard to do everything just the way Chroma had done, but nothing worked. The musicians played on, faster and faster, and the purple sun raced quickly across the sky. In less than a minute it had set once more in the west and then, without any pause, risen again in the east. The sky was now quite yellow and the grass a charming shade of lavender. Seven times the sun rose and almost as quickly disappeared as the colors kept changing. In just a few minutes a whole week had gone by.

At last the exhausted Milo, afraid to call for help and close to tears, dropped his hands to his sides. The orchestra stopped. The colors disappeared, and once again it was night. The time was 5:27 A.M.

"Wake up, everybody! Time for the sunrise!" he shouted with relief, and quickly jumped from the music stand.

"What a marvelous rest," said Chroma, striding to the podium. "I feel as though I'd slept for a week. My, my, I see we're a little late this morning. I'll have to cut my lunch hour short by four minutes."

He tapped for attention, and this time the dawn proceeded perfectly.

"You did a fine job," he said, patting Milo on the head. "Someday I'll let you conduct the orchestra yourself."

Tock wagged his tail proudly, but Milo didn't say a word. To this day no one knows of the lost week but the few people who happened to be awake at 5:23 on that strange morning.

"We'd better be getting along," said Tock, whose alarm had begun to ring again. "There's still a long way to go."

Chroma nodded a fond good-by as they started back through the forest. In honor of their visit, he made all the wild flowers bloom in a breathtaking display.

Think About It

1. How is the symphony orchestra in this story different from a regular symphony orchestra?
2. Describe what happened when Milo tried to direct the sunrise.
3. Why do you think the musicians went out of control?
4. *Chromatic* is a word that describes both the use of color and a musical scale. Why is Chroma a good name for the conductor?
5. What purpose did Chroma serve for the orchestra and for the colors of the day?
6. This story associates music with color. What colors can you think of to go with a song you know? Explain in writing what the colors of your song would be and why.

LEARN NEW WORDS

1. There was no way she could have **anticipated** running into a lion on the sidewalk this morning.
2. The young couple **cherished** their only child like a rare and priceless gift.
3. The woman was so gaunt and lifeless that she looked like a **corpse**.
4. We enjoy our monthly **excursions** to the city because we sometimes feel so solitary living out on the farm.
5. We all agreed that his monster costume for Halloween should win a prize for **hideousness**.
6. After we spent the weekend with her family, we wrote a note thanking them for their **hospitality**.
7. "Biting the hand that feeds you" is a saying that describes **ingratitude**.
8. After much begging, he finally **persuaded** us to come with him to the horror movie.
9. They ate dinner at exactly the same time as they had the **previous** evening.
10. She **resolved** not to be late again.

GET SET TO READ

What do you think of when you hear the word *monster*? Are the monsters you've heard of always evil and frightening?

Read this story to find out what happens when a man stays at the house of a mysterious creature.

The Beastly Creature and the Magical Flower

a Mexican folktale retold by JULIET PIGGOTT

Once there was a widower who had three daughters. As the daughters grew up, while they did not take the place of their dead mother in the household, they did look after their father very well indeed. Most important of all, they gave him much affection. It can be said that they cherished their father; and it can equally be said that he cherished them. A flower was responsible for one of the daughters leaving home. A single flower.

The father of the three girls (and they were young women, for the youngest was sixteen and the middle sister was eighteen and the eldest had just turned twenty) used to leave them alone in their country home once a month. This was because he was a merchant and had to go to the city to attend to his business. And every time he returned from one of these excursions (which he always made on horseback, for it was long after the Spaniards first came to Mexico bringing horses with them) he would give each of his daughters a present.

Just before the merchant set off on one of his excursions, he asked his daughters, as he always did, what they would like him to bring back for them. And the eldest asked for a new dress, a red one this time.

"Very well, my dear, you shall have it. I shall choose for you the brightest and most beautiful shade of red I can find."

He turned to the middle daughter and smiled at her, and she said, "Please, Father, may I have a new dress too, and may it be a yellow one?"

He said he would find for her in the city a dress of the brightest and most beautiful yellow.

And then he said to his youngest daughter, "Tell me, my littlest one, what color dress would you like?"

To his surprise, and that of her sisters, the youngest member of the family said she did not want her father to bring her back a dress at all. She wanted him to pick a single flower and bring her only that.

"What kind of flower? There will be many to choose from as I ride home from the city, and why should I not pick a whole bunch of flowers for you, my child?"

But the youngest daughter said she really only wanted one flower. "You will see a flower and know it is the one that will please me most."

"How shall I know? There are many flowers in blossom now. How shall I possibly be able to tell which particular blossom will be truly pleasing to you?"

"I cannot explain how you will know, but you will."

And with that her father had to be content.

The merchant finished his business in the city within a few days. Then he spent a whole morning looking for a red dress for his eldest daughter. He finally selected one of the purest scarlet, as bright as a flame and very beautiful.

In the afternoon he began his search for the yellow dress his second daughter wanted. It was late before he found the dress he liked better than any of the others he had seen. It was a vivid yellow, bright as a yellow flame is bright. It, too, was very beautiful.

The following morning the merchant carefully packed the two dresses in his saddlebags and set off for home. He could not ride quickly, for he was looking at the flowers by the road, searching for the one his youngest daughter had assured him he would recognize, the one that would please her most.

The sun had nearly finished its downward journey across the sky when he realized he would not be able to reach home that evening. Suddenly, in the growing darkness, he saw a light ahead of him. When he arrived at the light, he saw it was in the entrance to an empty stable.

He called out a greeting several times, but his voice echoed back and there was no reply. So he unsaddled, watered, and fed his horse, carefully hanging up his saddlebags. He resolved to leave money in payment in the morning if he could not find his unknown and unseen host.

Then he saw an open door with a light beyond it at the furthest end of the stable. This he had not noticed before, and

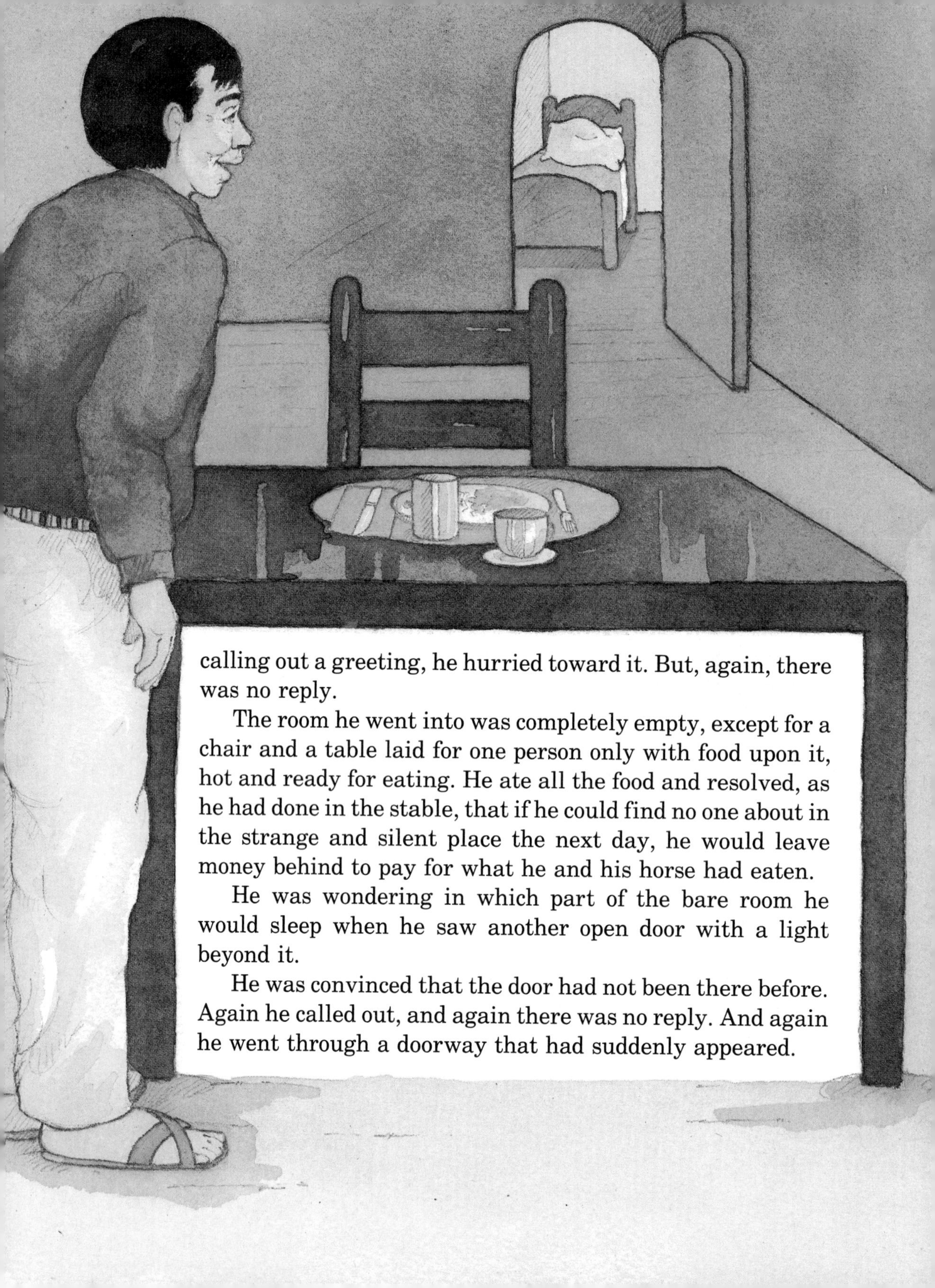

calling out a greeting, he hurried toward it. But, again, there was no reply.

The room he went into was completely empty, except for a chair and a table laid for one person only with food upon it, hot and ready for eating. He ate all the food and resolved, as he had done in the stable, that if he could find no one about in the strange and silent place the next day, he would leave money behind to pay for what he and his horse had eaten.

He was wondering in which part of the bare room he would sleep when he saw another open door with a light beyond it.

He was convinced that the door had not been there before. Again he called out, and again there was no reply. And again he went through a doorway that had suddenly appeared.

The room he entered was bare, as the other one had been, except for a bed, freshly made up and ready for use, and a chair. The merchant did what it seemed he should do: he undressed, put his clothes on the chair, and got into bed. He fell into a dreamless and deep sleep immediately.

The first thing he noticed when he woke up in the morning was that his clothes were no longer on the chair. In their place was a brand-new set of clothes and a new pair of riding boots. The door was open, as he had left it the previous evening, and he had heard nothing during the night. It was all very strange. There was nothing else to do but put on the new clothes. They fitted him perfectly, even the boots.

Then he went into the room where he had eaten the night before. The table in the bare room was once again set for one person, and, as the man half anticipated in that strange, silent, and magical house, breakfast was on the table, hot and steaming. Yet he had heard no one go into the room.

He ate the meal and went into the stable. All was as it had been the night before. Then, for the first time since the merchant had arrived, he felt the cold and prickly sensation of fear. His horse was not in the stall where he had left it, and the saddlebags containing the red dress and the yellow dress had disappeared.

Quickly he went out into the sunshine and there, peacefully flicking its tail and whisking away a few early morning flies, was his horse. It was saddled and the bags holding the dresses were in position. The merchant's fear fell away from him.

"Is there no one at home?" he called. The horse moved nervously at the sudden sound. Otherwise there was no reply. He called out again and again, but there was no answer. He decided that he would walk around and look for his silent host.

He had barely set off in the direction of the house when he saw a blaze of color, just beyond the stable. Never in his life had he seen so many flowers in such a profusion of colors. When he got closer, he saw they were not ordinary flowers. They were more transparent, as though they had been fashioned from a rainbow.

They were real flowers, but shaped differently from any he had ever known. The merchant gazed at them inquisitively, marveling at their beauty and breathing in the sweet scent that rose from them like a silver vapor shot with gold. Then he realized that each individual flower was different from the rest.

And as he looked at the beautifully colored glory spread out before him, the present for his youngest daughter came into his mind. He looked down and there, at his feet, was the flower he knew, as his daughter had told him he would know, that would please her most.

It consisted of a single petal, white with a blush of the palest mauve. It was in the shape of a tube, but spiraled. It shimmered in the sunshine as though it were filled with crystal.

The merchant stooped and picked the flower. At once it withered between his fingers. As he watched, the flower

became smaller until all that was left of it was a little moisture in the palm of his hand. For the second time, he felt the cold and prickly sensation of fear.

"Do not move," said a harsh voice.

The merchant turned and saw a beastly creature, a creature unlike any other. It was partly human in that it had arms and legs. But instead of hands and feet it had the scaled claws of a parrot. Its body was covered with curly grey fur. Its face was human, but of great hideousness. Long stringy brown hair covered its head, concealing its ears and forehead. The straight hair also grew over its cheeks and chin, and thus its mouth could not be seen. The creature's nose was very large, and its eyes flashed as though they were shining from inside the creature's head.

The beastly creature spoke again. "You have accepted my hospitality, put on the new clothes I gave you, eaten my food, and fed your horse. And then you attempted to steal my beautiful flower. I shall eat you, and eat you alive, for that act of ingratitude."

The merchant begged for his life. He tried to put money into the creature's clawlike hands, in payment for the hospitality he had received. But the offer was refused.

Then the anxious man said he had not tried to steal the flower for himself but for his youngest daughter. And the monster demanded an explanation. It made no sound while the merchant told of the presents his daughters had asked him to bring them. But the monster grunted and closed its eyes while the man spoke of how his youngest daughter had told him he would know which flower would please her most and of how he had known.

The creature opened its eyes and said, "You have persuaded me, by telling me of your youngest daughter, that your act of ingratitude was not purposeful. You may return to your

daughters. But for three days only. On the third day you will bring your youngest daughter to me and leave her here."

"How long do you wish my child to stay with you?"

"That is for me to decide, and perhaps your daughter herself will help me in my decision. If you do not bring her to me on the third day, I swear to you that by my magical powers I shall search for you, I shall find you, and then I shall eat you. Alive."

The man could think of nothing to say, for he knew he could not bargain with the beastly creature.

"Go now, and remember, my instructions must be obeyed if you wish to live to old age. And, furthermore, you shall not take a flower for your youngest daughter. That she shall choose and pluck for herself."

And so the merchant walked back slowly to his horse. When he looked back toward the place where the flowers had been, both they and the beastly creature had vanished. The cold and prickly sensation of fear came upon the merchant with increasing force. He quickly mounted and urged his horse into a gallop.

His fear had passed by the time he reached home. The loving welcome his daughters gave him and the pleasure of being with them again drove it away.

The two elder girls were delighted with their dresses. They fitted perfectly, and the eldest looked as beautiful in her flaming red dress as the younger did in her yellow one.

"And, dear Father, did you find and pick the flower you knew would please me most?"

He then had to tell the girls the whole story of his overnight stay in the silent house of the beastly creature. When he reached the end and spoke of the threat the monster had made, the cold and prickly sensation of fear came upon him again, and upon his elder daughters. But the youngest was not in the least afraid.

"The creature will not try to find you and eat you alive, for I shall go to him. I want to see the house in which he lives so silently. I want to see the magical flowers in his garden even more."

The man was terrified of taking his daughter to the silent place. But he was more fearful for his own life, for the monster had not threatened to harm her at all. The daughter continued to have no fear about going. On the third day she persuaded her father to take her.

The cold and prickly sensation of fear was upon the man as they saddled their horses and set off. It remained with him until they reached the place after darkness had fallen. When he saw the lamp at the stable entrance, his fear suddenly left him. All was as it had been on his previous visit: food and water for the horses, a meal waiting in the room beyond. But this time there were two places set at the table. There were two open doors in the room instead of one, each leading into a room with a bed and a chair in it.

And so the merchant and his daughter spent several days there in luxury, hearing no sound except that of their own

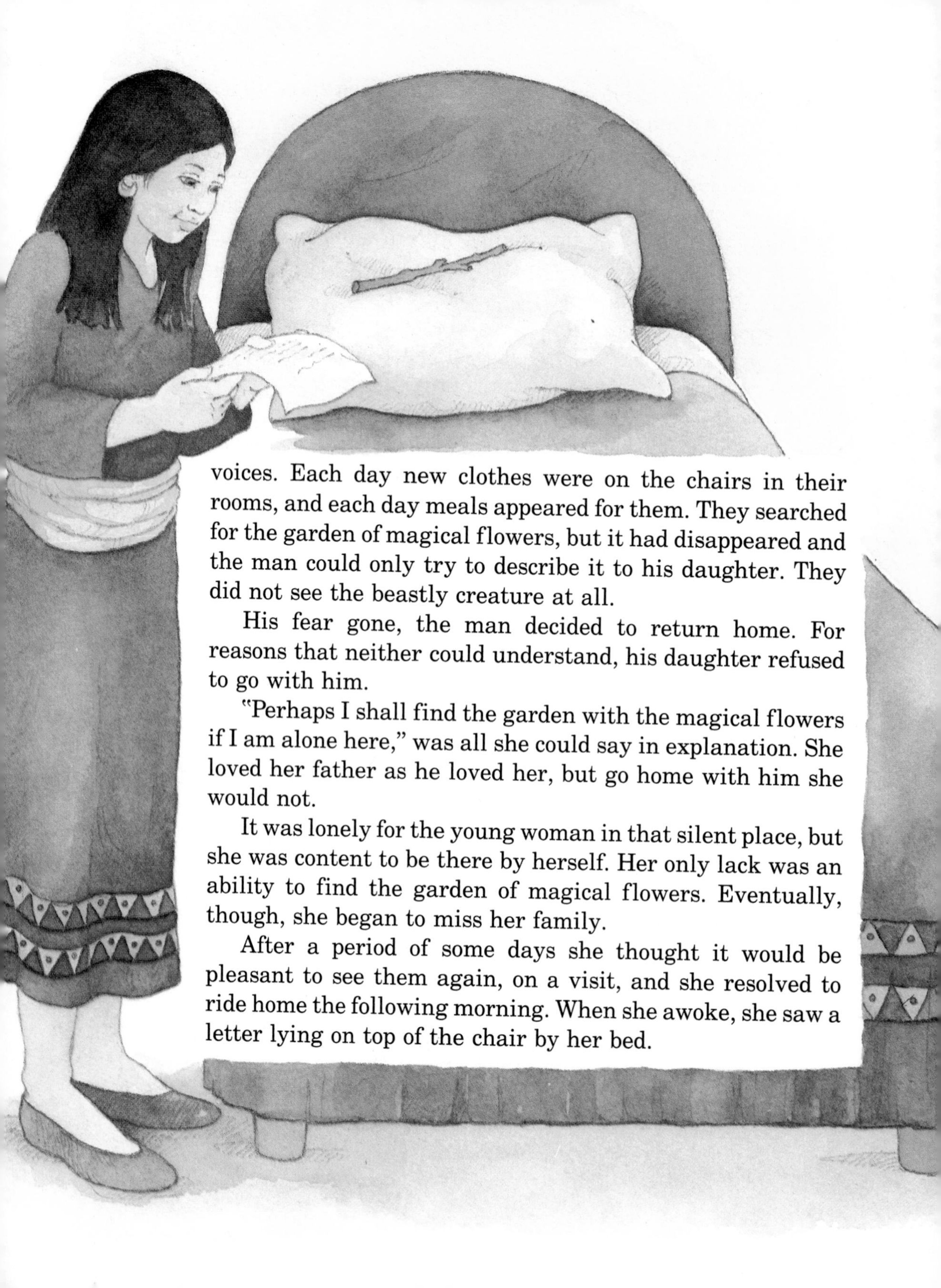

voices. Each day new clothes were on the chairs in their rooms, and each day meals appeared for them. They searched for the garden of magical flowers, but it had disappeared and the man could only try to describe it to his daughter. They did not see the beastly creature at all.

His fear gone, the man decided to return home. For reasons that neither could understand, his daughter refused to go with him.

"Perhaps I shall find the garden with the magical flowers if I am alone here," was all she could say in explanation. She loved her father as he loved her, but go home with him she would not.

It was lonely for the young woman in that silent place, but she was content to be there by herself. Her only lack was an ability to find the garden of magical flowers. Eventually, though, she began to miss her family.

After a period of some days she thought it would be pleasant to see them again, on a visit, and she resolved to ride home the following morning. When she awoke, she saw a letter lying on top of the chair by her bed.

The letter said that there was a little stick on her pillow. She glanced down and there it was; she was sure it had not been there before. She read on. The writer of the letter told her that if she bit the little stick, she would find herself with her family. On the third day of her stay, she was to bite the stick again and it would bring her back. The letter made no mention of the silent and strange place where she was staying, but she knew in her heart that it was to be her new home. The letter was unsigned. But the writer said that if she did not return in three days he, her unseen host, would die.

The young woman did not doubt the truth of all that was written in the letter. She put on yet another set of new clothes and then bit on the little stick. Immediately she found herself upon her horse outside her father's house.

Her family was overjoyed to see her, and they spent three happy days together. They could not understand her contentment at the silent place. Even though she had neither seen nor heard the beastly creature and had never been afraid of it, they begged her not to return.

On the third day her father and sisters were with her all the time, begging her not to leave them, for she had said that that was the day she would go back to the silent place. Not until after dark was she able to slip away. She took the little stick from the pocket of her dress and bit on it. At once she was mounted on her horse outside the stable of the silent place. The lamp at the entrance was lit, and she dismounted and led her horse inside.

For the first time since she had heard her father's story of the beastly creature, she felt the cold and prickly sensation of fear. But it was not for herself that she was fearful. She hurried through the stable to the room beyond. There, as she had anticipated, was a meal awaiting her. But stretched out

on the floor was the monster her father had described. It was dead.

Her fear left her and her only feeling was one of intense sorrow. To her the beastly creature was not a hideous or fearsome monster: it was something that had died alone and unloved. She cradled its head and wept for its loneliness.

After several hours she fell asleep on the floor beside the corpse. She dreamed it was alive again and that it spoke to her, saying, "Go and pick the flower that pleases you most and pour the liquid from its heart onto my head."

She was still weeping when she woke up. She saw the creature was dead indeed and not alive as in her dream. But she wondered about the dream as she wandered through the stable out into the sunshine.

In front of her she saw a blazing mass of color. Here at last was the garden of magical flowers of which her father had spoken. She walked toward it and marveled at the beauty of the flowers, each one different and unlike any other. Her eyes were dazzled and her mind was dulled by the perfumed vapor that rose from the colored glory. And then she saw by her foot one flower that seemed quite lovely. It was white, faintly tinged with mauve. The hollow spiral petal shimmered with a glow. It was the flower that pleased her most. She plucked it. It was cool against her cheek. As her dizziness left her, she saw there was liquid inside the flower, and the memory of her dream flooded back. Quickly she returned to the corpse and poured the contents of the flower onto the shaggy head.

The beastly creature suddenly moved and got up. But it was not the monster standing there. In its place stood a handsome and kindly looking young man. He held out his arms to the young woman and took her hands in his. He kissed first the flower and then her hands. "At last, my love, at last," he whispered.

And she kissed the flower and his hands and answered him. "At last, my love, at last."

And they held the flower together in their cupped hands and smiled at each other and murmured, "The flower that pleases us both the most."

Think About It

1. Why did the beastly creature let the merchant go?
2. In what ways did the creature use his magical powers to do good?
3. The story refers in several places to "the cold and prickly sensation of fear." How was the young woman's fear upon returning to the creature's house different from the fear felt by others in the story?
4. How was the young man brought back to life?
5. Write about what might have caused the young man to turn into a beastly creature in the first place.

The Winged Colt of Casa Mia

by BETSY BYARS

Coot Cutter, a former stunt man in the movies, lived alone on his Texas ranch, the Casa Mia. Then two things happened to change his life: his nephew Charles came to live with him, and a palomino colt was born with wings.

Charles looks up to his uncle as a superhero. He also loves the colt and names him Alado, which means "winged" in Spanish. But Coot remains puzzled and a bit worried about the colt. Together Coot and Charles try to raise Alado like a regular horse, but neither they nor the colt seems to know what to do about his wings.

The story begins when the colt is about a year old. So far, Alado has flown twice in his life, but awkwardly and only for a short time when he was frightened by something. Coot tells what happens next.

In this part of the country anything seems possible in the summer. The colors are brighter than any you ever saw, and the bare mountains against the sky look like their names—Cathedral Point and Weeping Women and Devil's Back. A desert arroyo, dry for years, rushes with water after a rain, and a light burns in the desert and no one can find it. A winged colt doesn't seem strange at all in the Texas summer.

June started slow and easy. Charles was out of school now and spending most of his time with Alado.

One day Charles decided to take Alado to the mesa, which was about two miles behind the house. A mesa, which means "table" in Spanish, is just a flat-topped piece of land with steep sides. It used to be a hill, I guess, only the sides washed away and the top wore smooth, leaving a piece of land like a platform. There was a stream that ran by the mesa after a rain, and that was why Charles had decided to go.

Charles and Alado set out, and right away Bones the dog came crawling out from under the porch and started after them. He never liked Alado to go off without him.

At three o'clock I was outside working on the truck, and I happened to glance up and see a glider flying overhead. The glider was low, circling about a mile north of the corral. I straightened up quick.

"Hey, Charles!" I called, in case he had come home without my seeing him. "Charles!" I wanted him to see the glider because that was all he had been talking about since Sunday, when we had gone into town. The National Gliding Championship was being held there, and since these were the first gliders Charles had ever seen, he couldn't quit talking about them.

A glider, in case you never saw one either, is an airplane that flies without an engine. These gliders have races and distance tasks, and when the contest is going on, you can see gliders and glider trailers everywhere you look.

"Charles!" I called again. I knew he was going to be disappointed.

I watched the glider and, from what Charles had told me, I figured the pilot wasn't doing too well. He had gotten low and was moving toward the road.

In this part of Texas there aren't many places to land a glider because most of the land has yucca and mesquite on it. So sometimes the pilots land their gliders on the road.

By now the glider was so close overhead I could hear a funny eerie noise as it passed, a whistling sound. The pilot moved closer to the road. I got in my truck and drove as fast as I could. I got to the main road just in time to see the glider land.

I went over and helped the pilot pull his glider to the side of the road, and then I looked it over. The pilot leaned in the cockpit and did something to the instruments. Then he glanced at me. I was standing at the back of the glider, by the T-shaped tail.

"You own that ranch over there?" he asked.

I nodded. "What is this for?" I asked, pointing to a metal thing that was sticking out of the tail. And then the pilot asked something that stopped me cold.

He said, "What was that thing I saw flying back there?"

"What?" I asked. My hand dropped to my side.

"Back there at the mesa behind your place. I couldn't get a good look at what it was, but it was flying. It looked as big as a horse. I don't suppose you folks raise flying horses around here." He laughed.

I got a funny feeling in the pit of my stomach. I said quickly, "Look, if there's nothing I can do for you here, I better get back to the ranch." I knew that Charles was in trouble.

He said, "Sure, here comes my crew now." We looked up the road at a car pulling a long white trailer.

I got in the truck and drove back to the ranch as fast as I

could. I jumped out and saw Bones coming toward the house. He was just a streak he was going so fast, and his tail was between his legs and his ears were flattened against his head. He ran around the house and went under the steps. I heard him work his way back under the porch. He was panting as if his lungs would burst.

As soon as the pilot had mentioned seeing something fly back at the mesa, I had known something was wrong. It was confirmed now. Unless something had happened to frighten him badly, the dog would never have left Alado.

My horse Clay was already saddled. I started out as fast as I could in the direction Charles and Alado had taken. I rode all the way to the mesa without seeing a trace of them.

"Charles! Charles!"

There was no answer. I turned Clay and rode to the right. I had the feeling that something had happened to Charles, and I suddenly got a sickness in my stomach.

I rode, stopped, and called again. "Charles, where are you?" I threw back my head and bellowed, *"Charles!"*

I waited a minute, and then I heard his voice in the distance. I rode around the mesa.

"Here I am," he called.

I looked up and saw Charles clinging to the side of the mesa. He hadn't gotten far, and he appeared to be stuck.

"What are you doing up there?" The relief of seeing him safe made me yell louder than was necessary.

"Uncle Coot?" He was stammering so badly I could hardly recognize my own name.

"What happened?" He swallowed, and I said, "Now, come on, Charles, what are you doing up there? What's going on?"

"I don't know exactly," he said, still stuttering a little. "We were coming down to the stream, Bones and Alado and I, just like we planned."

He stopped and I said, "Go on, Charles. The three of you were coming to the stream."

"Yes, and just then I looked up and saw a javelina ahead with her babies."

"Go on." A javelina is a wild pig. They can be mean, but

there's not much danger as long as you let them alone. "You didn't bother them, did you?"

"No, as soon as I saw them, I started backing up. I was going around to the other side."

"So what happened?"

"Well, when I stepped back, I stepped right on Bones. He was behind me, see, and as soon as I did this, he let out a terrible howl and leaped forward and landed directly in front of the javelina." He paused and shook his head. "After that I just don't know what did happen. It was like a tornado. Pigs were charging—it seemed like there were a hundred of them—and Bones was howling and running—and I was trying to grab Bones and we all rolled right into the path of Alado."

"And Alado flew," I said with a sinking feeling.

"It was terrible at first, Uncle Coot. I was never so scared in my life. And then all of a sudden he was flying. He was *really* flying."

"Well, that's great." I knew there was something that he hadn't told me yet. "If Alado can get control of himself, he'll be safe. We won't worry about him."

"I thought he was never going to stop, Uncle Coot. He flew and flew and *flew*."

Suddenly a terrible thought came to me. I said slowly and carefully, "Where is Alado now, Charles?"

At that question Charles's face sort of crumpled.

"Where is he now?" I asked, hitting at every word.

Without a word Charles lifted one hand. He pointed to the top of the mesa. With a sort of sick feeling in my stomach, I looked up and saw standing on top of the mesa, about fifty miles above us—anyway that was how it looked—the colt Alado.

Charles raised his head, and we both looked up at the colt for a moment. The height gave him a frailness, and Charles looked away quickly. He said in a rush, "But he flew real good, Uncle Coot. I wish you could have been here. He really flew!"

"I can see that."

"I mean he can really *fly,* Uncle Coot. He—"

"I can see that, Charles. There's no other way he could get up on top of that mesa."

There was a moment of silence, and then Charles said, "How are you going to get him down?"

All at once I felt tired. I felt so tired I could have just dropped out of the saddle. It was Charles's last statement that did it, I think, that "How are *you* going to get him down?"

Charles said again, "How are you going to get him down?"

"Well," I said finally, "I reckon he'll have to get down the same way he got up." To tell the truth I didn't know what to do about the colt. The sight of him up on the mesa had made me feel like I'd had too much sun.

"You mean fly down?" he asked.

"Yeah, I guess he'll have to fly down."

"But, Uncle Coot, he only flies when he's startled or frightened. He would never just fly on his own. He can't reason that out. You told me yourself that horses can't reason. You told me that horses do foolish things sometimes because they can't reason. I remember your saying that horses will run

straight into a fire instead of away from it."

"But flying is an instinct with this horse."

"I *know* he won't fly down."

"Well, we can wait and see, can't we? We don't have to start risking our lives this second." I wanted some time, but I could see I wasn't going to get it.

"You can wait if you want to." Charles started scrambling up the side of the mesa. His position hadn't been good to start with, and what with all the sliding and slipping he ended up even lower than he had started.

"I'm not going to wait around for him to fall off and kill himself. There's no need your trying to stop me." He said it like he was trying to give me an idea.

The last thing in the world I wanted to do was get off my horse and climb that mesa, particularly when I didn't know what to do when I got up there. I sat a minute more, leaning forward on my saddle. I shifted, and then before I could say anything, Charles blurted out, "You don't care about Alado at all, do you?"

It caught me by surprise, the way he said it and the way he was looking at me. "What?"

"You don't care about Alado." He paused. "You don't care about anything."

"Now just hold on a minute," I hollered. I wanted to say something then—he was listening—but for some reason I froze. All my life I've been troubled by not being able to say what I wanted.

He waited, and the moment for me to speak came and went. He said, "You don't care about anything," in a low voice. Then he added, "Or anybody."

Suddenly I remembered when I was six years old and I came galloping across the front yard on old Bumble Bee, standing up, arms out, yelling, "Pa, look at me!" Later, when I hit the ground and lay there half dead, my pa came over and started pulling my belt to get the air back in me. He said, "You want to get yourself killed? Is that what you're trying to do?" It was the first summer I had seen my pa since I was a baby, and I wanted him to notice me so bad I would have tried about anything. Every time I got near him I'd put his hand on my head or his arm over my shoulder or I'd try to climb on his back or swing on his arm. I broke my wrist two times that summer trying to make him show he cared about me.

I said, "I'll go up and get the colt."

Charles wiped his nose and climbed down a few steps. He slid the rest of the way to the ground, and said, "How will you get him down?"

"I don't know." I rode Clay all the way around the mesa until I found a place where I might, with a lot of luck, be able to climb up without killing myself.

Charles came running over, out of breath. "Is this where you're going up?" he asked, squinting at the mesa.

"This is where I'm going to *try* to go up, yes."

"You can make it. I know you can."

I never felt less like a superman in my life. I said, "The cameras are not rolling now, Charles." I got off the horse and threw the reins over a bush.

Charles paused, and then he came over and rested one hand on Clay's neck. He hesitated. He said, "Maybe we could wait a little while, Uncle Coot. What do you think? Maybe he *will* fly down."

I started up the side of the mesa without saying anything. I'm not much of a climber. My bad hip bothers me when I have to put a lot of weight on it, and I slipped twice before I went ten feet.

"Uncle Coot, if you want to wait for a little while, it's all right with me."

I kept going. I managed to get about halfway just by going real slow, one step at a time, the way a little kid goes up stairs. I stopped to rest against an outcropping of rock. "Are you doing all right?" Charles called from the ground.

"Wonderful."

"You look like you're almost a fourth of the way to the top."

I had thought I was bound to be a good bit farther than that, but I didn't say anything.

"The rest of the way looks like it's going to be a little harder though," he called. "It's steeper and there don't seem to be as many bushes to hold on to."

So far the total number of bushes I had found was one prickly-pear cactus which I would not advise holding unless it was a life-and-death situation. I rested a moment longer, and I started thinking how much easier things are in the movies. Like sometimes in a movie when somebody is supposed to be climbing up a cliff, they will just let him crawl on his stomach on the ground, and they will film this at a steep angle to make it look like he's climbing.

"Why are you stopping, Uncle Coot?" Charles called up. "Is there any special reason?"

The hurting in my hip had begun to ease. I looked down at him. "No, nothing special."

I started climbing again. I can't tell you exactly how long

that climb took me, but it seemed like the longest afternoon of my life. And all the while Charles was calling things about my progress. Once I guess he looked away, because he called, "What happened? Did you slip?"

"Slip?"

"Yes, I thought you were farther up than that."

"No," I said, "I'm not any farther than this."

"Well, it just seems like you're lower now than you were, Uncle Coot."

"Lower in spirits," I said.

"What?"

"Nothing!"

"What? I couldn't hear what you said."

"Nothing!"

He must have known from the way that "nothing" rumbled down the side of the mesa that it would be a good idea for him to shut up. He didn't call to me any more, just gasped once when I did slip a little. I looked down at him right before I pulled myself up on top of the mesa, and he was standing there with his hands raised against his chest like a small church steeple.

The top of a mesa isn't anything beautiful—just dry grass and rocks and a few straggly

plants—but it looked good to me. I lay there on my stomach for a moment and then I stood up. My hip was hurting so bad I thought I wouldn't be able to walk. I shook my leg a little, which sometimes eases it, and tried to put weight on it.

Across the top of the mesa Alado was standing watching me. "Here, boy," I said.

He came over slowly, tossing his head. He was like any animal in a strange situation, and he shied away a few times before he came. I patted him and scratched his nose. "When you fly, boy," I said, "you really fly, don't you?"

"Hey, Uncle Coot?" Charles called from below.

"What?"

"Is he all right?"

"Yes."

"He's not hurt or anything?"

"*He's* not."

"Are you sure?"

"Yes."

"Well, how are you going to get him down? Have you got any ideas yet?"

"No."

"As soon as you get an idea, will you let me know?"

"Yes."

I looked at the colt and I scratched his nose again. "Alado," I said, "we are stuck." Then I shook my leg and rubbed his neck and tried to think of some way to do this impossible thing before dark.

The sun gets the color of desert poppies at sunset out here, but this evening it was something I dreaded seeing. I had been stuck up on the mesa with the colt for three hours, and I was no closer to getting him down than I had been at first. I was also bone tired and hungry, and I did not have an idea in my whole head.

When I first got up, I had tried to startle Alado a few times by waving my arms at him and tossing my hat under his feet. All I got for my trouble was a crumpled hat. The thing was that Alado wouldn't get near the edge of the mesa. As long as Charles and I had both been on the ground he had looked over constantly, coming right to the edge. Now that I was up here with him, he stayed in the exact center.

I didn't blame him really. If he went over the side, he wouldn't have to fall far before he struck the rocks, and it turned me cold to think about that. Still, if he got a good running start, I kept thinking— Then I would give him the old hat under the feet a few more times. Nothing doing.

It stays light a long time out here—sunset is usually about nine-thirty—but once the sun drops it gets dark fast. By this time the sun was disappearing below the horizon. I got up, went to the edge of the cliff, and called, "Charles!"

His head almost snapped off his neck he looked up so fast. "What is it, Uncle Coot?"

"I want you to take Clay and go back to the house, hear?"

"I don't want to."

"Well, do it anyway. There's no need both of us spending the night out here."

"I don't want to leave Alado," he said. He looked down at his feet and then back up at me. "I don't want to leave you either."

Sometimes a man's life shifts in a moment. It's happened to me more times than most men because I've had a hard, fast life. I felt it happening again.

"Did you hear me, Uncle Coot? I don't want to leave you out here either."

I nodded. We kept standing there and I knew somehow that Charles, looking up at me from that distance, suddenly saw how little separated us. I wasn't so much of a superman at that moment, and when I looked down at him, I could have been looking back over the years at myself. The truth slithered up to us like a sidewinder. Separated by the height of a mesa, we were the closest we'd ever been.

"All right," I said, "go home, then, and get a blanket."

"Thanks, Uncle Coot." He untied Clay quickly and rode off toward home. I watched till he was out of sight. Then I lay down and tried to get some rest.

"I'm back, Uncle Coot," he called after a while.

I got up, walked to the edge of the mesa, and watched him spread out his blanket in the moonlight.

"I'll be right here if you need me."

"Fine, Charles."

I went back and lay down. There's no getting comfortable on top of a mesa—I had already found that out—but I got settled for a long night the best I could.

Alado was standing near my feet. He was so still I thought he must be asleep. About midnight—although I didn't think it would ever happen—my eyes closed too.

I woke up and it was two o'clock in the morning and I couldn't see the colt. I got up slowly. My hip had stiffened while I was asleep, and I limped forward a few steps.

I whistled and called, "Alado!" The sky was as bright with stars as I'd ever seen it and the moon was big. I looked around and I still couldn't see the colt. "Alado!"

For a moment there was silence and then I heard a whinny to my right. I hobbled over and saw what had happened.

On this side of the mesa there was a gentle slope. At the bottom of the slope was a steep cliff, straight down to the rocks, but the colt didn't know this. The moonlight made everything look different, and I could see why he had been fooled. The colt had seen the slope, started down, and now he couldn't get back up.

"Here, Alado, come."

I reached down to take his halter and lead him back. Sometimes all a horse needs is a familiar hand to help him do something he couldn't do on his own. As I reached down, though, my hip gave way. It just buckled.

I yelled, more with surprise than pain, and then I slipped down the slope. I hollered and scratched and grabbed at whatever I could find. I went wild for a moment. I knew that if I didn't stop, I would slip right off the cliff, take the colt with me, and both of us would end up on the rocks below.

My fingers dug into the ground like steel hooks, but I kept slipping. I was right by the colt's legs now, and although I hadn't touched him, he started slipping too. He was scared, I knew that, and for a moment I thought we were both lost. I squirmed around to avoid hitting him, and right then my foot found a rock ledge and I stopped.

"It's all right, Alado. It's all right, boy," I gasped.

He whinnied now, a loud high whinny. I turned over on my back and looked up. His pale legs were flashing by my face, thumping against the earth. Alado wasn't slipping anymore, but the dirt was still sliding down the slope and over the cliff, and that gave him the feeling he was. I tried to reach up and hold him, but at that moment his wings flashed out. The wind from them beat against me. I drew back.

Alado paused a moment, the wings lashing at the air, covering me when they came down. It was a strange, eerie thing. The wings blocked out the sky, the whole world. I couldn't move and I couldn't speak. The colt slipped again. I was frozen against the ground. Then he slid a few more inches down the slope, and he was in the air.

I managed to sit up then and look down the cliff. For a second the colt seemed to drop straight down. He just sank. The huge white wings flashing in the night seemed powerless. His body was turned a little sideways. It was like a fever dream. Then, at the last moment, just when I thought he was going to crash into the rocks, an updraft of wind rose beneath his wings and he flew.

He flew away from the cliff, his pale wings powerful now, sure. This was the way I had dreamed he would fly. I couldn't move for a moment and it wasn't my hip either. It was the sight of that colt in the air. In all my life I have never seen anything like that, terrible and awesome at the same time. It was something that was going to be with me the rest of my days.

Then Alado landed about two hundred yards away and, without a break, ran off into the night.

I stayed there a moment, hanging on the slope like a kid halfway down a sliding board. I was still too caught up in what I'd seen to move. Finally I made myself turn and work my way back up. I limped over, picked up my hat, and put it on my head.

I've heard men say that coming down a mountain is harder than climbing up, but it wasn't for me. After I climbed down the first part, which was red rock, I slid down the rest of the way—or fell sitting down, whatever you want to call it. I was rolling down the last part when Charles ran up and threw himself on top of me. It stopped me from rolling anyway. I hesitated a minute, and then I put my arms around him and he started crying. He didn't make any noise doing it, but I knew he was crying because his tears were rolling down my neck.

"It's all right, Charles. It's all right." I patted him on the back.

He said, "You could have been killed."

For some reason his seeing me as I was, just a plain person, made me feel like crying too. I patted his back again. "It's all right." I waited until he was through crying, and then I said, "Did you see Alado?"

He nodded against my chest.

"You saw him fly?"

"Yes."

We stayed there a minute. "It was something, wasn't it?" I said.

"Yes."

"It was really something." I took a deep breath and slapped him on the back. "Well, let's get Clay and start for home. Give me a hand up." Charles helped me to my feet, and I dusted myself off. We started walking toward where Clay was standing by the stream.

Then we heard the sound of a horse, and I saw Alado coming toward us. Alado went to Charles and nuzzled him and started walking beside him.

I looked at the colt and the boy. I said, "I'll tell you something, Charles. One day that colt is going to fly as easy as he walks."

Charles looked at Alado. Without glancing at me he said, "I know." I knew he was seeing again the pale wings in the dark sky just as I was. Seeing the colt fly like that, being the only two people in the world to have shared that awful and beautiful sight, touched us so much we couldn't speak of it any more. I knew he was thinking as I was, "One day . . . "

I lifted myself into the saddle. Then I turned. "Here, Charles, take my hand." I pulled him up behind me. "Let's go home." And we rode off together on Clay with Alado following behind.

READ ON!

The Wizard in the Tree by Lloyd Alexander. An old wizard and an orphan girl battle some evil characters in this fanciful adventure story.

Dragons and Other Fabulous Beasts by Richard Blythe. Read these entertaining folktales about some strange creatures that have been amazing, and sometimes scaring, the world for centuries.

Behind the Attic Wall by Sylvia Cassedy. Twelve-year-old Maggie is lonely and bored living with her great-aunts in their big house. Then she discovers the magical place that exists behind the attic wall.

The House of Dies Drear by Virginia Hamilton. In this house, a hundred years before, Dies Drear and two slaves he was hiding were murdered. Now, strange and frightening things begin to happen to the new family living there. Read this fascinating book to find out why.

Journey to the Planets by Patricia Lauber. Information and photographs from recent space probes make this book exciting reading.

Lizard Music by Manus Pinkwater. To his surprise, Victor sees a lizard band. And they sound good too! Laugh your way through Victor's zany adventures on a strange island inhabited by very charming and musical lizards.

UNIT 2

This Growing Time

LEARN NEW WORDS

1. I felt totally **disgraced** because I struck out every time I got up to bat.
2. They made **disparaging** remarks about the way the boy was dressed, saying that his clothes were funny-looking.
3. After he decided to become a **hermit**, he moved to a quiet place and lived his life alone.
4. The proud girl felt **humiliated** when everyone teased her and made disparaging remarks.
5. The children dressed in costumes and masks to go to the **masquerade** party.
6. Susan was **monopolizing** the phone, leaving little time for anyone else to make calls.
7. When my great-grandmother was young, she entertained her friends in the **parlor** of her parents' home.
8. His mother said his odd behavior was just a **phase** he was going through that would stop as quickly as it began.
9. He opened the **transom** above the door to let in more air.

GET SET TO READ

What would it be like to have a brother or sister do something embarrassing? What could be done about it?

Read this story to find out what Tom and two of his brothers do when their oldest brother adopts a new style.

The Great Brain and the Dude

by JOHN D. FITZGERALD

Growing up in the small town of Adenville, Utah, in 1898 was great if you had a brother with a great brain and he used it to play tricks on others but not on you. Eleven-year-old John tells one story of how he benefited personally from his twelve-year-old brother's great brain.

My brother Tom knew the ABC's, could write numbers from one to one hundred, spell a lot of words, and read simple sentences before he started school. He did get some help from Papa and Mamma and my oldest brother Sweyn, but he learned most of these things by himself.

Later, the schoolteacher let Tom skip the fifth grade. I guess that proves how smart my brother was.

Everybody laughed when, at the age of eight, Tom started telling people he had a great brain. But after he began to use his great brain to fool people, nobody laughed at him anymore.

With Christmas coming up Tom temporarily gave up trying to trick people. Sweyn was coming home for the Christmas holidays. We all went down to the depot to meet him.

When Sweyn left to go back east for his first year of high school, he was wearing a blue serge worsted suit with knee-length britches and a cap like all boys in Adenville wore until they were sixteen. A fellow didn't get a pair of long pants until he was sixteen.

But when Sweyn, who was only fifteen, returned home, he had blossomed out into a full-blown dude. He was wearing a light-gray checkered wool suit with long pants, shoes without laces that you pulled on, a derby hat, a blue-and-white-striped corded-front shirt, a purple necktie with a handkerchief to match in the breast pocket of the suit, and silk embroidered suspenders, all the likes of which had never been seen in Adenville, and maybe not even in all of Utah.

You can bet that Tom, my younger brother Frankie, and I held our heads down with shame as we walked toward home. People on the street turned around to stare at my oldest brother, peeked out of windows, and came out of stores to watch. It was a sight never seen before in Adenville, a full-blown dude walking down Main Street. I had never felt so humiliated in my life.

Sweyn had arrived on the eleven o'clock morning train on Monday, December the nineteenth. He would be home for ten days. Boy, oh, boy, the thought of having the fellows see my big dude brother with his fancy duds for ten days was enough to make me want to run away from home. It was bad enough when Sweyn had disgraced us by starting to go with

a girl at the age of thirteen. And now at the age of fifteen he had turned into a real dude.

Sweyn was in such a hurry to show off his fancy duds to his girl, Marie Vinson, that he excused himself from the table as soon as we finished lunch. He got his derby hat from the hallway hat rack and came back into the dining room.

"*Adieu* and toodle-oo," he said with a wave of the derby.

Tom stood up. "And a cockle-doodle-doo to you," he said, flapping his arms as if they were the wings of a rooster.

That made everybody but Sweyn laugh.

"*Enfant,*" he said and left.

Tom sat back at the table and looked at Papa. "What is that 'adieu,' 'toodle-oo,' and 'enfant' business?" he asked.

"Your brother is just showing off some of the French he learned during his first term in high school," Papa replied. "*Adieu* means good-by and *enfant* is French for infant."

"I'll infant him," Tom said frowning. "And what about that 'toodle-oo'? What kind of an insult is that?"

"It isn't an insult," Papa said, chuckling. "It is a rather common expression back east, just as we say 'so long.'"

Tom shook his head. "Are you and Mamma going to let Sweyn run around Adenville wearing those fancy duds and giving people that 'adieu' and 'toodle-oo' business?"

"Why not?" Papa asked.

"I'll tell you why not," Tom said. "People will think he has turned into an eighteen-karat sissy for sure."

"Don't be too hard on your brother," Papa said. "It is a phase every boy goes through during his first year of high school."

"Not me," Tom said. "I'm not going through any phase. If I have to wear fancy duds like that to go to high school in Pennsylvania next year, I'm not going."

"You will change your mind when you get there," Papa said. "All things, including clothing, are relative to time and place."

"What do you mean by that?" Tom asked.

"Well," Papa said smiling, "I wouldn't walk down Main Street and go to work at the newspaper office wearing my nightshirt because it is the wrong time and place to wear a nightshirt. But it is perfectly proper to wear my nightshirt to bed because that is the time and place for it."

That made us all laugh.

"Seriously, Tom," Papa said, "you would be just as much out of place wearing clothing suitable for Adenville at high school back east as your brother is wearing his eastern clothing here in Adenville."

"Then why don't you make him stop wearing those fancy duds while he is home?" Tom asked.

"Let him enjoy himself by showing off his new wardrobe to his girl," Papa said.

"Maybe Sweyn will enjoy himself," Tom said, "but John, Frankie, and I sure won't. The fellows will really make fun of us for having a dude for a brother."

After lunch, I sat on the railing of our corral fence with Tom.

"Why are we sitting here?" I asked. "It's Christmas vacation. Let's go to Smith's vacant lot and play."

"I don't feel like listening to the fellows rub salt in our wounds because we've got a dude brother," Tom said. "I'm going up to my loft and put my great brain to work on how to make Sweyn stop wearing those fancy duds while he is home."

I didn't want to just sit on our corral fence for my Christmas vacation. I decided to go to Smith's vacant lot. Tom was sure right. All the fellows stopped playing and crowded around me.

"Who was that fancy pants your family met at the train this morning?" Parley asked.

"You know it was my brother Sweyn," I said.

Danny Forester grinned. "I'll bet he uses perfume."

Hal Evans got in his licks. "If I had a sissy dude brother like that," he said, "I'd go hide in the mountains and become a hermit."

Seth Smith patted my shoulder. "I feel sorry for you and Tom," he said. "It must run in the family. That means both you and Tom will become dudes when you are fifteen."

"We will not," I said. "Tom is up in his loft right now putting his great brain to work on how to make Sweyn get rid of all those fancy duds."

I thought they would leave me alone after that but they didn't. They kept making disparaging remarks about Sweyn until I got disgusted and went home. I waited for Tom until he came down from his loft to help with the evening chores.

"Boy, oh, boy," I said. "You were sure right. The fellows let me have it with both barrels until I couldn't stand it anymore and came home. Did your great brain figure anything out yet?"

"Not yet," Tom said. "But it will. I'm not going to let Sweyn spoil our vacation."

"If your great brain doesn't do something," I said, "I'm going to pretend I'm sick and stay in bed for the whole Christmas vacation."

That evening Sweyn went up to his room. He didn't come down to the parlor until after Mamma and Aunt Bertha had finished the supper dishes. He had on a brand-new dude outfit. He was wearing white flannel trousers, a thing he called a blazer that was like a coat only it was made from light material that had big red and white stripes on it, and he was carrying a straw hat in one hand and a tennis racket in the other hand.

Tom stared at him bug-eyed. "Have you gone plumb loco?" he asked. "There aren't any tennis courts in Adenville and you can't play tennis in the dark anyway."

"I promised Marie that I'd show her my tennis outfit," Sweyn said. "And if I do say so myself, I learned to play a very good game of tennis back east.

And next summer I'm going to get some young fellows together and build us a tennis court here in Adenville."

"But you can't go walking down Main Street in that outfit," Tom said. "People will think you are crazy wearing white flannel trousers and a straw hat and carrying a tennis racket in winter."

"You're just jealous of my outfit," Sweyn said.

"How can I be jealous of a jerk?" Tom asked. Then he turned to Papa. "Please stop him. He'll make us the laughingstock of Adenville."

But Papa just smiled. "I think you're making a mountain lion out of a kitten," he said.

Mamma agreed. "And so do I," she said.

Sweyn gave us a wave with his straw hat. "Toodle-oo, everybody," he said as he left.

Right on the spot I decided to become a hermit and not to show my face outside the house until Sweyn went back to high school. Some of the fellows were sure to see him and boy, oh, boy, would they rub it in. I continued playing checkers with Frankie, but he beat me because I didn't have my mind on the game. Tom was reading a book, but I knew his mind wasn't on what he was doing either. Then Mamma spoke.

"The ragbag is almost full, Bertha," she said. "I think we should start making another patch quilt."

Aunt Bertha looked up from the sock she was darning. "Can't start tomorrow," she said. "The Ladies Sewing Circle meets, remember?"

"Of course," Mamma said. "But we will start the day after tomorrow on the quilt."

I was surprised to see how interested Tom had become in the conversation. He stopped reading and just sat there. I knew his great brain was working on something because of the furrows in his forehead.

I couldn't see why the ragbag would interest Tom. Mamma never threw anything away. When our clothes wore out, she laundered them and put them in the ragbag in the bathroom closet. When she needed a rag she always took out something white, like a worn-out suit of underwear. All the colored pieces in the ragbag she kept to make patch quilts. I was so curious as to why the ragbag interested Tom that I stayed awake that night until he came up to bed.

"Why are you so interested in the ragbag?" I asked.

"My great brain has come up with a plan to make Sweyn stop wearing those fancy duds," Tom said. "We'll put the plan into action tomorrow afternoon when Mamma and Aunt Bertha leave for the Ladies Sewing Circle. Don't ask me any more questions. There are a few details my great brain has to figure out."

I was as curious as all get out, but I didn't learn any more until the next afternoon. I was sitting on the back porch steps with Tom and Frankie. Mamma opened the kitchen door.

"Bertha and I are leaving now," she said.

We walked to the side of the house and waited until we saw Mamma and Aunt Bertha going down the street.

"Everything is working out perfect," Tom said. "Mamma and Aunt Bertha are gone. Papa has Sweyn helping him at the newspaper office. Let's go."

Tom got the ragbag and dumped its contents on the floor.

"What's the idea?" I asked.

"Sweyn's girl, Marie Vinson, has been away at school in Salt Lake City," Tom said. "She hasn't seen any of us since last summer. Now do as I tell you and stop asking questions. Strip down to your underwear and take off your shoes and stockings."

Tom began looking through the pile of stuff from the ragbag. Mamma had a system. When we got a new suit it became our Sunday best, which we wore to church. When it became too worn for church we wore the suit to school. When it became too worn for school we wore the suit for playclothes and it remained playclothes as long as Mamma could mend and patch it. Then it was put in the ragbag.

Tom picked out an old suit of Frankie's that was worn and patched. Then he picked out a worn-out suit for himself and one for me. He hunted until he found us all worn and patched shirts, and he tore a few of the patches off before he handed them to us. All the clothes were too small for us because we'd grown. When we got dressed, we looked like three ragamuffins from the poorest family in town.

"Now here is the plan," Tom said. "I want Marie Vinson to think Papa and Mamma are spending so much money buying Sweyn fancy duds that the three of us have to wear rags. Let's go."

We sneaked down alleys without being seen until we were in back of the Vinson home.

"We know Mr. Vinson is at work," Tom said, "and Mrs. Vinson is at the Ladies Sewing Circle meeting. That means Marie must be alone. Follow me."

He led us to the back porch and knocked on the kitchen door. A moment later Marie Vinson opened the door.

"We didn't want to disgrace you by going to the front door," Tom said. "But I've got to see my brother, Sweyn, and ask him if I

can use his horse, Dusty. Is he here?"

Marie stood bug-eyed and tongue-tied for about a minute before she could speak.

"You . . . you can't be," she finally said. "No, I know you are Sweyn's brothers. Why are you dressed like that? Are you going to a masquerade party?"

"No, we're not going to a masquerade party," Tom said, sadly shaking his head. "These are the clothes we wear to school and all the time now. You see, it has cost Papa and Mamma so much money to send Sweyn back east to school and buy him all those fancy clothes, there just isn't any money left to buy clothes for us."

"But that isn't fair," Marie said.

"Papa and Mamma can't help it," Tom said. "Sweyn is their pet. They give him everything he wants even if it means we have to wear rags. I guess he isn't here. I wonder where he could be."

"He told me that he had to help your father at the newspaper office," Marie said.

"Thank you," Tom said. "I'll see him there."

"And when you do," Marie said, "just tell him that I never want to see him again, the selfish thing."

She shut the door. Tom winked at Frankie and me. We had a hard time not laughing until we reached the alley. Then we laughed all the way home. We put the old clothes back in the ragbag and got dressed in our regular clothes.

"She went for it hook, line, and sinker," Tom said grinning. "The first part of my great brain's plan was a success."

"But won't Sweyn be mad?" Frankie asked.

"If my plan works," Tom said, "he will not only be angry but also heartbroken. We can't take a chance of Marie Vinson seeing us dressed like this. We'll have to play in our own back yard today."

That evening after supper Sweyn got all dressed up in another new suit, new shirt, and new necktie. He sat in the parlor staring at the clock on the mantelpiece.

Papa noticed. "Calling on your girl again tonight?"

"At seven o'clock," Sweyn said.

"Time moves slowly for sweethearts when they are apart," Papa said.

That made Sweyn blush.

Mamma and Aunt Bertha finished the supper dishes and came into the parlor. Mamma looked at Sweyn.

"Aren't you going to spend one evening at home during your Christmas vacation?" she asked.

"I'll stay home Christmas Eve and Christmas night and of course the night before I go back east," Sweyn said.

"You'll do better than that," Papa said. "We do not mind sharing you with Marie Vinson but we don't want her monopolizing all of your time. I think seeing her every other night is enough."

Sweyn looked as disappointed as a dog would if you took away its bone.

"All right, Dad," he said as he stood up. Then he gave us a wave of his derby hat and that "toodle-oo" business and left.

About twenty minutes later Sweyn returned. Papa was reading a farm magazine. Aunt Bertha was knitting. Mamma was crocheting. Tom was reading a book. Frankie and I were playing dominoes on the floor. We all stared at Sweyn. He walked, no, he staggered, as if he were dazed, to a chair and slumped down in it. His face was pale. He looked positively sick.

"Are you ill?" Mamma asked.

Sweyn pressed his hand to his heart. "Only here," he said. "You won't have to worry about Marie monopolizing any more of my time."

Mamma was the first to speak. "What happened between you and Marie?" she asked.

"I rang the front doorbell," Sweyn said as if he were reading a funeral service over a grave. "She opened the door. She gave me a nasty look and said she never wanted to see me again because I was the most selfish person in the world."

"Selfish?" Mamma asked.

Sweyn nodded sadly. "That is what she called me just before she slammed the door in my face," he said.

"Are you sure she wasn't just teasing you?" Mamma said.

"I'm sure," Sweyn said. "I rang the doorbell again. This time her mother answered it. She told me that Marie never wanted to see me again. I just don't understand it. We've been going together since I was thirteen. We wrote to each other every week while we were both away at school. We had a sort of understanding that some day . . ." He didn't finish the sentence as he stood up. "I think I'll go up to my room," he said.

We watched him leave and heard him go upstairs to his room. Mamma looked concerned.

"I'm going to phone Ida Vinson and find out what this is all about," she said.

I thought for sure Mamma was going to blow Tom's plan sky-high but Papa saved the day.

"People who interfere in young sweethearts' quarrels are asking for trouble," he said.

"But I don't understand the selfish part," Mamma said.

"I think I do," Papa said. "Sweyn had promised to go horseback riding with Marie this afternoon. He was quite upset when I told him I needed him at the office. He phoned Marie, and I guess she considered it selfish of him not to keep his promise."

Later Tom surprised me by going upstairs with Frankie and me when it was our bedtime. He could stay up an hour later if he wanted.

"Now for the second part of my plan," Tom said. "You two wait here."

"No," I said. "We want to listen."

"All right," Tom said, "but take off your shoes."

Frankie and I took off our shoes. We followed Tom to the door of Sweyn's bedroom. The transom was open. We could hear Sweyn sort of crying and groaning at the same time.

"Got him," Tom whispered.

Then he motioned for Frankie and me to stand on the side of the doorway so we wouldn't be seen when the door was opened. Tom knocked on the door.

"Just a minute," Sweyn said.

It was more than a minute before he opened the door. Tom entered the bedroom and closed the door behind him.

"I heard you crying," Tom said. "You really must be stuck on Marie Vinson."

Frankie and I could hear perfectly through the open transom.

"I know I'm only fifteen," Sweyn said, "but I've been in love with Marie for two years. And now it is all over. I think I'll run away to sea."

"It's too bad you aren't old enough to join the French Foreign Legion," Tom said. "But I guess you are old enough to become a cabin boy on a ship."

"I don't care what happens to me," Sweyn cried out. "Without Marie life has lost all meaning."

"You've really got it bad," Tom said. "I guess you would do just about anything to fix things like they were before tonight."

"I'll say I would," Sweyn said.

"Would you stop wearing all those fancy eastern duds and just wear your old blue serge suit until you go back to school?" Tom asked.

"What has the clothing I wear got to do with Marie?" Sweyn asked.

"Do you want my great brain to fix things between you and Marie or not?" Tom demanded.

"Sure, if you can," Sweyn said.

"I can," Tom said. "But first you will have to give me your word of honor you will never mention it to Papa or Mamma."

"I'm beginning to smell something," Sweyn said.

"Smell all you want," Tom said. "I came here to help you make up with your girl. But you don't want my help. So go back to your bawling."

"Wait," Sweyn said. "I'll do anything you say if you get me back my girl. I give you my word I won't say anything to Papa or Mamma."

"And will you also give me your word that you'll stop wearing all those fancy duds you bought back east?" Tom asked.

"I don't know what my clothing has to do with it," Sweyn said, "but I give you my word."

"All right," Tom said. "Tomorrow morning after breakfast we'll straighten this whole thing out. And remember to wear your old blue serge suit with the knee britches."

The next morning Tom, Frankie, and I got dressed in our Sunday best suits. Sweyn wore his old blue serge. Mamma was goggle-eyed when she saw us enter the kitchen.

"Why are you three boys all dressed up?" she asked. "And Sweyn, why are you wearing your old suit?"

"We'll do the chores later," Tom said. "But first we have to call on Marie Vinson and convince her that Sweyn isn't a selfish person."

Papa wasn't fooled. "I have a feeling," he said to Tom, "that this is another one of your great brain schemes."

Sweyn spoke before Tom could. "I don't care what it is as long as Marie and I make up," he said.

After breakfast the four of us went to the Vinson home. Mrs. Vinson opened the door.

"We must talk to Marie," Tom said.

"She is up in her room," Mrs. Vinson said. "I'll call her."

In a couple of minutes Marie came to the front door. She looked at Sweyn and then stared at Tom, Frankie, and me.

"I'm sorry," Tom said, "but we played a mean joke on you and Sweyn yesterday. We dug those old clothes out of our ragbag. We have plenty of clothes to wear. Our father can afford to send Sweyn back east to school and buy him the latest fashions in clothing."

"I don't understand," Marie said. "Why did you let me think you had to dress like ragamuffins because of Sweyn?"

"To make him stop wearing those fancy duds in Adenville," Tom said. "Being a girl maybe you won't understand. But all the fellows are making fun of John and me because they say we've got a sissy dude for a brother. It's humiliating. We will both be getting into fights every day as long as Sweyn wears those fancy clothes. Anyway, if you love him it won't make any difference what kind of clothes he wears."

Marie stepped out on the porch. She took hold of Sweyn's hand and smiled at him.

"I wouldn't care if you called on me wearing overalls," she said. "I cried all night."

"So did I," Sweyn said.

And that is how The Great Brain got rid of a dude. And for my money, if being in love can make you stay awake and cry all night, I hope I never fall in love.

Think About It

1. What was new about Sweyn when he came home from school?
2. Why were Sweyn's brothers bothered by this?
3. What did the brothers do to make Sweyn stop dressing like a dude?
4. Why did Sweyn do exactly as Tom said and not tell their parents?
5. What are some of the ways people's attitudes change as they grow up?
6. Write a paragraph telling whether you think the boys were fair to Sweyn.

LEARN NEW WORDS

1. They ate lunch every day in the school **cafeteria**.
2. In her **commentary** on the election, the reporter praised one of the candidates.
3. The art, religion, politics, and social customs of a group of people help make up its **culture**.
4. Her jeans were made of blue **denim**.
5. A grandfather, a father, and a daughter represent three different **generations.**
6. One way Navajo children learn about their **heritage** is from the stories passed down from generation to generation.
7. The wheat we planted is **maturing** early this year and will have to be harvested sooner than planned.
8. The minister called the Bible "the **sacred** book."

GET SET TO READ

Many Navajos continue to live much as their ancestors have for generations. What changes in the outside world do you think would affect people with a very traditional way of life?

Read these poems to see how Alice Yazzie's life is a mixture of old and new ways.

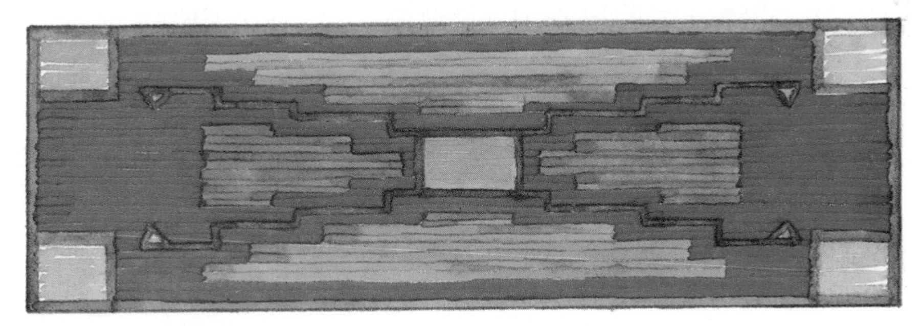

from Alice Yazzie's Year

by RAMONA MAHER

Δ JANUARY Δ YAS NILT'EES Δ

The snow slowed the world,
the Navajo world.
"Go see if the sheep are fine,"
Grandfather Tsosie tells Alice Yazzie.
"The hay is frozen
and so is the ground," says Alice, returning.
"The horses look like they blame me
for causing this cold."

Her nose red, her chin buried in sheepskin,
she carries the smallest lamb
into the hogan.
"Just for the night," says Alice Yazzie
holding the lamb.
"He's all new and starry.
He's too new to be cold."
Grandfather grunts.
He doesn't say no.

Alice heats milk in a bottle
over burning piñon.
Grandfather watches.
The new lamb sucks.
The piñon burns low.
The lamb goes to sleep.
His nose is a black star.

"It *is* cold out there," Alice tells Grandfather
as she goes to bed.
Grandfather nods.
He wears a red flannel shirt Alice gave him
for Christmas.
He looks at the low fire.
He looks at the lamb.
Grandfather says
to Alice Yazzie,
to Alice Ben Yazzie,
"It was almost this cold
the night you were born."

Δ APRIL Δ T'AACHIL Δ

Jimmy Benally had a pet coyote
with yellow eyes.
Nobody else wanted it.
It grew up to be
a long, gold shadow—
no more yellow pup.
He took off one day.
"That's just the way
them coyotes do," said Mr. Benally.

"He had to go," said Jimmy to Alice.
"He's smart, that fellow.
He can tell his shadow
from all of the others.
He was my coyote,
a different fellow.
He can hide and then smile.
He's out there teasing rabbits,
walking on his blue feet."

Alice Yazzie knows that Jimmy Benally
watches for shadows, listens to howls.
"He'll never come back.
He just grew up," said Jimmy Benally,
"and he had to go."

Δ SEPTEMBER Δ BINI'ANT'AATSOH Δ

Alice pulls her hair back into one long braid.
Last year's gym shorts are too short. She's grown.
Her toes won't even wiggle
in last year's tennies.
It's a mile through the dust
to the yellow bus stop. In winter: through mud.
Her pup seems to beg with his eyes:
"Stay home. Let's us play, Alice Yazzie.
The two of us."

Grandfather frowns.
"We do what we must.
I see you must go to school. This year—
not so many hot dogs in the cafeteria.
More books in the learning center.
We'll see to that."
Grandfather sits on the school board
and helps decide about classes and buildings.
The oldest school board man, he sees change happening.
He says it must come.
He even voted for girls to play football
if they want to. And study mechanical drawing.

Alice starts off in her tie-dyed T-shirt
and a denim skirt faded canyon blue.
Grandfather calls. He gives Alice a ride
behind him, on his horse,
to the bus stop shelter.
Alice is surprised.
"Remember," says Grandfather,
nudging the old mare until she faces around.
"You don't have to take mechanical drawing
if you don't want to."

"Thank you, Grandfather."
As they move off, old man on old horse,
Alice feels winter coming.

The Navajo Country and Ways of Life

a commentary by CARL N. GORMAN

Alice Yazzie's Year, by Ramona Maher, is a wonderful month-to-month story about a Navajo girl. I would like to add a commentary to tell you something about our culture.

Navajos call January "Yas Nilt'ees," which means crusted snow. It gets very cold in January, and when you walk on frozen snow, you can hear it crunch under your feet. In Navajo, "yas" means snow and "nilt'ees" could also mean roast or cook, but today most Navajos say "yas nilt'ees" means crusted snow. Our language is very old, and in the early days "yas nilt'ees" could have meant boiling or thawing snow for water.

Navajos call April "T'aachil," which means the reawakening of plant life in the spring after the winter sleep.

September is called "Bini'ant'aatsoh," which means the maturing of late crops.

Now let's go back to January, Yas Nilt'ees, and learn a little something about some of the things mentioned in the story that you may like to know more about.

Alice's name, Yazzie, is a word that means little or tiny in Navajo. Her grandfather's name, Tsosie, means slim. These names are heard a lot in Navajoland.

Navajos raise sheep, and children frequently herd them. They raise sheep for wool, and they sell their lambs in the fall for money. They shear their sheep in the springtime when the weather gets warm. Some of the wool they sell and some they save to weave beautiful Navajo rugs. Navajos also raise goats and cattle. The sheep and cattle are sometimes sold for their meat. Lamb is the Navajos' favorite meat.

Alice lives at a place called Black Mountain in the southwestern United States. The mountain is a sacred mountain to the Navajo.

Navajo children like to have dogs for pets. Coyotes, however, are not usually considered for pets. There are many stories about a character called Coyote. Most of the stories picture him as a trickster. When he does play tricks, he always ends up the loser. He is the symbol of all the desires that can get someone into trouble. This may be why no one else wanted Jimmy Benally's coyote pup.

Many Navajo children go to schools run by the United States government and known as Indian schools. Many of

them are boarding schools. Some schools on the reservation now have parents and other community members on school boards. This was not always so. Some are now teaching Navajo culture so that students may have a good foundation in the Navajo way as well as white people's way. This is very important for youngsters, because when they have a good feeling about their heritage, they do better in other school subjects. Girls have always enjoyed an important place in Navajo culture, and so Grandfather would be glad to have Alice do some of the things that the school may have planned just for boys.

Think About It

1. Many of the images, or word pictures, in the poem about January describe the cold. Find one or two examples.
2. How did Jimmy Benally feel about his coyote? Tell how you know.
3. How does the poem about September show the mixture of old and new ways in Alice's life?
4. What is Alice's relationship with her grandfather like? Give lines from the poem to prove your point.
5. How do you think growing up on a Navajo reservation is different from growing up anywhere else in the United States? How is it the same?
6. Write about why it is important for children everywhere to learn about their culture and heritage.

LEARN NEW WORDS

1. It was her **ambition** to be president of the company.
2. He felt such **compassion** for the prisoner that he decided to let him go.
3. The two **conspirators** plotted to rob the bank.
4. The famous spy was able to **decipher** the secret code in about an hour.
5. Denim is such a strong material that it's unlikely it could have **disintegrated** in the washing machine.
6. You can hunt for seashells during **ebb tide,** when the water is low and the sand is dry.
7. The answer **eluded** me, so I was forced to ask for help.
8. She spoke more **emphatically** when the girl wouldn't listen.
9. The words in the code should not be taken in a **literal** sense but should be examined for a hidden message.
10. She wanted to get **revenge** for all the wrongs they had done her.
11. The music was so loud it **surged** through the concert hall.

GET SET TO READ

Even within one family, people can have very different kinds of talents. What are some examples of this?

Read this story to see how Louisa uses her gift for words to solve a long-standing mystery.

The Keynote Clue

by KRISTEN RANDLEV MORSY

What could be worse than spending a vacation at my Great-aunt Lydia's old house in San Francisco while my parents vacationed in Hawaii? I could have taken care of myself at home. I'm eleven and very responsible. But no. Instead, I was stuck in a creepy house with an aunt who insisted on daily piano lessons.

I thought I'd go nuts before the end of the week. No kids my age, no TV, not even any books. The bookcases were stuffed with sheets of music. No wonder Aunt Lyd spent all her time at the piano. She called it her inspiration and her comfort. I called it torture!

I told her I'm tone deaf, but Aunt Lyd insisted everyone in the family must be musical. Music was almost sacred to her. I could read music because I sang in the choir at home. The choirmaster required only that you show up and sing loud. When I played that piano—*disaster!* Even Ramsey, the Great Dane, hid his head under the cushions of the sofa.

Whenever Aunt Lyd played the piano, music surged through the house until the walls vibrated. One evening I curled up next to Ramsey on the rug near the fire as she performed her favorite, Chopin.

"You play beautifully, Aunt Lydia," I said when she had finished. "I really wish I could play that way."

"But you can, Louisa," she replied emphatically. "You must cultivate that talent of yours."

"But I have no talent," I protested.

"Tut! Every one of the Alexanders has talent."

"Every one?"

"Well . . ." A shadow of memory pleated her forehead.

"Not really *every* one, right?" I pursued.

"Harrison Alexander was never very accomplished," she sighed. "But I think Father's expectations were unrealistic."

"Who was Harrison?" I asked.

She wearily rose from the piano bench and settled into the sofa closer to the fire. "Let's not discuss him."

"Come on, Aunt Lydia. I don't know anything about my own family."

Her eyes flickered in the firelight. I could see her resistance fading. "All right, Louisa, since you are named after my dear sister, your grandmother." Her long, slim fingers twirled the fringe on the sofa cover.

"Louisa Georgina and I were twins. Harrison was our little brother. When he was born, Louisa and I were already serious about our music. But Harrison was the male heir destined to carry on Father's famous name."

She peered at me over her eyeglasses. "You did know that my father, your great-grandfather, was a world-class conductor, did you not?" When I shrugged, she spoke more emphatically.

"A world-class conductor. He personally knew the great musicians of the day and frequently invited them here, to this house, for wonderful parties. What a chance to show off, to audition! But in those days young ladies were not encouraged to perform except for the family. Father said we both played well, even brilliantly. But he insisted that a performer's life was not suitable for his daughters. It would be the son who would dazzle the world as he matured. How Louisa and I resented it."

"But what happened?"

"We all grew up. The end." Aunt Lyd smiled at me.

"But I want to know what happened! Did you become a concert pianist? Did Harrison?" I asked.

"Perhaps if I'd been a modern girl," she said, "I might have followed my ambition. But I obeyed my father instead, as daughters were supposed to do—in those days anyway," she smiled. "Father was a dear and talented man. I loved and respected him."

"What happened to Harrison?" I asked.

"Oh, Louisa. That is a painful story. I haven't the strength tonight."

"When, then? You know, it wasn't his fault he was a boy," I told her. "Maybe he wished you were the favorite."

"You are probably right. You feel compassion for him. But when I was your age, I felt only envy and anger. And Harrison certainly did little to make us love him. He was spoiled, selfish and . . ."

"Lonely, too, I bet. It's not easy being a crummy piano player in this house," I added.

She laughed again. "Oh, Louisa, you are a relief. I do take myself too seriously."

The next morning during my practice period I pounded away at the grand piano. I wanted to please Aunt Lyd. I liked her better each day. But my supposed hidden talent eluded me like a ghost. My mind wandered from the music in front of me to the memory of Harrison. I bet he had to practice more than an hour and a half.

Bored with the technique exercises, I shuffled through the papers in the music bench. Maybe I could find something more popular. I was tired of classical, but I didn't expect any top ten either.

One sheet stuck to a piece of old music. I wondered how long the bench had remained shut. The loose sheet was hand-ruled with the music staff. The notes were marked in with a fountain pen. I smoothed out the page and tried to play it. Maybe it was an original composition by someone now famous!

I may be tone deaf, but the composer had been stone deaf. The piece sounded weird, without an ending. I replayed the notes, but the exercise still sounded incomplete. I glanced at the top where the word "Coda" had been printed carefully. In Italian, *coda* means "end of the music." But there was no ending.

I read the music note by note:

F-G-A F-G-A F-G-A A-A-A/ F-E-B G-A-G/ C-A-F-E E-G-G C-C-C/ D-A-D D-A-B E-B-B B-A-E C-A-G-E/ F-A-C-E B-A-E F-G/ B-A-C C-A-C-E/ B-E-A-D B-A-G/ B-A-B-E C-A-D/

Musically, I could make no sense of the "Coda," but maybe. . . . I glanced over the

sheet again. The groups of notes were clustered almost into words. Maybe I had discovered a code, not a coda! This music wasn't music at all!

"Louisa!" sang Aunt Lyd from the kitchen. "I can't hear you practicing!"

"I'm working out the fingering," I called back. I folded the sheet into my pocket. I could examine it later. I wouldn't need the piano next time.

"Hurry a bit, dear. It's almost time for your lesson."

Ramsey moaned and lazily laid his heavy head in my lap. "Don't worry, boy," I comforted him. "I may be a better detective than a musician!"

After lunch, I curled up on my bed to work on my musical mystery. I spread the paper out across my knees and studied it.

Then I noticed another peculiar thing about the music—the key. The music was written in the key of B-sharp. But B-sharp is the same as C. It must mean something. Be sharp! That's it! An instruction!

The time of the music was weird, too. It said 4/4 but the measures in the piece itself

didn't follow. I figured they must have their own meaning and order. The time must mean something different. I thought the way the B-note was squeezed in, it could say "for before." That means something. But what?

I pulled out a school tablet of paper and began to write the notes down. I wrote the clusters together as if they were words. I wrote the measures as if each were a sentence. It's a good thing I read a lot of mystery books. I stared at the result.

FGA FGA FGA AAA
FEB GAG
CAFE EGG CCC
DAD DAB EBB BAE CAGE
FACE BAE FG
BAC CACE
BEAD BAG
BABE CAD

A few words popped out, but most of the "Coda" I couldn't decipher. I sounded out each "word" as a first grader reads a primer, but no luck. The meaning still eluded me. Oh, well. The adventure had saved me from complete boredom for a while. Maybe Aunt Lyd would tell me more about Harrison that afternoon.

"Louisa, I'm beginning to believe you are tone deaf," confessed Aunt Lyd that afternoon after our lesson. She skillfully built a fire in the hearth. The March dusk arrived early with a blanket of fog.

"I guess Harrison and I have a lot in common," I suggested. I hoped to prompt her into the rest of the story.

"Please! Don't ever say such a thing!" she scolded. "He was, as I told you, dreadfully spoiled."

"What could a little kid do to you? It wasn't his fault the grownups favored him."

"Let me tell you!" she retorted. "On our eighteenth birthday, when your precious little Harrison was eleven, Father gave a splendid party for us. It was on Valentine's Day.

"As we dressed in our gowns, Father presented each of us with a set of gems that had been in the family for many, many years. Father gave me topazes, and to Louisa, garnets."

"After the party, we arranged our jewelry on a velvet tray on the dresser. In the morning, the gems and my crystal beaded evening bag had disappeared!"

"What does that prove?" I wondered aloud.

"It proves Harrison stole our jewels to spite us!"

"I don't get it."

"Who else had access to our room and a reason to steal?"

"Did you ask Harrison about the jewels?"

"Of course! He just laughed. He said if we were so smart, we could find them ourselves."

"Didn't you tell your father?"

"We were about to but . . ." She stopped suddenly.

"But what?"

"Louisa, we were afraid. Well, it doesn't matter now. Neither Harrison nor Father can care any longer." She paused, gathering her strength as I had seen her do before tackling a difficult piano piece.

"Harrison's birthday fell, appropriately enough, on April Fool's Day. For his twelfth birthday party, Father invited some distinguished musicians. Harrison was scheduled to give a concert first. An audition, really. Then the cake and presents would follow. Father had purchased a red racing bicycle that Harrison had wanted for nearly a year. It was to be a surprise."

"That party sounds boring," I commented.

"Why? What do you mean?"

"For my last birthday, I invited a bunch of my friends, and we went miniature golfing and got something to eat. Why couldn't Harrison have his own friends?"

"Harrison had no time for friends. He was always busy."

"Practicing, right? Poor Harrison," I muttered.

"Poor Harrison, indeed. I would have adored such a party. But not Harrison. He played terribly and embarrassed Father on purpose. He was sent to his room."

"Without cake?"

"Without cake or punch. He lost his bicycle as well."

"What a creepy thing to do," I protested. "Maybe he was just nervous."

"Maybe. Father obviously didn't think so. After he had apologized to the guests, he excused himself and visited Harrison in his room. But . . ."

"Go on!"

"We only overheard the story. Something about the curtain cord."

I shuddered.

"We decided he had run away, using the cord to lower himself out of the window. Perhaps he ran off to sea. He loved reading sailing adventures and visiting the ships down at the wharf whenever he could. In any event," she said, "we never saw Harrison again. It was out of the question to mention the jewels, and Father never asked us."

"I'm sure Harrison meant to return them," I insisted.

"Perhaps he did. However, our lives changed considerably. Father sold off most of the furniture to hire a detective. Mother died a year later."

"Which was Harrison's room?"

"The topmost. He wished to be as far away from the piano as possible."

I resolved to be up early the next day and explore Harrison's room. Usually, I waited for Aunt Lyd's early morning playing to waken me. But on that day, curiosity and excitement banged me into consciousness. I slipped into my jeans and sneaked out the door.

Aunt Lyd's house resembled a stack of boxes. Up through the center spiraled a narrow staircase. Harrison's room perched on top like a crow's nest.

The roof sloped sharply so that I could stand upright only in the middle of the room. I could understand why Harrison loved it up there. Sunlight exploded through the double windows, revealing a breathtaking view of San Francisco Bay.

Most of the upstairs rooms had been emptied years ago, but Harrison's room looked as though he might reenter it any moment. The window seat was fitted like a berth with a musty comforter still tucked in. An orange crate tilted with the weight of mystery books and sea adventures. On the wall, an oil painting of the bay at ebb tide tilted at a slight angle as if the whole room were a cabin rolling with the waves. Harrison obviously loved the sea more than the piano. I felt lucky. My parents would never make me be something I wasn't.

"Louisa!" Aunt Lyd's voice shattered my daydream. She peeked around the corner of the door, breathing heavily from the effort of the climb. "I've been calling you for your lesson."

"I'm sorry. I didn't hear you."

"Yes, I'd forgotten how cut off this room is," she remarked as she wandered about. "What made you come up here?"

"Oh, I don't know. Maybe to understand Harrison better. And I think I do. Why is this room kept like this?"

"I suppose Mother hoped for a while that he would return. The room was the one place he loved."

"Did you ever search here for the jewels?"

"Once. But Father discovered us. He forbade us to invade the privacy of Harrison's room."

"I think the clue must be here."

"Clue to what?"

"Clue to the code!" I pulled the "Coda" out of my pocket.

She barely glanced at it. "That's scrap paper. Come, it's time for your lesson."

"Not yet, Aunt Lydia," I said. "Could this be Harrison's handwriting?"

She glanced at the paper again. "I suppose so. But there is so little actual writing."

"Did Harrison ever compose anything?"

"Oh, yes," she laughed. "He reasoned that if the piece were his own composition, he could play it however he pleased, and no one could criticize. He rarely noted pieces down."

I pointed to the orange crate brimming with books. "Harrison liked to read mysteries, didn't he?"

"Yes. Anything to escape music."

"And he liked words and mysteries." I kept fitting the

jigsaw pieces of Harrison's personality together in my mind.

Aunt Lyd was staring at the "Coda." "I remember this piece. Harrison presented this trash to Louisa and me for our eighteenth birthday."

"Maybe that's it." I smoothed the paper out on the bed. "See the signature and the time. It's a sentence. 'Be sharp. For before.' Did you do anything to Harrison he might want revenge for?"

"Well," she hesitated. "We emptied his Christmas stocking and took all the name tags off his presents. He thought he'd received nothing."

"OK, so maybe he planned hiding your jewels as his revenge." My mind raced. I could almost hear the puzzle clicking together. Aunt Lyd stared at me.

"The jewels? How do you figure the jewels are involved?"

"I think he *meant* for you to get them back."

"His usual revenge required writing some horrid murder story in which we were killed and stuffed into a piano."

I laughed with delight.

"I hardly find my own murder amusing," Aunt Lyd scolded.

"I just feel as though I know Harrison. And if he could write stories, he could write codes."

"Your imagination is overactive, Louisa."

"No, Aunt Lydia. I'm more like Harrison than you know. That's why I can figure out the code—you didn't even recognize it as a code at all!"

Like two conspirators, we examined the page carefully. "The first line is the worst. F-G-A F-G-A F-G-A A-A-A. What could that be?" I asked.

Aunt Lyd thought for a moment, then revealed, "Because our initials were both *L,* Harrison sometimes used our middle initials as well. He called me *L-F* for Lydia Frances. He said it was short for 'elephant.'"

"And Grandmother's middle initial would be *G* for Georgina," I said. "So F and G could stand for you and your sister, since there's no L on the keyboard."

"Albert was Harrison's middle name. He called himself the HAHAHA."

"That fits. The first line addresses you. Maybe A-A-A is like laughter. Let's go on to the next line: F-E-B G-A-G."

"Obviously a dead end."

"You're too literal, Aunt Lydia. F-E-B could be the abbreviation for February. Didn't you say your birthday party was in February for Valentine's Day? Remember Harrison was really limited by the keyboard. There's only A-B-C-D-E-F-G—not the whole alphabet."

"It was quite enough for Chopin," she interrupted.

"Chopin wasn't hiding your jewels. Come on, cooperate! This is the trail. I feel it!"

I pointed to the paper again. "A gag is a joke," I went on. "Harrison wanted you to know he took the jewels as a joke. He didn't mean to hurt you. Now, look at the next line: C-A-F-E E-G-G C-C-C. What did the topazes look like?"

"The pendant in the necklace was as big as an egg and a rich, glittery brown. The earrings..."

"That's enough. Isn't *café* coffee? And coffee is dark brown. C-C-C could be see, see, see!"

Aunt Lyd caught my excitement. "Perhaps you are correct, Louisa. I do believe you have a gift for words, if not for music."

"And so did Harrison. But nobody ever gave him a chance. I think Harrison hid your jewels

and gave you the directions to find them in this 'Coda.' You would have to be able to think like Harrison did in order to figure it out. He wanted you to understand him. And maybe even to like him a little."

"D-A-D D-A-B E-B-B B-A-E C-A-G-E," she read. "Well, not much progress, eh?"

"You're being too literal again. Listen to the sounds of the words the way you would listen to the sounds of music." I read on. "Dad must be your father. What could a 'dab' be?"

"Father painted as a hobby, but called his oils 'dabs' so that no one would take them seriously. That painting," she said, pointing at the landscape on the wall, "is Father's."

"And that picture is a dab of the bay at ebb tide," I said.

"What is the cage then?"

"We'll have to come back to that. The next line reads: F-A-C-E B-A-E F-G. That must mean 'face the bay, Frances and Georgina.' You better obey Harrison this time, Aunt Lyd."

She turned to the window.

"I don't think that's right. The real water wouldn't always be at ebb tide. Face the painting instead." She turned, a conspirator's twinkle in her eyes.

"OK. The next line says B-A-C C-A-C-E. Back Case."

"How do you get 'Back Case' from those notes?"

"You sound it out. Remember, there's no K or S on the piano," I explained. "B-E-A-D B-A-G is pretty clear."

"Indeed. Did I tell you my beaded evening bag disappeared the same night the jewels did?"

"Yes, I remember." I puzzled over the last line. "B-A-B-E C-A-D has me stumped."

"But it shouldn't, my dear. Harrison was the babe of the family and obviously knew what we thought of him." When I still looked confused, she explained, "A cad is the opposite of a gentleman. Someone who does bad things."

She and I laughed together. "You have deciphered the code, Louisa. Congratulations."

"But if I solved the code, then where are the jewels?"

"Ever the romantic, Louisa." She sat on the bed. "You credit Harrison with more goodness than he deserves."

"No. He did everything right. I goofed." I concentrated on the painting.

"Tut! Look at that old painting," she fussed. "This house has settled so much since it was built. The walls even tilt now." She tried to straighten the painting. "Odd," she murmured.

"What's wrong?"

"The painting seems to be fastened to the wall."

I leaped to her side and ran my fingers along both sides of the picture frame. A series of tiny hinges scraped my left hand. My right caught against a tiny hook that broke off. With a squeak, the hinges sagged, and the picture swung out from the wall like the door of a medicine chest.

"The cage!" I cried. "And look there!" I pointed to a moldy beaded evening bag wedged into the corner of the shelf.

"My beaded bag! This is a shadow box," she marveled. "Harrison substituted a painting for the glass door so that no one could see into it. My evening bag!" She grabbed for the bag. The rotted cloth disintegrated in her hand, and beads bounced over the floor.

"Those aren't all beads, are they, Aunt Lydia? They're too big!" Rolling about the floor were gems as big as my finger tip, as big as an egg, dark brown and blood red.

"Garnets and topazes!" she cried as we scrambled about the floor on our knees. Her lap full of sparkling gems, she ran her fingers through the treasure. She bit her lip, but tears streaked the powder on her face.

"I'm glad you got your jewelry back," I said awkwardly.

"You gave me back something more important than gems, Louisa. You gave me compassion for a little boy I never really knew. You showed me the torment I caused him." She breathed deeply and smiled. "I feel young again, as though a chain were lifted. Thank you, Louisa. Your gift to me is more precious than all these jewels. But the garnets shall be yours. After all, they belonged to your grandmother."

She handed me the earrings. I put them on and felt very grown-up. After all, I was eleven and very responsible.

Think About It

1. What story did Aunt Lydia tell about Harrison?
2. Why do you think Harrison's family didn't understand him?
3. How did Louisa solve the mystery?
4. What did Louisa have in common with Harrison?
5. What did Aunt Lydia learn from Louisa?
6. Make up your own coded message telling the location of a hidden object. See how many of your friends can decode the message.

LEARN NEW WORDS

1. We listened as the **comedian** told joke after joke.
2. The **conceited** boy couldn't imagine that anyone might dislike him.
3. The **deranged** character ran away screaming and shouting.
4. Her **haughty** smile disappeared when she realized she wasn't going to win first prize.
5. With remarkable **insight**, the child was able to explain the true reason for her own behavior.
6. You are **liable** to get into trouble if you keep on doing that.
7. While demonstrating the vegetable chopper, the salesperson kept up a steady stream of **patter**.
8. Even without a microphone, her voice **projected** to the back of the auditorium.
9. No longer able to **repress** her feelings, she laughed out loud.
10. I **sprinted** across the floor to catch the child as he fell.
11. He swore **vengeance** against the person who had hurt him.

GET SET TO READ

Sometimes people get carried away when they do something. It can be playing ball or singing a song or even watching a movie. What does it mean to "get carried away"? What do you think it's like when this happens?

Read this story to see what happens when Lenny gets carried away by his first opportunity to make a dream come true.

Lenny Kandell, SMART ALECK

by ELLEN CONFORD

The year is 1946. Eleven-year-old Lenny is the neighborhood smart aleck. He dreams of one day being a stand-up comedian, but so far all he's gotten into is trouble.

The story opens after Lenny has angered the class bully, Maurice "Mousie" Blatner, by tripping him in a dark movie theater. Not only did he trip Mousie, but Lenny caused him to spill a drink on Georgina Schultz's dress. Georgina got mad at Lenny and now refuses to speak to him. But Mousie would like nothing better than to get his hands on Lenny.

Lenny spends the next few days avoiding Mousie and thinking of a way to make up with Georgina. With the help of his friend Artie, he decides to put on a comedy show to raise the money to replace Georgina's dress. The show is also his start in show business. It takes place on the roof of the apartment building where Lenny lives with his mother and sister.

Lenny stood at the iron door as his audience gathered on his rooftop theater.

If only I had a white tuxedo, Lenny thought, everything would be perfect. Well, maybe not exactly perfect.

There were no chairs on the roof, so the audience had to sit right on the hot tar surface.

And Lenny had to collect the ten-cent admission himself, because Artie was standing downstairs inside the lobby, letting the kids in so they wouldn't be punching people's apartment buzzers to get the lobby door open.

And Lenny would have to do his own introduction, because

Artie would be too nervous to talk.

But the sun was shining like a spotlight, and none of the kids was trying to get by him without paying, and no one was leaving, and it was going to be a big audience. An old wooden orange crate was there. Lenny told everyone it was the stage, and the audience was forming into sort of a horseshoe around it, giggling and chattering and looking toward Lenny, yelling, "When's the show gonna start?"

Lenny didn't have a watch, but Artie did, and they'd planned that Artie would come up at two o'clock and give Lenny the high sign to start. Unless there were a whole lot of kids still coming; then Artie said he'd wait a few minutes more.

"Pretty soon now," Lenny said. It must be close to two o'clock, he thought. The box wasn't exactly overflowing with dimes, but there were about thirty kids in the audience already. No one who came through the iron roof door looked at all like a show-business big shot—in fact, there were no adults at all, but it was unreasonable to expect a talent scout to be there the first time. Word hadn't gotten around yet.

It was just as well. This would be the first time he tested his act on a real live audience. A talent scout showing up now was liable to put too much pressure on him.

Not that Lenny had stage fright. (Or orange-crate fright, he thought, chuckling.) He felt pretty good. Excited, eager to get started . . . maybe just a little bit nervous. But it was a good kind of nervousness. It made him feel tingly and alert and full of energy.

"Thank you, thank you, the stage is over there, the show's about to start in just a few minutes, pull up a piece of roof and sit down."

"Thank you, thank you." Lenny kept up a steady patter as bunches of kids came through the door and dropped their dimes into the box.

Lenny looked toward the stage. There must be forty people on the roof!

He turned as he heard two more dimes hit the box. "Thank you, th—"

Lenny's patter stopped suddenly. Georgina Schultz stood in the doorway, holding on to a little kid. She tilted her head and gave Lenny a haughty stare. "My little brother wanted to come." She marched off toward the orange crate.

Lenny gazed after her, hardly believing she was there. Even though she'd looked interested from the first moment the show was mentioned, Lenny hadn't really expected her to come. He thought she was too mad at him, and too haughty to give him the satisfaction.

Lenny wasn't falling for that "my little brother" line. The kid was hardly old enough to walk, let alone read a sign on a lamppost.

Wait till she sees the dress I'm going to get her! Lenny thought. Wait till she finds out that practically all this is for her!

"Hey, when's the show gonna start? We want the show! We want the show!"

The kids began clapping and chanting. Lenny waved an arm at them. "Just a couple minutes more, folks. It's not two o'clock yet."

"It is too! It's ten after. WE WANT THE SHOW!"

"Okay, okay, keep your shirts on. We're just about ready to—"

"WE WANT THE SHOW *NOW*! WE WANT THE SHOW *NOW*!"

"All right already!" Lenny put the box down next to the iron door. He wondered, briefly, why Artie hadn't come up to the roof yet.

But Lenny had kept his audience waiting long enough. There was no time to wonder where Artie was, no time to wonder whether he would have stage fright.

It was show time. Lenny took a deep breath.

"And now, ladies and gentlemen, the moment you've all been waiting for. Here he is, that talented comedian, that star of stage, screen, and roof, the one, the only—ME!" He sprinted over to the orange crate and swooped down in an exaggerated bow, to show the audience that the introduction was supposed to be sort of a joke, and not meant to be conceited.

The audience clapped politely. Lenny jumped onto the orange crate and stood for a moment, just looking out at the expectant, upturned faces. He felt a surge of excitement, as if he were suddenly charged with electricity, and he knew it was because this was how it felt when a dream finally came true.

He thought he could almost spring off the orange crate and go flying around the roof like Superman. And when he started to talk, all the confidence and energy that he felt pulsing through his veins charged his voice with a power that projected it booming across the roof.

"I want to thank me for that very kind introduction," he said. The kids giggled.

"And let me tell you, it's a miracle I'm here at all. What a week I had. My teacher asked me why geese fly south in the winter. I said, 'Why not—it's too far to walk.' Then she asked me to use the words *defeat, deduct, defense,* and *detail* in one sentence. So I said, 'Defeat of deduct go over defense before detail.'"

The kids giggled appreciatively. He was just warming up.

"What a week," Lenny went on. "Last night my brother wakes me up at two in the morning, screaming that there's a mouse in his bedroom. I go into his room to look, and I say, 'I don't see any mouse.' And he says, 'I'm telling you there was a mouse in here, I heard it squeaking.' So I said, 'Well, what do you want me to do, oil it?'"

There was an encouraging burst of giggles. Lenny had enough insight to know not to start out with your best stuff, but to build up to it, holding out the really good jokes for the big finish.

"Then yesterday I went for a drive in the country with my Uncle Fred. Well, the car broke down and he went out to look under the hood, and this old horse comes trotting by. And the horse says, 'Neighhh. Better check the gas line.' And he trots off.

"Well, my uncle is the nervous type, and he gets so frightened, we run to the nearest farmhouse. He tells the farmer what happened, and the farmer says, 'Was this an old horse with one floppy ear?' And my uncle says, 'Yeah, yeah.' And the farmer says, 'Aw don't pay any attention to him. He doesn't know a thing about cars.'

"And speaking of horses, did you hear the one about the horse who walked into a restaurant and ordered a steak two inches thick with sour cream and caraway seeds on top of it, and sliced onions on top of that, and then on top of the onions a piece of tomato and an artichoke with a cherry in the middle? Well, the waiter goes to the kitchen and brings the horse the steak and the horse eats it and says to the waiter, 'Say, didn't you think it was strange for me, a horse, to come in here and order a steak two inches thick with sour cream and caraway seeds and sliced onions and tomato and an artichoke with a cherry in the middle?'

"And the waiter says, 'What's so strange about that? I like my steak the same way.' "

More laughter. The audience was really warmed up now, and so was Lenny. He picked out Georgina's face. She was grinning, but when she saw him looking at her, she bit her lip and began fussing over her brother.

Lenny smiled broadly. She wasn't fooling him a bit!

"Thank you, thank you. But let me tell you some more about my Uncle Fred. Like I said, my Uncle Fred is a really nervous type, and he was driving his wife to the hospital to have a baby and he was so nervous about getting her there in time that he lost control of the car and drove into a tree."

The roof door opened and Lenny saw Artie come in. Lenny grinned at him and Artie closed the door quietly behind him and tiptoed toward the audience. Artie looked sort of—nervous, or sick or something. Lenny only had time to wonder briefly what was wrong, and to hope Artie was okay. The kids were leaning forward, waiting for him to go on.

"So the next thing he knows, my uncle is in a hospital bed and wakes up yelling, 'My wife! My wife! Is my wife okay?' And the doctor sprints in and says, 'Your wife's fine, and congratulations, you're the proud father of twins. A girl and a boy. They're fine, too. The only thing is, you were unconscious for ten days after the accident, and your wife was unconscious for two days, and we had to get names for the birth certificates, so your wife's brother named the babies.'

"And my uncle says, 'Oh, no, my wife's brother is an idiot! I can just imagine the names he picked out.' And the doctor says, 'He named the girl Denise.' And my uncle says, 'Hey, Denise? That's not bad. That's kind of pretty. Denise. Okay, what did he name the boy?'

"And the doctor said, 'Denephew.'"

Even Georgina laughed out loud now, and she didn't try to repress it. Lenny felt the warmth of the sun and the warmth of his audience's response, and wished, just for a minute, that his sister and his mother were there to see him; to see for themselves that his dream wasn't crazy, that it really could come true.

Lenny told joke after joke, not waiting for the laughter to completely die down between punch lines, but just starting another story while the kids were still giggling. And the laughter built and built, getting harder and louder, the way he'd planned it, till Lenny was so flushed with success and self-confidence that he stopped wondering why Artie kept glancing nervously at the roof door.

Then he heard a metallic thunk. The roof door swung out, and there, at the top of the stairwell, frozen for one eternal moment like an ancient statue of vengeance, stood Mousie Blatner.

All Lenny could see were the backs of heads, as his audience watched Mousie advance toward the stage. A few braver kids dared a "Shush! You're ruining the show," but mostly they just watched in fascination, as if Mousie were part of the act.

"I owe you somethin', Lenny Kandell, and now you're gonna get it," Mousie yelled.

Suddenly Lenny was aware of a strange, almost unnatural calm settling over him; as if he had already faced the worst terror imaginable and had somehow gotten beyond it and reached a distant point where he didn't recognize the familiar sensations of fear. In fact, he felt hardly any sensation at all, except a distinct irritation at Mousie for interrupting his act.

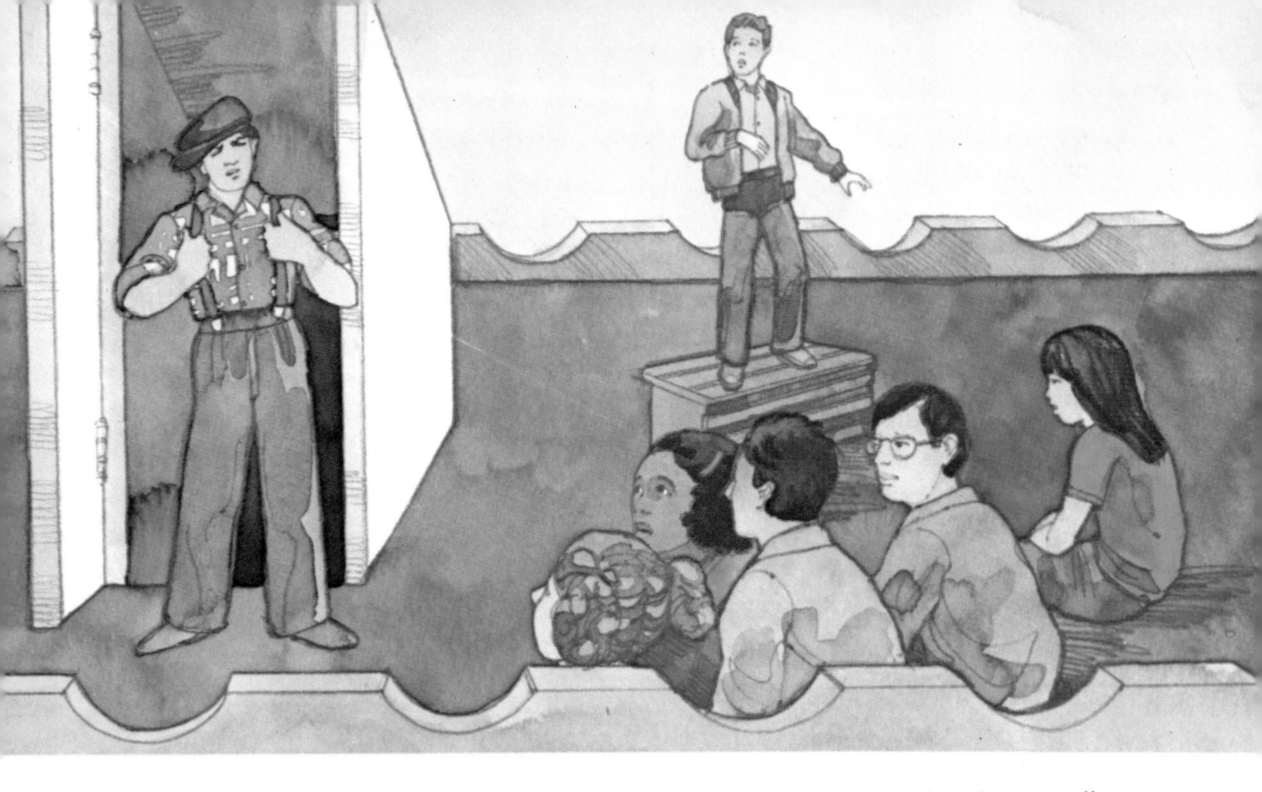

"You owe me a dime if you want to see this show," Lenny said.

Out of the corner of his eye, Lenny saw Artie shrink back. He thought, absently, that Artie was looking a little green.

"A smart aleck, aren't you?" Mousie sneered.

"It's better than being a conceited dumb *Maurice.*"

There were barely repressed giggles from the audience, even when Mousie glared around at the kids and sputtered, "You shut up if you know what's good for you!"

"Thank you, thank you," Lenny said. He bowed. "You're a wonderful audience." Mousie was wading through the semicircle of kids now, moving heavily toward the orange crate, with vengeance in his eyes.

Lenny watched Mousie come toward him with his huge fists clenched, and he had that strange, dreamlike feeling that he was watching himself watch Mousie come toward him. Here I am, he thought admiringly, and there's Mousie, who's going to kill me in about one minute, and I'm still on stage making wisecracks and laughing in the face of death.

What a trouper I am! Lenny marveled. If only my father were alive and could see me now.

And then, Mousie was two feet away from Lenny's stage, and Lenny saw him lower his shoulder in preparation for a flying tackle, and Lenny jumped off the orange crate and ran to the edge of the roof.

"Hah! Ya coward!" Mousie yelled. "Ya yellow coward! Come on and fight like a man."

Lenny never did remember how he actually did it, or even why, but the next thing he knew, he was standing on the ledge of the roof, far above the ground, arms folded across his chest, and snarling, "You wanna fight? Come and get me, Blatner."

He had a moment to consider adding a Jimmy Cagney impression to his act before the shrieking began.

All the kids were on their feet now—some were screaming for him to get down, some just staring mutely.

Mousie squinted up at him, shading his eyes from the sun with his hand. He didn't seem to know what to do next.

"What're you, crazy? Get down from there and fight."

"Come on up here and fight," Lenny yelled.

Don't look down, he told himself. He remembered the times he'd merely stood near the edge of the roof, remembered the scary sensation he'd felt looking down to the sidewalk.

And now, here I am, he thought hazily, doing probably the scariest thing anybody can do, liable to fall off and plunge to my death if a little breeze comes up or I lose my footing. Boy, this audience is certainly getting their money's worth!

"You're crazy!" Mousie howled.

"Yeah, that's right, Mousie, he is," Artie cried. "He's deranged. You better get out of here. You never know what he's going to do next."

"I'm not deranged!" Lenny called cheerily. Oh yes I am, he thought. I'm standing on the edge of a roof.

"That's the sure sign of an insane person!" Artie yelled.

"When they say they're not crazy. Lenny!" Artie's voice cracked. "Get off there! You'll kill yourself!"

"I'm waiting, Maurice," Lenny sang out. "Come and get me."

Then, in a dazzling flash of insight that he would remember even when he couldn't remember anything else about that afternoon, Lenny thought: This isn't brave, this is *stupid*! What am I *doing* up here? *What in the world do I do now?*

At that moment, a whole lot of things happened at once.

Mousie Blatner howled, "I'm gettin' outta here. You're outta your mind!"

A familiar scream pierced the air. "LENNY! WHAT ARE YOU DOING UP THERE?" He'd know his sister Rozzie's scream anywhere.

And Uncle Joe's voice, sounding unfamiliar because of an odd quaver in it, as if he were talking under water. "Don't startle him, don't make any sudden movements. Lenny, Lenny, don't do it!"

And his entire body breaking out in a cold, prickly, sickening sweat, as all the sensations of terror and reality returned in a dizzying whoosh, and he swayed and pitched forward and the black tar surface of the roof came rushing up to meet him.

Think About It

1. Why did Lenny decide to put on a comedy show?
2. How did the show go at first?
3. How did Lenny react when Mousie appeared at his show?
4. Why do you think Lenny dared Mousie to come onto the edge of the roof?
5. What did Lenny finally realize about challenging Mousie from the edge of the roof?
6. Write a paragraph about what type of performer you would choose to be and why.

HOW TO TELL A JOKE

by JOVIAL BOB STINE

"This joke is never going to end!"

"When already? When already!"

"I hope I never hear another joke as long as I live!"

Do people say these things when you're telling a joke? If not, you need more practice with your joke telling.

A truly unforgettable joke should be so long, so confusing, and so unbearably tiresome that the listener can't wait to start laughing at the punch line.

Wilma Wallaby is known as the best joke teller in her school, and is widely avoided for that reason. Wilma has been known to stretch a two-line grape joke into a three-day activity, leaving her audience so desperate to get away that they'll laugh at every word she says.

Here is Wilma now, telling one of her shorter jokes. Follow her technique—then practice it yourself on anyone you can force to listen.

Stop me if you've heard this one before. A bear goes into a restaurant. No—it was two bears. That's right. Two bears go into a restaurant, and—wait a minute! No, I got it wrong. It was a giraffe. That's right. A giraffe goes into a restaurant. Only it wasn't really a restaurant. It was a shoe store.

This giraffe asks the clerk for a tuna fish sandwich. Oh, I guess it was a restaurant after all. Well, it was more of a diner. There was a counter and a few seats in back, and it was called Joe's Diner. Or was it Jim's Diner? No, I think Jim owned the shoe store. Well, this is the wrong joke anyway.

A bear goes into a diner and orders a tuna sandwich. He wants to play the juke box, but there isn't one. "How come you don't have a juke box?" the bear asks the waiter.

"I don't know," the waiter tells him. "You're the first one to ask me that question."

"Well, that's okay," the bear says. "It isn't part of this joke anyway."

Well, the waiter brings the bear his peanut butter sandwich. Oh, wait—the bear ordered a tuna sandwich. I guess it was the giraffe that ordered peanut butter. That's another joke. Do you know the joke about the giraffe and the peanut butter sandwich? I'll tell that one when I finish this one.

So the waiter says to the—uh oh. I think it was a waitress. That's right, a waitress. She says to the giraffe—er, to the bear, "Are you the one that ordered the snoo?"

And the bear says, "Snoo? What's snoo?"

And the waitress—oh no—that's another joke. Wait. I'll get this right. The waitress brings the bear his tuna fish sandwich. Or was it peanut butter? No, it was a tuna sandwich with a banana. You haven't heard this joke before, have you? Oh, good.

Well, the waitress goes back to see the boss. Joe. Or Jim. No, Joe. And she says, "What shall I charge him for the pair of knee boots?"

And Joe says, "This is a restaurant—not a shoe store."

And so the waitress says, "What shall I charge him for the sandwich?"

And the owner says, "Well, he's only a bear. He probably doesn't know much about what things cost. So charge him five dollars for it."

The bear eats his sandwich. Well, almost all of it. I think he left the banana. Of course, I know a great joke about a bear and a banana peel. Remind me to tell it to you when I'm finished. The waitress tells the bear, "That'll be five dollars."

The bear pays the five dollars. I believe he had five one-dollar bills. Or was it four dollar bills and four quarters? Three quarters, two dimes, and a nickel? No, no—I remember! That's right—he had traveler's checks.

Anyway, he pays the five dollars. And as he's walking out, the waitress asks him—

Oh, wait. I think it was a giraffe after all.

No. No. It was a bear. And the waitress asks him, "Why did you choose this restaurant? We don't get many bears in here."

And the bear says, "Nothing. What's snoo with you?"

Oh, no. That isn't right. The waitress says, "Why did you come here? We don't get many bears in here."

And the bear says, "Well, with these prices I can see why!"

Hahahahaha hahahahahaha!! Funny? Hahahahaha!

Joke-Telling Rules

How can you tell jokes as well as Wilma Wallaby? By following these simple rules of joke telling Wilma was kind enough to write down for you:

1. Always begin by saying, "Stop me if you've heard this one before." If someone says "I've heard it," go right on telling it anyway.
2. Gesture a lot with your hands. Stand very close to the person you're telling the joke to, and poke him or her in the ribs to emphasize every third word of your joke.
3. Never tell a joke that takes less than twenty minutes.
4. Never tell a joke that involves a gorilla and a wise old farmer.
5. If you must tell elephant or grape jokes, never tell fewer than thirty at a time.
6. Always be the first to laugh at your own joke. Laugh as hard as you can so that the others will know just how funny it is.

QUESTION FOR REVIEW

Was it a bear or a giraffe?

LEARN NEW WORDS

1. He was **astounded** when the vase suddenly disintegrated in his hands.
2. She **calculated** that there was just enough time to finish her work.
3. I like to drink hot apple **cider** in the wintertime.
4. The writer **condensed** the message by taking out unnecessary words and shortening sentences.
5. Some of the **dialogue** in the play was rewritten to sound more like everyday conversation.
6. The **eruption** of the volcano was a spectacular sight.
7. In the **manual** alphabet, the hands form letters and spell words.
8. The room was a **moderate** size—not too big, not too small.
9. He **painstakingly** went over the wagonload, taking time to make sure each box was closed and tied down.
10. Thinking that everyone must have understood the joke, he **smirked** knowingly at the person sitting next to him.
11. All her muscles were **taut** as she strained to lift the weight.

GET SET TO READ

Do you think people always like surprises? Think of an example of a time when a person might not like a surprise or a joke.

Read this story to find out how his father feels about Harry's surprise.

Harry's Joke

by MARY RISKIND

Author's Note

I am a hearing person, but I grew up in a family with hearing-impaired parents. I learned to talk with my hands before I learned to talk with my voice. The characters in this story are hearing-impaired, like my mother and father, and they use sign language, just as we did at home. As you read this story, you will find that what Harry and his family say to each other is not like everyday speech. One of the problems I discovered in writing about hearing-impaired children is that it is hard to translate sign language into English. So I would like to tell you a little bit about how I have done that here.

One of the things you will notice is that words in the dialogue sometimes are spelled out, or finger-spelled. In the manual alphabet each letter is represented by a particular hand shape. Some of them look like the written letter: *O* and *C* are examples. But the letter *S* is made by a fist. You can say anything you want with the manual alphabet. But people usually finger-spell only at certain times: if there is no sign for a word, to say the proper name of a person or place, or to stress a word—a little like raising your voice.

Hearing-impaired people typically use some combination of signs and finger-spelling. A person who speaks sign language well can go as fast as (even faster than) you can say the same things aloud.

Sign language is very condensed. Often word endings (*-s, -ly, -ed, -ing*) and little words (*is, am, are, has, had, I, the*) are omitted, and a single sign will do the work of two or more English words to communicate an idea. In the dialogue you will also see many hyphenated words, like 'thank-you' and 'show-me.' These are words said by a single sign.

I hope you enjoy getting to know Harry.

This story takes place around the turn of the century. Harry, his mother, father, brother, and two sisters live on an apple farm near the town of Muncy, Pennsylvania. During the school year, Harry goes to a special boarding school for the hearing-impaired in Philadelphia. One of the things Harry learns at this school is how to speak.

For a boy like Harry, who has never been able to hear any sound, speaking is a difficult, sometimes painful thing to do. His teacher is able to show Harry how sound works by yelling Whoa! *to stop a horse. By the end of his first school term, Harry has learned to say* whoa.

When Harry returns to his family for the holidays, he wants to surprise them with what he has learned at school. Alone in the barn one day, he practices stopping the family horse by saying Whoa! *He even decides to name the horse Whoa. Now Harry is ready for his joke.*

Harry rose as the gray light of morning tiptoed across his bed. He prickled with excitement. This morning they were going to Mr. Russell's cider mill to press apples. The Muncy schoolhouse was very near the mill, and with any luck he calculated he'd at least have a chance to peek in and wave hello to his hearing friends. He couldn't wait to see their astonished faces when they saw him again.

Outside the window a dense fog rested on the Pennsylvania farmlands, rolling down be-

tween the hills like puffy mounds of freshly shorn sheep's wool. Harry's father strode from the mist toward the barn. He had been to the orchards to check his trees. He painstakingly checked them first thing every morning like an anxious parent.

But then maybe that's why his apples are so good, Harry thought. His father was one of the few Mr. Russell let pay in cider for pressing his apples. The rest had to pay cash, a cent and a half a gallon.

Harry waved from his high perch but his father didn't see him.

Through the floorboards he felt footsteps behind him. It was his brother, Ray. 'Mother say must hurry. Dress. Eat. Father angry i-f wait long,' Ray said. Harry reached right away for the trousers that hung on his bedpost.

Over breakfast his father solemnly cautioned the children to keep their hands low when they signed in town. 'Like-this.' He motioned in small gestures at his side. Harry's father looked directly at him. 'Understand?'

Harry nodded out of habit. They were the same instructions his father always gave. His father was suspicious of hearing people, expecting the shopkeepers in town to shortchange him, or blaming the friends Harry made there for anything he did wrong. He wanted Harry to stay away from the hearing.

Harry left the table, having barely touched his plate, and ran with the others to help hitch the wagon. The day before, they had loaded it with sacks of apples and an empty cider barrel. Harry's sister Veve led the roan out of his stall, and she and Harry held him still while Ray fastened the harness. Ray drove to the house, then they hopped over the seat and scrambled for places among the bags.

Climbing aboard, Harry's mother handed him a napkin folded around two biscuits. 'Eat very little. Must calm-down. Not want thin—' She drew a long bean with her fingers. Harry grinned and accepted the sweet-smelling rolls thankfully.

The reins slapped the horse and they were off. Down into the fog they drove, over the bumpy lane, between the two large piles of stones marking the entrance to the farm, and off the lane onto a wider, rutted road.

As usual, Harry's father was wearing his broad-brimmed felt hat. Harry leaned out over the side behind him to see, straining for a particular tree or a gully he knew. On an occasional curve he caught a glimpse of the horse's red flanks glistening in the moist morning. His father urged the horse to move faster, but the horse would not be hurried.

Perhaps Whoa really was a suitable name for this horse, Harry smiled. He realized he'd forgotten to tell Ray about how he'd learned to say *whoa.* His sisters and brother sat facing backward toward the road they

left behind. He tugged Ray's shirt sleeve.

'What want?' Ray answered.

'That horse have name?'

'No. J-u-s-t call Horse.'

'I have name for,' Harry said.

'What?'

'W-h-o-a.'

Ray wrinkled his nose. 'Silly. Where find that name?'

'Can't tell now. Wait. Big surprise. Will show-you.' Harry smirked, but Ray looked crosser by the minute, waiting for something to happen. 'After-while. Can't now,' Harry said when Ray nagged him to see the surprise now.

Ray gestured, 'Bah. Can't believe you. You make fun. Not any surprise.' He folded his arms and stared out of the wagon.

'You see,' Harry retorted.

They were coming to a level place in the road. Harry pursed his lips. His throat vibrated a little, then more, and stopped. He waited, every muscle taut.

The roan continued his lumbering pace.

Harry looked in disbelief. Holding his throat this time, he gave a big push from deep in his stomach. He could feel a powerful eruption spread through his chest and throat. Whoa slowed to a standstill and nibbled the grasses by the side of the road.

When Ray turned around, startled, Harry smiled knowingly at him, but Ray didn't seem to grasp what had happened.

'Why make stop?' asked Harry's mother.

Harry's father shrugged. 'Not,' he answered. 'Horse. Self.'

'Maybe horse tired. Steep-hill, many people and many apples. Hard work pull. Rest.'

Harry's father agreed with his wife's suggestion and let the animal rest for a few minutes, but he soon was impatient with the wait and started up again. Harry sat solemnly; inside he danced with merriment.

The wagon bounced steadily, up and down hills, in and out of the fog. Reaching a hilltop they burst upon the sun and later waded into patches of thinning moisture. The farther they rode, the itchier Harry became to try his trick again. The fog was burning off and he saw a clearing ahead.

Now! He rounded his mouth and once again felt a mighty eruption in his chest. His heart pounded. A few beats later Whoa pulled to a stop.

Harry's parents glanced uneasily at each other. His father climbed down from his seat. He patted the horse and brushed his hand over the velvety rump. He examined the animal's mouth. The bit was in place. He signed to his wife. 'Horse not look tired.'

'Look-at shoes. Maybe losing one.'

'Good idea.' Harry's father lifted each hoof and studied it, while Whoa waited patiently. No, Harry's father shook his head. He wiped his forehead and looked the roan over once more. As he walked back to the wagon, Harry ducked behind the seat.

Whoa started the wagon rolling. Up front the two adults puzzled over the strange behavior of their horse. Harry's father touched two fingers to his nose. 'Something funny.'

'Why you laugh?' Ray said to Harry.

'I d-o.'

'What?'

'Stop horse.'

'You? No. Can't believe. Lazy horse, that's-all.'

'I yell.'

'Yell?'

'Yes. School teach-me. Watch.'

Past the clearing was a small stand of evergreens, then there were a few farms and another turnoff onto a dusty road that followed the river like a weary companion into Muncy. The river road often was crowded with other vehicles. Harry calculated he had one more chance.

For the third time, he took a deep breath and he could feel the yell escaping. For the third time Whoa stalled.

'You d-o?' Ray was goggle-eyed. Harry smirked.

The wagon had barely come to rest when their father jumped down, ripped off his hat, and snapped it against a wheel. Whoa pawed the ground. Again his father painstakingly examined the horse, his mouth, the shoes, the harness. Then he examined the wagon wheels and the axles. 'Nothing wrong,' he signed to himself.

Then one by one he fixed his gaze on the children draped over the side. A smile tugged at Harry's mouth, and he tried not to look for too long.

Thinking and in slow motion, Harry's father mounted his seat. He turned deliberately to Harry. His right hand crashed to his left palm. 'Stop! No-more! You think funny, you can stay. Get-off wagon. Off! Wait here.'

Harry was stunned. He crawled over his brother and sister—Veve was near tears and Ray was pale with fright—and

dangled a moment at the end of the cart before he dropped to the dirt road. As the wagon pulled off, his mother was signing to his father, but he ignored her protests. Whoa rounded the corner and disappeared.

Harry walked to a nearby fence post and drooped against the rough wood. He felt lost, though it was a place he knew.

The morning fog was completely gone now. The sun was full and the sky glowed blue. In a few minutes they'd be at the cider mill. He kicked the dirt, covering the toes of his shoes with dust.

Soon a wagon appeared on the main road and his hopes leaped. Maybe they would give him a ride to town. He cut himself short. No, they were hearing for sure. That would anger his father more. He picked up a fistful of pebbles and threw them at the fence post.

Probably Ray was on his way to the schoolhouse already. Or the bridge.

He stuck his hands in a coat pocket and pulled out the rolls. Maybe if he ate, he'd feel better. He broke off a hunk of roll. The roll was dry and stuck in his throat like the bitterness he felt.

He scuffed his shoes again. He wasn't going to wait here forever with nothing to do. He'd walk, he resolved. But to Muncy? Or home?

He turned his back on the river road and started out at a moderate and constant pace, the way his father had showed him to hike on the farm without overtiring himself. Avoiding the deep ruts, he strode past one farm. Then another.

The air was cool, but the sun was hot. Soon his undershirt was damp and clung to his body. He removed his coat and tied it around his waist. The dry, parched feeling in his mouth was becoming more insistent. He hesitated at the next farmhouse, thinking of asking for a drink of water, then decided against it.

After a while, he reached the stand of trees near the clearing where he had stopped Whoa the second time. He climbed up the tallest tree like a fleeing chipmunk. On one side, he saw the rough up-and-downhill trek ahead of him. On the other, he saw how far he'd come. The river road was barely visible.

Then in the distance he noticed movement on the road. He recognized it as his parents. He could see his father pull up the wagon and get out, probably near the place where he left Harry. They were looking for him.

For a long time—it seemed like hours—his father just stood there. At last he climbed back into the wagon. Harry was astounded by what he saw next. The wagon turned in at each farm and drove up to the farmhouse. After a few minutes they were on the rough dirt road again, rolling very slowly closer and closer to him.

As the wagon approached, he could see his family's worried expressions. Even Anna was searching the road for some trace of her brother. But no one glanced up, so no one spied him. The wagon inched along.

Harry wanted to fly down from his hiding place, but an angry part of him held back. He

twisted from the right to the left of the tree trunk to get a better view. They were directly beneath him. Now moving away. Soon they would be gone.

Harry held tightly to the tree and drew up his lips. With all the strength he could summon he pushed out the biggest *Whoa!* he'd ever made.

The horse jerked short. Immediately, Harry's father stood up in the wagon and looked about. 'Come-back,' he said with a generous motion that even the hearing would know as a welcome.

Harry clambered down out of the tree so fast he skipped the lower branches entirely. He pressed hard against his father.

His father patted his blond hair, then lifted his chin gently. 'You much like father. Stubborn.' A wrinkle creased the corners of his mouth. He removed his felt hat and pulled it over Harry's ears. 'Come. Better wear coat. Riding not warm like walking. B-a-c-k to apple mash house. Not finished.'

Harry ran to the rear of the wagon where Ray moved over to make room for him. The wagon started up. 'You right,' Ray remarked shyly to Harry, their shoes trailing in the dust billows, 'true surprise.'

Think About It

1. What was Harry's joke?
2. Why do you think his father reacted the way he did?
3. Why was Harry astounded that his father would ask about him at every farmhouse?
4. Why do you think Harry stopped the horse by yelling *whoa* again instead of going out to meet his family's wagon?
5. What did Harry's father mean when he said, 'You much like father. Stubborn.'?
6 Write about the difference between Harry's joke and Lenny Kandell's jokes.

In the Mood

The two stories "Lenny Kandell, Smart Aleck" and "Harry's Joke" have similar themes. Both Lenny and Harry get carried away by their own performances, and in each case this causes a conflict with someone else. One of the things that makes the two stories different is the **mood** of each one. The mood of a story is the feeling that it creates in the reader. The mood of "Lenny Kandell, Smart Aleck" is comic, whereas "Harry's Joke" has a more serious mood.

In general, all elements of a story contribute to the mood. Part of the comic mood of "Lenny Kandell, Smart Aleck" comes from the many jokes sprinkled throughout the story. Other parts that add to a story's mood are its setting and the characters' actions and feelings.

Lenny performs his comedy show on a warm, sunny afternoon. On page 145 you'll find this description: "the sun was shining like a spotlight." Why is that a good simile to describe the setting of this story?

Many descriptions of Lenny's actions and feelings also help create the comic mood of the story. Read this description and answer the questions below it.

> Lenny jumped onto the orange crate and stood for a moment, just looking out at the expectant, upturned faces. He felt a surge of excitement, as if he were suddenly charged with electricity, and he knew it was because this was how it felt when a dream finally came true.

1. What does Lenny's action tell you about how he feels?
2. What is Lenny's feeling compared to?
3. Why is this moment in Lenny's life so special?

"Harry's Joke" is a very different kind of story from "Lenny Kandell, Smart Aleck." However, it opens with a similar sense of excitement. Turn to page 160 and read the first two paragraphs of the story. What kind of morning is it? How does Harry feel? What does the description of the fog as "puffy mounds of freshly shorn sheep's wool" tell you about how Harry feels about the fog on that morning?

After Harry's father gets angry with him, the mood of the story changes. Harry is sad and resentful that he won't get to go to the cider mill. Read these two paragraphs, detailing what happens after his father drives off with his family and leaves Harry behind. Then answer the questions that follow.

> Harry walked to a nearby fence post and drooped against the rough wood. He felt lost, though it was a place he knew.
>
> The morning fog was completely gone now. The sun was full and the sky glowed blue. In a few minutes they'd be at the cider mill. He kicked the dirt, covering the toes of his shoes with dust.

1. How is the setting in this paragraph different from the setting at the beginning of the story?
2. What do Harry's actions tell about the way he feels?
3. Find other sentences on page 166 that tell how Harry feels.

Despite this low point in the mood of "Harry's Joke," the story ends on a happy note. Read the last three paragraphs of the story. Find sentences that tell you that the conflict between Harry and his father has been resolved happily.

LEARN NEW WORDS

1. They learned how to build furniture by working as **apprentices** to a skilled cabinetmaker.
2. **Carpentry** is a good field for those who enjoy making things from wood.
3. Because of our moderate prices, we sell more typewriters than our **competition** across the street.
4. Mr. Green **consults** several trusted advisers before making any important business decision.
5. He must learn how to **convert** yards into meters.
6. The carpenters will first **erect** the frame for the new addition to the cafeteria.
7. It was her ambition to be an **executive** heading a major company.
8. The doctor gave me a **prescription** for medicine for my cold.

GET SET TO READ

An important part of growing up is thinking about what you want to do for a living. What careers do you think would be interesting?

Read this article to find out about a number of interesting jobs.

AND WHAT DO YOU DO?

by GEORGE ANCONA

Air Traffic Controller

The vast sky above an airport is filled with airplanes, some ready to land as others take off. Keeping this traffic flowing safely is what the air traffic controller does. The job calls for a person with steady nerves, good judgment, and a clear voice.

This controller talks with the pilot by radio from the time a plane leaves the loading gate, moves out to the runway, takes off, and is on its way. She can see incoming flights as lights on the radar screen long before she can see the planes from the control tower. She keeps these planes circling in the air in a "holding pattern" until a runway is clear. Then she instructs the pilot to land.

The Federal Aviation Administration trains people for this job in a special school. An air traffic controller works as part of a crew that is responsible for the lives of many people.

Carpenter

Carpenters work mostly with wood. A carpenter must know the many different kinds of lumber and must know how to use power and hand tools, install hardware, and do math.

These carpenters are building the frame of a house. Working from the blueprint, they measure and cut lumber with a power saw. The wall frames are nailed together on the floor and then raised into place. Floor beams and roof rafters are nailed to the standing walls. Next, the inside walls are framed. Then the frame is covered on the outside with a roof, windows, doors, and panels. Other carpenters and skilled workers finish the inside of the house with walls, floor, and ceiling.

Carpentry is taught in trade schools, but many people learn carpentry as apprentices on the job. Some carpenters specialize in building houses and others in making furniture.

Costume Designer

Actors and other performers wear costumes created by a costume designer. A costume will convert a player into a cowhand or a princess, a soldier or a ghost, a baker or an astronaut, or anything else the script calls for.

This designer consults with the director and set designer of a play to understand what the characters must look like. She spends many hours searching through books, paintings, and photographs that show how people dressed at the time of the play's story. The designer then makes sketches to show the director. The costumes are made up, rented, or bought according to her designs.

Costume designers need artistic talent and an understanding of theater or film. They learn the craft by working in the theater, by studying, or by assisting a designer. This is just one of the many crafts that go into producing a play, a ballet, or an opera for stage, film, or television.

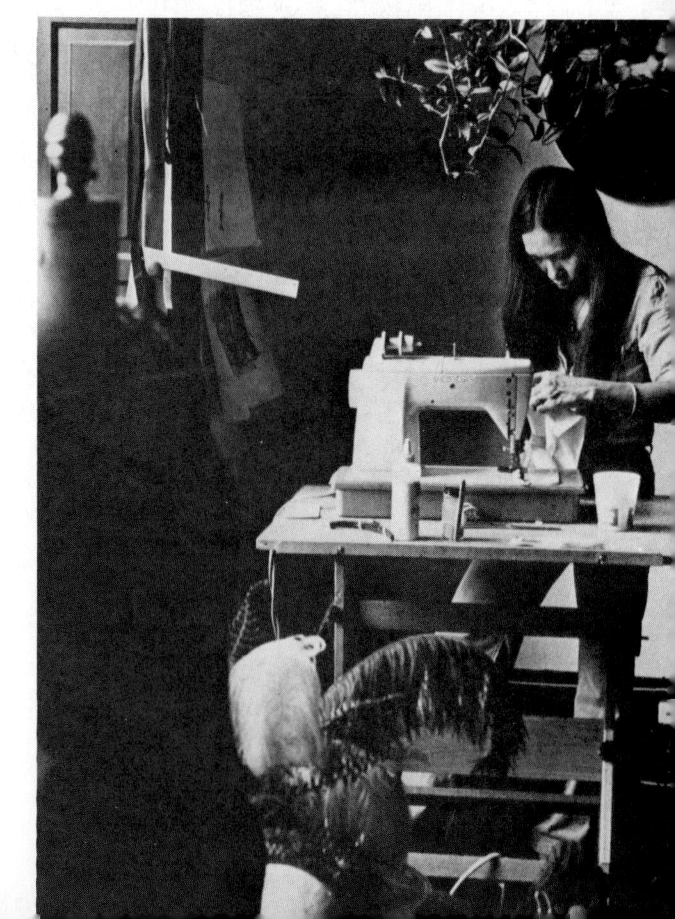

Day-Care Worker

Someone who enjoys being with and caring for children can become a worker in a day-care center. This day-care worker helps the teachers look after the children while they play and eat. She reads them stories and gets them ready for a nap. She may take them to the playground or the zoo. If a child gets hurt, she is there to give comfort. She also talks to the parents in school or goes to their homes. In this way she can help the child at the center. For most children, this is the first time they are away from home.

A worker at a day-care center must be sensitive to children and trained to meet their needs.

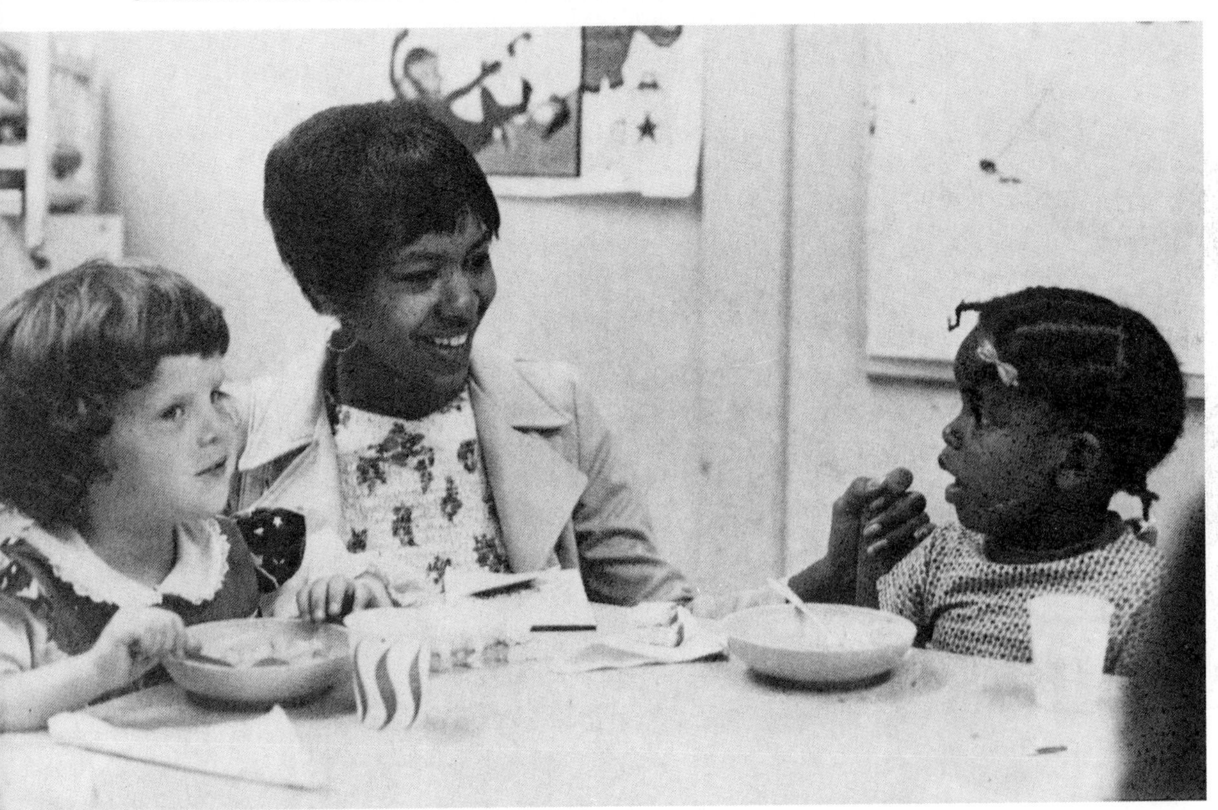

Illustrator

Artists who draw pictures for books and magazines are called illustrators. After reading a story, this illustrator sketches the pictures and characters as he sees them. Once the sketches are approved by the advertising agency or the publisher, the illustrator does a finished drawing or painting, using a variety of materials—ink, crayon, paint, magic marker, cutout paper.

The most important tools an illustrator has are imagination and the ability to draw. To become an illustrator, you can start as an apprentice in an art studio. Another way is to go to an art school.

Once this illustrator learned his craft, he put together a portfolio of his best work. On the basis of this selected work, he receives assignments. Some illustrators work in art studios. Others free-lance, which means they work on their own and are paid for each drawing they make.

Ironworker

Those who erect the steel sections of bridges, skyscrapers, and towers are called ironworkers. Each ironworker works as part of a team. An individual's life depends on the skill and ability of each one in the gang.

The raising gang erects the framework of a skyscraper. Using a guy derrick like the one in the photo, they raise each steel member from the street and guide it into its exact position. These steel columns, beams, and girders weigh as much as eighteen tons each. Once in place, they are bolted temporarily. The bolting gang then follows to bolt or weld each member permanently.

To become an ironworker, you must serve a three-year apprenticeship on the job while you also go to night school. Many ironworkers continue with their education to become structural engineers.

Nurse

A patient in a hospital is under nursing care day and night. Nurses work in shifts of eight hours. A chart is kept for each patient showing the illness and what treatments and medicines the doctor has ordered. The nurse follows the chart and writes down what has been done. The patient's condition is also noted so that the nurses and doctors have the latest information about the patient.

This nurse takes a patient's temperature, checks blood pressure and pulse, and gives medicines and injections. He often gives comfort and kindness to help the patient feel better. A nurse has the satisfaction of doing something for someone else.

After years of schooling, a nurse can take a state examination to become a registered nurse (RN). Many RN's study further to enter specialized nursing fields.

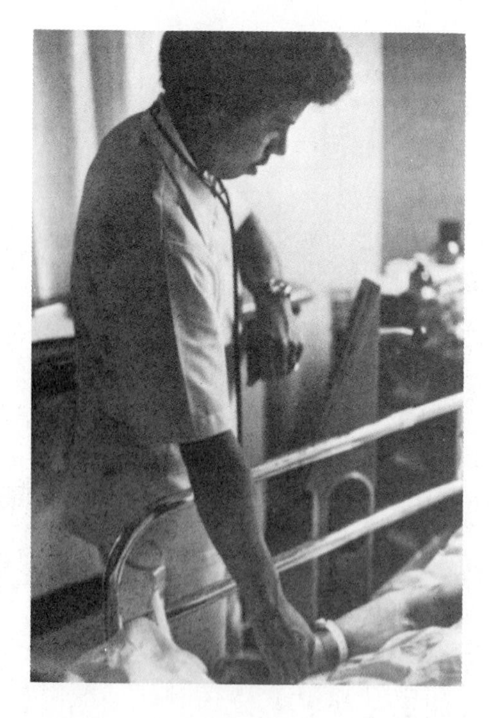

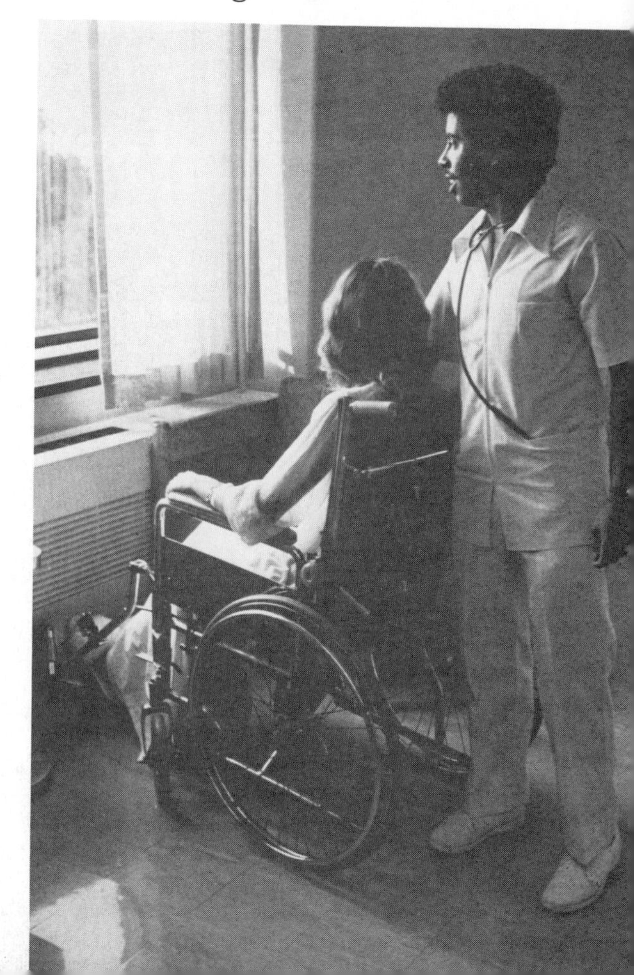

Optician

When an eye doctor decides a patient needs glasses, he or she makes out a prescription that the patient takes to an optician. The optician's job is to fill the prescription with the correct lenses and fit them into frames.

After helping the patient select the frames, the optician measures the distance between the centers of the eyes. This is done in order to position the lenses correctly in the frames. The lenses are ordered from a manufacturer who delivers two large, round, uncut lenses. Following a pattern, the optician grinds them down to fit the shape of the frame. Today most lenses are plastic. When glass is used, the lenses are heat-treated to make them impact-resistant. When the patient arrives for the glasses, the optician softens plastic frames in hot salt and shapes them to fit the person's face. Metal frames are fitted with special pliers.

This is a profession for those who enjoy working with their hands and dealing with people. After two years of on-the-job training and some courses in theory, the trainee takes a test for a state license to become a registered optician.

TV Production Assistant

Time—hours, minutes, seconds: these are the elements of television broadcasting. The production assistant is the one who makes things happen when they have to. The job varies with the type of TV show. This production assistant works with the producer and director. She reads the script and times the show to be sure that it fits into the time allowed. In the control room, she sits with a stopwatch during rehearsals and recording sessions.

The production assistant also casts the show; that is, she calls actors to be selected by the director. Sometimes she orders scenery for the show.

Part of this job is knowing how and where things are done, and who to get to do them. A production assistant will spend many hours on the phone coaxing and consulting with all the people responsible for putting a show together and getting it on the air.

People start in a variety of jobs in a television studio and then move into production. This job can be a steppingstone to the job of producer or director of TV shows.

Welder

The process of joining metal together is known as welding. Welding is used in making such things as automobiles, ships, bridges, and buildings.

One method is electric-arc welding. Here's how it works: One end of an electric current runs through the cable a welder holds. A slender rod called an electrode is clamped to the end of the cable. This electrode is brought close to the seam of two steel plates, causing a bright arc. The intense heat created by the arc melts the electrode and fills the seam, uniting the steel plates.

This man started out as a beginning welder, rated as third class. After six months to two years, he became a second-class welder. In about two more years he became first class and could weld pipes. With further study of metallurgy and theory, a welder can become a welding engineer.

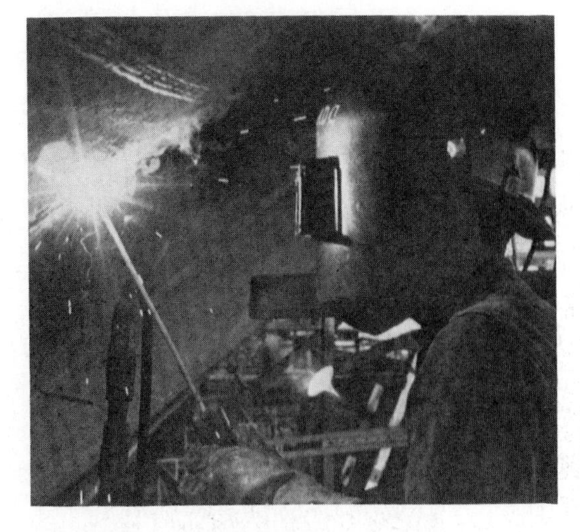

The Boy Who Learned To Sell Computers

by AMY A. HELLER

It's three o'clock in the morning in a dormitory at New York University. But upstairs in Room 704, Marc Mandel is wide awake . . . and working.

While everybody else sleeps, the college freshman sits at the keyboard of his computer, working rapidly. Marc isn't up late writing a paper or a program for class; he's preparing invoices for his mail-order computer company. And Marc doesn't mind losing a little sleep, because in the past year his company has made over $100,000 in sales.

At eighteen years old, Marc may not look like the average executive, but he's not new to the computer business. Marc started his first computer mail-order company when he was fourteen. Over the years he has built up the business that has made him so successful.

Marc describes his company as a "no frills" company. He buys computers and software at wholesale prices and sells them for less than the stores. Marc is able to undersell the competition by keeping his costs low. He works out of his dorm room and stores things in his parents' basement. Marc's main expense is the nearly $5,000 a month he spends to advertise his bargains in a number of computer magazines.

Because Marc is studying full time at NYU, he has to find time for business after he's finished his classes and his homework. Most nights he doesn't get around to processing orders until after midnight. On Fridays Marc usually travels to his parents' home in Huntington, Long Island, and ships out the week's orders.

Marc has big plans for his future. He wants to expand his company worldwide, attend law school, and eventually act as lawyer for the country's leading computer companies. But for now, he has to study for a test, process a batch of new orders, and catch up on his sleep—if he can find the time.

Think About It

1. What is the purpose of these two articles?
2. Choose one career from the articles and tell what kind of information is given about it.
3. Choose another career and explain what the photos tell you about it.
4. Which of the jobs in these articles seems the most exciting or interesting to you? Why?
5. What are some good ways to find out where your career interests lie?
6. What school subjects do you like most? Write a list of jobs that could be related to those subjects.

The Nit Nowns

by JOYCE HANSEN

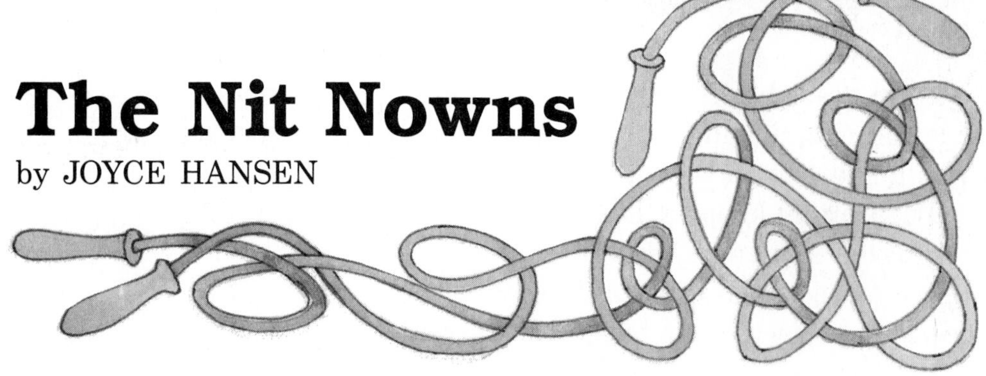

Doris can't do double-dutch when she jumps rope. She's the best rope turner in the neighborhood, but no matter how hard she practices, her feet keep getting tangled in the ropes. And now her best friends, Dotty and Mickey, want to have a double-dutch contest. Before she realizes it, Doris finds herself organizing a contest she wanted no part of in the first place.

"What do you want to have a double-dutch contest for?" I asked Mickey.

"For fun."

"I don't feel like it."

"You just don't want it 'cause you're not good at it."

"I can jump."

"But you're not good at it."

"I'll show you. Okay, let's have a contest."

"Don't back out."

"I won't."

Mickey and Dotty made me mad. They think they're the best rope jumpers in the world. I got some of the little girls on the block to turn for me so I could practice.

I twisted my ankle, tripped, scratched my legs, and scraped my knees. Those little girls started giggling, and I felt like wrapping the rope around their heads. I chased them away and sat on the stoop rubbing my legs.

Amir was across the street watching a stickball game. When I sat down he came over.

"You had a hard time with that rope, huh?"

"How do you know? I thought you were watching the ball game."

"Why get so upset?"

"I'm not upset. And I wasn't having a hard time. Those girls don't know how to turn."

"It's not that important. People aren't gonna hate you 'cause you can't jump rope."

"Why don't you mind your business, Amir? You want me to stand around and watch like you?"

"Sometimes it's more fun watching."

"I like to do the things my friends do."

"If your friends jump off a roof, you going to?"

"You know what I mean, Amir! I'm not like you!"

He shrugged his shoulders and went back across the street. Amir didn't understand.

We decided just to have the contest with the girls on our block. But word got over on Union Avenue, and who of all people but the Nit Nowns decided to enter the contest.

Now the Nit Nowns are five ugly sisters—Charlene and Charlotte, Pauline and Paulette, and Baby Claudette. They live on Union Avenue. Baby Claudette is two. She can't say "sit down." She says "nit nown" instead, so we call the whole family the Nit Nowns.

I've never known any of the girls on 163rd Street to play with them. None of us liked them.

One woman in my building said, "Those children look like they just reach in a box and put on whatever they pull out. They are some scruffy children."

And those Nit Nowns are always chasing someone home. I even heard that Baby Claudette slaps other babies. I don't believe that, though.

"They'd mess up the whole thing with their ugly selves," Mickey grumbled.

The big problem was who was going to tell them they couldn't be in it. Mickey said, "Well, I can't tell them 'cause I don't talk to people like the Nit Nowns."

I looked at Dotty but that was no use.

I said, "I can't tell them either because if my mama ever caught me talking to them she'd kill me."

Big-mouth Lavinia says, "How is your mama gonna see you talking to someone on Union Avenue?"

"She might be passing by."

"You're just scared."

"Why don't you tell them, Lavinia?"

"I'm not telling them."

I saw Amir coming up the street. "Hi, Amir," I said loudly. "Could you do us a favor?"

"What?"

"Could you tell the Nit Nowns for us that they can't be in the double-dutch contest?"

"Why?"

"'Cause nobody bothers with them."

"Why?"

"'Cause they're mean and ugly."

"How do you know they're mean and ugly if you never bother with them?"

"They act mean and anyone can see they're ugly."

"They chase people home and are always trying to mess with nice kids like us," Mickey said, putting an innocent look on her face.

"Maybe they just want to play with you. Did you make up rules for being in the contest?"

"Yes. It's only for the girls on 163rd Street."

"Tell them then. But maybe if you let them be in the contest they won't chase you home anymore."

"Amir, you're scared of them too," I said.

He just smiled and walked up the block.

Mickey said, "Maybe we can tell them it starts at five o'clock and when they get here it'll be over."

"Yeah. I can just see them coming down the street ready for the contest and it's over." We died laughing.

Dotty asked us, "But what are you gonna do when they find out you tricked them?"

"Let's don't have a contest," I said.

"But everybody is all excited about it. Even Mr. Sam said he'd give free treats to the winner."

"We got to have the contest. People been practicing like crazy," Mickey said.

Next day I was coming from the store for my mother and passed by the playground. I was sorry I did. I should've gone some other way. I saw the Nit Nowns playing on the seesaw. I turned my head and walked fast, hoping they didn't see me. Then I hear, "Hey, wait up." It was Paulette, the biggest one. She ran out of the playground.

"We can't wait to be in the contest. What time does it start again?"

"Twelve," I said.

"We'll be there. And we're gonna win too."

"Okay," I said all quiet like.

"Bye. We'll see you Saturday."

Baby Claudette looked up at me. "Bye," she said, waving her little hands.

Well at least they didn't run me home. I was glad no one heard me talking to them.

As the contest day got closer, I got more nervous. Now I wished my mother would make me stay in the house. I even thought about doing something so I could be put under punishment. But the thing was turning into a big block party. Even the grownups were looking forward to it. This is gonna be one big mess, I thought. Me falling. And the Nit Nowns messing things up. I was sorry I got mixed up in it.

Mickey and Dotty's mother bought us two new ropes. A lot of the grownups said they'd bring food. Lavinia's father said he'd give the winner a prize from the African jewelry he makes. Three of the older girls on the block said they'd be judges. Even old Mrs. Shepard said she'd make a pitcher of lemonade. And the whole block would be there to see me make a fool of myself.

When Saturday came I thought I had a fever.

"There's nothing wrong with you, girl," my mother said. "It's just hot out."

All morning I wished for something to happen to keep me in the house. Maybe it'll rain. I looked out the window. There wasn't a cloud in the sky. Not even a half a cloud. I looked down at the stoop. No one was out yet. But I could see myself down there in a couple of hours. Everybody laughing. Me twisted in ropes from my ankles up to my neck. I could get strangled.

"Hey, Ma, you could get hurt jumping double-dutch, huh?"

"You could get hurt jumping out of bed if you don't do it right."

I finally had to face it. We went outside. Some of the women were setting up tables for the food. Maybe I'll just stand here and faint, like they do in those old-time movies, I thought. Then they'll have to carry me upstairs and I can miss the contest. Why was I always in the middle of something dumb?

The stoop filled up like Yankee Stadium. Even all the boys were there. And those boys paid no mind to us jumping double-dutch until that day. Lavinia was the first to go.

She did her double-dutch twist.

Dotty spun in the ropes like crazy.

Mickey jumped and turned round and round on one foot.

Another girl did some steps that looked like tap dancing.

Everybody wanted me to turn for them. If you don't have someone good turn the rope, the jumper gets messed up.

I was miserable, though. Then, my turn to jump came. I felt like I had to go to the bathroom.

"Come on, Doris," Mickey said. "Go on and jump."

People were talking about how good Dotty was, and looking at me. Amir sat there with his head down like he was studying a crack in the sidewalk. I tried to look like I didn't care.

"I changed my mind. I'm not that good. I'll just turn."

Mickey looked shocked. Someone said, "Okay, but I want Doris to turn for me. No one can turn like her."

"Aw, Doris, come on," Dotty said. "We won't laugh. Try it."

It was funny, I really felt better. "Naw, it's okay. Bring the next jumper on. I'll turn."

I looked over at Amir again. He looked back at me with a smile in his big eyes.

I felt so good I forgot all about the Nit Nowns. We had two more people to go and the Nit Nowns hadn't shown yet.

"Maybe they're not coming," Mickey said.

But as the last person finished I see those five sisters cutting around the corner, carrying a big tray. Mickey looked at me and made a face.

Lavinia yelled. "The contest is finished."

Amir jumps up with his nervy self and says, "No, it's not. These sisters are in it too."

I was so mad at him. "Amir's mouth's getting big as his eyes," I said.

Charlene came over with the tray. "We made some sandwiches for the party."

My mother took them from her. "Oh, isn't this lovely. You're some nice girls," she said. Imagine my own mother telling the Nit Nowns they're nice.

Next thing I know people are coming out with card tables and all kinds of food and other goodies. And the Nit Nowns are getting ready to jump.

The minute they started I knew who the winner would be—one of those sisters.

Pauline looked like she had on special double-dutch shoes. They must've been turned over in just the right spots. The heels were worn down smooth. Her feet went so fast they looked blurry.

Charlene didn't move anything but her feet. The rest of her body was stiff and straight. She looked cool and calm. She smiled and jumped.

Charlotte and Paulette jumped together. They held

hands and did a double-dutch dance. Everyone cheered.

I was mad. Before they came, little Dotty had a good chance of winning. Now here comes these two Nit Nowns doing something I've never seen anyone else do before.

As the judges were deciding, I said to Mickey, "Maybe they won't pick those Nit Nowns. Nobody on this block likes them."

The judges got up. "Okay, everybody quiet. The winners are Charlotte and Paulette."

"I knew it, Mickey."

Everybody went over to them like they were special. Mr. Sam brought over some more treats from his store. We had a real party. One lady said to me, "You really know how to snap those ropes with a lot of rhythm."

People started talking about how we were gonna have another 163rd Street block party and double-dutch contest next summer.

The day after the party I was sitting on the stoop. Mickey comes running over to me.

"We're going to Union Avenue so Charlotte and Paulette can show us that double-dutch dance."

"What? You're going to play with those raggedy girls?"

"So? They're going to teach us that dance. We need you to turn for us."

"How can you play with them?"

"We're just going to learn that dance. Come on."

Since Mickey and Dotty were my two best friends and since I was kind of bored, I went too.

When we got over to Union Avenue, the Nit Nowns were jumping double-dutch. Paulette spun around on one leg. The baby laughed and clapped.

"Look how wild those girls act," I said to Mickey.

"You're just jealous," Mickey said.

"No I'm not. I don't care about double-dutch."

When the Nit Nowns saw us they grinned and waved. I whispered to Mickey, "They're acting friendly now, but those girls could turn on us in a minute and run us right back to 163rd Street." Mickey ignored me. Dotty was already in the middle of the ropes acting the fool with Paulette.

"Come on Doris, turn for us," Charlotte said. I tried to smile, but it was hard. Charlotte jumped in the ropes and she and Paulette did their dance. Mickey and Dotty watched, while Pauline and I turned. I got so interested in the dance they made up that I forgot about how I didn't like them.

Suddenly I felt something pulling at my shorts. I looked down. Baby Claudette was tugging at me. "Tun, tun," she said. We cracked up.

Charlene ran over to her. "Come here," she said.

I dropped the ropes and picked up the baby. "You're too little to turn," I said. "Go on Charlene, you turn. I'll mind the baby for you."

Claudette took my hand. I'd never noticed how cute she was. She had eyes that looked like they were always smiling.

Now Mickey and Charlene were turning while Dotty and Charlotte did the dance. "Hey, Dotty, you look like you're getting it," I laughed.

Charlene came back over to me and Baby Claudette. I noticed that she wore the prize necklace. She saw me looking at it.

"This is a beautiful necklace Lavinia's father made," she said.

"Yeah. Maybe we'll have another double-dutch contest and I can win one for turning."

"You want to wear it for a day?"

"No. That's Charlotte's and Paulette's. They won it."

"It's okay. I mean, all of us won it. The four of us made up the dance. We're like that with everything. You remember yesterday Pauline had on this belt at the contest? I'm wearing it today. We all own it."

I looked at the belt. But to tell you the truth, I never noticed the belt she wore yesterday. All I saw was her turned-over shoes.

Charlene sat on the steps and I leaned over the banister and played with Claudette.

"Doris, you want to wear the necklace?"

"I can't do that. You won that necklace; why should anyone else wear it?"

I felt so ashamed about the way I talked about the Nit Nowns. Charlene was so nice and Baby Claudette was cute and friendly. I reached down in my pocket and pulled out the raisins I was hiding from Mickey and Dotty and saving for myself.

"You want some raisins? Give the rest to your sisters."

"Thanks, Doris. I got to go upstairs now."

"For what?"

"It's my turn to cook. My mother works all day, so we take care of everything. Pauline, come here and get Claudette."

The baby sat down on the steps with her mouth full of raisins and a big smile on her lips. She looked up at me and pulled my hand.

"Nit nown," she said. Everybody laughed.

"Okay Claudette, I'll nit nown with you."

Well, we didn't have to worry about the Nit Nowns chasing us home anymore.

Daydreamers

by ELOISE GREENFIELD

Daydreamers . . .
holding their bodies still
for a time
letting the world turn around them
while their dreams hopscotch,
doubledutch, dance,
thoughts rollerskate,
crisscross,
bump into hopes and wishes.
Dreamers
thinking up new ways,
looking toward new days,
planning new tries,
asking new whys.
Before long,
hands will start to move again,
eyes turn outward,
bodies shift for action,
but for this moment they are still,
they are
the daydreamers,
letting the world dizzy itself
without them.

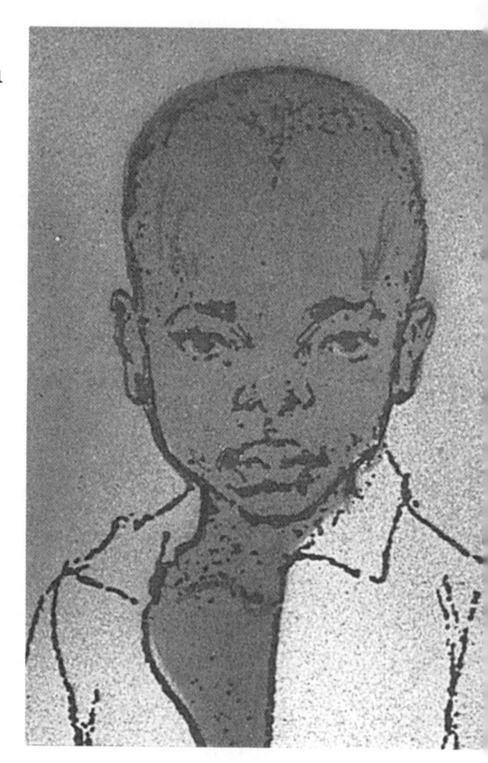

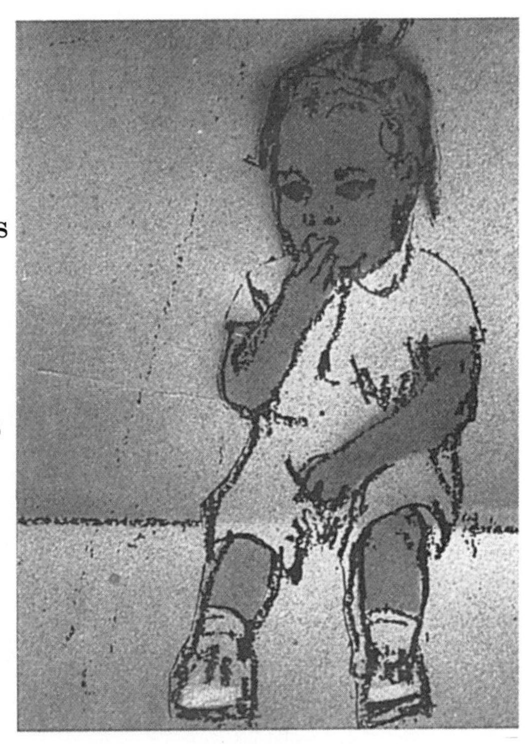

Scenes passing through their minds
make no sound
glide from hiding places
promenade and return
silently.
The children watch their memories
with spirit-eyes
seeing more than they saw before
feeling more
or maybe less
than they felt the time before,
reaching with spirit-hands
to touch the dreams
drawn from their yesterdays.

They will not be the same
after this growing time,
this dreaming.
In their stillness they have moved
forward
toward womanhood
toward manhood.
This dreaming has made them
new.

READ ON!

Just the Two of Them by Mary Anderson. When he first moves to New York City, Luis misses his homeland, Puerto Rico. But then he discovers interesting things to do in Central Park and finds a friend there.

The Great Brain by John Fitzgerald. If you liked the way Tom outsmarted a dude, then read more about what he's been up to. His brother, John, tells the stories in this first book of the Great Brain series.

Growin' by Nikki Grimes. The unlikely friendship between the new girl on the block and the class bully leads to a lot of growing for both of them.

In Charge: A Complete Handbook for Kids with Working Parents by Kathy S. Kyte. This humorous but helpful guide teaches you how to take care of yourself when your parents aren't home. Learn how to do chores, cope with emergencies, cook, handle laundry, and much more.

Growing Up Masai by Tom Shachtman. Photographs and text give a good account of what it's like to grow up as a member of the Masai tribe in Africa.

Help! There's a Cat Washing in Here! by Alison P. Smith. A fear of the big black cat that his little sister adopts is only one of Henry's problems. Read this funny story of what happens when Henry takes over the household for two weeks.

UNIT 3

Living With Nature

LEARN NEW WORDS

1. We **coordinated** our work on the garden: I made the rows, and she planted the seeds.
2. Every year we **cultivate** a beautiful garden of flowers and vegetables.
3. A violent thunderstorm **disrupted** our camping trip.
4. The fruit was spoiled; it was no longer **edible**.
5. We thought that they must have met with a **fatal** accident, because they were never heard from again.
6. There were **hysterical** shouts from the audience after the cry of "Fire!" disrupted the show.
7. After we had made a campfire and eaten, we put up a **makeshift** shelter for the night.
8. Many animals **perished** in the forest fire.
9. When he first saw the lion, the man was too **petrified** to scream for help.
10. The tiger that escaped from its cage **terrorized** the visitors at the zoo.
11. Slowly, the snake approached its next **victim**, a poor mouse that was too petrified to run away.

GET SET TO READ

What dangers might you encounter in a far-off land? How would you feel about these dangers if you had to live with them from day to day?

Read this true story to find out how a group of people face one of the greatest dangers of life in their small Vietnamese village.

Adventures of a Boy in Vietnam

by HUYNH QUANG NHUONG

The Land I Lost

I was born on the central highlands of Vietnam in a small hamlet on a riverbank that had a deep jungle on one side and a chain of high mountains on the other. Across the river, rice fields stretched to the slopes of another chain of mountains.

There were fifty houses in our hamlet, scattered along the river or propped against the mountainsides. The houses were made of bamboo and covered with coconut leaves, and

each was surrounded by a deep trench to protect it from wild animals or thieves. The only way to enter a house was to walk across a "monkey bridge"—a single bamboo stick that spanned the trench. At night we pulled the bridges into our houses and were safe.

There were no shops or marketplaces in our hamlet. If we needed supplies—medicine, cloth, soaps, or candles—we had to cross over the mountains and travel to a town nearby. We used the river mainly for traveling to distant hamlets, but it also provided us with fish.

During the six-month rainy season, nearly all of us helped plant and cultivate fields of rice, sweet potatoes, Indian mustard, eggplant, tomatoes, hot peppers, and corn. But during the dry season, we became hunters and turned to the jungle.

Wild animals played a very large part in our lives. There were four animals we feared the most: the tiger, the lone wild hog, the crocodile, and the horse snake. Tigers were always trying to steal cattle. Sometimes, however, when a tiger became old and slow it would go after humans. But a lone wild hog was even more dangerous than a tiger. It terrorized every creature in sight, even when it had no need for food. Or it did crazy things, such as charging into the hamlet in broad daylight, ready to kill or to be killed. The river had different dangers: crocodiles.

But of all the animals, the most hated and feared was the huge horse snake. It was sneaky and attacked people and cattle just for the joy of killing. It would either crush its victim to death or poison it with a bite. In some areas people called it the bamboo snake, because it was as long as a full-grown bamboo tree. In other regions, the people called it the thunder or lightning snake, because it attacked so fast and with such power that its victim had neither time to escape nor strength to fight it. In our area, we called it the horse snake, because it could move as fast as a thoroughbred.

Like all farmers' children in the hamlet, I started working at the age of six. I was twelve years old when I made my first trip to the jungle with my father. I learned how to track game, how to recognize useful and edible roots, how to distinguish edible mushrooms and fruits from poisonous ones.

My father, like most of the villagers, was a farmer and a hunter, depending upon the season. But he also had a college education, so in the evenings he helped to teach other children in our hamlet, for it was too small to afford a professional schoolteacher.

My mother managed the house, but during the harvest season she could be found in the fields, helping my father get the crops home; and as the wife of a hunter, she knew how to dress and nurse a wound.

I went to the lowlands to study for a while, because I wanted to follow my father as a teacher when I grew up. I always planned to return to my hamlet to live the rest of my life there. But war disrupted my dreams. The land I love was lost to me forever.

This story is one of my memories. . . .

The Horse Snake

One night a frightened friend of our family's banged on our door and asked us to let him in. When crossing the rice field in front of our house on his way home from a wedding, he had heard the unmistakable hiss of a horse snake. We became very worried, not only for us and our friend but also for the cattle and other animals we raised.

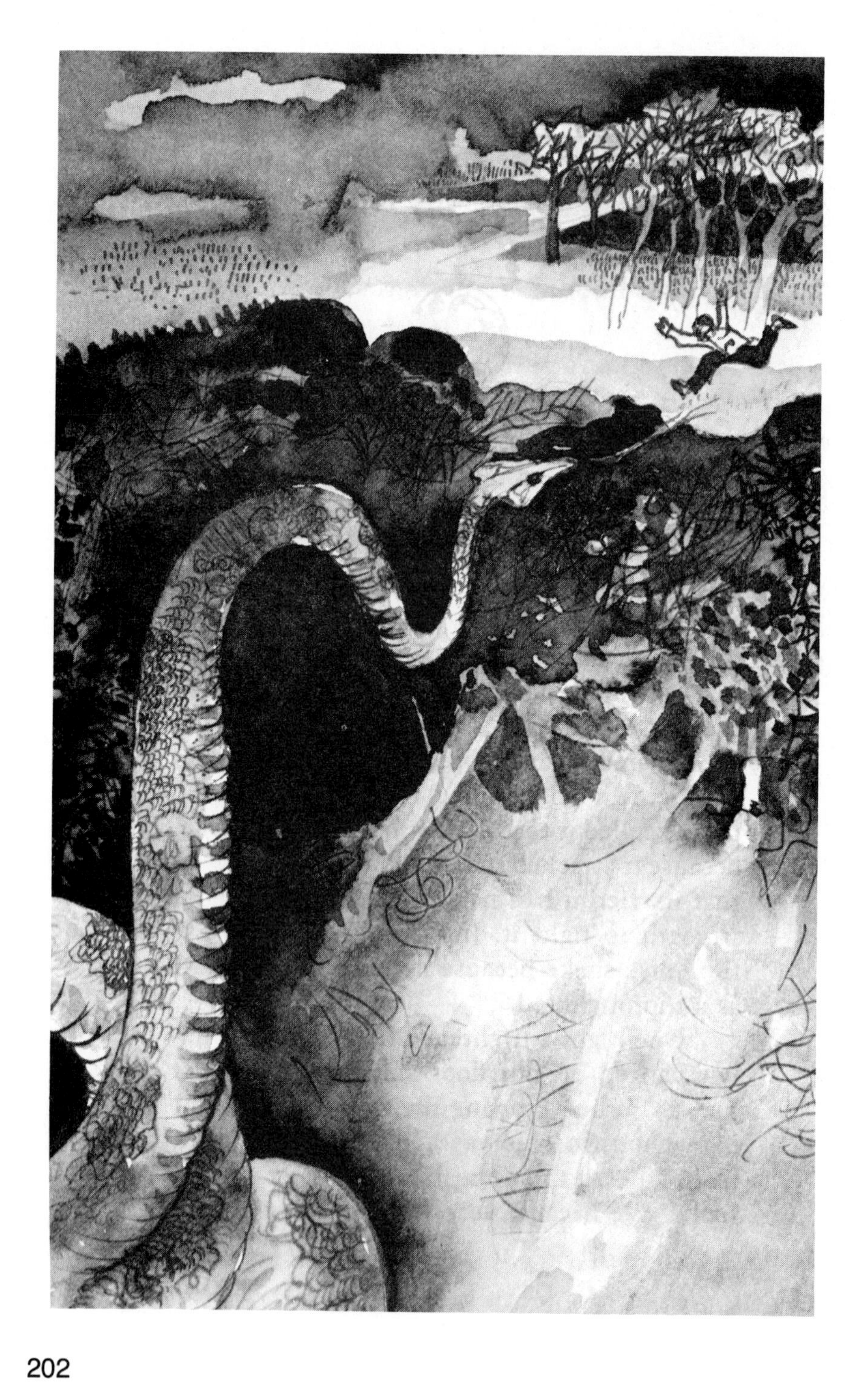

It was too far into the night to rouse all our neighbors and go to search for the snake. But my father told my cousin to blow three times on his buffalo horn, the signal that a dangerous wild beast was loose in the hamlet. A few seconds later we heard three long quivering sounds of a horn at the far end of the hamlet answering our warning. We presumed that the whole hamlet was now on guard.

I stayed up that night, listening to all the sounds outside, while my father and my cousin sharpened their hunting knives. Shortly after midnight we were startled by the frightened neighing of a horse in the rice field. Then the night was still, except for a few sad calls of night birds and the occasional roaring of tigers in the jungle.

The next day early in the morning all the able-bodied men of the hamlet gathered in front of our house and divided into groups of four to go and look for the snake. My father and my cousin grabbed their lunch and joined a searching party.

They found the old horse that had neighed the night before in the rice field. The snake had squeezed it to death. Its chest was smashed, and all its ribs broken. But the snake had disappeared.

Everybody agreed that it was the work of one of the giant horse snakes which had terrorized our area as far back as anyone could remember. The horse snake usually eats small game, such as turkeys, monkeys, chickens, and ducks, but for unknown reasons sometimes it will attack people and cattle. A fully grown horse snake can reach the size of a king python. But, unlike pythons, horse snakes have an extremely poisonous bite. Because of their bone-breaking squeeze and fatal bite, they are one of the most dangerous creatures of the uplands.

The men searched all day, but at nightfall they gave up and went home. My father and my cousin looked very tired when they returned. My grandmother told them to go right to bed after their dinner and that she would wake them up if she or my mother heard any unusual sounds.

The men went to bed and the women prepared to stay up all night. My mother sewed torn clothing and my grandmother read a novel she had just borrowed from a friend. And for the second night in a row, they allowed my little sister and me to stay awake and listen with them for as long as we could. But hours later, seeing the worry on our faces, my grandmother put aside her novel and told us a story:

Once upon a time a happy family lived in a small village on the shore of the South China Sea. They respected the laws of the land and loved their neighbors very much. The father and his oldest son were woodcutters. The father was quite old, but he still could carry home a heavy load of wood.

One day on his way home from the jungle he was happier than usual. He and his son had discovered a wild chicken nest containing twelve eggs. Now he would have something special to give to his grandchildren when they pulled his shirtsleeves and danced around him to greet him when he came home.

The father looked at the broad shoulders of his son and his steady gait under a very heavy load of wood. He smiled. His son was a good son, and he had no doubt that when he became even older still his son would take good care of him and his wife.

As he was thinking this he saw his son suddenly throw the load of wood at a charging horse snake that had come out of nowhere. The heavy load of wood crashed into the snake's head and stunned it. That gave them enough time to draw their sharp woodcutting knives. But instead of attacking the horse snake from the front, the elder shouted to his son to run behind the big bush of elephant grass nearby while he, who was a little too old to run fast, jumped into the front end of the bush. Each time the snake passed by him the old man managed to hit it with his knife. He struck the snake many times. Finally it became weak and slowed down; so the old man came out of his hiding place and attacked the snake's tail, while his son attacked the snake's head. The snake fought back furiously, but finally it perished under the well-coordinated attack of father and son.

When the snake was dead, they grabbed its tail and proudly dragged it to the edge of their village. Everyone rushed out to see their prize. They all argued over who would have the honor of carrying the snake to their house for them.

The old woodcutter and his son had to tell the story of how they had killed the snake at least ten times, but the people never tired of hearing it, again and again. They all agreed that the old woodcutter and his son were not only brave but clever as well. Then and there the villagers decided that when their chief, also a brave and clever man, died, the old woodcutter was the only one who deserved the honor of replacing him.

When my grandmother finished the story, my little sister and I became a bit more cheerful. People could defeat this dangerous snake. The silent darkness outside became less threatening. Nevertheless, we were still too scared to sleep in our room, so my mother made a makeshift bed in the sitting room, close to her and our grandmother.

When we woke up the next morning, life in the hamlet had almost returned to normal. The snake had not struck again that night, and the farmers, in groups of three or four, slowly filtered back to their fields. Then, late in the afternoon, hysterical cries for help were heard in the direction of the western part of the hamlet. My cousin and my father grabbed their knives and rushed off to help.

It was Minh, a farmer, who was crying for help. Minh, like most farmers in the area, stored the fish he had caught in the rice field at the end of the rainy season in a small pond. That day Minh's wife had wanted a good fish for dinner. When Minh approached his fish pond he heard what sounded like someone trying to steal his fish by using a bucket to empty water from the pond. Minh was very angry and rushed over to catch the thief, but when he reached the pond, what he saw so petrified him that he fell over backward, speechless. When he regained control, he crawled away as fast as he could and yelled for help.

The thief he saw was not a person but a huge horse snake, perhaps the same one that had squeezed the old horse to death two nights before. The snake had hooked its head to the branch of one tree and its tail to another and was splashing the water out of the pond by swinging its body back and forth, like a hammock. Thus, when the shallow pond became dry, it planned to swallow all the fish.

All the villagers rushed to the scene to help Minh, and our village chief quickly organized an attack. He ordered

all the men to surround the pond. Then two strong young men approached the snake, one at its tail and the other at its head. As they crept closer and closer, the snake assumed a striking position, its head about one meter above the pond and its tail swaying from side to side. It was ready to strike in either direction. As the two young men moved in closer, the snake watched them. Each one tried to draw the attention of the snake, while a third crept unseen to its side. Suddenly he struck the snake with his long knife. The surprised snake shot out of the pond like an arrow and knocked the young man unconscious as it rushed by. It broke through the circle of villagers and went into an open rice field. But it received two more wounds on its way out.

The village chief ordered all the women and children to form a long line between the open rice field and the jungle and to yell as loudly as they could, hoping to scare the snake so that it would not flee into the jungle. It would be far easier for them to fight the wounded snake in an open field than to follow it there.

But now there was a new difficulty. The snake started heading toward the river. Normally a horse snake could beat any human in a race, but since this one was badly wounded, our chief was able to cut off its escape by sending half his men running to the river. Blocked off from the river and jungle, the snake decided to stay and fight.

The hunting party surrounded the snake again, and this time four of the best hunters attacked the snake from four different directions. The snake fought bravely, but it perished. During the struggle one of the men received a dislocated shoulder, two had bruised ribs, and three were momentarily blinded by dirt thrown by the snake. Luckily all of them succeeded in avoiding the fatal bite of the snake.

We rejoiced that the danger was over. But we knew it would only be a matter of time until we would once again have to face our most dangerous natural enemy—the horse snake.

Think About It

1. Describe the setting of this story.
2. What dangers did the villagers face?
3. Why was the horse snake so deadly?
4. Why did the children feel better after the grandmother's story?
5. How did the villagers deal with the horse snake?
6. Why was a well-coordinated attack important in defeating the horse snake?
7. Write about why you think the author of this story loved his small hamlet and always wanted to live there in spite of the dangers.

LEARN NEW WORDS

1. With a score of 30–10 at the half, we were doing well in **comparison** to the other team.
2. If you looked closely, you could **detect** many weeds in the garden.
3. Ice melts when it is **exposed** to heat.
4. The buffalo had to be protected or it would have been hunted to **extinction**.
5. Wild geese **migrate** south in the autumn.
6. **Minerals** such as iron and zinc are important in our diet.
7. She felt too **sluggish** to exercise.
8. Cats and dogs belong to completely different **species** of animals.
9. The police officer fired off a series of questions in rapid **succession**.
10. An octopus uses its **tentacles** to grab or hold on to things.

GET SET TO READ

What is a champion? How does someone get to be one?

Read this article to find out about some living things that are champions in ways you may not have thought of.

NATURE'S CHAMPIONS

by ALVIN and VIRGINIA SILVERSTEIN

The Slowest Animal: The Snail

When something is happening very slowly, we sometimes say it is going "at a snail's pace." How fast does a snail go? It takes a lot of patience to find out. Snail watchers have found that garden snails at their speediest can cover as much as 55 yards in an hour, or about 0.03 mile per hour. But some snails creep along at less than 2 feet an hour—0.00036 mile per hour! The tortoise, another notedly sluggish mover, is a real speedster in comparison—when it's hungry, it can cover 5 yards in a minute (0.17 mile per hour). In snail races, a good winning time is 2 feet in three minutes. (The best human racers can run a *mile* in less than four minutes. A racing snail would take five and a half days to cover a mile.)

Of course, a race between a snail and a human would not only be silly, but unfair. The snail has only one foot, which is at the bottom of its body and is sometimes called a "belly-foot." A land snail moves by contracting the muscles in the sole of its belly-foot, one after another, in a rippling wave that moves forward along the foot. The animal glides along smoothly on a carpet of wet, slippery slime that it

dribbles out from an opening just under its mouth. After the snail has passed, shiny trails of slime mark its path.

A moving snail also has a heavy load to carry—you would move slowly, too, if you had to carry your house on your back! The snail's soft body is covered by a hard, coiled shell. When danger threatens—perhaps a rat, a duck, a blackbird, or a human being—the snail can pull all of its body into the shell, so that the sole of its foot neatly plugs the opening. It also retreats into its shell in the hot, dry summers and in the cold winters, sealing the edges of the opening with slime. Snails can stay inactive this way, without eating or moving, for months or even years.

A snail is a funny sight as it comes out of its shell. First the belly-foot comes out. Then, at the front end of this soft belly-foot, two pairs of tentacles begin to poke out, as if someone were pushing out the fingers of a glove that was inside-out. When they are all the way out, the tentacles look like horns on the top and front of the snail's head. At the tip of each of the two larger tentacles is an eye. Imagine having your eyes up on stilts! The snail can look around by moving its tentacles, without having to turn its head.

Garden snails eat mainly leaves and fruit. They saw off pieces of food with a long tongue. A snail has teeth on its tongue—15,000 of them!—and it uses its tongue like a file. Garden snails can find their way back to their favorite feeding places, even if a gardener has thrown them away over a wall. They may be slow, but they get there.

As a snail grows, its shell grows, too (otherwise its body would get too big to fit into its shell). The only place the shell can grow is around the opening. The snail needs minerals to build its shell. It gets them by cutting holes in limestone rocks with its file-like tongue and eating the powdery minerals it scrapes off. When the snail gets plenty of food and water and the minerals it needs, it can add an inch to its shell in just two weeks.

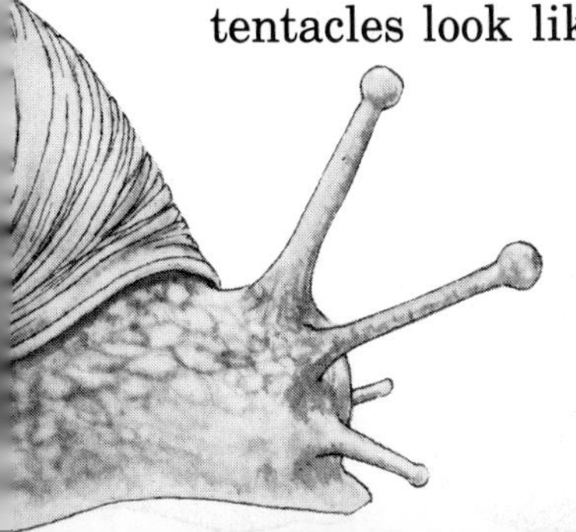

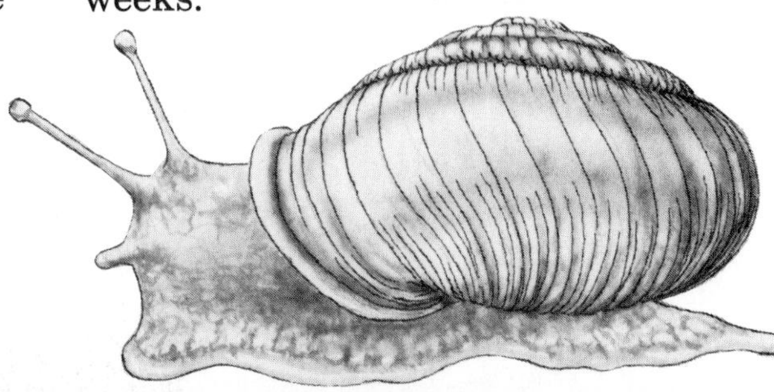

The Largest Animal: The Blue Whale

Just imagine an animal bigger than the biggest dinosaur! The blue whale is the largest animal that ever lived on earth.

The biggest blue whale that was ever caught measured more than 109 feet from the tip of its jaw to the end of its tail. No one weighed it, but it may have weighed as much as 200 tons! (That is as much as about twenty African bush elephants or more than 2000 people.) Even a newborn baby blue whale is bigger than most animals—about 25 feet long and weighing up to 3 tons. It is also the fastest-growing baby in the living world,

growing at an astonishing rate of 200 pounds a day.

No land animal could ever grow as large as a whale. And in fact, if a whale is accidentally stranded on land, it is crushed under its own weight. The water of the ocean helps to hold up the enormous weight of a whale's body.

Whales look like fish, but they are not fish. They are mammals, just like cats and dogs. Whales cannot breathe in the water as fish do. Though blue whales can stay underwater for about ten minutes at a time, they must then come up for a breath of air. A whale's nostrils form a "blowhole" on the top of its head. When the whale comes up to the surface and exhales, its moist breath forms a great spout above its head.

You might think that the world's largest animal would feed on other large animals—perhaps smaller whales or big fish. But the blue whale eats tiny shrimplike animals called krill. Each krill is only 2 inches long. The blue whale scoops in huge numbers of them—a ton of krill or more at one meal. Two sets of long plates called whalebone or baleen hang down from the roof of the blue whale's mouth. The whale sucks in a huge mouthful of water, then strains out the krill on the baleen plates. During the year, the blue whales migrate through the world's oceans. They move from the cold seas near the North and South Poles in the summer to warmer waters in the winter, following the schools of krill.

Unfortunately, during their migration these whales have been followed by human whalers, who chase and kill them on huge factory ships. Once there were hundreds of thousands of blue whales in the world's oceans. But for many years whalers killed them faster than new blue whale babies could be born. Finally, there were fewer than a thousand left. Scientists warned that the blue whale was in danger of extinction and might disappear from the earth forever. Now there are laws against killing blue whales, and their numbers are slowly increasing.

The Most Shocking: The Electric Eel

All living things produce electricity. In most animals and plants, the pulses of electric current are so tiny that special instruments are needed to detect them. "Brain waves," for example, can be detected by metal wires and disks pasted to a person's scalp. An electrocardiogram records the pulses of electricity from the heart. But some fish are able to produce enormous amounts of electricity—enough to stun or even kill. The most powerful of these electric fish is the electric eel. It can discharge up to 650 volts—enough to kill a person on contact. (By comparison, the electric current we use in houses is usually only 120 volts.)

Electric eels live in the shallow, muddy waters of the Amazon and Orinoco rivers of South America. They are not related to other kinds of eels and resemble them only in their snakelike shape. The electric eel has no dorsal (back) or tail fins, as other fish do. It swims with the aid of one long fin which runs nearly the whole length of the underside of its body. It can swim backward and forward, up and down, with equal ease. But most of the time it lives a lazy, sluggish life. It does not have to work hard to protect itself and catch its food.

The electric eel is like a living storage battery. All of its normal body organs are crowded

into the front fifth of its body. The remaining four-fifths is packed with more than 5000 tiny electric cells.

The electric eel uses its electricity in several ways. When it swims, a small "battery" in its tail sends out weak electric pulses at a rate of 20 to 50 a second. The eel uses these electric pulses to find its way. They bounce off objects and come back to special pits in the eel's head. The eel uses these electric "echoes" in much the same way that bats and whales use sound to find their way around. (It is fortunate that the electric eel has this ability to navigate by electricity. As it grows older, its eyes are damaged by electricity, and it becomes blind. Actually, eyesight is not too useful anyway in the dark and muddy waters where the eel lives.) Scientists think that the electric eel may also use its weak electric pulses to communicate with other eels.

If an enemy threatens the electric eel or prey is in the water nearby, the eel acts promptly. It turns on the powerful "main battery" that fills most of its body. Discharges, or jolts of electricity, lasting about 0.002 second are sent out in quick succession. An electric eel can continue discharging at a rate of up to 150 pulses a second without showing any signs of getting tired. Fish and frogs are killed by the eel's strong electric shocks. A larger animal—even a horse that has come down to the water to drink—may be stunned and drown. But except for the gradual damage to its eyes, the eel itself does not seem to be affected by the electricity at all. In fact, other electric eels are often attracted to an area where one of their species is discharging. They flock to join in the feast.

The breeding of electric eels is still a mystery. During the rainy season of the year, they disappear from their usual homes. Perhaps they go to the flooded swamplands. When they return, small baby eels are swimming along with them. The young electric eels produce very little electricity. The larger they grow, the more powerful their electric shocks become. A full-grown electric eel is one creature you want to stay away from!

The Largest Living Thing: The Giant Sequoia

The legends of many lands tell of giants who once walked the earth. A race of giants still lives on earth, but these giants do not walk. They are trees, firmly rooted to the ground. These are the giant sequoias of California.

The champion of all the giant sequoias is the General Sherman Tree. It measures more than 100 feet around its base and is over 270 feet tall. Its largest branch is 7 feet thick—a tall man could lie across it without even his toes hanging over. The General Sherman Tree is believed to weigh about 6000 tons.

Many other giant sequoias are nearly as large as the General Sherman Tree. The giant sequoias are not the tallest trees in the world. Their relatives, the redwoods, can grow to more than 350 feet. But they're not as wide as a sequoia. Some trees have trunks that are larger at the base. But those trees don't grow as tall as the sequoias. So in sheer mass, giant sequoias are truly the biggest living things in the world.

Of course, the giant sequoia does not start its life as a giant. It begins on a pine cone as a tiny seed only ¼-inch long. The cones may cling to the branches of the parent tree for as long as 20 years. But at last they fall, and new seedlings sprout from the seeds. A young giant sequoia looks like a Christmas tree. It has a cone shape, with branches reaching down to the ground. As it grows, its lower branches fall off, and its bark thickens. The bark of an old giant sequoia may be as thick as 2 feet!

The roots of the giant sequoias are surprisingly shallow. Most of them reach less than 8 feet down into the ground. But they spread out over an area of as much as three acres (an area about as big as four football fields), so the trees are in no danger of blowing over.

Giant sequoias are unusually strong, healthy trees. Their thick bark protects them from insects; and if they get burned, they can grow new wood over the scars. Many of them are 3000 to 4000 years old, and they still produce new crops of seeds. Not one giant sequoia has ever been known to die from old age or disease.

A giant sequoia is a lumberjack's dream. Just one tree could provide enough lumber to build eighty five-room houses. But so many have been cut down that only a small number of giant sequoias are left. Once they covered most of the land north of the equator. Now they are found in fewer than fifty groves, on the western slopes of the Sierra Nevada mountains. Groups of people are fighting to save the last of the giant sequoias.

The Oldest Living Thing: The Bristlecone Pine

The oldest living things on earth are not people or elephants or even the long-lived giant tortoises. They are trees—bristlecone pines. Many bristlecone pines living today in Nevada, California, and Utah were already old at the time of the Roman Empire, 2000 years ago. The oldest of all the living bristlecone pines, up on the White Mountains in California, is more than 4600 years old!

How can anyone know for sure how old a tree is—especially a tree as old as a bristlecone pine? As a tree grows, its trunk gets wider as a new ring of wood is formed. Growth rings show up clearly on the cut surface of a tree trunk. (Each ring represents a year's growth.) Scientists can study the succession of growth rings of a living tree without harming the tree by cutting out a thin core of wood, about the size of a pencil. A bristlecone pine's growth rings are much narrower than those of most trees, so narrow that a microscope must be used to count them. The tree grows very slowly, adding perhaps only an inch of width in 100 years. Even the oldest trees are only about 30 feet tall and perhaps 12 feet across the trunk.

Bristlecone pines *look* old. Their trunks and branches are bent and twisted. Grains of sand and ice crystals whipped by the winds on the high slopes have scoured them nearly bare. In trees more than 1500 years old, usually only a thin strip of living bark remains. This runs up the protected side of the trunk, away from the windy blasts. Water and food materials for the tree are carried along this strip of bark. The rest of the wood is dead. Some of the branches are bare; others are crowned with "bottle-brushes" of short green needles. The great roots may be partly bare, exposed over hundreds and thousands of years as the rocky soil was washed or blown away.

Not all bristlecone pines grow to such a great age. The trees living where there is plenty of soil and water and shelter

from the wind grow quickly and soon die and decay. The real champion ancients live high up on rocky mountain slopes. Their life is a hard one, but the longest of all.

Think About It

1. Why is the title of this article "Nature's Champions"?
2. How do the champions in this article differ from human champions you know about?
3. Describe one of nature's champions that you read about.
4. Which champion do you find most amazing? Why?
5. Which of these living things is in danger of extinction? Why?
6. Write a paragraph about what you can do to protect the wonders of nature from extinction.

SKILLS

Making an Outline

Making an **outline** is a good way of arranging information to help you understand it and remember it. An outline always follows a certain form. It has only the most important facts or ideas and a few details, often written in short sentences or phrases. An outline also shows how the main points of an article relate to one another.

Most of the time, an outline is divided into three parts or levels. The first level lists the **main topics** of an article. The second level lists **subtopics,** or the important points about the main topics. The third level lists **details** about the subtopics. Turn back to page 218 and read about the bristlecone pine again from the article "Nature's Champions." Then follow the outline of the section below.

First, find the main idea of the opening paragraph. This will become the first main topic of your outline. Try to state your main topics as briefly as possible, and always number them with Roman numerals. Next, think of points in the first paragraph that add to the main topic. These will be your subtopics. Indent them under your main topic and list them, using a capital letter to begin each subtopic. So far, your outline should look something like this:

I. Bristlecone pines are the oldest living things.
   A. Many are older than 2000 years.
   B. The oldest is 4600 years old.

Notice that subtopics A and B both directly support the main topic I.

The next paragraph in the article is longer and more complex. But you can follow the same process of finding the main points and the details that explain them.

II. Growth rings tell the age of a tree.
    A. Each ring equals a year's growth.
    B. Scientists cut a core to study rings.
    C. A bristlecone pine has narrow growth rings.
        1. It grows one inch in 100 years.
        2. The oldest are about 30 ft. tall, 12 ft. across.

Notice that the third level of the outline is numbered with Arabic numerals. The two details numbered 1 and 2 relate directly to subtopic C. Therefore, they are listed as details under a subtopic rather than as subtopics themselves.

Notice, too, how this outline so far follows the arrangement of information in each paragraph. In this way, an outline shows you not only how facts are related to one another but also how parts of a paragraph fit together.

An important thing to remember about an outline is that you can't have a I without a II, or an A without a B, or a 1 without a 2. Each level has to have at least two entries.

Here is an incomplete outline of the third paragraph. On a separate piece of paper, complete the outline by filling in your own sentences.

III. Bristlecone pines look old.
    A.
    B. Some have only a thin strip of bark.
        1.
        2.
    C.
    D.

Now finish the outline on bristlecone pines by outlining the last paragraph yourself. Remember: be brief but thorough. Because it is a short paragraph, you won't have many items.

LEARN NEW WORDS

1. The **barren** desert offered no source of shade.
2. We heard the squeal of brakes just before we saw the car **careening** around the corner.
3. The wind calmed down as the storm **diminished**.
4. After she won first place in the swimming competition, she felt **elated**.
5. When I saw the bicycle careening toward me, my first **impulse** was to jump out of the way.
6. The **inscription** on the bracelet read "Georgia, 1918."
7. One hot day I had an **irresistible** impulse to jump into the pool.
8. The waves slapped **monotonously** on the barren beach.
9. The auditorium **resounded** with loud applause when the famous ballerina pirouetted on stage.
10. He treated both people and animals cruelly; he was a **ruthless** person.
11. Even after spending all day on his job, my father still had the **stamina** in the evening to work on converting the basement into a family room.
12. Not one to waste words, my aunt always replied **tersely** to my questions.

GET SET TO READ

An animal can be a person's enemy, as in the first story in this unit. But an animal can also be a person's friend or helper. Can you give some examples of both?

Read this story to find out what happens when Alec tries to befriend a wild horse.

The Black Stallion

by WALTER FARLEY

The tramp steamer *Drake* plowed away from the coast of India and pushed its blunt prow into the Arabian Sea, homeward bound. Slowly it made its way west toward the Gulf of Aden. Its hold was loaded with coffee, rice, tea, oil seeds and jute. Black smoke poured from its one stack, darkening the hot cloudless sky.

Alexander Ramsay, Jr., known to his friends back home in New York City as Alec, leaned over the rail and watched the water slide away from the sides of the boat. His red hair blazed redder than ever in the hot sun; his tanned elbows rested heavily on the rail as he turned his freckled face back toward the fast-disappearing shore.

It had been fun—those two months in India. He would miss Uncle Ralph, miss the days they had spent together in the jungle, even the screams of the panthers and the many eerie sounds of the jungle night. Uncle Ralph had taught him how to ride—the one thing in the world he had always wanted to do.

But it was all over now. Rides back home would be few.

His fist opened. Lovingly he surveyed the pearl pocketknife he held there. The inscription on it was in gold: *To Alec on his birthday, Bombay, India.* He

remembered, too, his uncle's words: "A knife, Alec, comes in handy sometimes."

Suddenly a large hand descended on his shoulder. "Well, m'boy, you're on your way home," a gruff voice said, with a decidedly English accent.

Alec looked up into the captain's wrinkled, wind-tanned face. "Hello, Captain Watson," he answered. "It's rather a long way home, though, sir. To England with you and then to New York on the *Majestic*."

"About four weeks sailing, all in all, lad, but you look like a pretty good sailor."

"I am, sir. I wasn't sick once all the way over and we had a rough crossing, too," Alec said proudly.

"When'd you come over, lad?"

"In June, sir, with some friends of my father's. They left me with my uncle in Bombay. You know my Uncle Ralph, don't you? He came aboard with me and spoke to you."

"Yes, I know your Uncle Ralph. A fine man, too. . . . And now you're going home alone?"

"Yes, sir! School opens next month and I have to be there."

The captain smiled and took Alec by the arm. "Come along," he said. "I'll show you how we steer this ship and what makes it go."

The captain, the sailors, everybody on boat, was kind to Alec, but the days passed monotonously for the homeward-bound boy as the *Drake* steamed its way through the Gulf of Aden and into the Red Sea. The tropic sun beat down mercilessly on the heads of the few passengers aboard.

The *Drake* kept near the coast of Arabia—endless miles of barren desert shore. But Alec's thoughts were not on the scorching sand. Arabia—where the greatest horses in the world were bred! Did other fellows dream of horses the way he did? To him, a horse was the grandest animal in the world.

Then one day the *Drake* headed for a small Arabian port. As they approached the small landing, Alec saw a crowd of natives milling about in great excitement. Obviously it was not often that a boat stopped there.

But, as the gangplank went down with a bang, Alec could see that it wasn't the ship itself that was attracting all the attention. The natives were crowding toward the center of the landing. Alec heard a whistle—shrill, loud, clear, unlike anything he had ever heard before. He saw a mighty black horse rear on its hind legs, its forelegs striking out into the air. A white scarf was tied across its eyes. The crowd broke and ran.

White lather ran from the horse's body; his mouth was open, his teeth bared. He was a giant of a horse, glistening black—too big to be pure Arabian. His mane was like a crest, mounting, then falling low. His neck was long and slender, and arched to the small, savagely beautiful head. The head was that of the wildest of all wild creatures—a stallion born wild—and it was beautiful, savage, splendid. A stallion with a wonderful physical perfection that matched his savage, ruthless spirit.

Once again the Black screamed and rose on his hind legs. Alec could hardly believe his eyes and ears—a stallion, a wild stallion—unbroken, such as he had read and dreamed about!

Two ropes led from the halter on the horse's head, and four men were attempting to pull the stallion toward the gangplank. They were going to put him on the ship! Alec saw a dark-skinned man, wearing European

dress and a high, white turban, giving directions. In his hand he held a whip. He gave his orders tersely in a language unknown to Alec. Suddenly he walked to the rear of the horse and let the hard whip fall on the Black's hind quarters. The Black snorted and plunged; if ever Alec saw hate expressed by a horse, he saw it then. They had him halfway up the plank. Alec wondered where they would put him if they ever did succeed in getting him on the boat.

Then he was on! Alec saw Captain Watson waving his arms frantically, motioning and shouting for the men to pull the stallion toward the stern. The boy followed at a safe distance. Now he saw the makeshift stall into which they were attempting to get the Black—it had once been a good-sized cabin. The *Drake* had little accommodation for transporting animals; its hold was already filled with cargo.

Finally they had the horse in front of the stall. One of the men clambered to the top of the cabin, reached down and pulled the scarf away from the stallion's eyes. At the same time, the dark–skinned man again hit the horse on the hind quarters and he bolted inside. Alec thought the stall would never be strong enough to hold him. The stallion tore into the wood and sent it flying; thunder rolled from under his hooves; his powerful legs crashed into the sides of the cabin; his wild, shrill, high-pitched whistle sent shivers up and down Alec's spine. He felt a deep pity steal over him, for here was a wild stallion used to the open range imprisoned in a stall in which he was hardly able to turn.

Captain Watson was conversing angrily with the dark–skinned man; the captain had probably never expected to ship a cargo such as this!

Soon the *Drake* was again under way. Alec gazed back at the port, then he turned to the stall. The dark–skinned man had gone to his cabin, and only the excited passengers were standing around outside the stall. The black horse was still fighting madly inside.

The days that followed were hectic ones for Alec, passengers and crew. He had never dreamed a horse could have such spirit, be so untamable. The ship resounded far into the night from the blows struck by those powerful legs. The outside of the stall was now covered with reinforcements. The dark–skinned man became more mysterious than ever—always alone, and never talking to anyone but the captain.

The *Drake* steamed through the Suez into the Mediterranean.

That night Alec stole out upon deck, leaving the rest of the passengers inside. He listened carefully. The Black was quiet tonight. Quickly he walked in the direction of the stall. At first he couldn't see or hear anything. Then as his eyes became accustomed to the darkness, he made out the pink-colored nostrils of the Black, who was sticking his head out of the window.

Alec walked slowly toward him; he put one hand in his pocket to see if the sugar he had taken from the dinner table was still there. The wind was blowing against him, carrying his scent away. He was quite close now. The Black was looking out on the open sea; his ears pricked forward, his thin-skinned nostrils quivering, his black mane flowing like windswept flame. Alec could not take his eyes away; he could not believe such a perfect animal existed.

The stallion turned and looked directly at him—his black eyes blazed. Once again that piercing whistle filled the night air, and he disappeared into the stall. Alec took the sugar out of his pocket and left it on the window sill. He went to his cabin. Later when he returned it was gone. Every night thereafter Alec would steal up to the stall, leave the sugar, and depart; sometimes he would see the Black and other times he would only hear the ring of hooves against the floor.

The *Drake* stopped at Alexandria, Bengasi, Tripoli, Tunis and Algiers, passed the Rock of Gibraltar and turned north up the coast of Portugal. Now they were off Cape Finisterre on the coast of Spain, and in a few days,

Captain Watson told Alec, they would be in England.

Alec wondered why the Black was being shipped to England—perhaps to race. The slanting shoulders, the deep broad chest, the powerful legs, the knees not too high nor too low—these, his uncle had taught him, were marks of speed and endurance.

That night Alec made his customary trip to the stall, his pockets bulging with sugar. The night was hot and still; heavy clouds blacked out the stars; in the distance long streaks of lightning raced through the sky. The Black had his head out the window. Again he was looking out to sea, his nostrils quivering more than ever. He turned, whistled as he saw the boy, then again faced the water.

Alec felt elated—it was the first time that the stallion hadn't drawn back into the stall at sight of him. He moved closer. He put the sugar in the palm of his hand and hesitantly held it out to the stallion. The Black turned and once again whistled—softer this time. Alec stood his ground. Neither he nor anyone else had been this close to the stallion since he came on board. But he did not care to take the chance of extending his arm any nearer the bared teeth, the curled nostrils. Instead he placed the sugar on the sill. The

Black looked at it, then back at the boy. Slowly he moved over and began to eat the sugar. Alec watched him for a moment, satisfied; then as the rain began to fall, he went back to his cabin.

He was awakened with amazing suddenness in the middle of the night. The *Drake* lurched crazily and he was thrown onto the floor. Outside there were loud rolls of thunder, and streaks of lightning made his cabin as light as day.

His first storm at sea! He pulled the light cord—it was dead. Then a flash of lightning again illuminated the cabin. The top of his bureau had been swept clear and the floor was covered with broken glass. Hurriedly he put on his pants, shirt, and slippers and started for the door; then he stopped. Back he went to the bed, fell on his knees and reached under. He withdrew a life belt and strapped it around him. He hoped that he wouldn't need it.

He opened the door and made his way, staggering, to the deck. The fury of the storm drove him back into the passageway; he hung onto the stair rail and peered into the black void. He heard the shouts of Captain Watson and the crew faintly above the roar of the winds. Huge waves swept from one end of the *Drake* to the other. Hysterical passengers crowded into the corridor. Alec was genuinely scared now; never had he seen a storm like this!

For what seemed hours to him, the *Drake* plowed through wave after wave, trembling, careening on its side, yet somehow managing to stay afloat. The long streaks of lightning never diminished; zigzagging through the sky, their sharp cracks resounded on the water.

From the passageway, Alec saw one of the crew make his way along the deck in his direction, desperately fighting to hold onto the rail. The *Drake* rolled sideways and a huge wave swept over the boat. When it had passed, the sailor was gone. The boy closed his eyes and prayed.

The storm began to subside a little and Alec felt new hope. Then suddenly a bolt of fire seemed to fall from the heavens above them. A sharp crack and the boat shook. Alec was thrown flat on his face, stunned. Slowly he regained consciousness. He was lying on his stomach; his face felt hot and sticky. He raised his hand, and withdrew it covered with blood. Then he became conscious of feet stepping on him. The passengers, yelling and screaming, were climbing, crawling over him! The *Drake* was still—its engines dead.

Struggling, Alec pushed himself to his feet. Slowly he made his way onto the deck. His startled eyes took in the scene about him. The *Drake,* struck by lightning, seemed almost cut in half! They were sinking! Strange, with what seemed the end so near, he should feel so cool. They were manning the lifeboats, and Captain Watson was there shouting directions. One boat was being lowered into the water. A large wave caught it in the side and turned it over—its occupants disappeared beneath the water.

The second lifeboat was being filled and Alec waited his turn. But when it came, the boat had reached its quota.

"Wait for the next one, lad," Captain Watson said sternly. He put his arm on the boy's shoulder. Alec did his best to smile.

As they watched the second lifeboat being lowered, the dark–skinned man appeared and rushed up to the captain, waving his arms and babbling hysterically.

"Under the bed, under the bed!" Captain Watson shouted at him.

Then Alec saw the man had no life belt. Terror in his eyes, he turned away from the captain toward Alec. Frantically he rushed at the boy and tried to tear the life belt from his back. Alec struggled, but he was no match for the half-crazed man. Then Captain Watson had his hands on him and threw him against the rail.

Alec saw the man's eyes turn to the lifeboat that was being lowered. Before the captain could stop him, he was climbing over the rail. He was going to jump into the boat! Suddenly the *Drake* lurched. The man lost his balance and, screaming, fell into the water. He never rose to the surface.

The dark–skinned man was drowned. Immediately Alec

thought of the Black. What was happening to him? Was he still in his stall? Driven by an irresistible impulse, Alec fought his way out of line and toward the stern of the boat. If the stallion was alive, he was going to set him free and give him his chance to fight for life.

The stall was still standing. Alec heard a shrill whistle rise above the storm. He rushed to the door, lifted the heavy bar and swung it open. For a second the mighty hooves stopped pounding and there was silence. Alec backed slowly away.

Then he saw the Black, his head held high, his nostrils blown out with excitement. Suddenly he snorted and plunged straight for the rail and Alec. Alec was paralyzed, he couldn't move. One hand was on the rail, which was broken at this point, leaving nothing between him and the open water. The Black swerved as he came near him, and the boy realized that the stallion was making for the hole. The horse's shoulder grazed him as he swerved, and Alec went flying into space. He felt the water close over his head.

When he came up, his first thought was of the ship; then he heard an explosion, and he saw the *Drake* settling deep into the water. Frantically he looked around for a lifeboat, but there was none in sight. Then he saw the Black swimming not more than ten yards away. Something swished by him—a rope, and it

was attached to the Black's halter! The same rope that they had used to bring the stallion aboard the boat, and which they had never been able to get close enough to the horse to untie. Without stopping to think, Alec grabbed hold of it. Then he was pulled through the water, out into the open sea.

The waves were still large, but with the aid of his life belt, Alec was able to stay on top. He was too far gone now to give much thought to what he had done. He only knew that he had had his choice of remaining in the water alone or being pulled by the Black. If he was to die, he would rather die with the mighty stallion than alone. He took one last look behind and saw the *Drake* sink into the depths.

For hours Alec battled the waves. He had tied the rope securely around his life belt. He could hardly hold his head up. Suddenly he felt the rope slacken. The Black had stopped swim-

ming! Alec anxiously waited; peering into the darkness he could just make out the head of the stallion. The Black's whistle pierced the air! After a few minutes, the rope became taut again. The horse had changed his direction. Another hour passed, then the storm diminished to high rolling swells. The first streaks of dawn appeared on the horizon.

The Black had stopped four times during the night, and each time he had altered his course. Alec wondered whether the stallion's wild instinct was leading him to land. The sun rose and shone down brightly on the boy's head; the salt water he had swallowed during the night made him almost mad with thirst. But when Alec felt that he could hold out no longer, he looked ahead at the struggling, fighting animal in front of him, and new courage came to him.

Suddenly he realized that they were going with the waves, instead of against them. He shook his head, trying to clear his brain. Yes, they were riding in; they must be approaching land! Eagerly he strained his salt-filled eyes and looked into the distance. And then he saw it—about a quarter of a mile away was a beach. Only an island, but there might be food and water, and a chance to survive! Faster and faster they approached the white sand. They were in the breakers. The Black's scream shattered the stillness. He was able to walk; he staggered a little and shook his black head. Then his action shifted marvelously, and he went faster through the shallow water.

Alec's head whirled—what stamina and endurance this horse had! He was being drawn toward the beach with ever-increasing speed. Suddenly he realized the danger of his position. He must untie this rope from around his waist, or else he would be dragged to death over the sand! Desperately his fingers flew to the knot; it was tight, he had made sure of that. Frantically he worked on it as the shore drew closer and closer.

The Black was now on the beach. Thunder began to roll from beneath his hooves as he broke out of the water. Hours in the water had swelled the knot—Alec couldn't untie it! Then he remembered his pocketknife. Could it still be there? His hand darted to his rear pants pocket; luckily he had buttoned it. Alec's fingers reached inside and came out grasping the knife.

He was now on the beach being dragged by the stallion; the sand flew in his face. Quickly he opened the knife and began to cut the rope. His body burned from the sand, his clothes were being torn off of him! His speed was increasing every second! Madly he sawed away at the rope. With one final thrust he was through! His outflung hands caressed the sand. As he closed his eyes, his parched lips murmured, "Yes—Uncle Ralph—it did—come in handy."

Read more about Alec's exciting adventures with the Black in The Black Stallion *by Walter Farley.*

Think About It

1. Give clues from the story to tell how Alec felt about horses.
2. How did the stallion act when he was first brought onto the ship? Why?
3. How did Alec try to befriend the stallion?
4. How did Alec's treatment of the stallion differ from that of the dark-skinned man?
5. How did Alec's concern for the stallion save both of them from the shipwreck?
6. How did Alec's knife come in handy?
7. Pretend you are Alec. What will you do now that you are on the island?

LEARN NEW WORDS

1. We found out why the machine was **defective**: the blades were bent.
2. When stirred in cold water, the powdered milk **dissolved** quickly.
3. She was too **drowsy** to listen to his serenade, so she closed the window and went to sleep.
4. The man had to **exert** a lot of energy to repair the defective motor.
5. Someone was hired to take care of the **extermination** of mice in the building.
6. They banged on the door with all the strength they could exert; finally it gave way under the **impact** of the blows.
7. Their test scores showed how **intelligent** they were.
8. A **mechanized** household would most likely have a machine that dissolves dirt ground into a carpet.
9. We **transferred** the groceries from the cart to the car.
10. The program was interrupted with the **urgent** message that a tornado warning was in effect.
11. It was a **vertical** drop of only six feet, so the impact upon hitting the ground was not too great.

GET SET TO READ

Why is it important that neighbors help each other? How can people help their neighbors?

In this story, a group of rats think up a plan to help their neighbor, Mrs. Frisby. Read to see what happens when the plan develops a hitch.

Mrs. Frisby and the Rats of NIMH

by ROBERT C. O'BRIEN

This selection is taken from a book about the adventures of a group of super-intelligent rats and a few mice who learned from them. At a place called the National Institute of Mental Health (NIMH), the rats had been the subjects of secret experiments on animal intelligence. They learned so much from the experiments that they were able to escape from the laboratory at NIMH. The government's Public Health Service has been looking for them ever since.

The rats are so intelligent that they set up their own society in underground tunnels, complete with electric lights, elevators, and a library full of books. Mrs. Frisby is a mouse who lives with her children in a cinder block in Farmer Fitzgibbon's field, not too far away from the rats' society.

In this episode, Mrs. Frisby has asked the rats to find a way to move her cinder-block house to safety before Farmer Fitzgibbon plows his field. The rats agree to move her house, but first they must find a way to keep Dragon, the farm cat, from bothering them. Mr. Ages, a wise old mouse, makes up a sleeping powder. The plan is for Mrs. Frisby to sneak into the kitchen and put the sleeping powder in Dragon's food dish. One of the rats, Justin, goes with Mrs. Frisby and Mr. Ages up to the farmhouse.

Part One

Mrs. Frisby, Justin, and Mr. Ages walked together up the long corridor to the rosebush.

"Remember, when you come up through the hole in the kitchen floor," Mr. Ages said, "you'll be under a cabinet. It's low, but there's room to move. Go a few steps forward, and you'll be able to see out into the room.

"Mrs. Fitzgibbon will be there, getting dinner for her family. They eat at about six. When she has their dinner ready, she'll feed Dragon. He won't be in the kitchen, but he'll be waiting just outside the kitchen door on the porch. She doesn't let him in while she's cooking because he makes such a pest of himself, rubbing against her ankles and getting between her feet.

"If you look to your right, you'll see his bowl. It's blue, and it has the word Kitty written over and over again around the side. She'll pick it up, fill it with cat food, and put it down again in the same place.

"Then watch closely. She'll walk over to the door to let him in, and that's your chance. Her back will be toward you. She's got to walk about twenty feet—it's a big kitchen. The bowl will be about two feet away from you. Be sure the paper packet is open—then dash out, dump the powder into the food, and dash back. You don't want to be in sight when Dragon comes in. I can tell you that from experience."

"Is that how you hurt your leg?"

"I got there a few seconds late. I decided there was still time. I was wrong."

At the arch in the rosebush Mr. Ages left them. With a cast on his leg, he would not be able to climb through the hole to the kitchen; there was no point in his going farther.

Mrs. Frisby and Justin moved out of the rosebush and looked around them. It was still light, though the sun was low on the horizon. Straight ahead of them, perhaps two hundred feet away, stood the big white farmhouse. Dragon was already on the porch, sitting just outside the door, looking at it expectantly.

"We go under the right side of the house," Justin said quietly. "Follow me." They made their way around the edge of the yard, staying in the shadows, keeping an eye on Dragon. Justin still wore his backpack and had put the powder package in it.

There was a basement under the main part of the Fitzgibbons' house, but the big kitchen had been added later and stood on a foundation of concrete blocks, with only a crawl space beneath. As they approached this gray foundation, Mrs. Frisby saw that near the middle of it, a few inches off the ground, there was a square patch of darker gray. It was a hole, left for fresh air, and there was a screen over it. When they reached it, Justin caught hold of the screen and pulled the corner. It swung open.

"We already loosened it a bit," he explained, holding it open for her. Mrs. Frisby crept through.

"Careful," he said. "It's dark. There's a drop of about a foot.

Just jump. We put some straw at the bottom, so it's soft."

Holding her breath, Mrs. Frisby jumped blindly into the blackness and felt the cushion of straw under her feet. In a moment Justin landed beside her. They were under the Fitzgibbons' kitchen.

"Now," he said softly, "look to your left. See the patch of light? That's the hole. The light comes from the kitchen. We've piled dirt up under it, so it's easy to reach. Come on."

Mrs. Frisby followed him; as they got near the bright hole she could see around her a little. They were walking across bare earth, dry and cool to the touch; overhead there were heavy wooden beams holding up the floor, and above those the floorboards themselves. Under the hole rose a small round hill of dirt. They walked up this, and then Justin whispered: "This is as far as I can go. There's not room for me to get through. I'll wait here. Come back down as soon as you're finished. Here's the powder." He handed her the paper packet. "Remember to tear it open before you go out to Dragon's bowl. Hurry, now. I can hear Mrs. Fitzgibbon moving around. She's getting the dinner. Be careful, and good luck."

Mrs. Frisby first pushed the packet up through the hole. Then, as quietly as she could, grasping both sides, she pulled herself up and into the kitchen.

It was light there. But Mr. Ages had not been joking when he said the ceiling was low. There was less than an inch between the floor and the bottom of the cabinet, so that she could not walk properly but had to flatten herself out and crawl. She did, a few steps, and discovered that she was trembling. "Stay calm," she told herself. "Don't get panicky, or you'll do something foolish and spoil everything."

She crept forward again until she was near the edge of the cabinet. She stopped. From there she could see out into the kitchen fairly well. Straight across from her stood a big white stove, and in front of it, putting the lid on a pot, was Mrs. Fitzgibbon. Because the edge of the cabinet was so low, Mrs. Frisby could not see her head, but only up to her shoulders.

"There," Mrs. Fitzgibbon said, as if to herself. "The stew is done, the bread's in the oven, the table is set."

Where was the cat's bowl? Mrs. Frisby looked to her right as Mr. Ages had said. There it was, blue with words inscribed around the side. Yet something was wrong. It was not two feet from the cabinet, but more like four or five. In the corner, where it should have been, rose four round wooden legs. She realized that she was looking at the bottom of a kitchen stool.

No matter, she thought. The extra distance is just a couple of feet. Mr. Ages had not mentioned a stool, but perhaps they moved it around. She crawled to her right, as close to the bowl as she could get without showing herself, and tore open the package.

Just as she did this Mrs. Fitzgibbon walked over from the stove. Her hand appeared, picked up the bowl, and Mrs. Frisby heard it thump on the counter over her head. A cutting sound—a can opener—the scrape of a spoon, and the bowl was back on the floor. The strong fishy smell of cat food. Mrs. Fitzgibbon walked away.

Now.

Mrs. Frisby moved swiftly out into the room, across the open floor, holding the powder, her eyes intent only on the bowl. She was no longer trembling. She poured in the powder, which instantly dissolved in the moist cat food. Still clutching the paper, she turned and sped toward the cabinet.

With a bang, the lights went dim. The ceiling, which had somehow become curved, was filled with little round moons. Mrs. Frisby kept running, and her face struck a cold, hard wall of metal.

A voice shouted: "Mother! Don't let Dragon in yet. I've caught a mouse."

Billy, the younger Fitzgibbon son, had been sitting on the kitchen stool, his feet up on the rung, eating berries from a colander. The colander, upside down, was now over Mrs. Frisby.

Part Two

From a birdcage, Mrs. Frisby watched the Fitzgibbons eat dinner. There was dinner for her, too—bread crumbs, cheese, and bits of carrot—on the floor of the cage, along with a small bowl of water.

To get her out from under the colander, Billy had slid a piece of cardboard beneath it, pinching her foot sharply in the process, so that it hurt when she walked. She had been transferred first to a shoe box.

"Can I keep it?" Billy had asked his mother.

"What for? It's just a field mouse."

"For a pet. I like it." Billy had tried to look at Mrs. Frisby through some holes he had punched in the top of the box, but it was dark inside.

"I suppose so. For a few days. You'll have to feed it."

"I think I'll put it in the birdcage. I can't see it in this box. It must be hungry. It was trying to eat Dragon's food. Dumb mouse. It might have been killed."

No one had noticed the small torn piece of paper at first; then Mrs. Fitzgibbon had absently picked it up and tossed it into the wastebasket.

A few days! Mrs. Frisby felt sick. And after a few days—then what? Would they let her go? Or would Billy plead for a few more? But even if they did set her free—her children were alone; the rats were coming tonight to move her house. Why had Billy picked today, of all days, to sit on the stool? She had not the heart to eat the food that lay on the cage floor. She felt like weeping.

Paul came in for dinner, followed by his father. He looked at her in the cage.

"Why don't you let it go?" he said to Billy. "Poor little thing. It's scared to death."

"No it's not. It's just not used to the cage."

"I bet it will die."

"I bet it won't."

"You can't just put wild animals in cages. You have to catch them when they're babies."

"They do it in zoos."

"Yes, but they know more about it. Anyway, a lot of those die, too."

"It's strange that it was in here at all," said Mrs. Fitzgibbon. "I haven't seen any signs of mice. I didn't think we had any."

They sat at the table, and Mrs. Fitzgibbon served the stew. It was a long, square-cut farm table, big enough to feed, besides the family, the four hired hands who would be working with Mr. Fitzgibbon during the planting and harvesting. The Fitzgibbons sat together around one end of it.

Mrs. Frisby's cage hung from a metal stand in the corner on the opposite side of the room, quite high up, so that the floor where she crouched was above their heads. She could watch them, looking down; but if she retreated to the far side of the cage, they could not see her, nor she them. She kept hoping that Paul would resume the argument with Billy and win it, or at least convince Mr. or Mrs. Fitzgibbon that they should let her go.

But Paul was now busy eating. So, moving quietly, she crept to the back of the cage. There was a sliding door halfway up the side, which Billy had lifted to put her in. She looked at it, wondering if she could climb to it, and if she could get it open if she did. Not now, but later, when they had left the kitchen. Maybe. But it looked quite big and heavy.

She had one small satisfaction. Dragon, who had been admitted after she was safely caged, had eaten his bowl of cat food greedily, sleeping powder and all, purring as he licked the last scraps from the bottom.

Billy looked at the cage.

"There," he cried. "It walked. I saw it. I told you it was all

right." He started up from his chair.

"Billy, stay in your place and eat your stew," said Mrs. Fitzgibbon. "The mouse can wait."

"Speaking of mice," said Mr. Fitzgibbon, who had driven to town that afternoon, "there was quite a stir today at Henderson's hardware store."

"About mice?"

"No, but nearly. About rats. There was quite a group there talking about an odd thing that happened.

"It seems that six or seven rats got electrocuted there a few days ago. Very strange. Henderson sells motors—he has a whole shelf of them. The rats, for some reason, had got on the shelf. He says it looked as if they were fooling with one of the motors, trying to move it."

"That's a new one," said Paul. "Rats stealing motors."

Mrs. Frisby was listening to the conversation very closely. Dragon had stretched out on the floor, looking drowsy.

"Wait," said Mr. Fitzgibbon. "That's only the beginning. It seems that the local newspaper heard about it and sent their reporter over."

"Fred Smith," said Mrs. Fitzgibbon.

"Yes. Fred wrote a little article about it, with a headline, MECHANIZED RATS INVADE

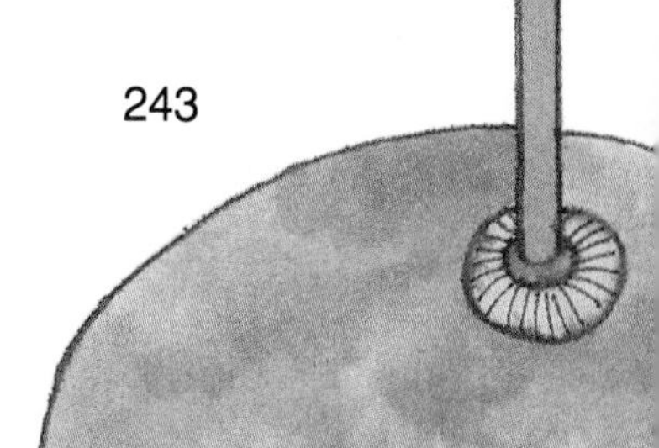

HARDWARE STORE. Something like that. Well, it attracted more attention than he expected. The next thing they knew, believe it or not, the federal government got into it. They sent a squad over there from the Public Health Service with a truckload of equipment."

"Just on account of seven rats?" said Billy. "They should send the truck over here. We've got more than that."

"That's just what I said," Mr. Fitzgibbon went on. "And do you know? They're going to. I was joking, of course, but the man in charge of the group didn't take it as a joke at all. He wanted to know where my farm was, how far away, how many acres, what I raised, how many rats I thought there were. He acted really interested."

"When are they coming?"

"Day after tomorrow, Saturday morning. The man in charge, a Doctor somebody, said they had some more checking to do in town tomorrow. They're coming with an extermination truck."

"I can tell them where to look," Paul said.

"Me, too," said Billy. "Under the rosebush."

"That's right," said Mr. Fitzgibbon. "In fact, they'll probably want to bulldoze that bush out of there."

Now Mrs. Frisby had another urgent reason to get out of the cage. Somehow, she had to warn the rats.

Dragon slept on the kitchen floor.

Part Three

At ten by the kitchen clock, the Fitzgibbons went to bed. Dragon was put out, the doors locked, the lights turned off. The first of these things was done by Billy, on instruction from his mother, not without some difficulty. He opened the door.

"Come on, Dragon. Out."

"He won't get up."

"I never saw such a lazy cat. He gets worse every day."

Finally Dragon, protesting with only the drowsiest of whines, was picked up and deposited on the back porch. He scarcely opened his eyes.

By that time it was dark. Mrs. Frisby waited a few minutes until she was sure they were really gone and until her eyes adjusted so she could see the bars of her cage. They were vertical bars, smooth and no thicker than match sticks, which made them slippery to climb; but by turning more or less sideways, she was able to grip them fairly well. She inched her way up to the sliding door and tried to lift it.

She could tell from the first pull that it was no use. The door was stiff and it was heavy, and she could not get a good enough grip on either it or the cage wall to exert much pressure. Still she kept trying, first lifting on the middle of the door, then on one corner, then on another, straining every muscle. In half an hour she admitted defeat, at least for the moment, and climbed back down. She sat there, shaking from the effort, and thought.

Somehow, she *had* to get out. Her children, even now, would be alone in the dark house, alone at night for the first time. What would they think? Since she had not told them about Dragon and the sleeping powder, she hoped that perhaps they would decide she was with the rats.

But at eleven, which could not be far off (she could not read the kitchen clock in the dark), the rats would arrive to move the house. Or would they, knowing—since Justin must have told them—that she had not come out of the kitchen? She thought they would. She hoped they would, and that Justin would go with them and talk to the children and try to calm their fear. There was something about Justin, a kind of easy confidence, that would help them.

She no longer had any doubt, of course, that the rats could move her house. It was a generous thing to do, especially when they were hurrying so to plan their own move. And they had no idea yet of how little time they really had, of the new danger that crowded upon them. If she could only get out! She would run and warn them, and it might still not be too late.

She heard a noise.

It was in the kitchen, near her cage, a small scuffling on the hard linoleum floor.

"Now what kind of a bird can that be, with no wings?"

It was Justin's voice, very soft, and he was laughing.

"Justin!"

"I thought you might like to come home. Your children are asking after you."

"Are they all right?"

"They're fine. They were worried, but I told them I'd bring you back. They seemed to believe me."

"But how did you know . . ."

"That you were here? You forget. I was waiting just under the cabinet. I heard what happened. But as soon as I heard that you were safely in the cage, I went and told the children you were all right, but that you'd be a little late. I didn't tell them exactly why. Now, let's get you out."

"I tried. I couldn't open the door."

"I'll get it open. I brought along a few tools in my backpack. Should I climb up the stand? No. It looks slippery. I think I'll try the curtain."

And in a matter of seconds Justin had swarmed up a window curtain a foot away, and she heard a thump as he leaped and landed on top of the cage, which swayed under the impact. The noise was slight, but they both listened intently for a moment to see if it produced another, from upstairs. All quiet.

"Now let me look at that door." Justin climbed easily down the side of the cage.

"Oh, I hope you can get it open."

"I can," Justin said, examining it, "easily enough. But I don't think I will."

"Why not?"

"Because *you* couldn't," Justin said, "and they'll know that. So they won't be curious, let's make it open itself. As I expected, it doesn't have real hinges." He had pulled a small metal bar out of his backpack, and was working as he talked. "Just like wire rings. Not good quality. Cheap, flimsy things. They're always coming apart." As he said that, one of them came apart; the door sagged and hung crazily by one corner. "There, you see? You couldn't help it if they put you in a defective cage. Come."

Mrs. Frisby climbed through and stood with Justin on the top of the cage.

"Now," he said, "we shinny down the stand like a fire fighter's pole. You go out the way you came in—under the cabinet and through the hole. I'll go out the way I came in—through the attic. I'll meet you outside."

"Justin," Mrs. Frisby said, "there's something I've got to tell you, something I learned . . ."

"Wait till we're out," said Justin. "We've got to hurry. You see, we're having a little trouble moving your house." He was off, running silently into the front of the house, from which the stairway led up two flights to the attic.

Mrs. Frisby crawled under the cabinet, searched in total darkness for the small hole, and finally felt one foot slip down. She dropped through. The square opening in the foundation was easier to find; it glowed palely ahead of her, lit with moonlight.

Justin was waiting for her as she came out of the corner of the screen. The night was warm, and a half-moon shone on the farmyard.

"Now," he said, "what was it you wanted to tell me?" He spoke seriously; he had heard the urgency in her voice. They hurried toward the garden, rounding the back porch. There, a dark heap in the moonlight, lay Dragon, no threat to anyone tonight.

"Some exterminators are coming to poison all of you." Mrs. Frisby told him, as briefly as she could, of the conversation she had heard at the Fitzgibbon's dinner table.

"When are they supposed to come?" Justin asked.

"The day after tomorrow."

To her surprise, Justin stopped. He looked at her in admiration.

"You know," he said, "I had a feeling the first time I clapped eyes on you that you'd bring us good luck."

"*Good* luck!" She was amazed.

"Oh, it's bad news. It's serious. We'll have to change our plans, and quickly. But think how much worse it would be if you hadn't overheard it. We wouldn't have had a chance."

They came into the garden.

"Now, we need your help to get started moving your house," said Justin.

"*My* help? What can I do?" Mrs. Frisby asked.

"You can talk to your neighbor, the shrew. She seems to think we're stealing your cinder block. She bit one of us in the leg."

Think About It

1. What was the plan that Mrs. Frisby was to carry out?
2. What went wrong with the plan?
3. What good came of Mrs. Frisby's imprisonment?
4. Why do you think that the Public Health Service was so interested in the newspaper story about the rats in the hardware store?
5. How did Mrs. Frisby escape from the birdcage?
6. How did Mrs. Frisby and the rats help each other to survive in their environment?
7. Write about what you think the rats will do to escape the new danger they face.

LEARN NEW WORDS

1. He was **apologetic** about disturbing us at dinnertime.
2. The house was filled with the irresistible **aroma** of turkey roasting in the oven.
3. Though she has been in a **coma** since the accident, we are hopeful she will regain consciousness and recover.
4. The cat held its head high with an air of **dignity**.
5. The **feline** transferred her baby kittens from the cold garage to a warm spot in our kitchen.
6. The **festive** cheer of the holiday season could be felt in the brightly decorated room.
7. The **rowdy** crowd continued to yell and whistle.
8. She brushed the cat to bring a **sheen** back to the dull fur.
9. The table was **superbly** set with beautiful silver and glassware.
10. The dog remained **unruffled** even though the cat was teasing it.

GET SET TO READ

What are some words you can think of to describe cats?

Read this account to find out how two cats can be very different from one another.

All Things Wise and Wonderful

by JAMES HERRIOT

James Herriot is a veterinarian who lives and practices in Yorkshire in northern England. This is a true story that he records in one of his best-selling books.

I know that my strongest memory of Christmas will always be bound up with a certain cat.

I first saw her one autumn day when I was called to see one of Mrs. Ainsworth's dogs, and I looked in some surprise at the furry black feline sitting before the fire.

"I didn't know you had a cat," I said.

The lady smiled. "We haven't. This is Debbie."

"Debbie?"

"Yes, at least that's what we call her. She's a stray. Comes here two or three times a week and we give her some food. I don't know where she lives but I believe she spends a lot of her time around one of the farms along the road."

"Do you ever get the feeling that she wants to stay with you?"

"No." Mrs. Ainsworth shook her head. "She's a timid little thing. Just creeps in, has some food, and then runs away. There's something so appealing about her, but she seems to resist letting me or anybody into her life."

I looked again at the little cat. "But she isn't just having food today."

"That's right. It's a funny thing, but every now and again she slips through here into the living room and sits by the fire for a few minutes. It's as though she was giving herself a treat."

"Yes . . . I see what you mean." There was no doubt there was something unusual in the attitude of the little animal. She was sitting upright on the thick rug that lay before the fireplace in which the coals glowed and flamed. She made no effort to curl up or wash herself or do anything other than gaze quietly ahead. And there was something in the dusty black of her coat that had no sheen, the half-wild scrawny look of her, that gave me a clue. This was a special event in her life, a rare and wonderful thing; she was lapping up a comfort undreamed of in her daily life.

As I watched she turned, crept soundlessly from the room, and was gone.

"That's always the way with Debbie," Mrs. Ainsworth laughed. "She never stays more than ten minutes or so. Then she's off."

Mrs. Ainsworth was a pleasant-faced woman and the kind of client a veterinarian dreams of—well off, generous, and the owner of three spoiled basset hounds. Whenever the normally sad expression of one of the dogs deepened a little, I was called there immediately. Today one of the bassets had raised its paw and scratched its ear a couple of times and that was enough to send its mistress rushing to the phone in great alarm.

So my visits to the Ainsworth home were frequent but undemanding, and I had many chances to look out for the little cat. On one visit I spotted her nibbling with an air of dignity from a saucer at the kitchen door. As I watched she turned and almost floated on light footsteps into the hall then through the living room door.

The three bassets were already in the room snoring on the fireside rug, but they seemed to be used to Debbie because two of them sniffed her in a bored, unruffled manner and the third just looked at her before flopping back on the thick rug.

Debbie sat among them in her usual posture: upright, intent, gazing into the glowing coals. This time I tried to make friends with her. I approached her carefully but she leaned away as I stretched out my hand. However, by patient coaxing and soft talk I managed to touch her and gently stroked her cheek with one finger. There was a moment when she responded by putting her head on one side and rubbing back against my hand, but soon she was ready to leave. Once outside the house she dart-

ed quickly along the road, then through a gap in a hedge, and then I saw the little black figure running over the rain-swept grass of a field.

"I wonder where she goes," I whispered.

Mrs. Ainsworth appeared at my elbow. "That's something we've never been able to find out."

It must have been nearly three months before Mrs. Ainsworth called me again.

It was Christmas morning and she was apologetic, "Mr. Herriot, I'm so sorry to bother you today of all days. I should think you want a rest at Christmas like anybody else." But her natural politeness could not hide the distress in her voice.

"Please don't worry about that," I said. "Which one is it this time?"

"It's not one of the dogs. It's . . . Debbie."

"Debbie? She's at your house now?"

"Yes . . . but there's something wrong. Please come quickly."

Mrs. Ainsworth's home was superbly decorated with tinsel and holly. The rich aroma of turkey and sage and onion stuffing drifted in from the kitchen. But her eyes were full of pain as she led me through to the living room.

Debbie was there all right, but this time everything was different. She wasn't sitting upright in her usual position; she was stretched quite motionless on her side, and huddled close to her lay a tiny black kitten.

I looked down, feeling puzzled. "What's happened here?"

"It's the strangest thing," Mrs. Ainsworth replied. "I haven't seen her for several weeks; then she came in about two hours ago—sort of staggered into the kitchen, and she was carrying the kitten in her mouth. She took it through to the living room and laid it on the rug and at first I was amused. But I could see all was not well because she sat as she usually does, but for a long time—over an hour; then she lay down like this and she hasn't moved."

I knelt on the rug and passed my hand over Debbie's neck and ribs. She was thinner than ever, her fur dirty and mud-caked. She did not resist as I gently opened her mouth. The lips were ice-cold against my fingers. I pulled down her eyelid. Then I put my stethoscope on her heart and listened to the increasingly faint, rapid beat. Then I straightened up and sat on the rug looking into the fireplace.

Mrs. Ainsworth's voice seemed to come from afar. "Is she ill, Mr. Herriot?"

I hesitated. "Yes . . . yes, I'm afraid so." I stood up. "There's absolutely nothing I can do," I said apologetically.

"Oh!" Her hand went to her mouth and she looked at me wide-eyed. When at last she spoke her voice trembled. "Well, you must put her to sleep immediately. It's the only thing to do. We can't let her suffer."

"Mrs. Ainsworth," I said. "There's no need. She's dying now—in a coma—far beyond suffering."

She turned quickly away from me and was very still as she fought with her emotions. Then she gave up the struggle and dropped on her knees beside Debbie.

"Oh, poor little thing!" she sobbed and stroked the cat's head again and again as her tears fell on the matted fur. "What she must have come through. I feel I ought to have done more for her."

For a few moments I was silent, feeling her sorrow, so out of place among the bright Christmas colors of this festive room. Then I spoke gently.

"Nobody could have done more than you," I said. "Nobody could have been kinder."

"But I'd have kept her here—in comfort. It must have been terrible out there in the cold when she was so desperately ill—I can't think about it. And having kittens, too—I . . . I wonder, how many she did have?"

I shrugged. "I don't suppose we'll ever know. Maybe just this one. It happens sometimes. And she brought it to you, didn't she?"

"Yes . . . that's right . . . she did . . . she did." Mrs. Ainsworth reached out and lifted the ragged black kitten. She smoothed her finger along the muddy fur and the tiny mouth opened in a soundless meow. "Isn't it strange? She was dying, and she brought her kitten here. And on Christmas Day."

I bent and put my hand on Debbie's heart. There was no beat.

I looked up. "I'm afraid she's gone." I lifted the small body, almost feather light, wrapped it in the sheet which had been spread on the rug, and took it out to the car.

When I came back Mrs. Ainsworth was still stroking the kitten. The tears had dried on her cheeks and she was bright-eyed as she looked at me.

"I've never had a cat before," she said.

I smiled. "Well it looks as though you've got one now."

And she certainly had. That kitten grew rapidly into a sleek, handsome cat with a rowdy nature which earned him the name of Buster. In every way he was the opposite to his timid little mother. Not for him the cold, hard outdoor life; he stalked the rich carpets of the Ainsworth home like a king and the fancy jeweled collar he always wore added something more to his presence.

On my visits I watched his development with delight, but the occasion which stays in my mind most was the following Christmas Day, a year from his arrival.

I was out on my medical visits as usual. I can't remember when I haven't had to work on Christmas Day, because the animals have never learned to recognize it as a holiday.

I was on my way home when I heard a cry as I was passing Mrs. Ainsworth's house.

"Merry Christmas, Mr. Herriot!" She was letting a visitor out of the front door and she waved at me gaily. "Come in and have some tea to warm you up."

In the house there was all the festive cheer of last year and the same glorious aroma of sage and onion. But there was not the sorrow; there was Buster.

He was darting up to each of the dogs in turn, ears pricked, eyes blazing with mischief, dabbing a paw at them and then streaking away.

Mrs. Ainsworth laughed. "You know, he's so rowdy he bothers the life out of them. Gives them no peace."

She was right. For a long time the bassets had led a life of peace and quiet; regular walks with their mistress, superb food in large quantities, and long snoring sessions on the rugs and armchairs. Their days followed one upon another in unruffled calm. And then came Buster.

He was dancing up to the youngest dog again, sideways this time, head on one side, teasing him. When he started boxing with both paws, it was too much even for the basset. He dropped his dignity and rolled over with the cat in a brief wrestling match.

"I want to show you something." Mrs. Ainsworth lifted a hard rubber ball from the shelf and went out to the garden, followed by Buster. She threw the ball across the lawn and the cat bounded after it over the frosted grass, the muscles rippling under the black sheen of his coat. He seized the ball in his teeth, brought it back to his mistress, dropped it at her feet and waited expectantly. She threw it and he brought it back again.

I could hardly believe it. A feline retriever!

The bassets looked on in disgust. Nothing would ever have persuaded them to chase a ball, but Buster did it again and again as though he would never tire of it.

Mrs. Ainsworth turned to me. "Have you ever seen anything like that?"

"No," I replied. "I never have. He is a most remarkable cat."

She snatched Buster from his play, and we went back into the house, where she held him close to her face, laughing as the big cat purred and arched himself joyfully against her cheek.

Looking at him, a picture of health and contentment, my mind went back to his mother. Was it too much to think that that dying little creature with the last of her strength had carried her kitten to the only comfort and warmth she had ever known in the hope that it would be cared for there? Maybe it was.

But it seemed I wasn't the only one with such ideas. Mrs. Ainsworth turned to me, and though she was smiling, her eyes were thoughtful.

"Debbie would be pleased," she said.

I nodded. "Yes, she would. . . . It was just a year ago today she brought him, wasn't it?"

"That's right." She hugged Buster to her again. "The best Christmas present I ever had."

Think About It

1. Describe what Debbie was like.
2. Why do you think Debbie stayed at Mrs. Ainsworth's home for only short periods of time?
3. Why did Debbie bring her kitten to Mrs. Ainsworth?
4. How was Buster's personality different from Debbie's?
5. Compare the feelings of the characters on the two Christmases in the story.
6. Why do you think some animals might prefer a harsh outdoor life?
7. Write about the personality of an animal you know or have seen or heard about.

CATALOG

by ROSALIE MOORE

Cats sleep fat and walk thin.
Cats, when they sleep, slump;
When they wake, pull in—
And where the plump's been
There's skin.
Cats walk thin.

Cats wait in a lump,
Jump in a streak.
Cats, when they jump, are sleek
As a grape slipping its skin—
They have technique.
Oh, cats don't creak.
They sneak.

Cats sleep fat.
They spread comfort beneath them
Like a good mat,
As if they picked the place
And then sat.
You walk around one
As if he were the City Hall
After that.

If male,
A cat is apt to sing on a major scale;
This concert is for everybody, this
Is wholesale.
For a baton, he wields a tail.

(He is also found,
When happy, to resound
With an enclosed and private sound.)

A cat condenses.
He pulls in his tail to go under bridges,
And himself to go under fences.
Cats fit
In any size box or kit;
And if a large pumpkin grew under one,
He could arch over it.

When everyone else is just ready to go out,
The cat is just ready to come in.
He's not where he's been.
Cats sleep fat and walk thin.

LEARN NEW WORDS

1. When we found out how much it would cost to mechanize our household chores, we **abandoned** the idea.
2. In newspaper and magazine articles, the art **critics** praised her work.
3. No wonder everyone feels so gloomy: the rain has made it a **depressing** day.
4. In order to get as many opinions as possible, we plan to speak to all the students **individually**.
5. The long line of trees went as far as the eye could see; it seemed to stretch to **infinity**.
6. The executive abandoned city life and moved to an **isolated** cabin in the woods.
7. The house was rebuilt to look **precisely** as it did a hundred years ago.
8. The small **proportions** of the house made it seem out of place in a neighborhood of huge homes.
9. The artist painted the scene so **realistically** that the picture appeared to be a photograph.
10. She received great **recognition** for her art work and won many awards.

GET SET TO READ

What kinds of pictures do you like to draw? Why?

Read to find out what subjects Georgia O'Keeffe found for her paintings in New Mexico.

Georgia O'Keeffe: An Artist Looks at Nature

by CAROL FOWLER

In the early summer of 1929 artist Georgia O'Keeffe traveled from her home in New York City to Taos, New Mexico. When she reached New Mexico, her artist's eye studied every detail of the mesas, or high desert tablelands. Deep canyons cut into the mesas and emptied onto the desert floor hundreds of feet below. Bright sunlight exposed every peak and valley of the mountains near Taos. The earth looked as naked as a skeleton, without a leafy tree or a single blade of grass to cover it. "Wonderful!" she exclaimed. "No one told me it was like this!" Those words were on her lips many times that summer.

Georgia O'Keeffe, then forty-one years old, had already gained recognition as an artist. Her paintings were exhibited regularly in New York galleries. Articles about these exhibits appeared in New York newspapers, and art critics wrote about her work in art magazines.

At the time, O'Keeffe was especially known for her paintings of flowers in large proportions. She would often cover an entire canvas with a single blossom. The large flower paintings were startling, and many times she was asked about their meaning. She said that if she painted flowers in normal proportions, just as everyone else had, no one would really look at them. But if she took a single blossom and enlarged it to an enormous size, then everyone, even busy New Yorkers, would take the time to look at it. They would really see the flower precisely as it was. Indeed, the flowers were noticed, and Georgia O'Keeffe had become famous for these paintings.

One painting of an enormous lily had sold for several thousand dollars in 1927. At that time it was a record price for a painting by a living American artist.

Then Mabel Dodge, a supporter of artists and writers, invited Georgia O'Keeffe to spend the summer of 1929 in Taos. Dodge had built a group of earth-colored adobe buildings at the base of Taos Mountain, and she hoped that artists would come there to paint in the clear light of New Mexico during the day. In the evenings they could talk about their work and ideas.

The desert excited Georgia O'Keeffe, and she enjoyed taking walks by herself behind the adobe buildings. Often, after a walk, she got out a canvas and painted the landscape. She never painted details as a camera might photograph desert rocks, but she recorded the landscape in simple, strong shapes and bright bands of color. The base of one painting is a band of gray-green, representing piñon and juniper trees. Beyond the trees arise the pink cliffs of mesas, then the indigo and violet of distant mountains. Her colors look as if she had mixed the clay and sand of the desert with oil and put them on the canvas. Her rock formations and mountains appear in shapes as bold as the windswept landscape.

That summer in Taos changed Georgia O'Keeffe's art and her life forever. Mountains and mesas became new subjects for her art. She made the New Mexico desert the focus of her life as well as her art. She still spent the winter in New York with her husband, the photographer Alfred Stieglitz. But she returned each summer to the desert. Because she preferred to work alone, she abandoned the art colony in Taos.

Someone had told O'Keeffe that the most beautiful spot in the United States was an isolated place called Ghost Ranch, New Mexico. By herself, she went there and rented a house.

Ghost Ranch was so dry that nothing but sage brush would grow there. But Georgia O'Keeffe loved the badlands that rolled away from her door to

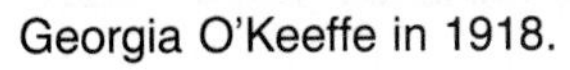

Georgia O'Keeffe in 1918.

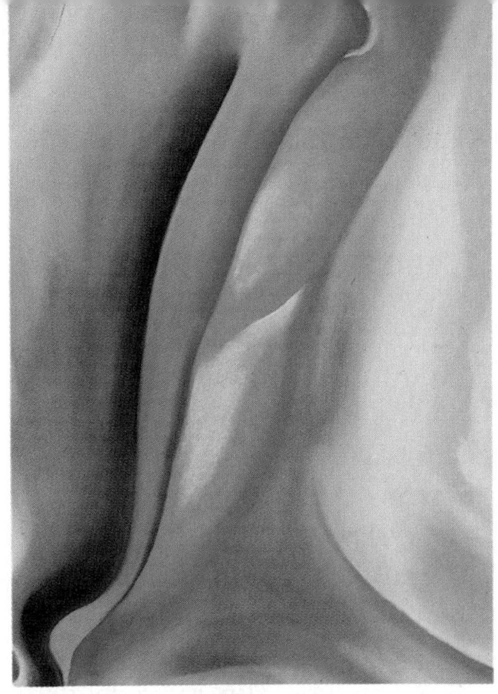

Shell No. 1, 1932, pastel by Georgia O'Keeffe.

Alfred Stieglitz, famous photographer, shown with
some of Georgia O'Keeffe's paintings in New York in 1936.

barren cliffs and mountains. The reds, purples, and copper green of the desert were as bright as the pigments of her oil paints. She painted the hills in a bright, pure way. Not everyone thought the hill paintings were as pretty as the flower ones, but she claimed that the hills touched her heart as much as the flowers. As she did in the flower paintings, she had a way of leaving out details and getting right at the heart of the landscape.

After she returned to her husband in New York for the winter, she sometimes painted the bones that she had collected on her desert walks. The bone paintings began to appear in her yearly shows. In one painting, a cow's skull is presented on a red, white, and dark blue banner. The horns of the skull and the banner form a cross. A later painting called *Summer Days* shows a deer skull with a small bunch of flowers floating over the red mountains and blue sky of New Mexico. The skulls were painted realistically, with great skill, much as the flowers had been.

When the skull paintings first appeared, some critics regarded them as strange, depressing symbols of death. But as the bone paintings appeared year after year during the 1930s, people began to regard them differently. The bones were seen as part of a whole cycle of life. Sometimes they were compared to wildflowers, because they were whitened by the wind and sun. The wear and tear of nature was not frightening or depressing to O'Keeffe. She said that she found the bones "more living than the animals walking around—hair, eyes, and all with their tails switching. The bones seem to cut sharply to the center of something that is keenly alive on the desert."

Her fame as an artist gradually spread far beyond the circle of people interested in modern art in New York. She was given many awards in the late 1930s and early 1940s. Also by that time her paintings hung in all the world-famous New York art museums.

During the early 1940s, she returned to the Ghost Ranch

Georgia O'Keeffe in 1949 in her studio and the cow's skull found in many of her paintings.

Georgia O'Keeffe and one of her skull paintings.

adobe house to paint each summer. She loved the isolation of the ranch, where days might go by without someone passing on the road. But since there was no water, all her food had to be brought in. She was getting tired of canned food. She ate simply, but she liked fresh fruits and vegetables. She thought that in the small village of Abiquiu, north of Taos, she could have a garden.

She had seen in Abiquiu an old tumble-down house with a marvelous view that seemed to stretch to infinity. She bought the crumbling structure in 1945. She found some women in the village who knew how to repair adobe, and she hired them to rebuild a cluster of rooms around a patio. Large windows provided a magnificent view of the valley. Even when she could not paint outdoors, the mesas and hills across the river were visible. Every room in the house had a fireplace, where fragrant piñon logs burned in cool weather. Now, in addition to the house at Ghost Ranch, she had a house in the village with a garden. Eventually, all the fruits and vegetables she needed were grown there. Her bread was homemade from wheat grown at her house.

In the summer of 1949, three years after the death of her husband, O'Keeffe settled permanently in New Mexico. During the cold months she lived in the comfortable adobe house in Abiquiu. Looking out of the big windows, she could see the winter-stripped cottonwood trees in the valley. She painted the trees to look like ghosts with tentacles looming out of the winter mists.

After a few years of the rhythm of living at Ghost Ranch in the summer and moving to Abiquiu for the winter, O'Keeffe was ready to travel. As an art student, and later during her career, she never had the urge to travel to Europe to see the work of the masters. Other artists never influenced her, neither old masters nor modern artists. When she chose to travel, in her mid-sixties, she was most interested in seeing the countries and the people. In 1953 she took her first trip to Europe. She liked Spain and returned the following year. In 1959 she traveled around the world, a trip that lasted three months, and she discovered that she liked the Far East better than Europe. The next year she went back to Japan and Southeast Asia.

Foreign countries were not the only thing that attracted her. In 1961, when she was seventy-three years old, she made her first raft trip down the rapids of the Colorado River. She found the trip so exciting that she repeated the adventure several times.

The experience of flying in airplanes on these long trips influenced Georgia O'Keeffe's painting. She painted rivers curving and cutting across the countryside, the way she saw them from the plane.

In the early 1960s she began to paint studies of clouds. The clouds appear as they would from an airplane. The first paintings in the series are of realistic, fluffy clouds. Then the size of the paintings became larger and the clouds became more individually shaped and precisely defined, like white rectangular stepping stones.

The final work of the series, *Sky above Clouds IV,* is twenty-four feet wide, the largest canvas O'Keeffe ever painted. She spent the summer of 1965 working on the massive painting in her double-garage studio at Ghost Ranch.

The clouds in the painting stretch out to the horizon, where they pass out of sight over the curve of the earth. The horizon, vastly far away, is rosy-colored like the dawn. The sky is a band of pale blue at the top of the painting.

This painting is considered O'Keeffe's masterpiece. Few people have seen it. Those who have say that they felt as though they were looking out at the endless sky from a high-flying airplane. The painting does not look exactly like the sky from an airplane, but Georgia O'Keeffe has captured the way it feels to look out of an airplane at the infinity of space.

All of these paintings continued to bring O'Keeffe recognition and honors during the 1950s and 1960s.

Many magazine articles have been written about her. Writers

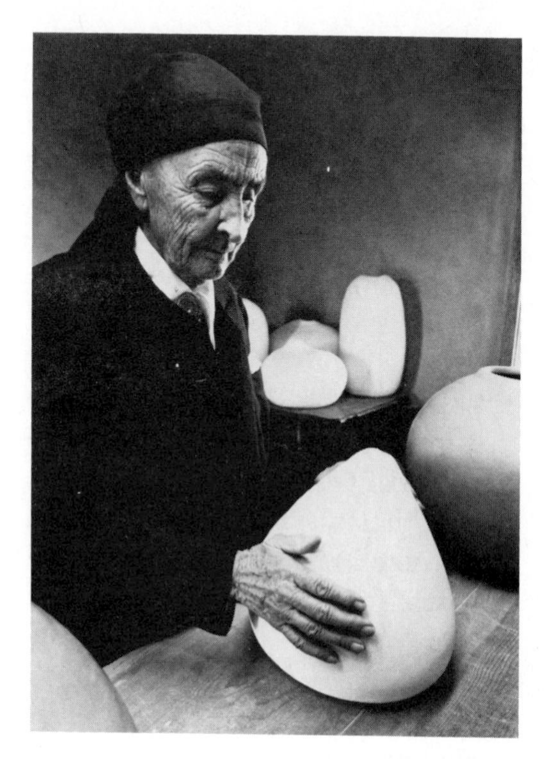

for art and fashion magazines are eager to visit her adobe home in Abiquiu to interview and photograph her. She is a favorite subject because of her striking appearance and her choice to live alone on the desert.

When interviewers ask her about her art, she says little. "Painting is my language," she says. "It is the way I speak." Modern American art is enriched by this language of timeless beauty and unique vision in the paintings of Georgia O'Keeffe.

Think About It

1. What was Georgia O'Keeffe known for painting before she moved to New Mexico?
2. What new subjects for her paintings did she find in New Mexico?
3. Why do you think O'Keeffe painted the bones she found on the desert?
4. How did she manage to live in the desert environment?
5. How did flying in an airplane give O'Keeffe another subject for her paintings?
6. Write a description of a picture you would like to paint.

Desert Person

by BYRD BAYLOR

Like any desert creature,
I build my own
safe shelter
with what the desert
gives.

I make thick walls
of mud and straw.
With my own hands
I shape the earth
into a house.

But when I say,
"This is my home,"
another desert person
always knows
that I don't mean
the *house*.

I mean
the farthest mountain
I can see.

I mean
sunsets
that fill the whole sky
and the colors
of the cliffs
and all their silences
and shadows.

I mean
the *desert*
is my home.

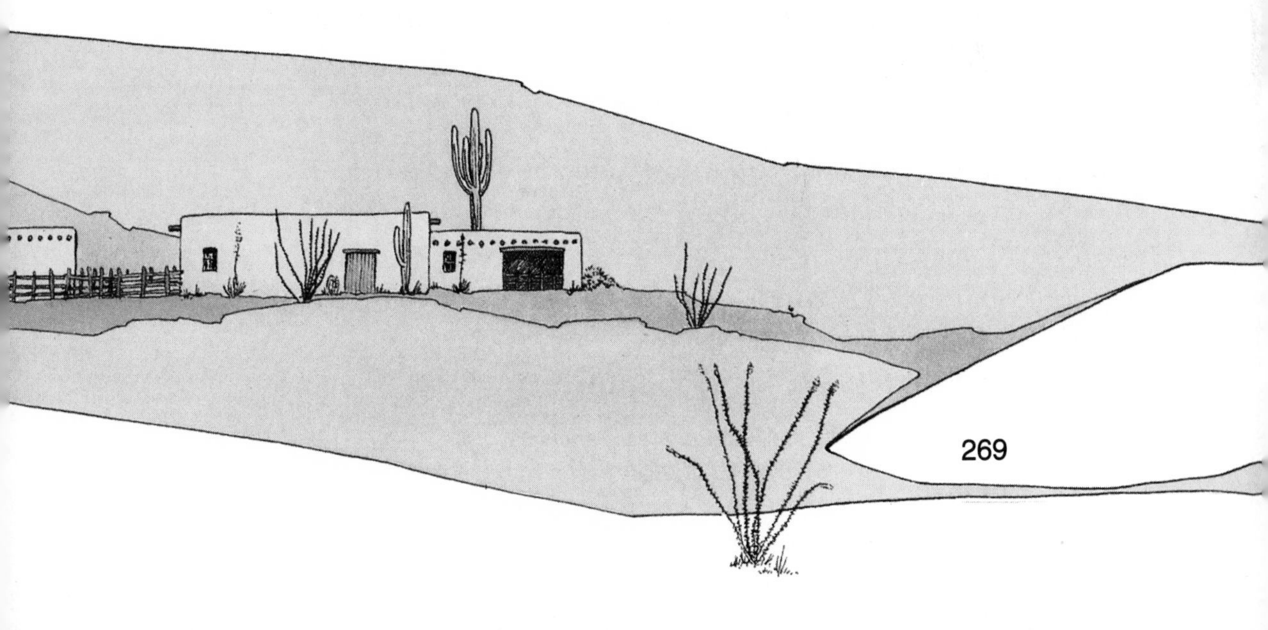

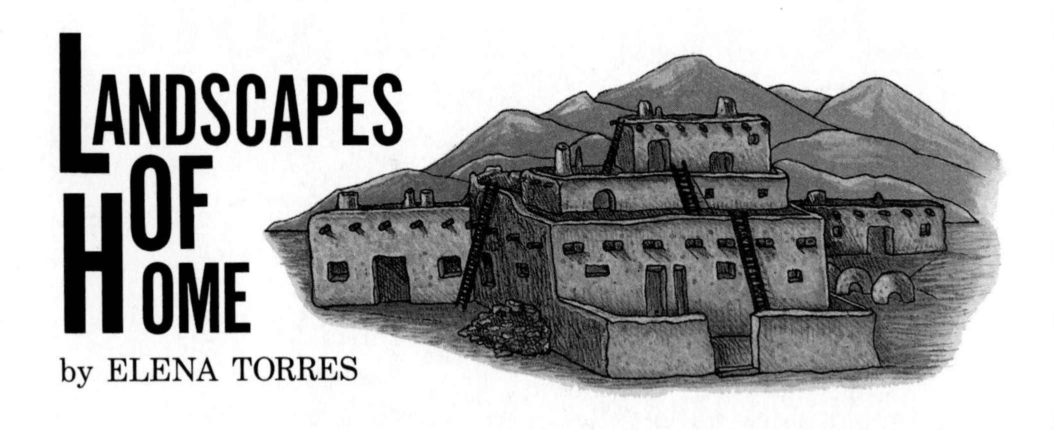

LANDSCAPES OF HOME

by ELENA TORRES

The painter Georgia O'Keeffe fell in love with the deserts of New Mexico and then made her home there. Here are some Mexican-American painters who were born in the Southwest. They recorded its landscape as their homeland and their heritage.

Joel Tito Ramírez, born in Albuquerque, paints the small villages of northern New Mexico. He sees his work as very much a part of the history of New Mexico. He says that "love for the history of our people is so embedded in my work that even [when] I paint the Southwest, and particularly the Albuquerque landscape, there [is a] flavor of the past . . . . This is part of me."

Joel Tito Ramírez, *Sanctuary,* 1969.
(Courtesy of the artist)

Margaret Herrera Chávez, *Sandía Mountain Spring Time,* 1970.
(Courtesy of the artist)

Margaret Herrera Chávez, who also grew up in northern New Mexico, used the area as subject for her paintings. She often painted with watercolors to achieve the effects of bright sunlight. The colors in her paintings are soft, even a little faded, as they would appear on a hot, sunny day.

Porfirio Salinas lives in San Antonio, Texas. He has become a favorite among Texans for his loving paintings of the Central Texas landscape. Unlike many modern artists, Salinas records exactly what his eyes see. In his paintings there are bluebonnets, cacti, and live oak trees—things familiar to most Texans as reminders of place and home.

Porfirio Salinas, *Bluebonnets,* 1956. *(Courtesy of Exxon Company, U.S.A.)*

Magic and the Night River

by EVE BUNTING

The cormorants squawked inside their bamboo baskets. Yoshi saw a flash of gray feathers through the webbing, the gleam of a black eye, the curve of a neck. It was important to look and to see everything clearly, because now each night on the river could be the last.

"Ready, Yoshi?" Grandfather asked, and Yoshi nodded.

Together he and his cousins loaded the baskets that held the cormorants onto Grandfather's boat.

Magic and the Night River

by EVE BUNTING

The cormorants squawked inside their bamboo baskets. Yoshi saw a flash of gray feathers through the webbing, the gleam of a black eye, the curve of a neck. It was important to look and to see everything clearly, because now each night on the river could be the last.

"Ready, Yoshi?" Grandfather asked, and Yoshi nodded.

Together he and his cousins loaded the baskets that held the cormorants onto Grandfather's boat.

The boat did not belong to Grandfather, though he had fished from it for forty years. The boat belonged to Kano, and because it did, half of their nightly catch went to him. Yoshi did not want to think about Kano. Kano was big and strong and he talked with a strong voice.

"Why is it, Yoshi, that your grandfather's boat always brings home the fewest fish?" Kano had asked as they stood on the riverbank. "Is it because your grandfather is now too old? I should rent my boat to a better fisherman. There would be more fish then for me to share."

"There is not anywhere a better master fisherman than Grandfather," Yoshi said fiercely. Kano shrugged.

Yoshi watched Kano load his cormorants onto his second boat. He threw the baskets down carelessly on the deck and the long, narrow boat swayed. Inside one of the baskets a bird screamed its rage.

Yoshi glared at Kano across the water space that divided the two boats. "You should be gentle with the birds," he shouted. "They are easily hurt and they work hard for us."

"Who worries about cormorants?" Kano asked. "The skies are full of cormorants for the taking."

"Grandfather says we owe them kindness. We . . ."

"What do I care what your grandfather says?" Kano sounded angry. "Let him think about other things. Tonight I will be taking careful count of the catch when the fishing is done."

Yoshi glanced quickly at his grandfather.

Grandfather was bent over one of the baskets, his hands moving across it, soothing the birds inside. Old hands with yellowed nails, gentle hands.

Yoshi swallowed. "Shall we ready the sail, Grandfather?" he asked, and Grandfather nodded.

The small breeze tugged at the canvas as Yoshi and his cousin Masa pulled on the ropes. It blew on the lanterns

that decorated the barge, on the other side of the river, filled with people who came to watch the fishing. Soon the barge would glide upstream with the working boats. The voices of the people drifted across the darkness and the lanterns spilled their yellow glow on the shine of the water.

Grandfather gave the signal and Yoshi's older cousin, Take, whose place was in the stern, poled their boat away from shore.

The other four boats pushed off too, fanning across the river, their sails opening themselves to the wind.

And there was only the contented lapping of the water, the ripple of the wind in the canvas, the splashing of the polers on the barge. The sounds of the night river. Remember them for always, Yoshi told himself.

Grandfather raised a hand and Yoshi knew it was time. He stared down into the dark water. There was nothing to see, but he knew it must be time.

He heard the scraping of the match and saw his grandfather hold its light to the wood in the iron cradle that hung out from the bow. The dry wood took the fire immediately, crackling and spitting. Smoke blew back, rising and drifting to the sky where the night stars hung. It was time.

One by one the bow fires blazed in the other boats.

Yoshi sniffed at the pine smoke. Who will light the first fire when Grandfather is gone, he wondered. He wanted to shout to Kano, "It is Grandfather who knows where the fish lie waiting. He has been lighting the first fire for forty years. Doesn't that mean something?" But he didn't shout anything, because all Kano cared about was counting the catch when the fishing was ended. He helped his cousin Masa take down the sails and mast.

They drifted slowly, pulled only by the river. The light from the fires danced on the water, calling the fish from

the depths to where the birds could reach them. There was a hiss and a shower of sparks as a piece of burning wood fell into the river.

Across the water the bargemen raised their poles. Yoshi saw the drops hanging like pearls from the poles, saw the blur of people's faces behind the railing.

"Should I release the birds now, Grandfather?" he asked, and Grandfather nodded.

Yoshi felt the simmer of excitement that came to him the same way each night. It was time.

He took from the box the wedges of wood with the cords wrapped around them. Then he opened the first basket and felt under the half-raised lid. His hand found Itchi-ban, their number-one cormorant, and eased it out. The ring around its neck gleamed silver and red, reflecting the flames. Quickly Yoshi passed the cord around the bird's breast and tied it.

"Grandfather?" he said, holding the bird toward the old man.

Grandfather leaned forward and touched the cormorant's head once. It was this way each night, with each bird. The old hands reaching out, warm and gentle.

"Go," he said, and Yoshi held onto the end of the cord and set the cormorant free.

The first second of flight was only a flurry of awkward wings. Then Itchi-ban surged away, the air thick about it, its body beating against the dark, the feel of life on a leash, spinning, cartwheeling to dive, crashing into the river.

Yoshi passed the cord to Grandfather. His smile answered his grandfather's smile. We know, he thought. We feel together. It could not be this way for his cousins, who handled only the boat and not the birds. The strength of

his feeling was almost an embarrassment, and he was glad to lean over and bring out the second bird.

Soon all the cormorants were in the air, swooping and diving, filling the night with their wings and their hoarse cries.

Fourteen birds.

Grandfather handled eight from the bow. He held the cords between his fingers, shifting them to the birds' needs.

Yoshi worked only six. He had not yet the skill to manage more.

Once Grandfather had been master of twelve birds. His fingers had moved so quickly then that to watch him was to watch a juggler at work. Now the fingers were bent and stiff.

"Fourteen birds for two handlers," Kano had said. "Am I a fool to rent my boat to two such fishermen?"

Yoshi remembered his words as he jiggled his cords. "Come on," he whispered. "Dive for us. Bring us back fish, fish, fish."

His grandfather reeled in one bird, its neck bulging with the fish it had caught but could not swallow. Grandfather held the cormorant's beak over a basket and ran his hand along its neck. The big fish spilled in a stream of silver from the bird's throat. Grandfather nodded toward Yoshi's cord. "Yours," he said.

Yoshi pulled in his fisher cormorant and stripped its throat into his waiting basket. When he had first come with Grandfather he had known little and had had to ask many questions.

"Why does the ring around the throat not choke the bird, Grandfather?"

"Because it is placed there with delicacy. It is tight enough so that the cormorant cannot swallow the big fish,

yet it is loose enough for the small ones to slip down. That way the bird is happy because it is not hungry. And we are happy too, Yoshi, because with the big fish to sell we are not hungry either."

"Pay attention to your cords, my Yoshi," Grandfather called now, and Yoshi nodded.

On the next boat, Kano was reeling in. His cormorants fought and pecked at each other, hanging in the air beside the boat, held tight on short lines. Too tight, Yoshi thought. Even I know better than to hold the lines like that.

Grandfather's birds were working well. Time and again they came with their catches and flapped away to fish again. Do they know how much we need a good catch tonight? Yoshi wondered.

The air was alive with the birds' cries and screams as the river was alive with their lights and shadows. Do they know? Yoshi wondered.

There was a flurry of work on all the boats. Once Kano shouted across, "We have one basket almost filled, old man. How goes it with you?"

Grandfather said nothing.

It was then that one of the other boats bumped theirs. Yoshi had seen this happen before, here where the river ran swift and narrow. But he'd never seen what happened next. One of the men on the other boat stumbled. His hands lost control of his lines and they tangled with the lines of another.

Now all the boats were nudging, brushing sides, and the birds were too close, flying in a jumble, their cords tangling.

A rustling, like a small wind, came from the watchers on the barge.

The birds squawked their rage, spinning in furious circles, almost strangling one another. The cords were a great shadowy cobweb that hung above the dark gleam of the river, the birds darting through it like monstrous flies caught in its maze. Yoshi tried to let his eyes follow the lines that ran from his fingers. Where was Itchi-ban? Which were their cormorants? If they would only stay still!

Panic urged the birds to greater struggle. One plummeted into the river, the cord a cocoon around its body. One hung upside down, the cord twisted on its neck. One dangled by a wingtip, its other wing flapping weakly.

Yoshi's throat felt tight, as if he too wore a metal ring.

"Grandfather?" he asked, and his grandfather nodded. It was the way it always was between them, the meaning clear without words spoken. Slowly Yoshi unclenched his hands and let the cords hang free.

A bird lifted itself from the web, screeching loudly, its line trailing behind it. Another pulled loose. Its cord caught, but the bird jerked and its wings pushed away the night as it rose to freedom.

Grandfather looked unblinkingly at Yoshi. Then he spread his fingers wide and stood motionless, his face turned to the sky.

Good-by birds, Yoshi thought. We will not need you again. There was a terrible sadness in him as he watched their cormorants skim away into the shadows. It was as though everything he and his grandfather had had together went with them. He rubbed the smoke sting from his eyes. Good-by birds. May kindness find you.

On the other boat Kano yelled and twitched his lines.

The men stepped from boat to boat, changing places as they tried to unravel the quivering web.

On Grandfather's boat there was only calm. The cousins had pulled in their poles. Grandfather sat quietly in the bow.

What is he thinking? Yoshi wondered. Does he remember all the years on the boat? The fish he's taken? The birds he's known?

Then, there was a sudden flurry of dark wings, a scrabble of clawed feet on the deck.

Yoshi gasped.

Itchi-ban was perched by the fish basket. Its eyes held no fear as Yoshi crept toward it.

Grandfather smiled. "Take what it offers us," he said, and Yoshi took the bird and emptied the fish from its throat.

He held Itchi-ban's warmth close against him. Should he put it back in its basket? Fasten tight the lid? Slowly he opened his hands and set it free.

A second bird came back, and a third.

Yoshi was dizzy with excitement. He and Masa and Grandfather worked together, taking the gifts the cormorants brought, releasing them to fish again.

Who could believe it? Grandfather had no need of cords to hold his birds. They were held to him by something stronger.

Their baskets bulged with the shine of their catch. The bargemen poled the barge closer so the people could see.

Kano shook his head and watched with amazement. Then he opened *his* hands and let the birds go. But his birds did not return.

Grandfather's baskets were full. Fish tumbled over their tops to wriggle back into the river.

"Shall we fish for you now, Kano?" Grandfather asked.

"No," Kano said.

"We are ready to go back then." Yoshi did not try to hide his joy. "We will wait for you on the riverbank."

He counted thirteen of their cormorants perched on the boat, waiting, and Itchi-ban standing proudly on the overhanging prow. All of their birds had returned. Yoshi watched as Grandfather gathered them one by one and placed them in their baskets. Tonight he was content to leave this job to Grandfather alone. He saw how Grandfather fondled the head of each bird before he closed the lid. Old hands with yellowed nails, gentle hands. He had left Itchi-ban till last. Grandfather held the big bird close. Yoshi saw his lips move but could not hear the whispered words. Then Itchi-ban too was settled into its basket.

"The old man has magic," Kano said, and there was a new sound to his voice.

Yoshi smiled. It might be that Kano would never understand what kind of magic had brought the birds back. For now there were other matters to think about as Masa and Take poled the boat toward home. Grandfather could train new birds. He could have eight on cords and others working free. With Yoshi's six, their cormorants would bring in many fish. Kano would like that.

Grandfather seemed to creak as he bent to examine the night's catch.

His strength grows less each day, Yoshi thought. But my strength grows greater. It is another kind of magic. Together we will have many nights on the night river.

READ ON!

The Animals of Farthing Wood by Colin Dann. A group of wild animals see their woods destroyed by humans and machines. Read what happens when Fox, Badger, and Toad lead the other animals on a long and dangerous journey to find a safer place to live.

The Absolutely Perfect Horse by Marylois Dunn and Ardath Mayhar. This story tells how a downtrodden horse named Dogmeat earns the new name of Chief. It's a family story of rescue and of loss and gain.

The Cry of the Crow by Jean Craighead George. Set in the Florida Everglades, this story tells how Mandy tries to protect a young crow and then learns how to communicate with it.

Creatures of Paradise: Pictures to Grow Up With by Bryan Holme. Enjoy this wonderful collection of pictures of animals, all painted by famous artists.

Flower, Moon, Snow: A Book of Haiku by Kazue Mizumura. This is a good introduction to haiku poetry and an explanation of the form, with illustrations of each poem.

The Sign of the Beaver by Elizabeth George Speare. Left alone in the Maine wilderness of 1760, Matt must depend on his Indian neighbors to survive. He grows to understand and eventually share their feelings for the land.

UNIT 4

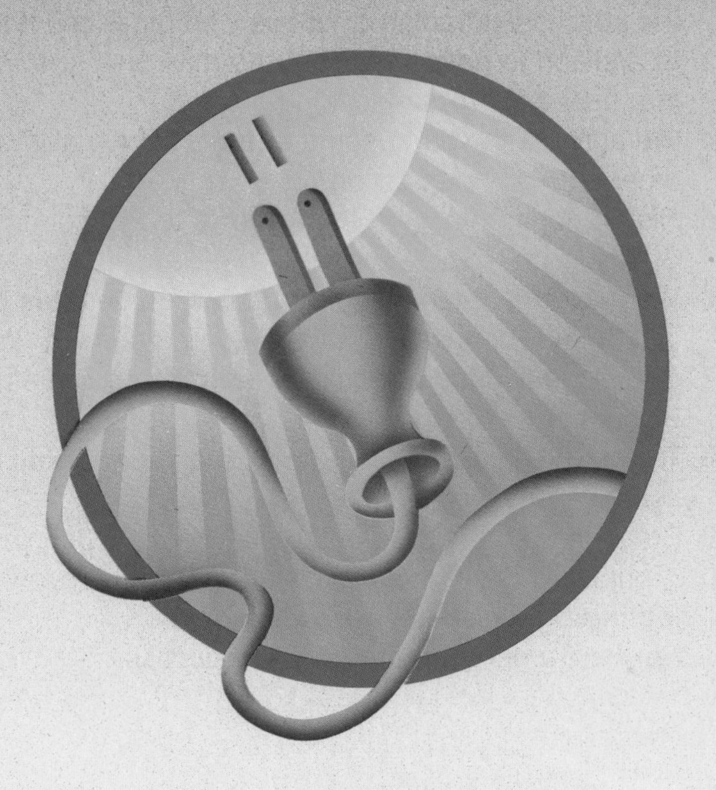

Connections

LEARN NEW WORDS

1. There was no **basis** for the rumors that spread through the school.
2. The **economy** of the United States depends, in part, on the successful trading of goods with other countries.
3. In addition to potato farming, the man was now involved in a new **enterprise**—cattle ranching.
4. We agree with you to some **extent**, but we also see the other side of the question.
5. His grandparents were **immigrants** to this country from Spain.
6. We had many reasons for starting a garden, but our **primary** reason was to have a source of fresh vegetables.
7. She explained the scientific **principles** behind airplane flight.
8. To avoid the construction, he took a **roundabout** way home.
9. Bread is a **staple** food in the diet of many people.
10. A primary task of these engineers is to improve the **technology** used in space exploration.
11. Her hard work **ultimately** led to success.

GET SET TO READ

Do you ever wonder where certain things come from? Think of your favorite foods or machines you use every day. How did we get these things?

Read this article to find out how some of the things we see every day made their way into our lives.

Back at the Beginning

by LEE SHERIDAN

Picture this: You sit down for dinner one evening in front of a plate of spaghetti. Armed with a fork, knife, spoon, and napkin, you struggle to get the long, slippery noodles from the plate to your mouth without dropping one in your lap. Then you wonder: Who invented spaghetti anyway, and why is it so much trouble to eat?

The answer to this question won't make eating spaghetti any easier, but it may surprise you. Spaghetti came from the Italians, but the Italians originally got spaghetti from China over 600 years ago. The Chinese have been making noodles for thousands of years; they say, the longer the noodle the longer the life. In Chinese restaurants today, you can find long noodles that you're supposed to eat with chopsticks!

Many other things we take for granted as belonging to one time and place had their beginnings in quite a different time and place. In our age of instant communication, where things happen so fast, it may be surprising to find out that the discoveries and inventions so important to the present actually developed very slowly and sometimes took a roundabout way getting to us. Let's take a long look back in history and find out when some things had their beginnings.

Made in China

Many early inventions that shaped our history to a great extent were first developed in China hundreds of years ago. In the year A.D. 105 a Chinese politician named Ts'ai Lun made the world's first sheet of paper. He did it by soaking and pounding the inner bark of a mulberry tree and then pouring the mixture into a flat mold to dry. Later, the Chinese made paper by pounding together old ropes, rags, or fish nets. Paper making remained a Chinese secret for over 500 years. It eventually spread to the Arab world in the eighth century. Europeans ultimately found out from the Arabs how to make paper in the twelfth century.

Printing was also first invented in China. In the eleventh century, the Chinese were already using block printing—a process whereby several signs were carved on large wooden blocks, then dipped in ink, and pressed onto paper. A Chinese printer also invented movable type, with a separate piece of wood or clay for each sign. It was over 400 years later, in 1440, that Johannes Gutenberg invented movable type in Germany and so introduced printing to Europe.

Knowledge of many Chinese customs and inventions was brought back to Europe by the Italian explorer Marco

Polo. He was only seventeen years old when he traveled with his father and his uncle to China in 1271. Twenty-five years later, Marco Polo returned to Italy and wrote a book about his travels throughout the Far East.

Marco Polo's book (written by hand because printing had not been invented in Europe) described such Chinese inventions as the magnetic compass, as well as paper making and printing. At a time when Europeans were using wood as fuel and heavy coins as money, Marco Polo's book also told of the mining and burning of coal as fuel and the use of paper money in China. This book became the most widely read book in Europe. It may have greatly influenced other early explorers, among them Christopher Columbus.

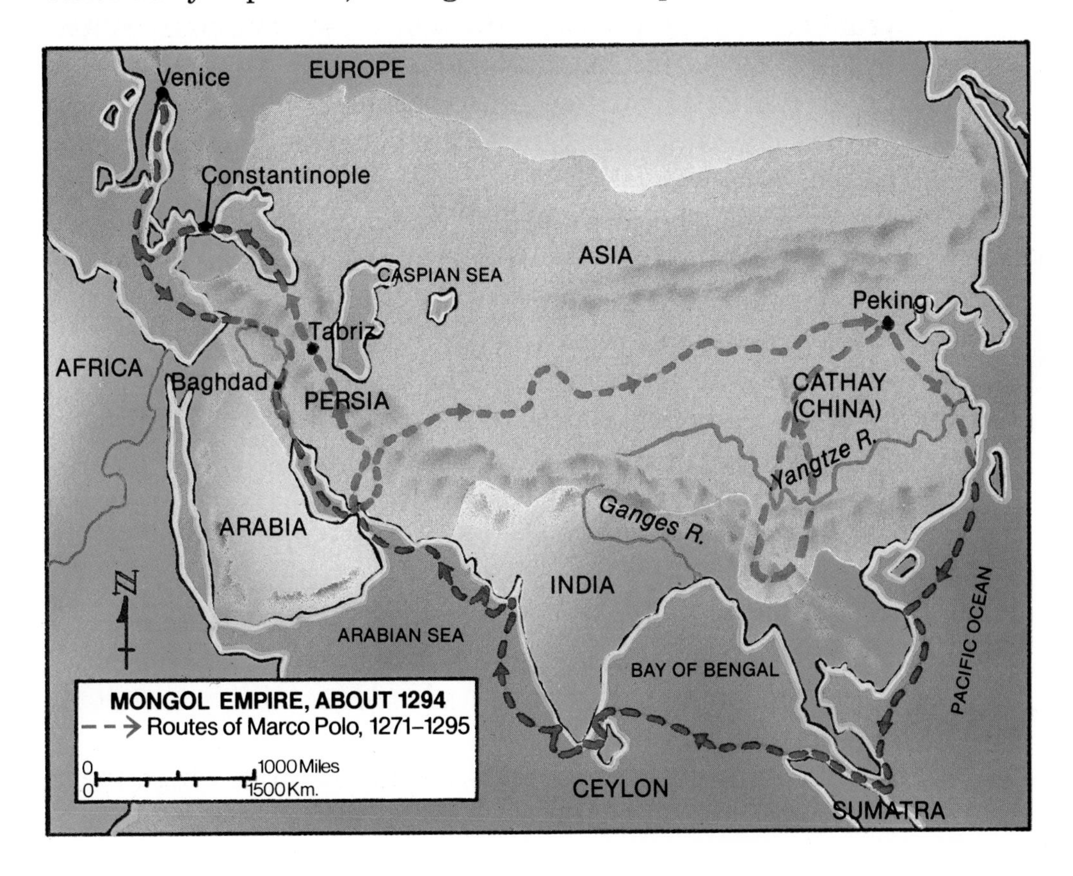

Homegrown Favorites

Marco Polo also brought back from China a thin noodle made from wheat flour that became a staple food in the Italian diet. And what would spaghetti be without tomato sauce? Surprisingly, tomatoes didn't originally come from Italy either; they were first grown by Native Americans in South and Central America. Many of our foods and even some of our treats came from Native Americans: squash, beans, avocados, pineapples, plums, cashews, pecans, peanuts, maple syrup, vanilla, and chewing gum. Most important, however, are two staple foods in our diet—corn and potatoes.

Corn was grown as early as 2000 B.C. in the warm, dry climate of Mexico where the first farmers of the New World lived. It took several thousand years for the cultivation and use of corn to spread among the peoples of both North and South America. By the time Christopher Columbus landed in 1492, corn was growing from Canada to the southern tip of Argentina. The corn the Native Americans originally grew formed the basis for all the types of corn we raise today, including popcorn.

Corn became as important to the early colonists as it was to the Native Americans. Not only was it sometimes the only steady food source in the new land, but corn was often used by the colonists as money to pay their rent and taxes. Today, much of the corn grown throughout the world is used as feed for cattle and pigs, although people in both North and South America still serve it with meals.

Potatoes had a more roundabout way of reaching our tables. About 400 years ago, the Incas grew what we know as white potatoes high in the Andes Mountains, where it is too cold to grow corn or wheat. The Spanish explorers brought some of these potatoes back to Europe, where they quickly became a popular crop.

The potato grew so well in Ireland and had such nutritional value that it became the primary food crop. Irish immigrants brought it with them when they settled New England in the early eighteenth century. So today, what we call the Irish potato is really the same white potato the Incas ate!

Home on the Range

For about 350 years, from the time of the Spanish explorers to the Mexican War in 1848, the southwestern part of the United States was part of Mexico. We owe much of the economy and culture of this area to its original Mexican settlers.

Mexicans founded many of the major cities of the Southwest—Sante Fe, Albuquerque, Los Angeles, San Antonio, and Tucson. More important, Mexican settlers developed methods of cattle ranching and irrigation that were necessary to the settlement of the dry grasslands and deserts.

Cattle ranching, in a way, began with Columbus. He brought the first cattle to the New World. Later, the Spaniards brought horses and pigs as well as cattle to the Caribbean Islands and Mexico. Before that, no one had ever seen such an animal as a horse or a cow in North and South America.

By the time the early settlers from the eastern United States came to Texas in the 1820s, cattle ranching was already a profitable enterprise. The Mexican ranchers taught the new immigrants about the breeding and pasturing of cattle. The *vaqueros,* or mounted herders, taught them how to tame wild horses and how to rope, herd, and brand cattle.

As a result, most of the dress, equipment, methods, and even the language of the Texas cowboy came from the Mexicans. *Corral, bronco,* and *sombrero* are all Spanish words. Other words came from Mexican ranching terms: *lariat* (from *la reata,* the rope), *lasso* (from *lazo,* a slip knot), *pinto* (from *pinta,* a spotted horse), and *stampede* (from *estampida,* a loud noise or crash).

In addition to cattle ranching, Mexicans in California taught the new immigrants important mining techniques. The Mexicans knew how to mine copper and silver when the first settlers from the East arrived. The thousands who came to California during the Gold Rush of 1849 also learned from the Mexicans how to pan for gold in rivers and streams. As a result, mining became very important to the economy of the Western states.

Vaqueros. *(The Granger Collection)*

When Inventions Finally Take Off

When looking back to the beginnings of things, you may find big gaps in time between an idea for something and its eventual use. Cattle ranching happened at the right time and in the right place for it to be a successful enterprise. But sometimes the time isn't right; an idea may be far ahead of the technology needed to carry it out.

This is what happened with the helicopter. Because so many helicopters stir up the sky these days, it's hard to believe that they've only been around for the past forty years. But the idea for the helicopter is very old. Hundreds of years ago the Chinese made toys called "flying tops" that flew like helicopters with the aid of two feathers as rotors. For the great Italian artist Leonardo da Vinci, however, the idea of a helicopter was more than just child's play. In 1500, he sketched a design for a vertical flying machine. Unfortunately, there was no such thing as an

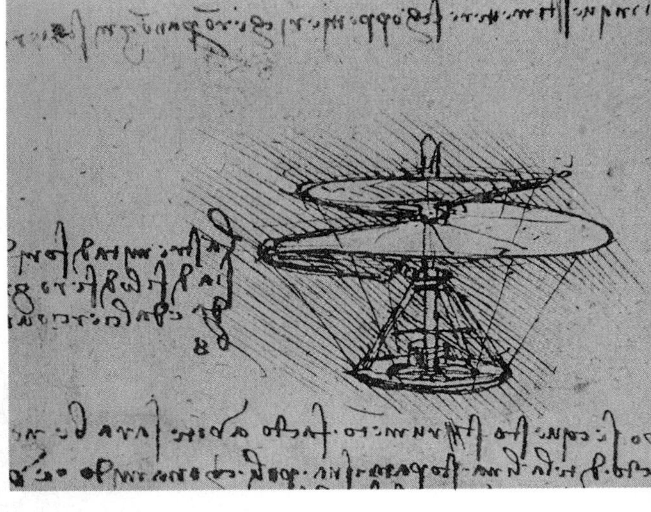

Leonardo da Vinci's *Mona Lisa* and sketch of a helicopter with notes he wrote backwards.

engine in those days, so da Vinci's flying machine never got off the ground. Still, his design was the first to show the principles of helicopter flight. Da Vinci created the design for the first helicopter at about the same time he painted the *Mona Lisa,* perhaps the most famous portrait in the western world.

Like the helicopter, the computer was thought of before the technology was available to power it. The first computer was designed in the 1830s by an English mathematician named Charles Babbage. The principles that Babbage developed for his computer—complete with punched cards, memory, and printouts—formed the basis of computers today. Even so, nobody paid much attention to the computer at the time.

The missing element in Babbage's design was electricity; he had no way to turn on his computer. Without electri-

cal switches and circuits to power it, Babbage's computer was just a big, clumsy machine. Babbage never finished it. Before the computer became the electronic miracle it is today, there were to be many years of electrical inventions: the light bulb, the telephone, radio, and TV.

Computers certainly will continue to change and improve throughout our lifetime. Ultimately, future historians will look back at us and say that computers changed the course of our lives to the same extent that paper making and printing changed everything so many years ago. Computers and communications satellites already link countries and cultures in the wink of an eye. Looking back to the time of great explorers like Marco Polo or Christopher Columbus, we might wonder if they ever imagined it would be so easy to connect the world.

Think About It

1. What is the main idea of this article? Write the sentence or sentences that give you clues.
2. Describe how one of the discoveries in this article made its way to us.
3. How did Marco Polo's book influence Europe?
4. Why are the foods we got from the Native Americans so important to us?
5. What did the early immigrants to the West learn from the original Mexican settlers?
6. Pretend you are an inventor. Describe an invention you would create and tell its uses. Try to convince someone of your invention's importance.

SQRRR

Have you ever spent a lot of time reading something, only to find out afterward that you didn't remember very much of what you read? This is a common problem for all of us, especially for students who must study for tests. **SQRRR**, or SQ3R, is a five-step study plan to help you understand and remember the major points of what you read. The letters SQRRR are the first letters of the five steps in the plan: Survey, Question, Read, Recite, Review.

If you practice the SQRRR method of study, you can learn more and remember it longer, probably in less time than it took you before. Here's how it works.

Step 1: Survey

Before you even begin reading an article or lesson, first look at its title, then glance through it and read all the headings. Headings are printed in special type and divide an article into sections. For example, in the article you just read, the phrase "Made in China" is a heading.

Don't spend too much time on this step. Your survey is meant to give you a general idea, or overview, of an article before you read it. One or two minutes is usually all it takes.

Step 2: Question

After you have surveyed an article or lesson, go back to the first heading and make it a question. The title of the article will help you know what kind of question to make out of the heading. For example, the first heading in "Back at the Beginning" can be turned into "What was first made in China?"

When you turn a heading into a question, you set a goal for your reading. That is, you can read the section to find the answer to the question you asked. You are more likely to find and remember information if you know what you are looking for.

Step 3: Read

After you have set a goal for your reading by turning the first heading into a question, you are ready to read that section. Concentrate on finding the answer to the question as you read. Taking notes on a separate piece of paper during this step also helps you remember what you read. First write down the question made from the heading; then write down the important points of the section in your own words.

Step 4: Recite

When you have finished reading the first section, stop. Then recite to yourself in your own words the answer to the question you made from the first heading. Use your notes to help you remember. This fourth step is very important in the SQRRR study plan. Spend about half your study time on this step.

Repeat the second, third, and fourth steps—Question, Read, Recite—for the rest of the sections.

Step 5: Review

To review an article or lesson, go back over the headings and try to recall the answers to the questions you made. Look over your notes, too. You will remember more of what you read if you review it the very next day. To prepare for a test, read your notes and review a lesson several times.

Now apply the SQRRR method to a selection from one of your textbooks.

LEARN NEW WORDS

1. The boy's constant complaining really **aggravates** me.
2. He went to see what the **commotion** was and found the dog chasing the cat through the row of garbage cans.
3. Rather than argue, we **compromised** and took turns being pitcher.
4. In the movie, the ruthless **gangster** was caught and sent to jail.
5. Every time I charge the net, she **lobs** the tennis ball over my head into the back of the court.
6. He might be late; he's always been **unreliable**.

GET SET TO READ

What kinds of things do people write in their diaries or journals?

Read this selection from Steve's journal to find out how his family makes a decision about whether or not to adopt another child.

EARL

by WALTER DEAN MYERS

Steve Perry, fourteen years old, lives with his parents in New York City. One summer, his parents consider adopting another child about Steve's age named Earl Goins. Thirteen-year-old Earl has been in several foster homes and orphanages.

There is a trial period during which Earl stays with the Perry family. This gives all of them, including Earl, a chance to decide whether to go through with the adoption. The adoption is a big decision for all of them.

During this time, Steve keeps a personal journal in which he records not only his feelings about Earl but some of his parents' feelings, too.

June 11th He came today. I said I was going out to play ball, and Mom asked me didn't I want to be home to greet Earl when he came.

"No," I said.

She gave Dad a look, and he said something about that being quite all right, and I left.

I went out and there wasn't anybody in the park. I found Hi-Note, and he was on his way to the movie so I went along.

"When's that guy supposed to come over to your place?" Hi-Note asked.

"He might be there now," I said. "He's supposed to show sometime today."

"How come you're not home checking him out?"

"I'll see him when I get home," I said. "It's no big thing."

"What are you gonna call him?" Hi-Note asked.

"Earl," I said. "That's his name."

"That's his real name?"

"Yeah, I saw it on his record," I said.

"You saw his records and everything?"

"Yeah, I did."

"What did they say?"

"The same old thing—you know, poor homeless kid, no family, no friends, no place to live," I said.

"Yeah, I get it," Hi-Note said.

When I got home there was a suitcase near the hall closet.

"Hi, Steve, how did your ball game go?" Mom asked. The way she asked, all cheery and bubbly, I figured that the guy must be around somewhere.

"I went to a movie instead," I said.

"Earl is in the room," she said.

The room, yesterday it was *my* room. Today it's *the* room. Okay. I went to check him out.

Gangster. I took one look at the guy and I knew he was a gangster. He was lying out on the bed with a toothpick hanging out of his mouth, looking like he was waiting to get somebody. I swear he looked like a bad dream at high noon.

"Hi," I said, extending my hand. "I'm Steve."

"I figured you were," he said.

He didn't move. He didn't stick out his hand. He didn't turn his head. Nothing.

"This is my room," I said. "I'm glad to share it with you."

"Yeah."

"What school you go to?" I asked, sitting on my bed. The bed my parents had bought for Earl was just like mine.

"I don't go to school."

"What do you do?" I asked. "Take a smart pill along with your friendly pill in the morning?"

Earl rolled out of bed slowly and stood up. I was positive this was the biggest thirteen-year-old in the world. He looked like King Kong with sneakers.

"What's that supposed to mean?" he asked.

"Nothing," I said.

"Look, let me get one thing straight. I didn't ask to come here. This place is no different than any other place I've been in, so don't think you're doing me a favor. If you mess around with me, I'm gonna bust you up no matter who you think you are."

I didn't say anything else. I lay on the bed for a while and tried to read a book.

Earl just stared at the ceiling. I thought of about five cool things to say, but I didn't get any of them out. Then Mom came and said that supper was ready, and we ate.

Earl was polite during supper, but he didn't put himself out to be friendly.

"Perhaps Steve can introduce you to some of his friends tomorrow, Earl," my mother said.

Earl gave a little nod.

"If you play ball you can come with me," I said.

"*If* I play ball?" Earl looked at me as if I'd said something stupid.

That was the last thing he said during supper. My mother was upset—I could tell—but my father looked pleased. After supper Earl went back into the room and closed the door.

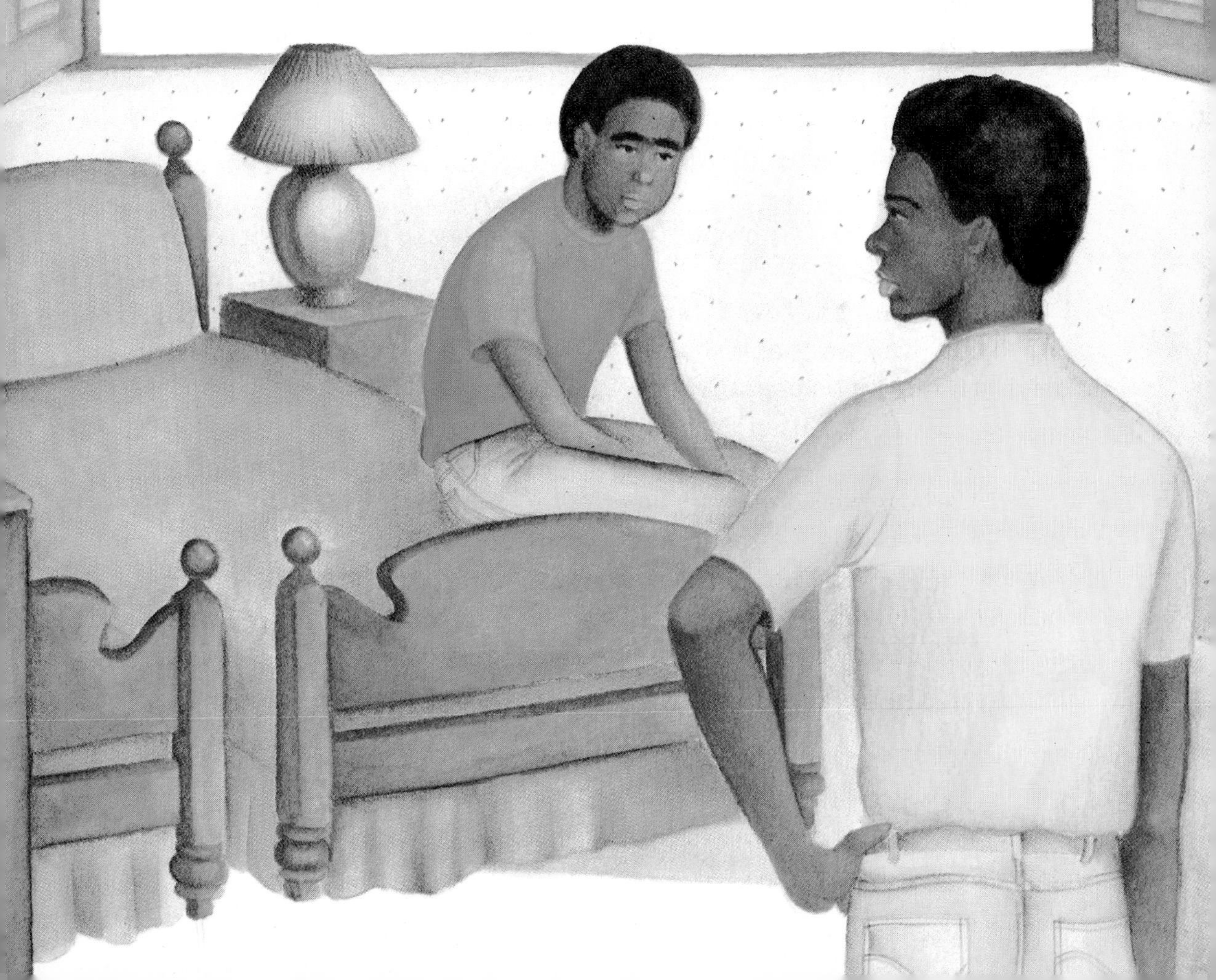

"So he thinks he can play ball," my father said. "Maybe, but at least it's something he's got confidence in."

Later on I watched a little television with my parents, and then I went to bed. Earl waited until I got undressed, and then he got into bed. But he didn't put the light out. I got up and put the light out and he asked me what I was doing.

"Putting the light out," I said.

"I don't sleep with the light out," he said. "I got a lot of enemies."

Then he got up and put the light back on.

"I can't sleep with the light on," I said.

"Why are you so anxious to get the light out?" he said.

"How about putting a lamp on? That way it won't be so bright that I can't sleep, and you can be looking out for your enemies."

That's how we compromised on our first night together. Sleeping with the lamp on so that King Kong could watch out for his enemies.

July 6th So it's Sunday morning and I get up and I'm feeling pretty good. Earl's still sleeping. We were up late last night watching an old movie. We had a pizza, and the pizza box was on the floor. Big night. The room looks like it just went through some kind of shock test.

Then, to top it all off, Earl wakes up and throws his pillow at me. Nothing hard, just kind of lobs it over. I know he's just fooling around. I lob the pillow back and follow it up with my own pillow. Before you know it the pillows are flying back and forth. Wham! Wham! What a commotion!

In comes my father and says that Mom doesn't feel well and isn't going to church. He says we should clean the room up and come and have breakfast, and then we'll go, the three of us, to church.

Only Earl doesn't help with the cleaning. I start gathering things up from the floor, including his stinky sneakers, and he's just lying there.

"You waiting for an invitation to the party?" I ask.

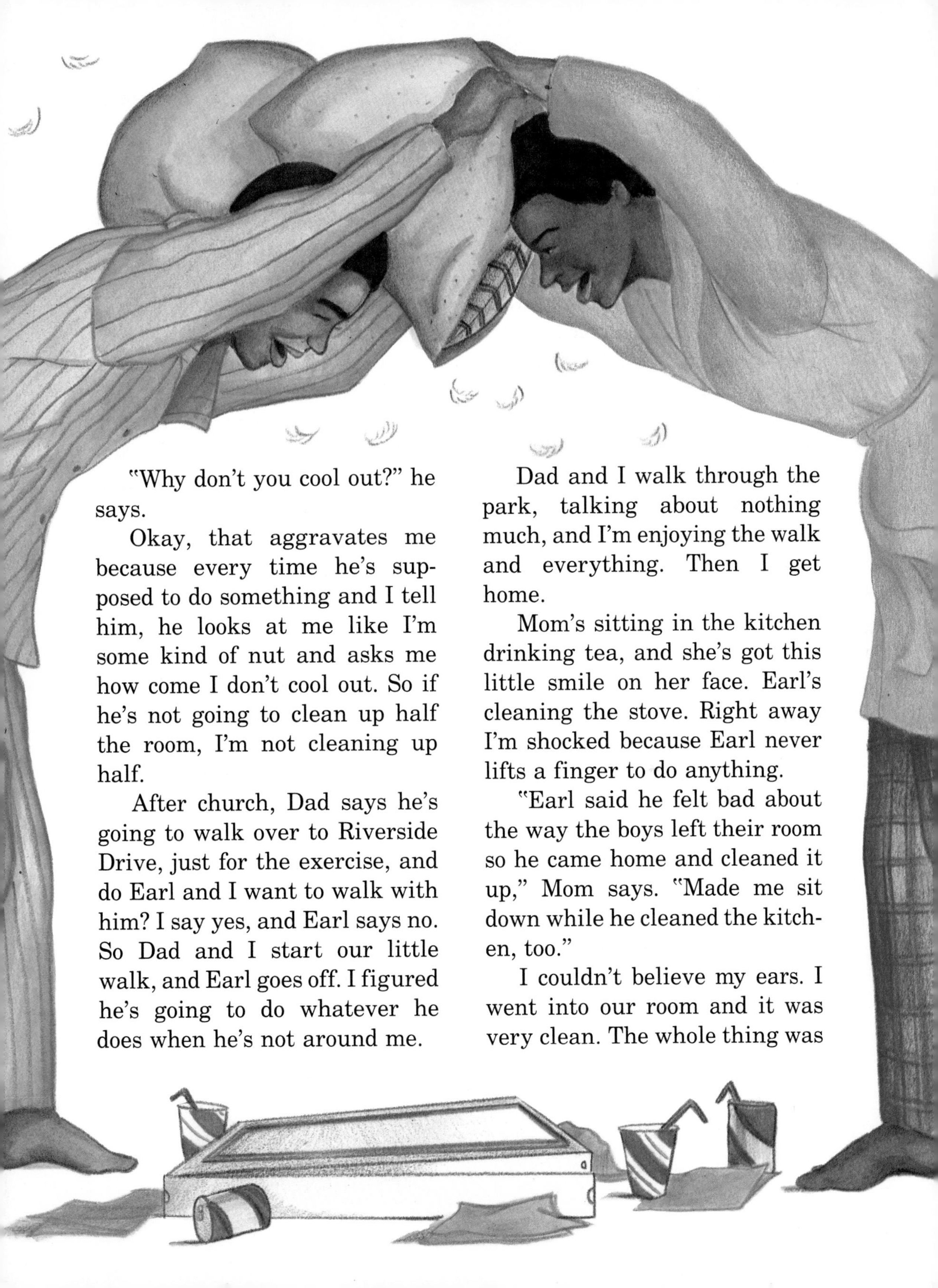

"Why don't you cool out?" he says.

Okay, that aggravates me because every time he's supposed to do something and I tell him, he looks at me like I'm some kind of nut and asks me how come I don't cool out. So if he's not going to clean up half the room, I'm not cleaning up half.

After church, Dad says he's going to walk over to Riverside Drive, just for the exercise, and do Earl and I want to walk with him? I say yes, and Earl says no. So Dad and I start our little walk, and Earl goes off. I figured he's going to do whatever he does when he's not around me.

Dad and I walk through the park, talking about nothing much, and I'm enjoying the walk and everything. Then I get home.

Mom's sitting in the kitchen drinking tea, and she's got this little smile on her face. Earl's cleaning the stove. Right away I'm shocked because Earl never lifts a finger to do anything.

"Earl said he felt bad about the way the boys left their room so he came home and cleaned it up," Mom says. "Made me sit down while he cleaned the kitchen, too."

I couldn't believe my ears. I went into our room and it was very clean. The whole thing was spotless. I go back into the kitchen and Earl's asking Dad if he would like some tea. Dad sits there and says yes. I wanted to throw up!

I was the one that wanted to clean the room in the morning in the first place. And I end up being the one that his lordship had to clean up behind! I was aggravated.

July 8th Sometimes I feel okay about Earl—at other times I want to break his neck. It's so different from what I thought it would be before he came. I imagined this cool little brother type hanging around and asking me questions about how to catch a baseball, that kind of thing. Also, I figured that he'd do just about anything I asked him to. What I got instead was a guy who was all set in the way he was and I was supposed to adjust to him as much as he was supposed to adjust to me. Earl's different from what I thought he would be, but I guess anybody would be. Maybe that's why people mostly adopt babies. You get yourself a baby and you know it's not going to give you a hard time.

July 28th Today is Thursday. Last Friday my father pops into the room and asks if Earl and I would like to do something different for the weekend.

"Like what?" I asked.

"I thought it would be nice to take a camping trip," he said.

A camping trip? My father doesn't even like grass! So now he says he wants to go on a camping trip.

When he asks, I'm supposed to say something good-doing like, "Gee, Dad, that's a great idea!" So I said something like that, and then he asked Earl and Earl said okay. It's supposed to be just the three of us. I don't know what this is supposed to show, but I go along with it. So he has us get up and go downtown with him to buy about one hundred and twenty dollars' worth of gear. Plus, I still had a lot of my stuff from when I was in the Scouts. Okay, so we're supposed to get up early and go to this place in Pennsylvania that he knows about.

July 28th (continued) Early? The moon was still out, and he's shaking us and talking about hop to it and stuff. I look at Earl when Dad goes out of the room and Earl looks at me and we both laugh. Okay, so a-hunting we will go.

We hop into the car and drive for three hours, and we come to a place where there's a man Dad knows. Get this, when we get to this place it's about seven-thirty. Seven-thirty! We leave the man and the car behind, and off we go into the woods. We have a compass and Dad is talking about how it's up to Earl and me to figure out which way we're going so we don't get lost. I figure like this, how lost can you get in Pennsylvania? The worst thing that can happen is that you find the road and have to stop at an emergency stop to ask the police where you are.

Every once in a while we stop and my father points out something that we might have missed, like a huge dead tree

lying right in front of us or something like that. We go on like this, walking through the woods until it's noon and I'm about as tired as I can get. Then I notice that Earl is getting a little up tight. And soon I realize that he really thinks we're going to get lost. He's looking around as if he's nervous. Then it comes to me; Earl couldn't sleep with all the lights off at our house. If we stay overnight in the woods, he might freak out.

Dad's walking about twenty yards or so in front of us, and I run up to him.

"Hey, look," I said, keeping my voice low. "I never told you this, but Earl sleeps with the light on. He really gets upset when it's really dark out. I just wanted to let you know in case you were thinking of spending the night here."

We walked on for a while longer, maybe fifteen minutes, and then Dad stops and says let's break for lunch. So we break out the food that Mom made—sandwiches, fried chicken, and jars of potato salad. I didn't know how long the food was supposed to last, but knowing my mother, I knew she'd pack at least twice as much as we'd need.

After we finished lunch and made sure that we didn't leave any garbage around, Dad turns to us and asks which way were we headed mostly. I look at Earl, and he looks at me.

"I don't know," I said. "Which way do you think?"

"We must have gone a little of every way," Earl said. "I'm not too good on a compass."

So we compromised and start walking due east. We're walking and talking and just being cool, and we're not getting anywhere that looks like anything, see. Then we take another break and eat up the rest of the food.

"We gonna sleep out here?" Earl asks.

"Well. What would you like to do?" my father asks, being cool.

"It doesn't make any difference to me," Earl says.

"Oh."

That from my father. Now he thinks maybe he was wrong, or I was wrong, about Earl being afraid of the dark. So he talks about when he was a kid and he was in the Scouts and whatnot, and meanwhile Earl is eating it up. Now my old man sees this, and he's going on because Earl likes it, and it's like I'm not even there. We finish eating and we start putting up the tents. Now this is cool, and I kind of like it, but my father and Earl are really enjoying the whole thing. We pitch two tents, one for Earl and me and the other for my father. We make a fire. For the rest of the evening we just sit around and talk a little, with my father doing most of the talking.

When it got dark, it really got dark. I have never seen it so dark that the darkness comes right down and gets on you, but that's how it got.

We had trouble keeping the fire going, and before you knew it, the blaze, which wasn't anything to brag about in the first place, had died down.

"Make sure you tie your tent flaps down tight," my father said.

"How come?" I asked.

"In case any animals start nosing around in the dark," he said.

Thanks. I needed that.

I'm not afraid of New York City darkness. New York knows how to get dark. The sun goes down, and you can say, "Hey, it's dark," but New York doesn't get ridiculous about it. Out there in the woods it got ridiculous! You could bring your hand toward your face and not know how close it was until your nose got bumped. I figured Earl must have been glad to be sleeping with me instead of alone.

Also, in New York the noises are cool. Maybe you hear a truck going past or once in a while somebody passes with a loud radio or they're laughing. Those are cool noises. Out in the woods you hear little chirping noises and things screeching. Then sometimes you hear a rustling noise that could be the wind. It could also be some long-haired, red-eyed thing with yellow teeth that runs around eating boys in tents. I was sure Earl was going to get nervous and start a conversation or something.

"Hey, Earl, are you tired?"

"I think I'm tired," he said, "and I want to go to sleep."

"How come you're scared to sleep with the lights out back

home and you don't care out here?"

"I'm not scared of anything," he said. "I just don't want my enemies sneaking up on me."

"They could get you out here," I said reassuringly.

"I'll take a chance. Go to sleep."

Then he went to sleep. I got another thing against Earl. He's unreliable.

My father was the first one up in the morning and he woke us up by banging on the top of the tent. He took the compass and we started due east again. We walked until my knees were beginning to hurt. When we finally got to the car, the man who knew my father said that we had had quite a trip for ourselves. This I knew already.

On the way home we stopped at a restaurant, and my father asked us how we liked the trip.

I said it was okay, but Earl started talking about how he really liked it, and I could see that he meant it, too. My father was glad Earl liked the trip, and they were really talking to each other.

I had a feeling, right then and there, that my father was going to adopt Earl. My mother had said that there was something we wanted to get from Earl, and I hadn't really known what she was getting to, but watching my father there I could see he was getting something from Earl now.

July 30th I had a heart-to-heart with Mom in the supermarket. We were picking up some odds and ends.

"Did your father have a chance to talk to you?"

"About Earl?"

"Yes."

"I guess he had a chance, but he hasn't said anything."

"Adopting a child is so different from what I thought it would be," she said. "I'd still like to share our home with Earl. But once we accept Earl permanently, we accept him as part of our family. Every time he fails or we fail with him, the family fails. I'm not so sure I have the confidence to handle that."

"Dad's not sure, either."

"I think he's almost sure, but it would help if he was positive that it was the right thing for Earl and for you. When you came back from that camping trip, he seemed to want to go through with the adoption very much. But then he did some more thinking. . . . As soon as you stick your head in it as well as your heart, you have a problem," she said as she paused and picked up an avocado.

"Your father said that the two of you got along just fine."

"Yeah, I guess so."

"What do you think? You want us to adopt Earl?"

"I don't know."

She smiled and turned quickly away, pretending to look at the labels of some canned mushrooms. I stepped around her and looked at her face. Our eyes met and we both smiled.

"How come you're smiling?" I asked.

"It's a hard decision," she said. "It makes us people."

"What does that mean?"

"That we're not machines. None of us. We can't just plug in the facts and come out with nice, neat answers. I think"—she looked at me, and the smile was gone from her face almost without her changing expressions—

"that your father will be better off when he realizes that. With people you just hope for the best."

"Just check out your heart and boogie on?"

"Something like that," she said, laughing. "Something like that."

August 13th Mom told me today that they had started the process to adopt Earl. What a relief! Now that the decision is made, it seems so natural and so right I can't even figure out what all the commotion was about. We went out to eat, not because of a celebration or anything like that, but because Mom destroyed our dinner.

She's forever trying out new recipes that she gets from the *Times,* only she sometimes wants to be a little inventive. Well, today she gets a chicken and beats up on it or something until you could hardly tell there are any bones in it. I'm watching her the whole time. Then she puts some water on it, some broth mix, and some onions, and sticks it in the oven. I go to my room to watch some television, and she tells me she'll be right back because she's going to the store to get something to make yellow rice.

I'm watching the TV, and all of a sudden I smell this smoke. At first I don't make too much of it, but then there's a knock on the door, and when I go to see who it is, thinking my mom has forgotten to take her keys, I see the house is full of smoke.

I open the door and it's Earl.

"What you doing, man?" he says, looking in the house over my shoulder.

"Nothing," I say. "Something must be burning."

It didn't take us long to figure it was coming from the oven. I ran over and turned the oven off. We opened the door and the chicken was black.

"Now what?" Earl asked.

"I don't know. What do you think?"

"If it's not a friend of yours, I think we should leave it," he said.

So we went into the room and I told him what my mother had done to the chicken. Then my mom came home, and I could hear her running to the oven. There was some scurrying around, and then she came to our room and asked what had happened.

"The stove started smoking and we cut it off," I said.

She looked real pitiful, and we all went out to the kitchen. The chicken was on the counter, one leg pointed up and one leg pointed kind of sideways. Most of it was black, but you could see that the inside wasn't even cooked.

"You beat it up like that?" Earl asked.

My mother nodded.

"You beat it up and then you burned it." Earl had this silly look on his face.

Mom began to laugh a little, and then we were all laughing.

That evening we went out to dinner at this Korean place. By this time Mom was pretty much okay. We got on her a little bit more about the chicken; then my father started talking about baseball. I knew that he didn't like to kid my mother too long, even if we were just fooling around. So I switched off and Earl did, too, which was good because it meant he knew what was going on.

The supper went fairly smoothly, except for my father, who insisted that he could eat with chopsticks even though most of the food fell back on the plate. Then, just as we were about to finish the meal, Dad dropped the bombshell.

"Earl, have you given any thought to what name you want to use?" he asked.

"What name?" Earl looked up at him. "You don't like Earl?"

"Earl's just fine," Dad said, "but how about a last name? You'll have to make a decision soon. You can continue to use Goins if you want, or you can switch to Perry."

"Or you can use both names, Earl Goins Perry." Mom smiled.

Earl didn't say anything. He put his head down a little and his jaw moved as if he was trying to chew. Then he swallowed hard.

"Is everything okay?" Mom asked.

It was, only Earl was so choked up he couldn't say anything. He just sat there and looked down at his plate.

"You do want to be adopted, Earl?" my father asked.

Earl nodded. Even though the way Earl was feeling was good, it bothered me.

Sometimes you can take something that seems so simple, like Dad making Earl feel good by telling him that we, or at least my parents, were going to adopt him, and it ends up not being simple at all.

August 15th Dad came in the bathroom while I was brushing my teeth and said something about how tall I was getting. Then he asked me if I wanted to hear something silly, so I said okay.

"I love you," he said.

Just like that. He just laid it out. I asked him how come he said that, 'cause he never says things like that.

"Just wanted to say it," he said. "Guess I've been thinking a lot about it."

You know I didn't know what to say? I just stood there looking at him, and he was there looking at me and looking like me, too, for a long minute. Then he gave me this quick little hug and left. I'm glad Mom didn't come in; she'd have cried or something.

Think About It

1. What were Steve's feelings about Earl when he met him?
2. Why do you think Earl acted the way he did when he first came to stay with the Perrys?
3. What does Earl's behavior toward Mr. and Mrs. Perry show about him?
4. What are some signs that a closer relationship is developing between Earl and the members of the Perry family?
5. Why do you think Earl and the Perrys decided to go through with the adoption?
6. Why do you think Steve's father told him "I love you" after the family decided to adopt Earl?
7. Write about why you think this story is written as a journal.

LEARN NEW WORDS

1. The woman was **bilingual**; she understood both English and Spanish.
2. We could tell from his confused look that he was not **comprehending** what we were saying.
3. We knew what the **consequences** of our decision would be, but we went ahead with it anyway.
4. To be a good homemaker, it is important to know how to do **domestic** chores.
5. Her brother was a perfect example of weakness, but she had always been the **embodiment** of strength.
6. She was **impulsive**, often saying things she later regretted.
7. He showed great **ingenuity** in the way he used parts from one machine to repair another.
8. The company my family started is small, but it has great **potential** for growth.
9. The **stability** of the airplane was affected by the strong winds.

GET SET TO READ

What makes people change their minds? Under what circumstances is it a good idea to change your mind?

Read this story to find out whether Magdalena's grandmother will change her mind about something that's very important to Magdalena.

Magdalena

by LOUISA R. SHOTWELL

Magdalena had tried and tried to convince her grandmother, Nani, to let her cut her long braids, which she felt were old-fashioned. But Nani, who takes care of Magdalena while her father is away at sea, refused. Nani wants her granddaughter to wear braids, as she had when she was a girl in Puerto Rico many years before.

Meanwhile, Magdalena befriended Daisy (known as Spook), a neglected, bright girl who was known for causing trouble at school. Spook introduced her to Miss Lilley, a kind but unusual old woman. Miss Lilley liked Magdalena and helped her by arranging to get her hair cut. This upset Nani greatly, and she blamed Miss Lilley for what happened. Now, some time later, Miss Lilley is coming to pay a visit to Nani, as she says, "to open her eyes to today's world."

Miss Lilley leaned more and more heavily on Magdalena with every step, and on the third floor landing she crumpled and slid to her knees.

"Are you all right, Miss Lilley? It's only one more flight."

"I am resting. A cautionary measure. No cause for alarm."

At that instant Magdalena was surprised to see Spook come pounding down the stairs from above. She avoided crashing into Miss Lilley and was brought to a sudden halt by Magdalena.

"Oh, Spook, I'm so glad it's you! Were you looking for me?"

"Not 'specially. What's the matter?"

"It's Miss Lilley." Magdalena lowered her voice. "She's determined to see Nani. I couldn't stop her. She has her mind made up to talk to Nani, and whatever

Nani will say I can't imagine. It's going to be awful. You will help me, won't you?"

"I don't see it's so awful." Spook dropped cross-legged to the floor beside the slumped figure and said companionably, "Hi, Miss Lilley. How are you? It's me, Daisy."

Miss Lilley welcomed Spook as if her arrival were perfectly natural, a most happy event, and quite to be expected. What Spook was doing there Magdalena had no time to wonder, nor did it matter. Together the girls eased Miss Lilley to her feet and the trio made it to the fourth floor. By the time Nani responded to their knock, Miss Lilley was thoroughly in command of herself and the situation.

She greeted Nani. "Señora Mendez? I am Esmeralda Lilley. The children will vouch for me. I hope this is not a bother. It may have been inconsiderate of me to come without warning. I have always been impulsive. I believe in direct action, though I confess it has at times been my undoing, and I've had to pay the consequences. What a charming room! May we sit?"

It was a difficult speech to interpret, and Magdalena did not try. Instead, she offered her own explanation in rapid Spanish.

"This is Miss Lilley, Nani. Now don't be angry. It's true she showed us the way to Peter John the barber but it was not her fault that I went. I wanted to. She bought us three oranges with her last forty-five cents, and she heats up soup on her radiator. She's tired from climbing our stairs. Please let her sit down. She wants to talk to you."

Nani gave no indication that she had heard a word. She stood in silent dignity, taking in her unlikely visitor from head to toe, all the way from her amazing hat to the shiny buckles on her shoes.

Unexpectedly, Spook put in a word of her own. "Miss Lilley is my friend."

Nani stirred. She glanced at Spook. When at last she spoke, it was in her usual Spanish. She made a sweeping gesture and said, *"Mi casa es su casa."*

Miss Lilley went to the center of the room and perched daintily on the wooden rocker.

Nani faced her from a straight chair at the kitchen table. The two girls sat side by side on the other side of the kitchen table.

Miss Lilley gave a slight cough. "Forgive me for addressing you in English. I am not skilled in your language, though I grasp it, a bit here, a bit there, if the words are distinct. You, I feel sure, do likewise, or better, in comprehending English. It is not so?"

"I am not a dunce," said Nani, clinging to her Spanish.

"Assuredly not."

The strange bilingual dialogue proceeded.

From the wall behind Nani, the portrait of Great-grandfather Mendez looked down upon the guest. To Magdalena, his eyes seemed to gleam at the unusual visitor.

Miss Lilley inclined her head in his direction and said, "Good

evening to you, Sir." This would have sounded very odd coming from somebody else, but Miss Lilley was not somebody else; she was herself, and it seemed entirely natural for her to greet Great-grandfather Mendez as if he were alive. To Nani she said, "Ancestors' portraits give tone to a household, I always say. Warmth. Stability. A link with the past. He is a relative, I suppose?"

"My father," Nani told her. "A man of consequence. A teacher. A man of letters. A leader in politics."

"Indeed! I detect excellent qualities in the face. Lively wit, gentleness, and energy. An admirable combination. You understand me?"

"Enough," said Nani.

Miss Lilley slid back in her chair and rocked delightedly.

Now it was Nani's turn to cough. "I understood you desired to talk to me," she said. "I await your pleasure."

"So I did, so I did . . . The present! That's it. Today's world. Now I remember. I came to bring enlightenment of today's world." She looked doubtfully at Nani. "You will not take offense at what I say?"

"How can I tell till you say it?"

"Touché!" Miss Lilley clapped her hands three times. "I had not anticipated meeting my match in a battle of wits. The fact is"—she squirmed in her chair—"to go bluntly to the heart of the matter, I came to open your eyes."

"In that case your journey is wasted. I have excellent eyesight."

"There are none so blind as those who will not see."

Nani seemed to be comprehending the bilingual conversation almost too well. She laid the palms of her hands flat on the table. She was irritated. "Do me the honor to state precisely why you are here."

Miss Lilley made a sucking sound with her tongue. "Tst, tst, now I have offended you. And I tried so hard to be tactful. Let me put it another way. My imagination has been captured by your granddaughter's potential for elegance."

"Potential for elegance? So that is the lure you used to lead astray my motherless Magdalena. Shame upon you!"

"Nani! It was my own fault, my very own. I hated my braids. You knew I did. I told you and told you. I wanted to be rid of them," Magdalena shouted.

Nani struck the table with her fist. She ignored Magdalena's outburst and continued accusing Miss Lilley. "What am I to believe? I recognize bewitchment when I see it, whatever form it takes. With you, it is especially wicked." She stretched out her arm and pointed a threatening finger at Miss Lilley. "You are the embodiment of the American influence!"

"No, no, no! It is not possible!" The hands in the black lace gloves flew up and fluttered, as if trying to push Nani away. "I could not be what you say." Miss Lilley looked suddenly old and shrunken.

Shriveled like the shell of a walnut, Magdalena thought.

"You are so mistaken. So frighteningly mistaken. I am not the embodiment of anything, above all not of the American influence. Why, I was educated in Switzerland!" Her back arched forward till her forehead touched her knees, and in this position she finished what she had to say. "All I am is Esmeralda Lilley, who is . . . impulsive . . . and rash . . . and so very . . . hungry." She slipped to the floor and lay still, like death.

Nani's first command was, "A blanket, Magdalena. Two blankets. Hurry!" Her second command was to turn up the gas under the teakettle and to brew the tea of sour orange, proper remedy for a fainting fit.

Spook had cleared the distance from the table in a single bound, flung an arm across the still figure, and there she crouched and stayed.

Spook spoke once, to Nani. "She's not wicked you know. Really she's not."

Nani, who was holding Miss Lilley's head and trying to make her swallow the sour-orange tea, said nothing.

Spook went on. "She's alone, that's all. She told me once. No relatives. Nobody."

They watched. They waited.

Miss Lilley made small murmurs and turned her head from side to side, but she did not open her eyes. She said no words that could be understood.

They waited some more.

"Will she die?" asked Spook.

After a minute, Nani answered, but doubtfully. "My *Pot-of-Gold Dream Book* has a proverb: 'It is part of the cure to wish to be cured.' I have done what I know to do—the blankets, the tea of sour orange. But to persuade her to wish to be cured, that I cannot do."

The cuckoo came out of its clock door. Seven times it struck.

When Nani spoke again it was with decision. "Magdalena, find Mrs. Candelario. Tell her it is time for the hospital, and why. Ask her to telephone for the ambulance. Quick, Magdalena, run, run!"

•

"I suggest you come, too, lady," said the young ambulance driver. "She shouldn't ride off to the hospital alone, not without somebody from the family."

"I'll go," said Spook.

"The hospital likes it to be a grownup," said the young man. "They need somebody to give information, answer questions, and reassure the patient."

"There's a card in her bag with her name on it," said Magdalena, "and her address and everything." She was about to go on and tell the driver that Miss Lilley had no family at all, when Nani cut in.

"I go, *naturalmente.* You think I have a heart of stone? Magdalena, find my coat."

Miss Lilley did not die. Five days in the hospital, five days at home with nursing visits from Nani, who took time off from the factory during the emergency, and the patient was a patient no longer. She was well. In Miss Lilley's own words, which Nani reported to Magdalena with a laugh, she was "fit as a fiddle." Plainly, the two ladies had come to be, in ten days' time, on excellent terms with each other.

"She is coming for dinner with us Saturday evening," said Nani. "A small *fiesta* to celebrate her recovery. Invite your friend *La Spook* to come also and make the party complete."

It was then that Magdalena remembered to ask Nani if Spook could keep Magdalena's blue-and-white polka-dot dress that she had loaned her. "May she keep it, Nani? She can wear it when she comes to dinner."

"But of course! I told her long ago the dress was hers."

"You already told her! When?"

"The day she came to see me."

"Spook came to see you? Without me?" Magdalena was thunder-struck, and more than slightly hurt. "She didn't tell me. When did she come? Why did she come? Where was I?"

"When was it? I must think. Yes, yes, now I recall. That is why I never mentioned it. The collapse of Miss Lilley drove it from my mind. It was that very day. We had a long visit."

So that was why Spook had appeared on the stairs like a rescuing angel, Magdalena thought to herself.

"I like that child," said Nani. "She has problems at school and at home. She has one very big problem with herself. She believes she cannot help being—what is the word she employs?—a stinker! I told her it is not necessary she be a stinker; it is necessary only that she be herself. This I made her repeat after me, three times. She needs to realize that she can be herself without being a stinker. It is a thing not easy to comprehend, but she is intelligent, that one. I think she begins to see."

"I hope so. Nani, why is it you understand Spook so extremely well but you don't understand me at all?"

"Magdalena! What do you mean? That is ridiculous! I understand you *perfectamente.* I love you!"

"I know you love me, Nani, but understanding is something different. You don't understand that I have to be myself, the same as Spook. You've never even tried to understand me—how I felt about my braids, for instance."

Never since she found out had Nani referred to the episode of the braids. During all those weeks any direct mention of her hair by Magdalena was turned aside or ignored by Nani. Now it was as if Magdalena were forcing Nani to listen to her.

Magdalena was feeling quite sorry for herself. Her words boiled up from inside. "You wouldn't believe I hated my braids. You thought it was like the chicken pox and I'd get over it. You thought I cut them off to hurt you, but I didn't, I didn't. You thought I didn't want to be Puerto Rican any longer, but that was not it at all. It was true what I said about feeling shame when the boys called me 'Miss Two Ropes,' but that wasn't the whole trouble. The rest of it was—and I tried to tell you this too—I wanted to look like other people in my class, not proper and quaint as if I'd stepped out of an old picture book. I still don't know if what I did was right or wrong. All I know is I had to do it, and the boys stopped calling me the foolish name, and I do feel more modern without any braids. But my hair grows and grows and it doesn't look elegant any more the way it did when Peter John first cut it. I know I need a second haircut, and I've been saving from my lunch money, but not very much. Peter John does not cut hair for peanuts. Barbers are expensive, and besides, what will you say when I come home with a second haircut? Oh, I'm so miserable, I don't know what to do!"

It was all true, and having announced that she was miserable, Magdalena suddenly felt better.

Nani seemed stunned, too stunned to speak, for a minute. What she finally said was no great help. "All I ever want,

Magdalena, is for you to be perfect. That is all. But who knows what is perfect? Ah, *quién sabe*?"

Exactly as planned, on Saturday evening in the Mendez kitchen Miss Lilley sat down to dinner. Mr. Candelario, at Nani's request, had brought her in his taxicab, accepting no money ("A free ride, it is my pleasure!"). Once inside the building Miss Lilley had taken the stairs slowly but definitely, one step at a time.

At the table set for four, Nani and Magdalena faced each other, and between them, on Nani's left, sat Spook, sparkling from a recent bath in the Mendez tub and wearing the blue-and-white polka-dot dress. The place of honor on Nani's right was occupied by Esmeralda Lilley herself, erect, rested, eager, and entirely at ease.

Nani eyed Miss Lilley's fork, which was poised above a Puerto Rican dish prepared by Nani expressly for this occasion.

Miss Lilley's first taste was hesitant. Her hummingbird tongue darted out and licked her lips.

"Delicious!" she said, and took a second and bigger forkful. "Is it permitted to ask what I am eating?"

"Codfish boiled with green bananas," Nani told her. "A specialty of this house."

"Codfish!" Miss Lilley ate some more. "How is it possible for codfish to become so tasty? Is it written somewhere in a book, the recipe? An invention of yours? A secret, perhaps?"

"No secret, but I always find it difficult to tell what I do with my codfish. The green bananas must be of a good variety. Of course the codfish must be soaked, cut in small pieces, the bones removed, and during the cooking the cook must taste, taste, all the time taste, and add the herbs. Each time is a little different. Always I put in the olives and a bit of lemon. It calls for skill, for judgment, for ingenuity. The cook must enjoy cooking and enjoy also eating. You will have more?"

"I enjoy eating," said Miss Lilley, passing her empty plate,

"but I do not enjoy cooking. I have no domestic instinct of any sort. Now you, you are quite different. You are a genuine homemaker. It is unbelievable what you have been able to do with the room where I live. A touch here, a touch there, and you transformed it from a hovel into a place it is a joy to come home to. How I envy you that gift!"

"No two of us are alike," said Nani, looking pleased. Then she added earnestly, "Domestic skill is not entirely instinct. Much of it is energy, a willingness to scrub and dust, the ingenuity to find places for things, and the pains to keep them put away. Anyone with a will can do it."

"Not I," said Miss Lilley. "It is too late. I am too old."

"My *Pot-of-Gold Dream Book* says not." Nani was emphatic.

"What exactly does your book say of scrubbing and dusting and keeping things in order? This I should be glad to hear."

Nani replied, "It says: 'It is always in season for the old ones to learn.' That reminds me. Magdalena, on Monday morning remember to ask me for the money."

Magdalena was mystified. "The money? What money, Nani? What for?"

"I may forget," said Nani. "Already it has waited too long."

"Nani, what are you talking about? What money?"

"Your hair," said Nani, "*naturalmente*! The money for Peter John the barber to cut your hair. What else?"

Think About It

1. Why didn't Nani and Miss Lilley get along when they first met?
2. Why do you think Miss Lilley fell to the floor while she was visiting Nani? Give some facts from the story to support your answer.
3. What do you think caused Nani to change her mind about Miss Lilley?
4. How can you explain the friendship that developed between Nani and Miss Lilley?
5. Why did Nani change her mind about Magdalena's haircut?
6. Make a list of things you think are old-fashioned. Choose one item and write why you think it belongs or does not belong in today's world.

LEARN NEW WORDS

1. I will **accompany** you on your walk so you won't be alone.
2. The person in **authority** ruled over several villages.
3. Don't **betray** my trust in you by telling my secret.
4. This is a **confidential** matter; it should be kept private.
5. When they started arguing, she stepped in to end the **dispute**.
6. My father is a science teacher, so in my family we place great **emphasis** on math and science.
7. As she sang a song of deep **lament** at the funeral of her friend, her voice projected throughout the room.
8. He continued **mocking** and teasing them even though he knew it was cruel.
9. The **mourners** at the funeral wept openly.

GET SET TO READ

Laughter is usually considered a good thing. When might laughter get you into trouble?

Read this play to find out how laughter causes trouble for a man who loves to laugh.

The Man Who Loved to Laugh

based on a Sudanese folktale
retold by CAROL KORTY

Characters

NARRATOR
MAN
WOMAN
BULLY SNAKE
LITTLE SNAKE
ANT VOICE 1
ANT VOICE 2
DOG
MOSQUITO VOICE
RAT
THE CHIEF
VILLAGERS

Time: any time
Setting: a Nuer village in the southern Sudan

Prop List (These things can be real or mimed.)

Hand Props	*Stage Props*
yellow feather	stool
work tools	sleeping mat
bowl and spoon	shutters
food	door
broom	grain barrel

NARRATOR: Hello! We'd like to tell you a story. It is a story about a man who loved to laugh.

(MAN *enters laughing with a little walk-about, gives greeting, and exits.* NARRATOR *or musicians can accompany all such walks with a drumbeat.)*

There is his wife,

(WOMAN *also enters with a little walk-about, gives greeting, and exits.)*

and some snakes,

(SNAKES *leap on, fighting, and hiss off.)*

some ants that you can hear,

(ANT VOICES *chatter off stage.)*

but they're too small to see; a dog,

(DOG *runs on and off again, wagging eagerly.)*

a rat,

(RAT *darts on, sees audience, and darts off.)*

and a mosquito. There he is now.

(MOSQUITO VOICE *buzzes from offstage while* NARRATOR *watches the imaginary flight.* NARRATOR *sees mosquito land and swats.* MOSQUITO VOICE *registers the slap and buzzes away limply.)*

Missed him!

(THE CHIEF *and* VILLAGERS *enter.)*

Oh, yes, and a chief and villagers.

(CHIEF *and* VILLAGERS *greet audience and exit.)*

Let's start at the beginning with the man who liked to laugh.

(MAN *re-enters, laughing heartily, and does his walk-about or little dance. He is easygoing.)*

Yes, he loved life, and he loved to laugh because he was very happy with the world and with the people in it.

(WOMAN *enters and approaches* MAN. *She is sweet.)*

He was happy with his wife, and she was pleased with him.

WOMAN: Why are you laughing?

MAN: I am laughing because the sun is shining, because you're pretty to look at, and because I love you.

NARRATOR: She was very pleased, and she said:

WOMAN: That is very nice!

*(*MAN *and* WOMAN *do a walk-about together.)*

MAN *(stopping their walk)*: It is time for me to go to work in the field.

(They do a turn-about, WOMAN *exits, and* MAN *starts his walk in the field.)*

NARRATOR: When he came to the field, he found two snakes fighting there.

*(*BULLY SNAKE *and* LITTLE SNAKE *leap on and fight in dance form. The small one is getting badly beaten.)*

MAN *(running between* SNAKES): Stop! Stop! Stop! I don't know how this started, but it had better stop fast, for this little snake will be killed. *(He separates them and chases the large one.)* Get out of here, you bully!

*(*BULLY SNAKE *exits.* MAN *continues his walk.)*

LITTLE SNAKE *(in wheezy, magic voice)*: Wait! I want to thank you.

MAN *(turns with great surprise and laughs)*: I just thought I heard a snake say, "Thank you!"

LITTLE SNAKE: Yes, I want to thank you, young man . . .

MAN: What?

LITTLE SNAKE: . . . and to give you a present. Come here.

MAN: Well, I'm glad I could help you. *(Stops and laughs.)* But I'm absolutely amazed that I can hear you talking to me, and that I can understand you.

LITTLE SNAKE: You were kind to me. I want to give you a magic yellow feather. *(Presents him with large yellow feather.)* With this charm you will always be able to understand what animals say.

MAN: What a wonderful idea! This is a really beautiful charm. Thank you very much.

LITTLE SNAKE: I'm happy that you like it. But here is a warning! You must not tell anyone I have given you the feather, and you must not tell anyone about the new power it gives you. Promise not to tell.

MAN *(good-naturedly)*: All right, if you wish. I promise not to tell anyone.

LITTLE SNAKE: It is important. Because, if you betray the promise, you will die.

MAN *(startled)*: Oh, thank you for the warning. I'll be very careful. I certainly don't want to die. *(Considers.)* I don't want to die. No, I don't want to die because I love being alive, and I would miss life.

*(*MAN *spins about with feather, while* LITTLE SNAKE *does its snake-about.)*

NARRATOR: Then the snake said:

LITTLE SNAKE: Good-by, friend. *(Crosses paths with* MAN.*)*

NARRATOR: And the man said:

MAN: Good-by, friend. *(Moves around* SNAKE.*)*

NARRATOR: And they each went their separate ways.

(They complete the walk-about together, and LITTLE SNAKE *exits.)*

MAN: What a happy present! *(Laughs.)* I am just amazed. A snake has just spoken to me and given me a magic yellow feather! *(He puts feather in his pocket.)*

ANT 1 *(offstage voice)*: Watch out, for goodness sake!

ANT 2 *(offstage voice)*: A monster!

MAN: Where's that? *(Looks about anxiously.)*

ANT 1: Quick, hurry.

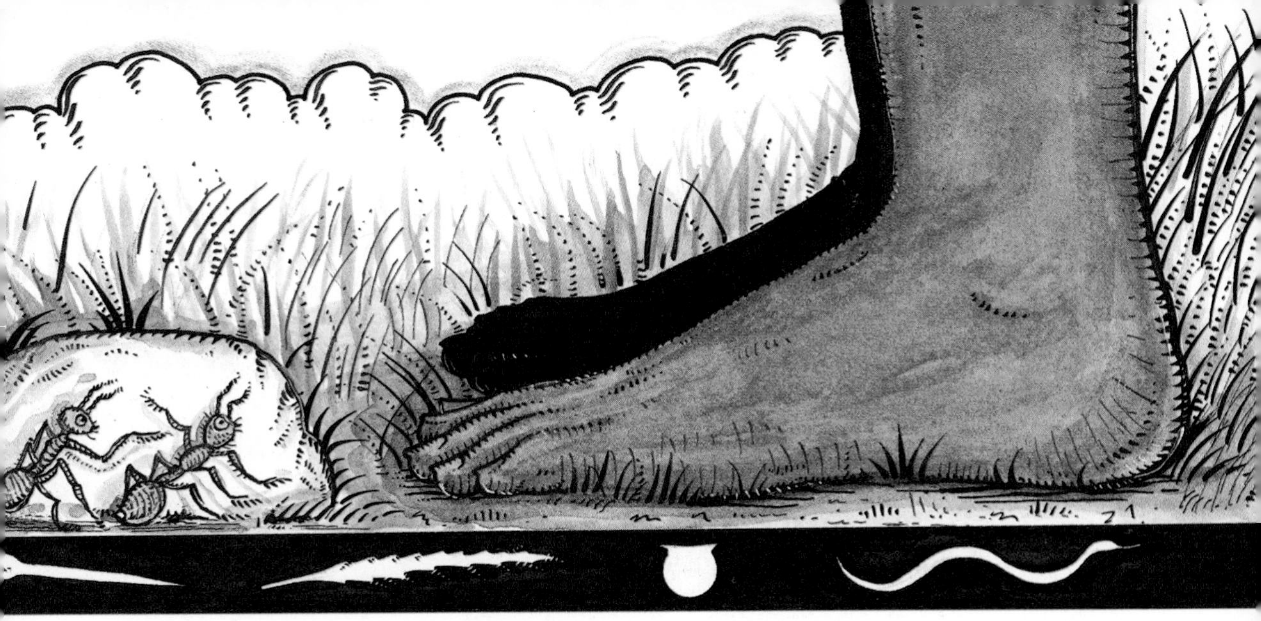

ANT 2: I'm running as fast as I can.
ANT 1: Over this way. Quick.
ANT 2: Oh, no! There's another part of him.
MAN: What's happening? Who's talking? Where's the monster? *(He moves his feet, and* ANTS *exclaim loudly.)*
ANT 1: Stop running, and hide.
ANT 2: Hide? Hide? Where?
ANT 1: Under this rock. Quick.
MAN: Rock? There's no rock here. *(Looking at the ground.)* The ground is absolutely flat.
ANT 1: Whew . . . It's good the rock was here. Grass is no good at a time like this.
MAN *(looking at grass)*: There's no monster here either.
ANT 2: Keep still now and watch for him to leave.
MAN *(looking down at a spot near his feet)*: Ants! *(Laughs.)* Ants! There they are, hiding under a pebble. *(Laughs.)* And I am the monster. How strange people must look to them. *(Laughs.)* I've heard ants talking!
NARRATOR: Then he did his work in the field.
*(*MAN *begins his work. His work can be acted out with real stage props, such as a hoe or a shovel, or*

pantomimed with imaginary objects. It can also be done as a dance, accompanied by a drumbeat.)

And when it was finished, the man went home to his wife and to his dinner.

*(*MAN *exits or circles while* WOMAN *and* DOG *enter to establish the house.)*

NARRATOR: When he came to his house, his dog ran out to greet him.

*(*DOG *barks and runs wagging up to him.)*

MAN *(patting* DOG*)*: I am hungry, hungry, hungry!

WOMAN: Good. I've made a special dinner for you.

NARRATOR: So he sat down to eat it.

*(*MAN *and* WOMAN *sit down and begin to eat.)*

DOG: Don't be so greedy. *(*MAN *is startled.)* If he eats so fast, there'll be nothing left for me. He looks like an old goat.

*(*MAN *finally realizes that it is the* DOG *speaking. He laughs and chokes.)*

WOMAN: Goodness, what's the matter?

MAN *(starts to tell her and stops, remembering that he must not)*: Nothing . . .

WOMAN: You choked on the food . . . *(*MAN *hands* DOG *some meat from his bowl)* and now you feed it to the dog. Isn't it good? I tried to cook it just right.

MAN: No, no. The food is delicious, my love. I choked because I was laughing.

WOMAN *(reassured)*: What made you laugh?

MAN *(again starts to tell, then remembers)*: Nothing.

DOG: I take it back. He doesn't look as much like an old goat as I thought.

*(*MAN *laughs again.)*

WOMAN: There you go again. What is it?

MAN: Ah . . . I thought of something funny.

WOMAN: What was that?

MAN: I can't say, really.

WOMAN *(helpless and perplexed)*: Can't say? You mean you won't say! I think you're making fun of me.

MAN: No, I'm not making fun of you. *(Goes to soothe her.)* Don't worry. It's not important. Let's not talk about it. It's time to sleep.

WOMAN *(calmed and loving)*: Please fasten up the door and shutters. I want to close the grain barrel and put this food away. *(*WOMAN *does these tasks. The activities can be mimed or done with real objects.)*

MAN: All right. *(To* DOG.*)* Out you go, friend. You've had enough to eat. It's time to sleep.

(He shoos DOG *outside and closes the door and shutters.* DOG *curls up outside door.* WOMAN *prepares bed or sleeping mat, and they lie down. The activity should be carefully timed so actors finish together.)*

NARRATOR: It grew quiet in the house until:

MOSQUITO *(offstage voice)*: Bzzzzzzzzzz.

DOG *(snapping at* MOSQUITO*)*: Leave me alone. Can't you see I'm trying to sleep? It's much too dark to be out flying around.

MOSQUITO *(buzzing)*: Don't worry. I'm not after you. I want to get inside to take a good mosquito bite from that woman's arm.

*(*MAN, *who has been overhearing the conversation, bursts out laughing.)*

WOMAN *(stirring)*: Laughing again!

DOG: The place is shut up tight. You can't get in now. You'll have to wait till the morning.

MOSQUITO: No, in the daytime she swats at me. I have to get her while she's sleeping.

DOG: I'm in no mood to argue. You'll never get in there with those shutters closed. Now get out of my ear. I want to sleep.

*(*MAN *laughs again.)*

WOMAN: What is making you laugh? Everything's quiet except for a few insects buzzing outside. *(Drops off to sleep.)*

*(*MAN *gets up, goes to window, and opens shutters.)*

MOSQUITO: Oh, here's my chance. See you later, Dog. Bzzzzzzzzzz.

*(*MAN *watches the* MOSQUITO *enter and slaps his hands together to catch it.* MOSQUITO'S *stunned buzz lets us know he's received the blow. He buzzes away weakly.* MAN *looks at* DOG, *laughs, and closes shutters.)*

WOMAN *(wakening at the slap and laughter)*: What are you doing, and what is so funny?

MAN: Nothing, really. Ah . . . some thought just struck me funny.

WOMAN: You said before that some thought struck you funny, but you won't say what you're thinking. I'm sure now that you're making fun of me.

MAN: Really I'm not. Please don't be angry. Why would I want to make fun of you? Don't think about it any more. *(He pats her reassuringly and lies down again.)*

NARRATOR: The man really didn't want to laugh again, so he tried very hard not to think about the things he'd heard. Then he finally went to sleep. And his wife went to sleep. And the dog went to sleep. *(*MAN, WOMAN, *and* DOG snore in turn.) It grew quiet again . . .

*(*RAT *comes running on right in front of* DOG, *sees* DOG *sleeping, turns on heel, and exits. Reappears, pretending to be very casual.)*

RAT: Good evening.

DOG: *(waking with a start)*: Evening. Looking for something?

RAT: Just out for a walk.

DOG: Good. Keep right on walking. No rats allowed. I'm on guard.
RAT *(tries new approach of being confidential)*: Actually, I'm out looking for a little grain. Do you have any?
DOG: Yes.
RAT: Where?
DOG: Inside.
RAT: Can I have a handful?
DOG: No!
RAT: Please. Just a handful. Look how small my hand is.
DOG: The people are sleeping inside. Can't wake them up. Come back tomorrow!
*(*RAT *starts to protest.)*
DOG: Come back tomorrow.
RAT *(starts to exit and spins around with a new scheme)*: How do I know you won't eat it before tomorrow?
DOG: Oh, me . . .
RAT: But I could come back tomorrow, and you'd say there was no grain left.
DOG: For goodness sake! I never touch the stuff.
RAT: Oh, then you won't mind if I take a little.
DOG: Oh, get out of my hair! Go on; take a little.
*(*MAN *has been listening. He gets up and is on hands and knees ready to meet* RAT. RAT *leaps up to run to the door.)*
DOG: Don't use the door. Use the hole in the wall and be quiet!

*(*RAT *runs in through hole and stops dead still when he sees* MAN *looking at him nose to nose. He spins around and runs out.* MAN *goes and gets the broom.)*

RAT *(to* DOG*)*: There's a man in there!

DOG: There's a man in there. Of course there's a man in there! Didn't I tell you he's sleeping and not to wake him up?

RAT: Sleeping?

DOG: Yes! Go on and be quiet.

*(*RAT *crawls back in.* MAN *is holding broom over his head, ready to hit the* RAT. RAT *stops short at* MAN'S *feet, slowly looks up his legs until he sees the* MAN'S *face, slowly looks down again, turns, and starts to sneak away.* MAN *bangs down the broom. A drumbeat can give additional emphasis here.* RAT *makes a lightning-fast exit past* DOG, *who looks up with surprise.* MAN *laughs heartily.)*

WOMAN *(wakening with crash of broom)*: What's going on?

*(*MAN *continues laughing.)*

WOMAN: What are you doing with a broom in the middle of the night?

MAN *(thinking quickly, starts to sweep)*: I'm just tidying up the house a little.

WOMAN: Ohhhhhh . . . of all the insults! You get up in the middle of the night to check up on my work!

MAN: There was just a little grain on the floor . . .

WOMAN: First you spit out the food I cook for you, and now you say I keep such a dirty house that you can't even sleep until you've cleaned it up!

MAN: No, love. You're wrong. Please don't be upset.

WOMAN *(in tears)*: How can I not be upset when you act like this?

MAN: I would like to explain, but I'm not allowed to. I never meant to insult you. I love you very much. Please believe me. *(They each lie down.)*

NARRATOR: That was all they said that night. They both felt very unhappy *(each turns over)*, but they finally went to sleep. In the morning the wife jumped up early and said:

WOMAN: It's time to get up. I want you to come with me.

(She opens shutters and door and shoos away DOG, *who exits.)*

MAN: What's the matter? Where are you going? Let's eat breakfast. *(He gets up sleepily.)*

WIFE: I won't eat breakfast this morning, and I'm not going to fix it either. I don't want to spend another day in this house with you mocking me. I'm going to the Chief to ask him to settle this dispute.

MAN: The Chief!

WOMAN: Come on. *(Exits or circles to village.)*

MAN: But . . . ! *(Follows her.)*

*(*CHIEF *and* VILLAGERS *enter, establishing the village.* MAN *and* WOMAN *enter.)*

NARRATOR: When they arrived in the center of the village, the wife found the Chief.

*(*THE CHIEF *stands or sits in a position to show his authority;* VILLAGERS *are there as witnesses or assistants.* MAN *and* WOMAN *exchange a greeting with* THE CHIEF *to show their respect for his authority.)*

WOMAN: Chief, I have come about a dispute; a matter that needs your settlement.

CHIEF: What is it?

WOMAN: My husband mocks me.

CHIEF: Mocks you? How?

MAN: I do not. I never mock my wife, because I love her.

WOMAN: He laughs at me. When we're alone, suddenly out of silence he bursts out laughing, and then he says it's nothing. He laughs when I give him food. He laughs when we sleep at night.

CHIEF *(to* MAN*)*: How do you explain yourself?

MAN: I am not laughing at my wife. But I cannot explain. I've promised to keep the reason confidential.

(Wife moves away from him to stand near CHIEF.*)*

VILLAGER: Why can't you tell? Are you ashamed?

MAN: No, my reason is a good one. But I'm not allowed to give it.

CHIEF: If it is a good reason, you can give it. If you refuse to give it, your wife will be taken away from you. She does not have to live with someone who makes fun of her. I will send her back to her own village to live with her parents.

MAN: Oh, Chief, please don't do that. I don't want to lose my wife. I love her very much.

CHIEF: This is my answer. Either you tell us the good reason for your laughter, or your wife will return to her village. *(To witness.)* Is this just?

(Witness nods yes.)

MAN *(turning aside to think)*: I would rather be punished for telling my secret than to have to lose my wife, so I will break my promise and tell. *(To* CHIEF.*)* Chief, I saved a snake from being killed. He thanked me and gave me a present, a magic yellow feather. *(Takes feather out of his pocket and shows it. All are amazed.)* With this charm, I can understand animals when they talk. Their talk makes me laugh. If you could only . . . *(He starts to laugh and collapses in the middle of his laughter.)*

*(*WOMAN *rushes to help him but finds him lifeless. She is stunned.)*

VILLAGER: He is dead.

CHIEF *(amazed)*: Dead?

*(*WOMAN *begins a dance lament with keening, a wailing done by mourners.* CHIEF *and* VILLAGERS *join in her lament, moving their heads, bodies, and arms in slow circles. While mourners dance,* LITTLE SNAKE *enters from offstage and approaches* MAN.*)*

LITTLE SNAKE: Young man, I warned you not to tell. You once saved my life, but now my gift has cost you yours. *(Keening continues softly.)* I did not wish it to happen. *(Coils beside* MAN, *who begins to stir.)*

VILLAGER *(noticing* LITTLE SNAKE*)*: Look at the snake!

LITTLE SNAKE: I know you had good reason.
WOMAN: What is he doing?
CHIEF *(signaling all to stand back from* MAN *and* LITTLE SNAKE*)*: It is his charm. Do not interfere with things you do not understand.
LITTLE SNAKE: Your love is strong. We need your love and your laughter, so I will help you this time. Wake up, dear friend.

*(*MAN *sits up, laughing, and sees* LITTLE SNAKE, *who picks up the feather.)*

LITTLE SNAKE *(interrupts* MAN *and gives him the feather)*: It is yours, but do not again betray the secrets that it gives you. Enjoy them through your laughter.

*(*MAN *continues his laughter and* LITTLE SNAKE *exits.)*

WOMAN: He's alive!
VILLAGER: He's alive and he's laughing!
WOMAN: Laugh all you want, husband.
CHIEF: Laugh all you want, and no one will ask questions.
WOMAN: And when you laugh, love, I will laugh with you.

(All do brief dance or walk-about and exit laughing. LITTLE SNAKE *re-enters at the very end in time to catch the eye of the* MAN *before he exits.)*

Think About It

1. Describe the character of the man in the play.
2. How did the man get the magic feather?
3. How did the man's laughter get him into trouble.
4. Why did he break his promise to the little snake?
5. Why did the little snake give the man a second chance?
6. Write about how useful it would be to understand what animals say.

LEARN NEW WORDS

1. Even though we were only **amateur** painters, we did as good a job as any professionals.
2. The park had been neglected for years until the neighborhood children undertook its **beautification**.
3. During the flood, the river **engulfed** the nearby farmland.
4. The city dump on a hot day is a **ghastly** place.
5. We could not afford to live in that **luxurious** high-rise apartment building.
6. She was so angry at what had happened that no one could **pacify** her.
7. Visitors were **prohibited** from entering the roped-off area.
8. He was a **refugee** who came to the United States after an earthquake destroyed his village in Italy.
9. My grandmother is looking forward to **retirement** so that she can spend more time working in her garden.
10. After dinner, we washed the dirty dishes and cooking **utensils**.

GET SET TO READ

Do you think people always appreciate help? Think of situations in which people might not want help.

Read this story to find out how Eddie feels when his friends decide to help him keep his home.

THE GLAD MAN

by GLORIA GONZALEZ

Melissa and her younger brother Troy discovered a man living in the woods at the edge of the city dump. His name was Eddie Bebberidge, and he lived in an old rusted bus with his dog Shadow. Years before, Eddie had traveled around St. Louis in his bus selling flowers. His specialty was gladioluses, so he was called "The Glad Man." But after his wife died, Eddie stopped selling flowers, drove his bus to a quiet place among the trees, and lived in peace with the neighboring farmers.

But St. Louis was expanding. The city began buying up the farmland around Eddie's bus. Before Eddie knew it, the land he was living on became city property. Eddie's life in the woods, where he said he could hear "the skunks square-dancing on the roof" at night, was coming to an end.

To save Eddie from being moved into a retirement home and losing his dog and his bus, Melissa comes up with an idea. She thinks that if the bus looks more like a house trailer and not a piece of junk, then Eddie will be able to stay where he is. So she organizes her school friends, her teacher, and her parents into an amateur work crew to fix up Eddie's bus. Materials and tools for the job, which were donated by local stores and neighbors, have been temporarily stored in Melissa's apartment.

On Saturday my father woke us at six o'clock in the morning for a quick breakfast before we began loading the truck. We agreed silently to let my mother sleep until the mess was cleared out of the apartment.

We wolfed down breakfast, and my father left to bring the truck to the front of the building. Troy and I started lugging boxes and crates downstairs. After about four trips up and down the three flights, I was ready to go back to bed.

"Some athlete you'd be," Troy commented, not even puffing.

By seven o'clock, some of the kids started arriving. It was impossible to keep the noise to a respectable level. My mother stumbled out of her room, waved to everyone, and groaned.

My friend Miriam immediately began organizing the caravan of movers. "The first person who breaks anything gets his head bashed in!" she called down the stairs.

Charming personality that girl has.

"I don't know how we're going to get everything in," my father panted, collapsing on the couch. "You guys are going to have to ride on top of the stuff."

A half-hour later, when most of the stuff was cleared out, our teacher, Miss Wilson, arrived.

I didn't recognize her at first. She was wearing blue jeans, a sweat shirt, sneakers, and her hair was covered by a scarf.

"Miss Wilson?" I stood at the door.

"This is the off-duty me," she said, walking past me and into the kitchen. She and my mother started packing pots and pans and cooking utensils.

"Okay. Let's roll out!" my father announced. He was awfully cheerful for someone who had been working since dawn.

Soon all the furniture and equipment was loaded into the back of the truck—the kids too. Miss Wilson and my mother rode inside.

"This will be good experience for me when I decorate my own home." Kelly fluttered her eyelashes.

Miriam told her, "You won't have to worry about that. The zoo keeper will do it."

Kelly shoved her and a fight almost broke out. My father shouted at us. "Be quiet! All of you." Then he leaned out and called back, "Melissa, did you tell Eddie we were coming over today to do the work?"

Oh, no! In all the excitement I had never mentioned it. I hadn't even been to see him.

"Did you?" asked Troy.

I gulped. "Dad."

"Well?" he shouted.

"I forgot."

Everybody groaned. My father said something under his breath and whipped the truck into gear.

Troy was hopeful. "The worst that can happen is he'll throw us out."

Miriam said, "I hope he's not the type that wakes up grouchy."

I silently agreed. All of a sudden my great idea didn't seem so hot. What would Eddie say when he saw us? I had the frightening feeling that maybe my mother was right after all. Eddie might be very offended by this caravan descending upon him. I pushed the thought out of my mind.

People in passing cars looked at us in amazement. Some even laughed. Troy responded by sticking out his tongue and crossing his eyes.

Soon, up ahead, was the cut-off to the dirt road. We crossed the highway, headed into the trees, and bounced down the road.

Within minutes, we came to a stop in front of the bus. Eddie was nowhere to be seen. Shadow ran out to greet us and then backed away, confused by the crowd.

Troy leaped out of the truck and hugged Shadow.

"It really is a bus!" said Miriam. For the first time in her life, something amazed Miriam.

Everyone got out of the truck. Surely, with all the noise, Eddie had to know we were here. And now I panicked. What if he was watching us, his temper flaring, ready to pounce on us and throw us out? How would I ever explain it to the kids after all the work they did?

"Well," my father said, eyeing me.

"Well, we're here!" I smiled. Why was everyone staring at me?

"Melissa," my father whispered, "I think you and I should go in and break the news."

I swallowed. "Okay." He nudged me in front of him. I don't know why he couldn't go in alone. Grownups are good at these awkward things.

Just as we raised our hands to knock on the accordion door, Eddie stepped out. He took us by surprise and no one said anything right away.

"You folks going on a trip?"

That did it. Everybody laughed and started talking at once. My father ordered everyone to be quiet.

"Morning," my father told Eddie. "I brought some friends along for a visit."

Eddie eyed the mob with suspicion. "Looks more like you cleared out the whole city."

Miss Wilson stepped forward. "How do you do, sir? I'm Miss Wilson, Melissa's teacher, and these are some of my students. I'm very pleased to meet you."

He nodded in her direction. A very strange silence engulfed

the whole group. No one knew exactly what to do next, or who should do it. I felt people looking at me. Even Eddie was now staring at me, expecting some type of explanation. I wanted to say something but couldn't think of anything.

Troy came strolling up to the bus with Shadow prancing alongside.

"Eddie," he said casually, "if you get out of the way, we can get to work."

The old man blocked the entrance. "Hold on, there," he said from the doorway. "Seems to me this place is getting to be more popular than Fort Knox. I mean to know the reason for all this commotion. What do you people want here?"

I turned helplessly to my father, but it was obvious he wasn't going to get involved. It was the old "you made your bed, you sleep in it" routine.

Troy backed up and stood near me.

"Melissa has something to tell you," he said.

No one in the crowd breathed. It was like being in a museum surrounded by statues.

"We worked all week collecting all this equipment," I said nervously, "and these people have volunteered to fix up your bus."

Eddie eyed us suspiciously. "There's nothing wrong with my bus."

"I know that," I told him. "But those people in City Hall

think there is, and we're here to keep them off your back."

"I like it just the way it is. If it needs fixing, I imagine I can do it myself, if I had a notion to." He looked at me squarely. "And I don't."

He sure is a stubborn man.

"We're going to fix the bus so they don't take Shadow away and put him in the pound," Troy spoke up. "If you don't care about yourself, then think about him."

My father said, "That's enough, Troy. You talk to Mr. Bebberidge with respect. He's right. He didn't ask for our help. We came here without telling him." Then he turned to Eddie, "I'm sure I'd react the same way if I were you."

Eddie spoke to my father. "Was this your idea?"

"Nope! I'm just a hired hand. Melissa's running the show. If you want us to leave just say so."

"Eddie," I said. "We worked very hard all week to get all this stuff and the people. We even got up at six in the morning. You can't throw us out."

"That isn't the question. You know you're welcome here anytime. You and your family. But this—"

I tried one last approach.

"Eddie. It's going to be all right. Trust me."

That struck me as the world's stupidest remark. But a slight smile crossed his face. That's all. Just a hint of recognition. A tinge of understanding.

"Looks like those young'uns mean to do something here," Eddie observed, none too happy.

"Sure looks that way," my father grinned.

"You better not break any of my stuff!" Eddie shouted. "And don't go touching everything."

That did it! Within minutes people were running in and out, throwing out things, carrying in things, shouting back and forth, unloading the truck and barking orders.

Eddie started to follow the group into the bus but my mother quickly grabbed his arm.

"Mr. Bebberidge, I wonder if you can give me a hand lifting these boxes," she said, leading him to the rear of the truck.

Blankets, furniture, newspapers, utensils, pillows, and mattress were hoisted out of the bus.

My father started prying the wood slats off the windows. Larry climbed on the roof of the bus and began scraping the rust. Kelly swept out the inside, and Troy organized a human chain to unload the truck.

"Just hold on! Hold on one minute!" Eddie sprang to his feet. My mother tried unsuccessfully to pacify him. "Hold it right there!" Eddie went up to Miss Wilson, who was carrying his rocking chair. "What are you doing with my chair?"

"I'm taking it outside to paint it. That's all."

Eddie growled, "It doesn't need paint. Chair is fine just the way it is." He tried to pry it from her.

Miss Wilson held on tightly. "Mr. Bebberidge, I am just going to put on a fresh coat of paint to match the new cushion we bought for it."

"I have never sat on a cushion," he shot back.

"Well, when I'm done, if you don't like it, you can throw the cushion away. All right?"

Eddie thought for a moment and then released his hold. He seemed pacified. "All right! Fine! And if I don't like the color of your paint, you can scrape it back off, too." With that he stalked back to join my mother.

Eddie sat stunned under a tree. At one point, he broke away again and marched up to my father. "Look here. I know why you people came here. I know these kids mean to do well by me, but I got to tell you something just the same. After they get through destroying here, if I don't like it I want them here tomorrow morning at six o'clock to put everything back the way it was before!" With that he marched away before my father could answer.

Eddie was whipped. I knew it, and it hurt to see him that way. I silently prayed that what I was doing was the right thing. I realized in that moment that if someone came into my room and started throwing out things and bringing things in, I'd be pretty hysterical. Like Eddie, I really don't have much, but I have my room. It's very important to me.

Troy announced to one and all who cared to listen that his first order of business was the beautification of Shadow.

"I'm going down to the brook with Shadow. We'll be gone a couple of hours, and I don't want anyone coming to bother us." He then leaned over and whispered to Eddie, "Are you all right?"

Eddie nodded. Leave it to Troy to remember another person's feelings and to be so bold as to actually mention them. I wish I wasn't such a coward. I have feelings just like everyone else but I can't talk about them. If I can't talk about my own, how can I talk about someone else's?

Troy stalked off, carrying a load of stuff and whistling for Shadow to follow. The dog did.

The next hours were filled with activity, shouts, anger, laughter, and sweat.

"Melissa," my father called, "bring me a can of oil from the truck."

I found it and rushed over to him. He had the hood of the bus

opened and was peering inside at a globby mess of black gunk.

"What's that?" I pointed.

"That," he said, wiping his sweaty face, "is the engine."

A spider crawled out lazily and stretched its legs in the sunlight. Probably the first time it had been out in years.

"Get me the kerosene," he said. "This motor is in need of a bath."

I lugged the can of kerosene, all the while silently praying that he knew what he was doing. I got away as fast as I could before he asked me to help. I wasn't going to stick my hand into that black cave.

A bunch of the kids were tying chains to the bus, and they yelled to me to get out of the way. I saw Larry rolling the new tires toward the bus.

Back by the tree, Eddie was still sitting silently, watching the confusion. I waved—weakly—half-heartedly—somewhat embarrassed and apologetic. He merely stared.

My mother, I noticed, had the table set up with a large paper cloth and napkins and plates. Our large water cooler was standing at the end of the table and she was handing out drinks.

"How's it going?" I whispered to her.

"Just fine," she smiled.

I wanted to ask her if Eddie had said anything but was afraid he'd overhear.

"Take this cup of lemonade to Mr. Bebberidge," my mother said.

Wouldn't you know it? Now I'd have to face him. I tried to approach Eddie cautiously. He didn't seem to hear me.

"Eddie. Would you like some lemonade?"

He spun around quickly. He hadn't heard me walk up.

"Lemonade," I smiled. When in doubt—do!

"Why?" he said, not making a move to take the cup.

"I thought maybe you'd be thirsty."

He took the cup and put it on the ground next to him. "Why would all these people—strangers—want to come out here and do whatever it is they're doing?"

"Well . . . we figured if we fixed up the bus real nice, the people at City Hall couldn't complain about you living here, and you wouldn't have to go into a retirement home. You and Shadow could stay together and nobody would bother you."

Eddie sighed and mumbled something. Then he reached over, lifted the paper cup, and drank from it. Then he turned his face to me—looked at me for a long time, it seemed—and said, "Thank you."

I'm smart enough to know he wasn't just talking about the lemonade!

I ran and told my father. "Eddie isn't mad at us! He's happy we came! He really is! He even said thank you!"

My father tossed the kerosene rag on the ground. "This engine must be seventy-five years old!"

I looked down at the ghastly mess. It looked worse now that some of it was cleaned. The dirt was six inches thick.

"Can you fix it?" I asked.

"I'm a mechanic—not a magician," he snarled.

Brother!

I slipped away and went over to my mother. "Do you need any help?"

"Nope. Go see if Miss Wilson can use you."

I was starting to feel like a Ping-Pong ball.

I dashed into the bus. Miss Wilson was humming and papering the walls. "Don't you just love it?" she beamed, swabbing glue on the wall.

I wasn't sure, but I said, "Sure do," and ran back out.

Troy dashed past me. He was a vision in white. His hair, face, and chest were totally engulfed in soap bubbles.

"Who's getting the bath?" My mother laughed.

Troy stood in front of Eddie. "That is a stubborn dog you have. I told him I was going to tell you." With that he disappeared back in the woods.

Eddie laughed. He threw back his head and wiped his eyes.

My father found Kelly hiding under the truck and eased her out. "What are you doing under there?"

"Trying to stay out of trouble."

"I have just the solution," he said, handing her a can of paint and brush. "Melissa," he called, "you and Kelly climb up on the roof and start painting. The top has been scraped. By the time you get done, we'll have the sides sanded down. Go to it!"

We took a lunch break in the afternoon. I was too tired to even lift my arm to eat the sandwich, but I didn't dare show it. Everyone else was talking and laughing and planning what they'd work on next.

Even Eddie was joining in. He and my mother dished out the food and made sure everyone had plenty.

"Brings to mind the days when I hired on as a cattle rancher out on the Arizona plains," he said. He sat down and told us ghastly stories about rattlesnakes and vultures and the night the water barrel sprung a leak out in the desert.

Troy burst into the circle, proudly leading a soaking-wet, miserable-looking, downcast dog.

"Doesn't he look and smell terrific?" Troy boasted.

I noted the flea collar wrapped around the bony neck.

Shadow looked as unhappy as any dog I'd ever seen. He could've been a refugee from a flood.

"Look what that feller went and did," Eddie laughed. "Why, if I didn't suspect it was Shadow that went into the woods with him I'd never believe this is the same critter who's been occupying my life these past years!"

Troy helped himself to two sandwiches and a big cup of lemonade.

"You're going to stay right next to me until you dry," he informed the weary dog. Shadow responded by dropping his head and sinking to the ground.

"Everyone—back to work!" my father said.

Finally, it was nighttime. We had put in a long day. Our troops were stretched out on the ground like combat refugees. The dark air was nippy, and we hung close to the campfire that Eddie had made to cook dinner.

"Good soup," my father told him, finishing his second bowl.

"It doesn't take much talent to make soup," said the old man. "Just patience."

"And energy," my mother groaned.

I smiled. She had been in charge of the open-air canteen all day, feeding and watering the work crew, and she looked as beat as the rest of us.

"I, for one, think these kids did a great job," my father announced.

As if on signal, we all struggled up to a sitting position and looked at the bus. It was a most amazing sight.

The bus gleamed brightly—a vision of orange paint in the glint of the firelight. The cement blocks were gone and it rested proudly on thick, black rubber tires. The glass windows sparkled, reflecting the red-orange licks of flame.

None of us had gone into the bus since midafternoon. The beautification of the inside had become Miss Wilson's special project and all visitors were prohibited. Kelly had been called in a few times for hurried conferences but evidently had been sworn to secrecy. That in itself is impossible.

"What say we go in and look around." Miss Wilson stood up. She walked over to Eddie and helped him to his feet. His legs were stiff from sitting on the ground all day.

Everyone stood and waited politely for Eddie and Miss Wilson to go first. We formed an outer circle of expectation. I looked behind me to see my father standing with his arm around my mother's waist. They were whispering quietly.

"The tour starts here," Miss Wilson took Eddie's hand and led him through the darkness. He walked slowly up to the bus and paused to take in the entire view. It was eerie, quiet. I had this strange feeling I might cry—I don't know why.

My father lit a small gas lamp and handed it to Larry to lead the way. Larry shone the light over the bus entrance while Eddie was shown the fresh, new lettering over the door: The Glad Man. It was painted in large, blue strokes.

"Kelly and Miriam did that," Miss Wilson smiled. "It was quite a job to trace over the faded old lettering."

Eddie looked up at it. "They did a fine job." His voice grew very soft. We had to strain to hear him.

THE GLAD MAN

"Shall we go in?" Miss Wilson suggested.

"Wait. Let me go light the lamp first," my father said. He darted into the bus and lit the kerosene lamp.

In our eagerness to get inside we came close to knocking Eddie right through the door.

He was pushed forward by the crunch of the mob as we struggled to get a look at the room.

The sight froze us. We were stunned!

The walls were papered in a bright orange design with yellow flowers that matched the starched curtains framing the windows. The new couch was covered with a quilt and decorated with fluffy pillows.

A soft brown rug was thick under our feet. It covered every inch of floor space and gave the room a luxurious air.

The wooden refrigerator gleamed with hand polishing and now supported a glass bowl of shiny wax fruit. The rocking chair was there, but painted a soft brown and wearing a new stuffed orange cushion. A bright, hand-painted yellow flower decorated the headrest.

It was a room of gold and rust-colored hues softened to perfection by the orange glint of

the overhead kerosene lamp. It was a beautiful, warm, inviting, comfortable home.

Shadow, confused by the soft rug under his feet, huddled next to Eddie. Eddie, sensing his bewilderment, stroked his neck.

"Not bad for a bunch of amateurs," Miss Wilson said.

None of us looked directly at Eddie. It was a very private moment, and I suddenly felt that we shouldn't be there.

Eddie turned to me and Troy. He wanted to say something. We could feel it. I could see the struggle in his face. I couldn't find any words to break this silence.

Just then the bus started buzzing, a loud noise whirred through the room, and we felt the walls vibrate.

My father jumped up the stairs into the room.

"Guess I am a magician after all," he boasted.

Think About It

1. Why did Melissa and Tony want to fix up Eddie's bus?
2. Why didn't Eddie like the idea at first?
3. Did Melissa understand Eddie's resistance to her plan? Find the part of the story that tells you.
4. What made Eddie change his mind about accepting the help?
5. How did Melissa, her family, and her friends help Eddie in ways he couldn't help himself?
6. Pretend you have offered help to someone who resists it at first. Write about what you would do and why.

LEARN NEW WORDS

1. Because my brother's disease was **contagious**, we were prohibited from visiting him in the hospital.
2. She was unreliable, but I always **credited** him with a good sense of responsibility.
3. He was **deprived** of a college education because he couldn't afford it.
4. Our **eccentric** neighbor always wore a luxurious mink coat with tennis shoes.
5. That artist is no longer alive, but her works are **immortal**.
6. His **passion** for music left him little time for anything else.
7. In her flowing white dress, the pale woman walked alone in the moonlit garden like a **phantom**.
8. The many workers on the **plantation** were busy in the fields harvesting the crops.
9. The great jazz musician recalled that his childhood friends used to **ridicule** him for practicing the piano after school.
10. She described the scene in such detail that I could **visualize** it exactly.

GET SET TO READ

Why do people sometimes ridicule others? What are some different ways people react to being ridiculed?

Read this story to find out what happens when Meg gets to know a woman who is ridiculed and avoided by her neighbors.

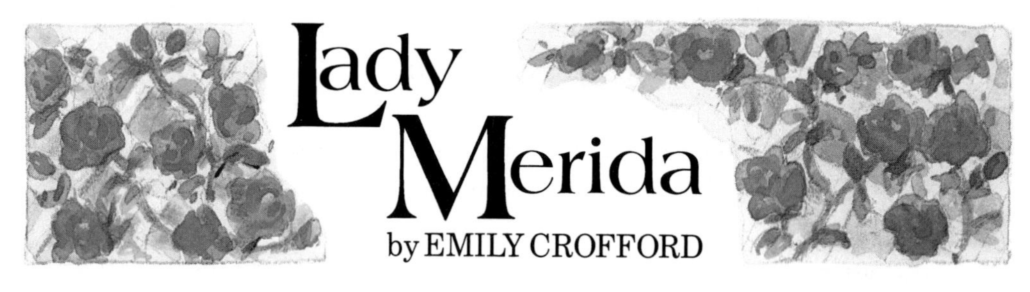

Lady Merida

by EMILY CROFFORD

"Cross over," Josie said.

Her commanding tone aggravated me, and I didn't see any reason to walk on the far side of the road just because Mrs. Merida was playing the piano. But which side of the road we walked on didn't seem like a big enough reason to fight with my best friend. I crossed over.

Mrs. Merida had come from England with her daughter, who had married the plantation owner, Mr. Limon. Josie remembered the first Mrs. Limon, who had died before my family moved to Arkansas. "It depressed him so bad," Josie had told me, "that he went across the ocean for a vacation—and came back with a new wife." People didn't say anything in front of Mr. Limon—times were too hard to chance getting put off the plantation—but his mother-in-law made a fine subject for talk behind his back. Some said Mrs. Merida was moonstruck; others came right out with crazy. And she had cancer.

Mrs. Merida never visited neighbors or went to the store or to the post office, but some of the kids had seen her walking in the Limons' flower garden. And everybody had heard her playing the piano, which they said was proof of her madness. Not that we hadn't heard pianos—including the one at school, there were four on the plantation—but none of them sounded anything like Mrs. Merida's. Her music whispered and thundered, stroked and lashed, danced and wept. It made me dream, made me restless, made my heart and my mind yearn for something beyond their ken.

"She's really . . ." Josie traced a circle by her temple when we were past the house.

Set in a grove of oak trees, the Limon house was painted

white and had a screened front porch. There were shrubs too, and roses climbing a trellis, and a curving sandy walkway to the front steps. I looked back over my shoulder at the house.

"Mother says she's just eccentric," I said.

Josie bounced her hair, which was thick and wavy and the color of a red squirrel. "Well, Papa says she's crazy—and I guess he knows."

Josie's father, Mr. Tomkin, was a ginner, an important position on the plantation. She said that was why he knew all about the lives of the other important people. I liked Mr. Tomkin, but I didn't think it was very nice of him to talk about Mrs. Merida.

Josie put her face so close to mine I could count her freckles. "And furthermore, he says that terrible disease she has is contagious." She bounced her hair again. "That's why she never visits anybody."

Josie's know-it-all attitude and her bossiness really bothered me. Lately it had gotten worse, as if she were trying to see how far she could push me. But I didn't like to argue, and I didn't know what to say in Mrs. Merida's defense—for all I knew, maybe Mrs. Merida's disease *was* contagious.

After I got home I waited until my two brothers went outside to play. Then I told Mother what Mr. Tomkin had said about Mrs. Merida's illness being contagious. Mother was setting up the ironing board and she jerked the legs so hard I thought they would break.

"That's bosh and nonsense!" she exploded. "Cancer is not contagious!" Pulling one of my

school dresses over the ironing board, she said, "Meg, would you sweep the kitchen? The clothes have been sprinkled so long they're going to mildew if I don't get them done."

"Sure," I said. I knew she would return to the subject. She only wanted to make the right sentences in her head.

Mother took a flatiron off the stove and touched it with a tongue-moistened finger. The moisture sizzled, she began to iron, and the kitchen filled with a clean, starchy smell.

"People don't mean to be cruel," she said. "It's just that Mrs. Merida and her music are different, so people don't understand them. What they don't understand, they fear; and what they fear, they disparage."

I didn't know the word *disparage,* but if I asked what it meant she would just tell me to look it up. I had a fair idea about the meaning from the way she had used it, though, so I nodded and reached the broom under the table to sweep out some cornbread crumbs.

"Actually," I told her, "I think Mrs. Merida's music is wonderful, even if you can't clap your hands or sing to it. I don't care what Josie says."

Mother worked the iron around the dress collar. "So do I. Sometimes late at night, when it's still, I can hear it through the bedroom window—so beautiful, so filled with passion." She gave a sad little sigh. "I think Mrs. Merida must play when she's in pain."

"I'd give anything if I could play the piano like that," I said.

"Then why don't you ask her to give you lessons?"

I stopped sweeping and stared at Mother. Even though I didn't believe most of the stories, considering the number of them, Mrs. Merida must be at least a wee bit mad. Besides, she was a very important person, and she lived in a very important house. Just thinking about going there was scary . . . and kind of exciting.

Mother set the cooled flatiron back on the stove and picked up the other one. "Meg, believe me—there's nothing to be alarmed about. In fact, Josie's own mother visits Mrs. Merida."

This time I figured Mother had gotten some wrong information. I couldn't visualize Josie's spiritless little mother being so bold as to see Mrs. Merida without Mr. Tomkin knowing about it.

"Mrs. Tomkin and Mrs. Merida are friends," Mother was saying. "But you must not mention that to anybody—especially Josie."

I was going to ask her to repeat slowly what she had just said, but the boys charged through the back door, one chasing the other, and ran right through my nice pile of dirt. I threw the broom after them, but I wasn't really all that angry. Now I knew how to stand up to Josie! And I would learn to play the piano at the same time.

The next afternoon I left Josie standing on the other side of the road and went up the sandy walkway through the grove of oak trees to the Limon house. Josie had tried to talk me out of it and said she might walk with Peggy's group from now on if I went. That scared me, but it also made me more determined.

It was reassuring to find that the Limons' screened porch creaked just like the porch on our Blue Road house. Mrs. Limon answered my knock. Up close I could see why Mr. Limon had brought her from England. She looked like a movie star, with creamy skin and cornflower-blue eyes.

Clutching my books so tightly that my arm cramped, I stammered, "I—I'm Meg Weston. I wanted to—to talk to your mother about, uh, taking piano lessons."

"Why, yes," she said. "If Mama—that is, nothing like this has happened before."

"Dorothy," a voice behind her said, "will you get out of the doorway so the girl can come in." I liked their accents and wished I could talk that way.

"Hello, Mrs. Merida," I said.

"Lady Merida. Lady Rose Merida."

"Yes, Ma'am, Lady Merida."

She was wearing a soft and shimmery gray dress that went all the way to the floor, but it was only old-fashioned, not crazy or eccentric. She had not torn out hunks of her own hair, as I had heard, and there was no blood dripping from her fingertips either. Her nails were just painted with bright red polish.

Feeling more confident, I continued my inspection. I wanted to be able to describe Lady Merida to Mother. She was terribly thin. Her gray, tightly curled hair topped a small face, and her pale skin was drawn tight over her bones. Then Lady Merida stepped toward me and my confidence dissolved. Her fierce gaze made the hairs on the back of my neck stand straight out.

"Well, I—I didn't think you would, I mean could, Ma'am. I mean, Lady Merida. I know you're busy." I backed toward the door, ready to run the instant I reached it.

She thrust out a bony hand as if to grab me. "Wait!"

I stopped in my tracks, too terrified to move, and stared at

the hand. Blue veins stood out beneath thin white skin, the sinews from her knuckles to her wrists looked like cords, and her red fingernails were filed almost to the quick.

"You want to learn to play. You shall learn!" She pointed her index finger at the piano bench, and on legs more wooden than the bench's I moved to it. She sat down beside me. "Put down your books," she said, and added scornfully, "The piano is played with *both* hands."

My hands were shaking so badly, I was sure she'd say something about them, but she didn't. I quickly forgot my terror during the next thirty minutes as she taught me the connection between the notes on the music sheet, the keys, and my fingers. I was learning fast, I thought. Soon I would be playing like Lady Merida. Once I laughed aloud with the joy of my accomplishment and she smiled a little.

"Did you know I was a concert pianist?" she asked suddenly. She scooted me off the end of the bench and ran her fingers up and down the keyboard. Her hands no longer looked ugly but incredibly graceful. I visualized my own hands moving swiftly over the keys, imagined people around me gasping with admiration.

It started then, the kind of music that made people walk on the other side of the road. "What am I playing?" she demanded.

Drops of sweat crept down from my hairline. Somewhere buried inside all the extra notes I recognized the tune to a song I had heard, but I couldn't remember the title.

"Well, what?"

"It's something about she misses him," I said.

Her hands stopped in midair; her mouth opened with such horror that it pulled the skin even more tightly over her face.

"That," she said in a quiet, dreadful tone, "is Beethoven's great and immortal Concerto No. 5. The Emperor Concerto." She folded her fingers into her palms, then flung them outward. Then she began to play with the force of her whole body. The piano seemed to be alive, to be breathing its own fury and passion.

The notes swelled, vibrated, wrapped themselves around me, filled my ears, burst into the space behind my eyes.

Mrs. Limon came in quickly from another room, took my arm, and guided me toward the door. Lady Merida, although she didn't turn to look at me or slow her racing fingers, ordered, "Come back tomorrow. Same time."

The next day I learned to stretch my fingers beyond their reach. When I protested that they wouldn't spread any further, Lady Merida took my hands and showed me that they would. Then she placed my fingers on the keyboard. "Practice!" she said. "Stretch them. Practice!"

Since I didn't have anywhere else to practice playing except at Lady Merida's, she made me spend part of each lesson running up and down scales and playing the same pieces over and over. I didn't mind at first, but after two weeks of the same exercises, it seemed to me that Lady Merida should let me stop doing them.

She wouldn't. In fact, when I complained that the exercises were boring, she made me practice an extra ten minutes.

But I kept going for the lessons, almost every day except for the times Mrs. Limon met me at the door and told me her mother didn't feel well.

Josie tried everything to get me to quit. I told her playing the piano was important to me and that she might as well give up.

Actually, I was tired of going so often for the lessons. I missed out on a lot of after-school talk. I especially missed standing around in the post office with Josie and the other kids, including boys, while we waited for the postmistress to come back with the mail after meeting the afternoon train.

I had been going for the lessons for a month when I realized that I hadn't really wanted to learn to play the piano. I had wanted to make the piano sound like Lady Merida made it sound. If Josie would stop bullyragging me about going for the lessons, I could quit. I didn't think Lady Merida would mind too much.

Sometimes she got a pained expression when I played.

Josie didn't give up, though. She got angry every time I told her good-by at the Limon house. And finally she said, "I'm going to get myself a new best friend."

I shrugged as if I didn't care, but the truth was that it made me feel sick all over. Josie liked to get her way, she had a quick temper, and she could be mean. But she was more fun than anybody I knew, and she always stuck up for me. There were times when I felt closer to her than to my own family. We could freely tell each other our hurts and dreams, be silly or serious, say we hated somebody without feeling guilty. But even as I told myself that all I had to do was say I wouldn't go anymore, I turned into the Limons' without a word.

Josie kept walking. I stopped before I reached the oak grove to watch her back and the way the sun seemed to set her hair aflame, and she turned.

"I was"—and I heard a quiver in her voice—"going to ask you to stay all night."

"Sure," I said. "If it's all right with Mother." I took a deep breath. "I'm still going for the lesson, though."

"Okay," Josie said. "Come as soon as you can."

I thought about running to hug Josie and talk with her about what we would do that night.

If I hadn't told Lady Merida I would be there, I would have gone home. I had won! I had made Josie understand that my letting her be the leader didn't mean she could bullyrag me. Besides, the air had become light with spring, the sun gifted everything with lazy warmth, and taking a piano lesson was the last thing I wanted.

Before I reached the porch, I heard the piano and knew immediately that someone other than Lady Merida was playing it. This music was timid and sweet. Starting across the creaky porch, I peered through the partly opened front door. The woman sitting at the piano saw me, jumped up, and darted through the kitchen and out the back way like a phantom. Mrs.

Tomkin, I thought dizzily. Josie's mother! She did visit Lady Merida. She not only visited, she played the piano! She could make music. I realized that Lady Merida was watching me and I closed my mouth.

"Since you're here," she said angrily, "come in."

The minute I walked into the living room, she pounced. "You're just like the rest! Insensitive! She"—she pointed a withered arm in the direction Mrs. Tomkin would be taking home through the field—"has the soul of an artist. If she hadn't been deprived as a child, if she wasn't married to that, that . . ."

"He is not either," I said, which surprised me because I never talked back to grownups. "Mr. Tomkin is funny—and nice." It was true. Mr. Tomkin had never ignored me like some adults did. He asked me kindly about school and my grades and my favorite subjects.

Her eyes still locked with mine, Lady Merida seemed to be asking herself a question. "Yes," she said. "Yes, I'm going to show you something."

She left the room and returned with a small, framed watercolor. It was so lovely—mountains and sky and sunlit grasses and wildflowers swaying in a breeze—that I sucked in my breath. Lady Merida knew that I thought the watercolor was beautiful.

"Sarah Tomkin painted this from a childhood memory of her Ozark Mountains," Lady Merida told me. "Up until now I have been the only one on this plantation who knows she has this talent—because she's been ridiculed so often."

We were silent for a minute, and when she spoke again her voice sounded squeezed out. "She can't even read. I don't try to teach her, but she's drawn to the piano like a hungry, deprived child."

Instead of giving me my lesson, Lady Merida served us tea in china cups and not-very-sweet cookies that she called biscuits. She talked of her childhood, told me about concerts she had played, and described how the British countryside looked in the spring.

"Meghann," Lady Merida said, and I didn't tell her Meg came from Margaret, "there's nothing wrong with playing the old familiar songs, but listen to great music, with your senses and with your heart, all the days of your life."

I knew what she was saying, that I would never become a good pianist, and I didn't think it was fair. I had done everything she had told me. Besides, it was one thing for me to think about quitting. It was quite another for Lady Merida to suggest it, and I was certain she was about to.

"You mean you want to stop teaching me?"

She looked into her teacup, which was almost empty, and with a strange little smile said, "No, ducky, I don't want to stop teaching you." She went with me to the door, something she had never done before. "But perhaps not so often, eh! Say—once a week?"

I ran most of the way home, until I got a stitch in my side, and asked Mother if I could spend the night at Josie's. When she said yes, I quickly did my chores, tossed my toothbrush, nightgown, and a change of underwear into a pillowcase, and left for Josie's.

The minute I walked into her big, two-story house, I sensed the excitement and smelled chicken frying. I loved the commotion there, the seven children talking two and three at a time, the laughing and singing, even the arguing.

Mr. Tomkin sat in his easy chair making jokes and asking questions about school. Mrs. Tomkin, as always, moved like a phantom, constantly busy, seldom speaking. I had never really noticed her before, but now I realized that the faded hair she wore in a bun at the nape of her neck had probably once been as lush and red as Josie's. I kept looking for a chance to speak to her in private before supper, but the only time I came close, just as I was about to follow her into the pantry where she stored quarts of fruits and vegetables, Danny and James Lee, Josie's big brothers, came rushing into the kitchen and started teasing me.

For supper we had fried chicken heaped high on platters at each end of the table, mashed potatoes, with milk gravy, two quarts of Mrs. Tomkin's butter beans seasoned with bacon drippings and chopped onion, and watermelon rind preserves. We all said how good it was, Mr. Tomkin first.

"I would like a bit of variety, though," he said, then beamed around the table as if he had a wonderful idea. "I tell you what, let's all save our pennies and buy Mother a cookbook for Christmas."

He had always made remarks like that, and I had credited him with a fine wit, never before seeing below the surface. Knowing as I did now that Mrs. Tomkin couldn't read, I thought I should have let Lady Merida call Mr. Tomkin whatever bad word she'd had in mind that day. The kids laughed, as they always did when he said something he expected them to laugh at. But this time I understood that some of them—especially Danny and James Lee—laughed out of nervousness. They were afraid to displease Mr. Tomkin.

After supper I got my chance to speak alone with Mrs. Tomkin. Mr. Tomkin and the boys had gone out to slop the hogs. I had drawn scraping the dishes, so I'd finished first. The girls were washing and drying and putting away. I heard Mrs. Tomkin going upstairs and quietly followed her. She had her hand on the doorknob to her and Mr. Tomkin's room when I reached the upstairs hall.

"Mrs. Tomkin," I said in a low voice, "Lady Merida showed me the watercolor you did."

She looked around like a frightened deer to see if anybody had heard.

"It's very beautiful," I said.

She blushed and a delicate smile fluttered over her lips.

"Thankee," she said.

When I went to Lady Merida's the next week, I had made up my mind to tell her I couldn't come anymore until fall. After-school softball season had started, and I was trying out for sixth grade pitcher. Josie was trying out for pitcher, too, and I really wanted to beat her out.

Mrs. Limon came to the door. "Mama won't be able to give you lessons anymore, Meg," she said in a shaken voice. "She's very ill."

As I walked toward home, the gravel crunching under my shoes seemed to be saying,

"She's dying, she's dying." I looked out over the flat land to where the tree line seemed to cut jagged pieces out of the sky and wondered why I was so upset. Lady Merida had never been patient with me like my teachers at school. She hadn't smiled with pride the way my parents did when I tried hard. We hadn't been friends like Josie and I were. She was not kin I was bound to love whether I liked her or not.

Still trying to figure it out, I turned onto the Blue Road and the crunching changed to a softer, sadder, earthy sound. I went down the grassy bank to the drainage ditch. Violets were growing beside the water. I picked a bouquet and wrapped their stems in a maple leaf I caught as it floated past.

All the way back to Lady Merida's I kept making up speeches, but when Mrs. Limon opened the door, all I said was, "These are for Lady Merida."

"How did you know?" she said. "Violets are her . . . her favorite."

She was going to cry. I glanced away and caught my own reflection in a window glass. My face was streaked with dust and tears.

Nothing had ever stirred the plantation up like what happened when Lady Merida died. She left her piano to Mrs. Tomkin. Not only that, but when Mr. Tomkin tried to sell it, Mrs. Tomkin told him that if he did he'd never get another meal in that house. Now people began to walk on the other side of the road when they passed the Tomkins'. I could sort of see why they did. Take the day Mrs. Tomkin told Josie and me to get our hoes and help weed the garden. She started hoeing and singing like she had a fever. She had changed her hair too. Instead of the bun at the back of her neck, now she plaited it into a crown.

Scowling at me, Josie said, "You might have come out all right, but she caught it—at least the crazy part. She's been like

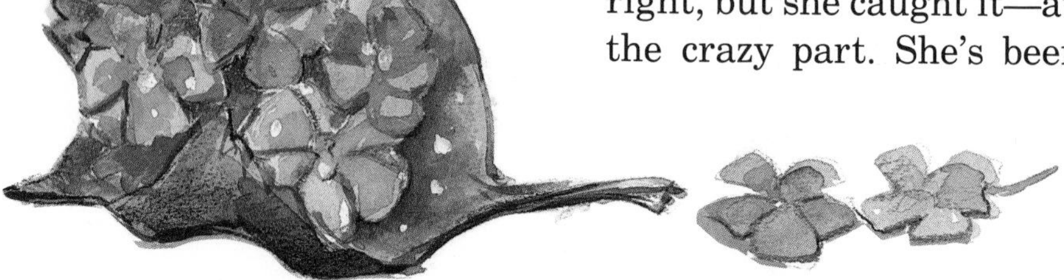

this ever since that lady passed on."

Mrs. Tomkin must have heard her, because she leaned her hoe against the garden fence and said, "Come into the house, the both of ye. I'm going to play my pieanna. My pie-anna," she said again wonderingly, "what Lady Merida gave me."

She marched into the house. Josie and I trailed behind her, past Mr. Tomkin, who sat forward in his easy chair and asked nervously, "What's the matter, Sarah? Did it come on you again?"

"Hush up," she said.

She sat down at the piano and began to play, at first gentle and timid, like rabbits hopping, then so natural and sweet that it brought a vision of flowers swaying in the wind.

"What's she playing?" Josie whispered.

Josie might have beaten me out for pitcher on the softball team, but she didn't know music.

"A concerto," I whispered back, and stood there listening with my senses and my heart while the music rose and soared out the window and climbed toward heaven.

Think About It

1. Why did the neighbors say that Lady Merida was crazy?
2. What made Meg decide to take piano lessons from Lady Merida?
3. Describe the friendship between Meg and Josie.
4. What did Meg discover about Lady Merida after she got to know her?
5. Why do you think Lady Merida befriended Mrs. Tomkin?
6. How did Lady Merida's death change things at the Tomkin household?
7. Write about how the friendship between Meg and Josie was different from the friendship between Lady Merida and Mrs. Tomkin.

To Catalina

by FRANK HORNE

Love thy piano, Oh girl,
It will give you back
Note for note
The harmonies of your soul.
It will sing back to you
The high songs of your heart.
It will give
As well as take . . .

Finn Magic

a Scandinavian folktale
retold by ETHEL JOHNSTON PHELPS

Far to the north, on the bleak coast of the Northern Seas, there once lived a lad named Eilert. His family were fisherfolk, and they lived beside a rocky headland jutting out into the sea. Their nearest neighbors, who lived some distance along the shore on the other side of the cliff, were a family of Finns.

Both Eilert's family and the Finns used the same fishing grounds, but there was no friendliness between them. Eilert's family were Nordlanders, and they were sure the Finns used their special magic against them.

Eilert's father muttered angrily, "Evil charms and spells!" when the Finns hauled in a good catch and his own was small.

The Nordlanders along the coast thought the Finns were strange folk and credited them with knowledge of ancient magic. The Finns had black hair, wore odd clothes, and talked among themselves in a peculiar language. All their habits and customs were strange, and their burial ground in the village was separate and apart from the Nordlanders' graves.

Eilert did not share his father's fear of the Finns' magic. When he was a small child playing on the rocky headland, he had met Zilla, a Finn girl his own age. They had become friends, and he had often gone home with her to the Finns' place on the other side of the headland. Zilla was thin and wiry, but she was strong. She could run like a hare and handle a boat as well as he could.

The Finns were kind to him. He saw no evil in them. Nonetheless he thought it best not to tell his family where he had been whenever he returned from a visit to Zilla's place.

Nor did he tell his family of the strange tales the Finns told of Mermen and Draugs who dragged fishermen under the waves to their homes at the bottom of the sea. The Mermen had heads like seals; the Draugs were evil creatures with heads of seaweed.

Eilert and the Nordlanders knew of course that Mermen lived under the Northern Seas, waiting for victims. But the Finns seemed to have an uncanny knowledge of this kingdom beneath the sea, and claimed that their ancestors had often visited there.

Walking home across the headland after hearing these tales, Eilert shivered and wondered if the Finns did indeed have a strange power over the sea. But the lass Zilla was friendly and merry, and the Finns seemed to be kind, cheerful folk, so he put the thought away from him.

Now it happened that one autumn Eilert's family was having a very lean time of it. Day after day on the fishing grounds his father's lines caught next to nothing, while not far off, a dark-haired Finn pulled up one fine catch after another. Eilert's father swore the Finn was making strange signs in the air and using magic spells against him.

"I'd use our counter-charm," cried his father angrily, "but I don't dare. It's said the Merfolk take a terrible revenge on those who do!"

Eilert became very troubled. Was the Finn using magic to lure all the fish to his lines? He felt guilty about his secret friendship with Zilla and the Finns—could this be the cause of his father's bad luck?

He stopped his visits to the Finns' place, and he no longer walked with Zilla under the pines on the headland. But this did not help at all. Day after day, Eilert's father set out his lines and drew them in almost empty of fish.

Eilert knew the counter-charm was dangerous, for it put the user in the power of the Merfolk. But he made up his mind that he himself must use it. He must take earth from the grave of a Finn and rub it on his father's fishing line.

Late the next night he went off secretly to the Finn graveyard and put a handful of earth from a Finn grave into his pocket. When he returned home, he rubbed the earth on all his father's fishing lines.

The very next day his father hauled in a fine catch, and this good luck continued day after day. The counter-charm had worked. But each day Eilert's fear of the Draugs and Merfolk increased. To avoid their revenge, he went back to the Finn grave one night to beg forgiveness. But he also took care to carry a piece of iron in his pocket at all times, as protection against sorcery.

One day Eilert went out alone to fish for Greenland shark, for the fish brought a fine price at market. As he rowed, he did not look in the direction of the Finns' place, nor did he notice the lass Zilla watching him from the shore. He rowed on out of sight.

When a shark at last took his line, it was a huge one. Although the boat was small, Eilert would not give up his efforts to pull the shark alongside. At last the shark tore off with Eilert's line taut behind him. Then, unable to lose

the fishing line, the shark twisted and plunged suddenly down to the depths of the sea. The boat tipped.

Faint and numb with cold, Eilert clung to the hull of the overturned boat as it tossed in the rough sea. Suddenly he saw, sitting on one end of the boat, a large creature with a seaweed head and a neck like a seal. The two reddish eyes glared at him. The Draug slowly forced its end of the boat down under the water.

"You rubbed your lines with grave earth," hissed the Draug. "Now the people of the sea seek their revenge."

Eilert closed his eyes in despair. He felt himself sinking down under the waves. When he opened his eyes, the frightening Draug was gone, but he saw that he was standing on the bottom of the sea near his overturned boat.

The floor of the sea was of white sand, and the light around him was pale gray, but strangely he did not feel cold or wet. Then he saw a Mermaid beside him.

"I have rescued you from the Draug," she said. "Come, now I must take you to my father, the king of the Merfolk."

The Mermaid's black seaweed hair floated out from her head; her face was pale, with dark, gleaming eyes. Her form was clad in a greenish substance, and the silver brooch she wore had the same strange design the Finns used.

Eilert walked with the Mermaid along the sandy bottom. On either side were meadows of sea grass and bushes of thick seaweed. They passed brightly colored shells and broken hulls of boats half-buried in the sand.

At last they came to a house made from the hulls of two ships. The Mermaid led Eilert through the door, which she closed behind him. Inside, seated on a rough chair, was a large Merman. His head and neck were like a seal's, but his face resembled that of a dogfish. The fingers on both hands were webbed together, his feet covered in old sea boots.

"Well, Eilert," said the Merman, grinning, "you've had a very bad time of it up there today. Sit down, sit down."

Eilert saw nowhere to sit but on a pile of old nets. When he was seated, the old Merman shook his head sadly. "You should not have taken our grave earth to rub on your lines. But you're here now, so you might as well make the best of it."

Eilert could think of nothing to say; he put his hand into his pocket to touch the piece of iron.

At last the Merman sighed, leaned back, and closed his eyes. Without a sound, he slid slowly to the floor and slept.

"Come," said the Mermaid. "He will sleep like that for hours."

He followed her back along the sea floor until they reached his boat where it lay on the sand.

The Mermaid turned to him. "If I am to help you escape and return to the world above, you must lie down in the boat now and sleep."

Eilert hesitated, but the Mermaid's eyes were as kind as Zilla's and he was very tired. He lay down in the boat and closed his eyes. He felt her black seaweed hair spread around him like a dark curtain. As he drifted off to sleep, he heard her chanting a strange song.

When Eilert opened his eyes, he looked about in wonder. He was safe in the Finns' house, and Zilla and her father sat close by. Zilla's long black hair lay over her shoulders; her dark eyes stared at him from her pale face.

"I was under the sea with the Merfolk," he cried. "How—how—"

The room was still. Zilla and her father exchanged glances. Then the old man said evasively, "Aye. Our Zilla brought you back. She knows a thing or two about the sea, does Zilla!"

So it was Zilla who had saved him! Eilert wondered what powers she had used. He thought it best not to question; it was enough to know she rowed out to sea to bring him home.

Now when a lass, Finn or Nordlander, sets about rescuing the lad of her choice—whether by magic or otherwise—there can be only one outcome. The following spring, Zilla and Eilert were married.

It was the first time a Nordlander had married a Finn, and everyone in the village was surprised. But Eilert's parents, on thinking the matter over, had concluded that if the Finns did indeed possess magic spells over fish and other creatures of the sea, it was much better to have them in the family than not.

READ ON!

Grave Doubts by Scott Corbett. Two boys suspect that a murder was committed for inheritance money. Join them in some suspenseful detective work that also turns out to be a treasure hunt.

Al(exandra) the Great by Constance C. Greene. Two girls who are best friends face their problems together with wit and humor.

From the Mixed-up Files of Mrs. Basil E. Frankweiler by E. L. Konigsburg. When they hide out in the New York Metropolitan Museum of Art, Claudia and her brother become involved in a surprising mystery.

Mojo and the Russians by Walter Dean Myers. Who are those Russian men who visit Willie? Dean and his friends try to find out and get themselves into some funny situations along the way.

Bridge to Terabithia by Katherine Paterson. Jess is surprised not only that the new girl in school can run faster than he can but also that she wants to be his friend. Together they share many real and imaginary experiences until the day of a tragic accident.

The Best Bad Thing by Yoshiko Uchida. Twelve-year-old Rinko discovers that an unwanted move to her aunt's California farm turns out to be a good thing after all.

UNIT 5

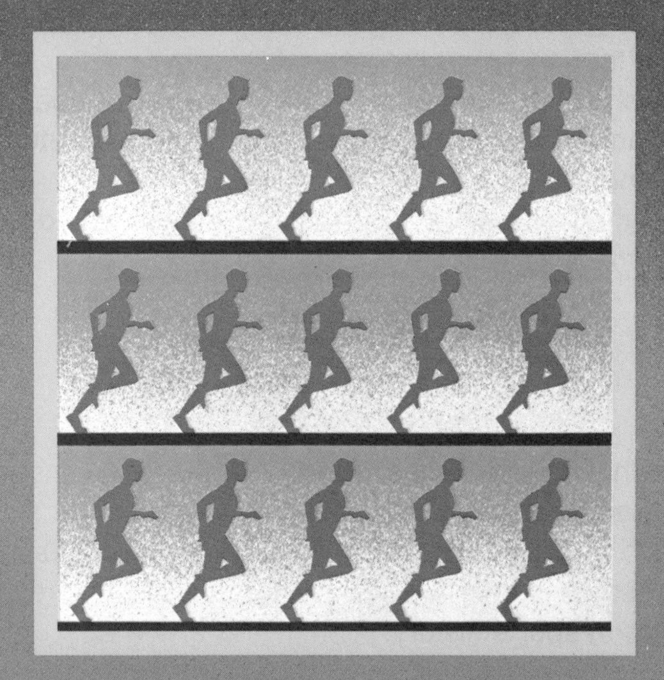

Set In Motion

LEARN NEW WORDS

1. Several species of plants on one side of the mountain were destroyed by an **avalanche** of snow and ice.
2. The game is very one-sided, as the Red Team is way ahead and has been **dominating** the Blue Team.
3. Our team is so far behind that **drastic** measures are needed for us to win.
4. A chair lift **enables** the skier to get up a slope.
5. Many hours of practice enabled her to **execute** that difficult dance step.
6. At the last minute, the exhausted team **rallied** and won the game.

GET SET TO READ

What is your favorite sport? Many sports fans have a favorite story about something funny or strange that happened at a sporting event. What's your favorite sports story?

Read this article to find out about some interesting moments in sports history.

Strange but True Sports Stories

by HOWARD LISS

Wrong-Way Goal

In February 1982, Dwight Anderson of the University of Southern California scored one of the strangest goals in basketball history.

A University of Washington player had missed a shot at the basket. One of Anderson's teammates got the rebound and fired the ball upcourt. Anderson raced after the ball, but by the time he caught up with it, he was almost out of bounds.

As his momentum carried him over the back line, Anderson flipped the ball over the *back of the backboard.* The ball swished through the net.

The basket counted because Anderson's feet had not touched ground, even though his body was out of bounds.

Taking Turns

Spartanburg County, South Carolina, was the scene of a strange basketball game in 1976. A girls' team from Mabry Junior High School took on a girls' team from D.R. Hill Junior High, and each team took turns dominating the other.

D.R. Hill dominated the first half by scoring twenty-six points while Mabry got nothing. In the second half Mabry rallied and racked up twenty-eight points while D.R. Hill's score was zero.

The final score: twenty-eight to twenty-six, Mabry.

The Lady Is a Champ

Great Olympic athletes are measured by the number of medals they have won. Using this measure, the greatest of all Olympic athletes is a woman.

Larisa Latynina, a young Russian gymnast, won a total of six medals in 1956. Four were gold medals, one was silver, and one was bronze. In 1960 Latynina won another six medals: three gold medals, two silvers, and one bronze. In 1964 she was again one of the stars of the Olympics, winning six more medals.

Larisa Latynina won a total of eighteen medals in Olympic competition. It is very difficult to imagine that *any* athlete will ever reach that total again.

Survivor

In the early days of championship skiing, one of the greatest skiers was Mathias Zdarsky. He was the first person in Austria to teach skiing on a regular basis, and by 1904 he had about 1000 students. Zdarsky is now considered by many to be the father of the Alpine technique. It was Zdarsky who introduced the snowplow to skiing. To execute the snowplow, both skis are pointed inward. This enables the skier to slow down. Zdarsky also introduced the stem turn, in which the skier changes direction by pushing one heel out while moving fast.

But Zdarsky contributed more than skiing maneuvers to snow sports. Once he was caught in an avalanche and suffered more than eighty fractures. But he survived and later wrote a book about avalanches that proved to be very useful.

All Tied Up at the Moment

Sandy Valdespino was a fast outfielder who made it to the major leagues with the Minnesota Twins. But when he was still playing minor-league baseball, he had difficulty running the bases. He would try to steal every time he got on base. Sometimes he wouldn't watch the coach's signals. As a result, he was often picked off first base. Or he'd be tagged out trying to steal an extra base, thus killing a rally.

Finally his manager said he would take drastic action. "Sandy," the skipper warned, "if you try any more silly base running, I'm going to tie a rope around you."

Sure enough, Valdespino ran through a coach's signal to stop and was thrown out at the plate. The manager decided his threatened drastic action was necessary.

The next time Valdespino got on base, the manager called for a time-out. He came off the bench carrying a rope. One end was tied around Valdespino's waist; the other end was handed to the first-base coach. The crowd went wild with laughter, but at long last young Sandy Valdespino got the message.

Gloves

Before 1875 the idea of a baseball glove was almost unthinkable. Anyone wearing protective equipment would have been considered a sissy. But that was the year Charles C. Waitt, the first baseman for a Boston team, became the first player to wear a glove. Because he didn't want the fans to notice it, Waitt's glove was flesh-colored.

Think About It

1. Tell about one of these stories that you found the most interesting.
2. Think of an adjective that describes one of the athletes in this article. Explain why you chose that word.
3. Why do athletes want to participate in the Olympics?
4. What does it take to be a good athlete?
5. Many athletes show great determination to succeed in their sports. Write about an individual you know who has shown determination in sports or in some other area.

More Amazing Achievements

by SHEP STENEMAN

Fast Ball

No major-league pitcher who ever lived could boast of having 110 no-hitters, 35 perfect games, and a fast ball clocked at 118 miles per hour. Not to mention a lifetime batting average of over .300. But between 1958 and 1976 one softball pitcher did put these amazing statistics together. Her name is Joan Joyce.

Leap into History

With one amazing jump in the 1968 Olympics, Bob Beamon made a fantastic leap into the record books. On this first try in the long-jump finals, the tall New Yorker raced down the runway and flew into the air. He came down 29 feet 2½ inches from where he'd started. That was more than 21 inches farther than anyone had ever jumped before.

It was a once-in-a-lifetime performance. Beamon himself never again came within two feet of his record leap. And no one else since has approached his record.

Analysis of Baseball

by MAY SWENSON

It's about
the ball,
the bat,
and the mitt.
Ball hits
bat, or it
hits mitt.
Bat doesn't
hit ball, bat
meets it.
Ball bounces
off bat, flies
air, or thuds
ground (dud)
or it
fits mitt.

Bat waits
for ball
to mate.
Ball hates
to take bat's
bait. Ball
flirts, bat's
late, don't
keep the date.
Ball goes in
(thwack) to mitt,
and goes out
(thwack) back
to mitt.

Ball fits
mitt, but
not all
the time.
Sometimes
ball gets hit
(pow) when bat
meets it,
and sails
to a place
where mitt
has to quit
in disgrace.
That's about
the bases
loaded,
about 40,000
fans exploded.

It's about
the ball,
the bat,
the mitt,
the bases
and the fans.
It's done
on a diamond,
and for fun.
It's about
home, and it's
about run.

LEARN NEW WORDS

1. That **architect** designs houses as well as office buildings.
2. The hungry animal **devoured** all the food.
3. His **genius** was seen in the design of his inventions.
4. Why didn't you **heed** my advice before you got yourself in trouble?
5. When the wind died, the large kite came **hurtling** to the ground.
6. This fascinating game must have been created by an **ingenious** person.
7. The entire island was the king's **realm**.
8. Her father said, "Obey the traffic laws, and don't be so **reckless** on your bicycle."
9. As she fell, her efforts to regain her balance were in **vain**.

GET SET TO READ

If you were a prisoner on an island, how would you escape?

Read this myth to find out how Daedalus and Icarus try to escape the island of Crete.

Daedalus and Icarus

a Greek myth
retold by ANNE TERRY WHITE

In the days when King Minos ruled Crete and his mighty navy ranged the seas, there lived in Athens a man by the name of Daedalus. And his name was known as far and wide as that of Minos. For Daedalus was the greatest architect and sculptor of his time. There was nothing his ingenious mind could not design or his skillful hands execute.

One day Daedalus left Athens with his only son Icarus and crossed the sea to Crete. King Minos was delighted to have the Athenian architect in his realm. The King had something in mind that called for the genius of Daedalus. Minos possessed a fearful monster, with the head and shoulders of a bull and the legs and trunk of a man. The creature was called the Minotaur—that is, the Bull of Minos. The King wanted a suitable place to keep the Minotaur. The building must be such that neither the monster himself nor any victim sent in to be devoured by him could possibly escape from it.

So, at the King's command, Daedalus designed the Labyrinth. This ingenious building was a bewildering maze of passages. They turned back upon themselves, crisscrossed, and went round and round without leading anywhere. Once someone went inside the Labyrinth, it was all but impossible to find the way out again. Even Daedalus himself was once nearly lost.

King Minos was delighted with Daedalus' work and held him in the highest favor as a great genius. Yet Daedalus was less than pleased, for he felt himself to be no better than a prisoner in Crete. The King was so afraid Daedalus would reveal the secret of the Labyrinth that he would not let him leave his island realm. And for that very reason Daedalus yearned to go. With what envy he watched the birds winging their way through the sky!

One day, as his eyes followed the graceful sea birds, an idea came to him.

"King Minos may shut my way out by land and by sea," he thought, "but he does not control the air."

He began to study the flight of birds and to observe how their wings are fashioned. He watched the little song birds fold and unfold their wings, watched how they rose from the ground, flew down from the trees, and went to and fro. He also watched the herons slowly flapping their great wings. He watched the eagles soar and swoop. He saw, too, how their feathers overlapped

one another—where they were large and where they were small.

When he thought he understood the secrets of flight, Daedalus went to a nesting place he knew of and gathered feathers of various sizes. In a chamber close to the roof, he began to build wings. First he laid down a row of the tiniest feathers, then a row of larger ones overlapping them, and yet larger ones beyond these. He fastened the feathers together in the middle with thread and at the bottom with wax. When he had built on enough rows, he bent them around into a gentle curve to look like real birds' wings.

His young son Icarus stood by and watched his father work. Laughing, the boy caught the feathers when they blew away in the wind. He pressed his thumb into the yellow wax to soften it for his father.

When Daedalus had finished the pair of wings, he put them on. He raised himself in the air and hovered there. He moved the wings just as he had seen birds do, and lo! he could fly. Icarus clapped his hands together in delight.

"Make me a pair of wings, too, Father!" he cried.

Then Daedalus made a second pair of wings and prepared his son to fly.

"Now I warn you, Icarus," Daedalus said, "not to be reckless. Be wise, not bold. Take a course midway between heaven and earth. For if you fly too high, the sun will scorch your feathers. If you fly too low, the sea will wet them. Take me for your guide. Follow me and you will be safe."

All the time he was speaking, Daedalus was fastening the wings to his son's shoulders. His hands trembled as he thought of the great adventure before them. At the same time, he was worried about the boy. He did not know whether he could quite trust Icarus to heed his warning and obey. As he adjusted his own wings and kissed the excited child, tears ran down Daedalus' face.

"Remember," he repeated for the last time. "Heed my words and stay close to me!"

Then he rose on his wings and flew from the housetop. Icarus followed.

Daedalus kept a watchful eye on the boy, even as a mother bird does when she has brought a fledgling out of its nest in the treetops and launched it in the air. It was early morning. Few people were about. But here and there a plowman in the field or a fisherman tending his nets caught sight of them.

"They must be gods!" the simple toilers cried, and they bent their bodies in respect.

Father and son flew far out over the sea. Daedalus was no longer worried about Icarus, who managed his wings as easily as a bird. Already the islands of Delos and Paros were behind them. Calymne, rich in honey, was on their right hand. But now Icarus began to yield to the full delight of his newfound powers. He wanted to soar and swoop. How thrilling it was to rise to a height, close his wings, and speed down, down, like a thunderbolt, then turn and rise again!

Time after time Icarus tried it, each time daring greater heights. Then, recklessly forgetting his father's warning, he soared higher still, far up into the cloudless sky.

"Not even the eagle soars as this!" the boy thought. "I am like the gods that keep the wide heaven."

As the words crossed his mind, he felt a warm stream of liquid over his shoulders. He had come too close to the blazing sun, and the sweet-smelling wax that bound the feathers was melting. With a shock of terror he felt himself hurtling downward. His wings, broken in a thousand parts, were hurtling downward,

too. In vain Icarus moved his arms up and down—he could get no hold on the air.

"Father!" he shrieked. "Father! Help! I am falling."

Even as he cried, the deep blue water of the sea—that ever since has been called Icarian—closed and devoured him.

"Icarus! Icarus! Where are you?" Daedalus cried in vain, turning in every direction and searching the air behind, above, and all around. Then his eyes fell on the sea. Tufts of feathers were floating on the crest of the waves.

Too well he understood their meaning. Folding his great wings, he came to earth on the nearest island and fixed his streaming eyes upon the sea.

"O Icarus, my son!" he wailed. He ripped off his glorious wings and stamped upon them. "Cursed be the skill that wrought my son's destruction!" he cried.

Days afterward, the body of Icarus washed to the shore. There, on the lonely island which bears the boy's name, Daedalus buried his only son.

Think About It

1. Why was the Labyrinth a perfect place for the Minotaur?
2. Why wouldn't King Minos let Daedalus leave the island?
3. What did Daedalus do to escape the island?
4. What warning did Daedalus give to Icarus?
5. Why did Icarus fly too high?
6. What do you think the moral of this story is?
7. Do you think the moral of this ancient myth applies to today's world? Write a paragraph explaining why or why not.

LEARN NEW WORDS

1. The man was thin, with very **angular** features.
2. The sunlight brought out the red in her **auburn** hair.
3. At night he **barricades** the door with a heavy bar.
4. The woman is a writer of high **caliber;** she has won many awards for her work.
5. Her **commitment** to politics was such that she decided to run for public office.
6. Because we **dallied** too long after school, we missed the bus and had to walk home.
7. The man was standing at the busy **intersection** waiting for the light to change.
8. It was no accident; I saw the girl with the auburn hair **maliciously** trip him in the movie theater.
9. When the **obnoxious** man shoved his way onto the bus, the little boy maliciously kicked him.
10. The old house was **renovated** to show the fine caliber of its original design.
11. The people who dallied at the theater while a taxi waited looked very **sophisticated.**

GET SET TO READ

What's the difference between someone giving you advice and someone pressuring you to do something? Why is it important to make up your own mind about what you want to do?

Read this story to find out how Kate comes to a difficult decision.

Maybe Next Year...

by AMY HEST

The New York Ballet Academy is located in a rickety old building on Eighty-sixth Street and Broadway. I've been studying there since fifth grade. That Christmas Mr. and Mrs. Schumacher took my sister Pinky and me to see *The Nutcracker* at Lincoln Center. I had never been to the ballet before, and the minute the curtain went up on the first act, I was hooked. I remember borrowing a dime from Mrs. Schumacher, and during the intermission I called my grandmother to ask for lessons. Lucky me, because she said yes. The surprising thing is that Pinky never wanted lessons, either.

"Hey, Kate!" I turn in time to see Peter Robinson dodge a blue city bus in the busy intersection at Eighty-sixth and Broadway.

"You'll kill yourself at that rate," I scold when he is safely at my side. But I'm smiling because it's good to see Peter, especially in one piece.

"Can't," he answers, "can't kill myself until after class."

"Wise guy."

Although I've never had the nerve to tell him, Peter is far and away my best friend. Sure, there are girls from school, like Patricia Mandella and Sabina Moskowitz, but the truth is I'd rather be with Peter. When I was younger I liked to pretend he was my big brother, but recently I've decided that I'm just a little bit in love with him.

First of all, Peter is the most handsome boy I've ever known. Not movie star handsome, just plain cute. He's a drop shorter than I am, and very thin. His eyes remind me of two aqua almonds, and his hair, a dark shade of auburn, has the nicest way of flopping in his eyes and around his ears, in layers so thick he needs to wear a bandanna during dance class.

"Guess who's been invited to take Ron's advanced ballet class?"

"Peter!" I jump up and clap my hands. I want to throw my arms around his neck. I want to kiss his cheek. Of course I do neither.

Peter has been studying ballet about six months longer than I, but right from the start he had a way of standing out. He's a boy, first of all, and there aren't too many at the academy. But the important thing is that Peter is the most incredible dancer.

I once heard Madame Dukowsky say that dancing is in Peter's blood. And when I watch him in class, I sometimes think he was *born* dancing. He doesn't seem to be struggling like the rest of us. There's something special about Peter, all right, and it's no secret that he is every teacher's favorite. I'm sure he'll be a star one day.

"Don't tell anyone, okay?" he is saying.

"If *I* were invited to take advanced, I'd be shouting it from the rooftops," I answer. "It's a good thing I like you, Peter, or I could easily hate you for being so good."

"You *are* a good dancer," he tells me.

"Not good enough."

We walk up the two dingy flights to the New York Ballet Academy. Piano music filters through long, narrow hallways. It is always extra-crowded here on Saturdays, and while waiting for class to start we clutter the halls, talking in huddles, stretching out across the floor. Some of the kids drink small containers of orange juice and eat yogurt as if it were going out of style.

I climb across a contorted body and peer into one of the dance studios. The door is open a crack.

A floor-to-ceiling mirror spans an entire wall. Opposite, a dozen timid children in first or second grade flounder at the *barre*. Most of them look rigid and unhappy. Their teacher, Corwin, paces up and back, pulling in a stomach, straightening a leg. He doesn't miss a beat as he drones on, ". . . and one, and two . . . heels together, Hilary . . . and three, and four . . . shoulders down, Marilyn . . . and one, and two . . ."

"Psssst." Peter waves to me from the announcement board. "Look at this," he half whispers, "tryouts for the best summer school in the city!"

I read the small printed bulletin.

ATTENTION SENIOR BALLET STUDENTS
Audition for National
Ballet Summer School
March 16

SEE MADAME DUKOWSKY AT DESK
FOR MORE INFORMATION
REMEMBER: SENIOR STUDENTS ONLY!

"This is it, Kate!" Peter is delirious. His dance bag slips off his shoulder to the floor and he absent-mindedly kicks it between his feet. He grabs my shoulders and looks me square in the eye.

I feel my face getting pink and warm.

". . . either now or never," he is saying. But I am concentrating on the blue-green of his eyes. His tone of voice is serious. "Here's our big chance! If we take summer classes at the National Ballet School"—he says the last three words slowly, and he hangs on every syllable—"we'll really be on our way."

"Sure, Peter," I interrupt. "They're just sitting there waiting for the two of us."

"We'll never know if we don't try," he says.

"I bet *hundreds* of kids will show up for that audition!" I exclaim.

"So what?"

"So what?" I repeat. But even as I say the words, my head is spinning.

I have just auditioned, and the judges remain pinned to their seats. Finally, they begin to whisper among themselves. *The tall blonde,* they buzz, *she is perfect. Don't let her leave the studio. She will start her professional training immediately. An ideal, a dream,* they ogle. *We will sculpt her into the ballerina of the century . . .*

"Are you there, Kate?" Peter is waving his hand in front of my eyes. "Daydreaming again?" His smile is smug.

"M.Y.O.B." I tell him. "Mind your own business."

"Don't forget," Peter answers, "March the sixteenth."

"Don't forget," I mimic, "March the sixteenth." Then I pat his shoulder and smile. "I'll tell you what," I say quietly, "*you* go to the audition and you can tell me all about it. Meanwhile, I'll go in here." I point to the yellow sign marked "Girls' Dressing Room."

I slip through the door but hear him call out, "I *am* going. But you're coming with me, you'll see!"

If only I were good enough, Peter . . .

The dressing room is noisy and crowded and smells as if someone forgot to open a window. Girls, everywhere girls. Sprawled across narrow wooden benches, they tug at jeans, pull on leotards and tights and sweat shirts and leg warmers.

I sit in the corner on the cool gray floor to unlace my sneakers. All around me they are talking about the National Ballet School bulletin.

"Madame says the auditions would be a waste of time for Ballet Two students." Susan Thorndike's voice has great authority.

"Naturally." That is Lucy Framington. Lucy has been studying at our school since kindergarten, and most of us agree she is one of the most obnoxious people in Manhattan. "Unless you've been on toe for two years, don't bother showing up."

"Are you going to audition?" Sarah Albright sits on the edge of the narrow bench in front of me.

Of course, I am! Everyone knows I'm good enough for that kind of competition. That's what I would like to say, and believe, but instead I answer with a shrug. "I don't know." I pull a bright yellow T-shirt over my head and my chest is labeled "Forever Dancing." "What about you?"

Sarah shakes her head. "Not me. I don't have a prayer."

"We'll never know if we don't try," I tell her, realizing that Peter said the same thing to me just five minutes ago.

It's important to stretch out before class, but today I have dallied too long. Our teacher, Ron, is already in the studio. Suddenly he looks up. All chattering stops. And the stretching. Ron gives the final sign that he is ready. I race to the *barre*, like the others, and squeeze between Ariane Dukowsky and Peter.

"We begin," Ron announces, unsmiling. "Left hand on the *barre*. And *plié*."

Ron Vlostic is a very mysterious and much-talked-about teacher at the academy. It's easy to see why. He is not only glamorous but exceedingly handsome—movie star caliber. His nose is so straight, cheekbones so high and angular, you would swear someone had chiseled them to perfection. He has olive skin and short black hair and eyes as dark as the Hudson River on a winter's night.

Ron claims he once danced with the Bolshoi Ballet in Moscow. Some people say he is rich and famous and that he is descended from Russian aristocracy.

"Hips under. Neck lo-o-ong." He places two cold fingers under my chin.

Battement tendu. My eyes are glued to the back of Ariane's head. As usual, Ron stops to praise her flawless extension. Ariane Dukowsky's mother happens to own the academy and Miss Darling Daughter is the most perfect person I've ever seen. Perfect face. A perfect skinny body. Worst of all, Ariane is a perfect dance student.

Frappé. From across the room the voice booms, "Kate! Point that foot until it hurts." I point my foot and it hurts. "*Now* you are working," Ron informs me as if I don't already know it.

Do I ever hate being singled out like that. Sometimes I wish Ron would just leave me alone, but Peter says I should be happy he corrects me. He says Ron wouldn't criticize so much if he didn't think I had potential. But of course, it's easy for Peter to talk.

". . . supporting leg straight, Sarah Albright."

The big hand on the studio clock creeps through our *barre* exercises. Twenty minutes. Twenty-three minutes. I am hot. I am sweaty. I am hungry. Ron walks by and I pray he doesn't see the bent knee or the hip that lifts. I pray that he doesn't see the mistakes I don't even know I'm making.

Later I peel off pale pink leg warmers and the yellow T-shirt. We have done our *battements, petits* and *grands,* on the floor and off. We have done all those exercises that are supposed to strengthen muscles in our feet, our legs, our backs, our fronts. We move out to center floor, which is a lot more fun, but also more difficult.

Away from the *barre* there's a whole new set of things to concentrate on, like the way we move our heads, the *port de bras* (arm position), and *épaulement* (shoulder position). Ron says this is when we begin to bring "an artistic life" to even our most basic ballet exercises.

During this part of class we usually work in three lines across the studio, with Ron choosing the day's stars for the first line, the flunkies for last. Peter and Ariane are always asked to go to the first row. Once in a while I am too, but mostly Ron sends me to the second. I hate not being best, but sometimes it's good to watch the others try out a new movement or position before I have to do it.

It isn't until the last ten or fifteen minutes of class, though, that I remind myself why I want so badly to be a dancer. There I am—jumping, leaping, spinning. (But of course everything has a fancy French name like *assemblé, jeté* and *pirouette.*) Finally, I am *going* somewhere, even if it's only across the floor of a run-down dance studio on the Upper West Side. Springing into *pas de chat*, I catch a glimpse of myself in the mirror and believe, even for a second, that I'm dancing. Dancing!

By the end of our *allegro* combination I am breathing heavily. My face is flushed scarlet, and the perspiration that started as a trickle on my forehead more than an hour ago leaves telltale splotches across my blue leotard as it creeps down, down, down to the sticky soles of my feet.

The official way to end a ballet class is with *révérence* (a bow or curtsy that makes you feel as if you have just performed at the Metropolitan Opera House). Then there's a round of applause for the teacher (by this time you remember where you really are).

We begin to file out of the studio. "Your attention, please," Ron calls to us. "Students who intend to audition for the National Ballet Summer School, stay a moment," he says.

Nobody moves.

"Shhhhhhhh!"

"Quiet! Ron is going to tell us something."

"Girls and boys." Ron speaks in a low monotone. "As you all know, March sixteenth is only two months away. In the spirit of giving you every advantage for a successful audition, I will be holding supplemental classes on Tuesday and Thursday afternoons at 3:30. Because of their specialized and intensive nature, I'm sorry to report they will be expensive—twice as costly as your regular classes."

"I'll pay anything!" shrieks Lucy Framington.

"But I have flute on Thursdays," somebody whines.

Ron inhales deeply. "A serious dancer will find a way to be here." He turns on his heel and leaves the studio.

We are dismissed.

"I wonder if my grandmother will go along with the extra classes," I say to Peter en route to our separate dressing rooms.

"I thought you didn't want to audition." He is smug.

"I never said anything of the sort, Peter Robinson. And besides," I add smoothly, "a few extra classes may be just what it takes to push me over the edge—and on to stardom."

Peter laughs and gives my shoulder a friendly nudge. "See you in a few minutes."

Jake's is a run-down but homey little diner near the corner of Eighty-eighth Street. It is squished in between a gourmet treat center and a fancy-looking health food store. Jake himself must be a hundred years old, and the story goes that he refused to sell his store for a million dollars, even though the rest of the block is being renovated into a glamorous shopping plaza.

A narrow and cluttered aisle leads to the back. Peter and I sit on two of the three wobbly stools.

"Yeah?" The teen-ager behind the counter looks as if he wouldn't know a bottle of shampoo if one fell on him.

"Orange juice, please."

"Lemonade and a rare hamburger," says Peter.

I put an elbow on the counter and rest my head on my hand. "You see," I say slowly, "it's finally beginning to dawn on me that I'm never going to be a star."

"How do you know?" Peter turns the bottle of ketchup upside down and barricades it with little cubes of sugar.

"I *know*. Sometimes you just feel these things. My grandmother always tells me I push myself too much," I continue, "and I think she's right."

"Yeah, but she never told you to *quit*." Peter flicks two fingers against the side of the bottle and spins it around and around.

"It wouldn't be quitting. I am not a quitter."

He turns to face me. "Then why won't you audition?"

"I thought you were my friend, Peter." I shake my head. "You act as if you wouldn't talk to me again if I decided not to audition."

"I *am* your friend," he insists. "That's why I think you should audition. You'll never get anywhere if you don't go through with this."

"So what," I mumble, thinking what a disaster it would be if Peter and Ariane went on to the National Ballet School without me. Why, I'd be nowhere. Nowhere! Peter would be too busy and too proud to bother with a flunky named Kate, and the two of them would dance off, never looking back, never feeling the tiniest little bit sorry for me . . .

"Are you sure you want to be a dancer?" Peter is beginning to sound slightly disgusted with me.

I blow the paper off the straw the greasy kid put in front of me. I wish I could think of something brilliant to say.

"I don't know what you're so afraid of," he tells me, and his voice is kinder.

"The way I see it," I begin, "the difference between you and me, and between creepy Ariane and me, is that the two of you are willing to give up *everything* to dance."

Peter takes a long strawful of lemonade. He stares ahead, at the ancient grill that sizzles his hamburger and the plastic cups piled in the sink. Right this minute he looks much older, like someone too wise and sophisticated to be associating with a kid like me.

"Well?" I say. "Aren't I right?"

He smiles slightly, as if he'd just awakened from a pleasant dream. "It's my life," he says simply.

Peter douses his hamburger with extras. Extra pickles from the tiny bowl on the counter, extra onions, and about a pound of ketchup. He carefully cuts it in half. Then, like the gentleman I always knew he was, he hands me my share. One thing about Peter Robinson is he always knows the right thing to do.

"Nana!" I have been stalling for an hour. My French text is open, untouched, to the chapter on pluperfect. Lounging across my bed, I reach for the door and call to my grandmother. "Nana!" I repeat. "Can you come here?"

"I'm busy," she replies.

Swell. Too busy to talk to her own granddaughter. I fall backward and raise my legs toward the ceiling. Scissor kicks . . . one and two. Maybe Peter is right; if I would just audition, my decision would be made for me. If the judges select me, I'll go on to the National Ballet School this summer. If they don't pick me, well . . .

The door opens and Nana comes in brushing a powdery layer of flour off her hands and onto her apron. "What's up?" She sits on the edge of my bed.

"I'm in a fix, Nana."

"What kind of fix?" she asks.

"I can't decide what to do about that audition," I tell her. "I'm just not sure I'm good enough."

"You're afraid you'll be turned down." She says it as if she were some kind of mind reader.

"That's part of it," I sigh. "The other part is I'm not even sure I *want* to study at the National Ballet School. Everybody says it's horribly competitive. They say the pressure is so great that kids are always having nervous breakdowns . . ."

"Kate," she frowns, "wherever did you hear such a ridiculous story?"

I shrug. "Just around."

"But you love your classes," she reminds me.

"I know, but I have a feeling it's kid stuff compared to the National Ballet School."

She nods.

"Peter says," and I stare down at the red plaid quilt on my bed, "maybe I don't want to be a dancer."

Nana makes a little clicking sound with her tongue. "One day you want something, and the next day you don't," she says slowly. "Grownups have that problem, too."

"Peter says I'd be a quitter."

"Nonsense!" She looks at me sternly. "Peter's whole life is ballet. He has made a total commitment, and nothing will stand in his way." Nana leans toward me and our faces are very close. "When he auditions on the sixteenth, it's because that's the right thing for *him* to do."

"I'm not a quitter, Nana."

"I know that," she smiles. Using her fingers like a comb, she pushes the hair away from her forehead. The soft white fluff reminds me of the snow before New Yorkers traipse all over it. "And there's something else," she continues. "You may not be ready to audition right now, but it's important to remember you're only twelve years old—not exactly over the hill, even for a ballerina. Peter is a little older, and so is that Ariane girl you keep talking about."

"And what happens when the two of them make the NBS? What happens to *me,* Nana?" I mumble.

Nana takes a deep breath, then lets the air out slowly. "You mean, what happens when the two of them start going places and you're left behind."

I nod.

"It would be hard to take, all right, but you would learn to accept it," she says, very matter-of-fact. "That's no reason for you to audition, Kate."

"You don't understand," I sigh, but I know she does, and she knows it.

"One thing I've learned from all the literature you bring me on being a professional dancer is you don't *have* to study at the National Ballet School at the age of twelve." Nana pauses briefly. "The point is, Kate, all won't be lost if you wait a year or two."

"Wait a year or two . . ." I repeat the words and suddenly they make sense. "Nana," I say softly, "maybe that's the answer—and I never even thought of it. I never even thought about next year."

When she hugs me it feels safe and good, like when I was little. When life was simple. "Sometimes we're so close to a situation that we can't see it clearly," she tells me.

"How will I know if I'm ready next year, Nana?"

"Suppose we take it one year at a time," she says. "It's easier that way."

I am sitting on a park bench across the street from the building that houses the National Ballet School. It is drizzly and cold and my eyes wander from outer space to the wide double doors across from me.

March the sixteenth. From my secret post I watched Peter enter the stark modern building at 10:00, and Ariane Dukowsky at 10:05. A few minutes later two or three others from the academy slip in—but where are the rest? How come more kids from Ron's classes aren't showing up?

By 11:00 I have eaten my sandwich, and the apple. My stomach churns the way it might if *I* were in there, doing whatever it is those kids are doing to get into the National Ballet School. I'm probably just silly to be sitting out here, but something inside me says to wait. So I wrap my arms around myself—and wait.

There's Peter! He pushes through the heavy doors and I am on my feet, waving excitedly. "Peter!"

He looks around, then spots me. I can tell he is surprised, and it's no wonder. We haven't spoken a word in days, since I told him I wasn't going to audition. Now he crosses Broadway slowly, after waiting for the traffic light to change.

"How did you do?" I ask when he is sitting beside me.

"What are you doing here?"

"Well? How did you do," I repeat, "in *there*?"

He looks puzzled. "You still haven't told me what you're doing sitting around in the rain."

"Maybe I just felt like sitting around in the rain," I answer.

"Sure."

"Well, actually," I begin quietly, "I came to wish you good luck, but then I didn't have the nerve. So I decided to hang around in case you had some nice news to tell me."

"Oh," he gulps. "But I guess it figures."

"What figures?"

"It's just that . . . what I mean is . . . when you do stuff like this, I realize . . . well, I realize what a good friend you are."

"I know it," I say lightly. "You're a lucky guy to have a friend like me."

But Peter doesn't allow himself to smile, even a little. "You didn't audition," he says quietly and without looking at me. "I can't believe you didn't audition."

"Believe it," I answer. "I didn't audition. Anyway, that's no reason to quit talking to me."

"I didn't quit talking to you."

"You've been pouting for days," I say sternly. "Very immature."

But then he is pushing up the brim of my yellow rain hat. He kisses my cheek. It's all over very fast, yet it's never a bad thing to be kissed by Peter. "Friends?" he says.

"Friends."

All of a sudden Peter's eyes are filling with tears. "I made it," he whispers. "I made the National Ballet School."

"Peter!" I shriek. Then I throw my arms around his neck as if I'll never let go. "Peter!"

We take the bus uptown to Jake's. I make Peter tell me everything that goes on at an audition for the National Ballet School. Once he gets going he doesn't stop talking, and I, the captivated audience, hang on every word.

"Who else made it?" I keep asking. "Who else, Peter?"

But he shrugs and insists he doesn't know.

"Let's take class," I say suddenly, tossing a quarter on the counter for the greasy one's tip. "We can make the 1:00 if we hurry."

"Are you kidding?" he exclaims. "I'm wiped out. First I've got to break the news to my father; then I'm going to sleep away the next two days."

"Too bad," I smile. "Ron's class is kid stuff compared to what you'll be doing at the NBS."

Everybody is in class today. Everybody. I can't hear myself for all the commotion in the studio. "What's going on?" I try to find out. "What's all the fuss about?"

The word is out. Ariane Dukowsky made the National Ballet School.

A hundred tiny hammers are pounding inside my head. I break into a sweat. And the tears I can't keep from coming are streaming down my face and my neck. I hate Ariane! I knew this would happen. She and Peter are in, and I am out. It's not fair.

I head for the aloneness of the *barre* at the far end of the room and swing my right leg up on it. Leaning toward the knee, I reach past pointed toes with my fingertips. I stretch until it hurts, and then I stretch a little more.

"Why didn't you audition?" The voice behind me is Ron's and it is ice-cold.

I lift my leg off the *barre* and stare ahead, at the dirty white wall where some long-ago person penciled the message "Jane loves Bryan."

"I am disappointed, Kate." I can barely hear Ron for the drumming in my head, and the quiet of his voice. "You had every reason to try." Still, I can't turn to look at him.

"Maybe," my voice is a cracked whisper, "maybe next year."

"Next year!" He laughs maliciously. "And next year you say, 'Maybe next year.' That, my dear, is not the stuff ballerinas are made of."

Then he is gone and I am breathing normally. Ron doesn't believe me. He doesn't understand a girl may just not be ready. Well that's too bad, Mr. Perfect. That's too, too bad!

But the arms are trembly as I resume my stretch. And I want to shout with all my might, *Ron Vlostic, you wait and see!*

Think About It

1. What decision did Kate have to make?
2. Why was it hard for her to decide?
3. What was the reasoning behind her final decision?
4. Contrast the different ways in which Nana, Peter, and Ron Vlostic try to influence Kate.
5. What do you think will happen when Kate gets the opportunity to audition for the National Ballet School again? Tell why you think as you do.
6. Write about what you think it takes to be a good dancer.

LEARN NEW WORDS

1. Press the "on" button to **activate** the copy machine.
2. The people were committed to saving the local forest, so the senator came to talk with them about **conservation**.
3. When my sewing machine isn't **functioning** as it should, I have to call someone to fix it.
4. "The Beast," as the name **implies**, is a very scary roller coaster ride.
5. If any part of the sophisticated engine **malfunctions**, the train will stop automatically.
6. That store has all kinds of **merchandise** related to sports.
7. The fallen trees and other **obstacles** at the intersection after the storm made it difficult to pass.
8. **Personnel** who sell souvenir merchandise at the amusement park wear special uniforms.
9. The motor **propelled** the boat up the river.
10. The workers will **reinforce** the new building with concrete.
11. The large waves created **turbulence** in the water, causing some people on the ship to get seasick.

GET SET TO READ

What are your favorite amusement park rides? Why do you like certain rides?

Read this article to find out how some of the most exciting rides in the country keep on their tracks.

Behind the Scenes at the Amusement Park

by ELIZABETH VAN STEENWYK

Scream If You're Scared

The safety bar snaps shut, and you are locked inside the car of "Greezed Lightnin'," the roller coaster at Astroworld in Houston, Texas. You hold the bar in a white-knuckle grip, thinking about what the roller coaster's name implies. You can hardly wait for the thrilling ride to come, but at the same time you're almost choking with fear. Why did you ever decide to get on this roller coaster in the first place?

But you can't back out now. The ride begins, and the train goes from zero to sixty miles an hour in less than four seconds. Before you can take a breath, you are launched with the force of more than four times the weight of gravity *upside down* into a loop eighty feet high. When the train has completed the loop and you are right-side-up again, it heads up a seventy-degree incline rising 138 feet into the air. It pauses at the top. You look down and discover there's nothing, absolutely nothing, between you and the ground. You are powerless to stop the scream erupting from your throat as the train is propelled *backward* from its highest point, down the same track and into the station.

It's over! You stagger from the car, giddy with happiness to have both feet on the ground. You'll never do that again—at least not for a few minutes. As you walk away, you wonder if any of the people waiting to board heard you scream. Then you realize that it doesn't make any difference. Screaming is part of the fun that goes with riding a roller coaster.

One hundred fifty tons of steel were used to build "Greezed Lightnin'," which gives guests at Astroworld an upside-down view of Houston's skyline.
(Courtesy of Astroworld)

Roller Coaster Maintenance

"Greezed Lightnin'" is similar to other roller coasters in amusement parks across the country. These complicated rides don't take care of themselves. Operators and maintenance personnel with lots of training and practical experience are needed to keep them functioning smoothly.

Even getting a roller coaster to go takes know-how. To start "Montezooma's Revenge" at Knott's Berry Farm in Buena Park, California, two release buttons must be pressed at the same time from different ends of the station, each by a different operator. If one operator sees something that looks like a problem, he or she doesn't push the button.

Even if everything is okay and both buttons are pressed, the train doesn't activate for two seconds. During those two seconds, a computer checks the roller coaster's sixty-two circuits for malfunctions.

If any system isn't functioning properly, the ride won't operate. A ride maintenance employee is then called in. A readout from the train's computer tells where to look for the malfunction. After the necessary repairs are made, the maintenance employee signs his or her name to say the ride is safe. At last "Montezooma's Revenge" is ready to be activated.

At Astroworld, a mechanic walks the wooden roller coaster, "Texas Cyclone," each morning, checking for weak places in the structure. It takes nearly an hour to walk the slopes and angles of this coaster. After the mechanic is satisfied that the track is all right, a safety card is signed, meaning the 3500-foot coaster is ready for guests.

Safety checks are a lot of trouble. But they are trouble worth taking. All amusement park personnel agree that their second consideration is guest satisfaction. Their first consideration is guest safety.

A Beast of a Roller Coaster

Someone once said you enter a roller coaster as a person and exit as a dishrag. If a roller coaster ride is so scary, why do

people take it? That's a question that's hard to answer. It's easier to explain how a roller coaster is built.

A team of designers, engineers, and construction workers at Kings Island, a park in Kings Island, Ohio, built the roller coaster called "The Beast." Before beginning the project, members of the team walked the park and decided that the rugged territory in the southeast corner would be a good place for a unique ride. They visited other parks, gathering information on rides already built. They rode on more than fifty roller coasters before they began to design their own.

"The Beast" at Kings Island is rated as one of the best coasters in the country. This first hill on the ride is a 135-foot drop into an underground tunnel. *(Courtesy of Kings Island)*

Over 4000 hours of exacting design work went into the blueprints for "The Beast." The plans were very precise, and little error could be made in the construction.

Work began in 1978 during the park's summer season. While guests were enjoying other rides, watching shows, and eating their favorite foods, a lot of hammering and sawing was going on in the southeast corner of the park. Altogether over 2400 yards of concrete were mixed and poured to form the firm foundation and giant pillars which support and reinforce the track. Nearly 38,000 pounds of nails were pounded into 850,000 board feet of lumber to make a wooden track over 7400 feet long. A computerized safety system was installed. Numerous test rides were conducted. Finally, in 1979, "The Beast" was opened for business.

As its name implies, "The Beast" is scary. But it's also fun. The coaster has two long vertical drops, eight banked turns, and three tunnels. The ride lasts almost four minutes, making it one of the longest rides on a wooden coaster track in the country.

Keeping the Green in the Greenery

Roller coasters are just one of the things at an amusement park that need constant maintenance and upkeep. At five o'clock in the morning, the landscape crew of Magic Mountain spreads across the park and begins to snip, clip, mow, and sow. About half the area, or 125 acres, is green, requiring constant care. Because Magic Mountain is located in a hot, dry area forty miles north of Los Angeles, nearly 12,000 trees have been planted to keep guests cool and comfortable. The trees need daily watering and, on a hot day, require 300,000 gallons of water to survive the heat.

Building Rapids That Roar

The hill where the Magic Mountain white-water ride, "Roaring Rapids," is located was covered long ago with oak, pine, pepper, sycamore, and other trees. It is still covered with those same trees. How they were preserved and replanted is an interesting story of conservation.

Before construction of the ride began, the landscape crew carefully removed approximately 500 trees to the Magic Mountain nursery. Even five massive oak trees were preserved. These rare, hundred-year-old trees weigh up to forty tons and stand twenty and thirty feet tall.

To build "Roaring Rapids," bulldozer operators cut a riverbed at least six feet deep. Grading crews sliced down through almost ninety feet of mountain to create a 1200-foot-long river course with a twelve-and-a-half-foot drop from start to finish.

While the river appears natural, it is artificial, constructed with modern technology. The riverbed is lined with reinforced concrete six inches thick. The canyon walls are made of a mixture of cement, sand, and water carved to look like rocks.

The river was widened in several places to form lakes. Islands have been left in the centers of the lakes to serve as obstacles for the large rafts and to create turbulence. More obstacles in the form of sandbars, chutes, and boulders were constructed to make the artificial river appear natural.

Hidden machinery provides the energy that keeps the water

Workers carefully move a pine tree before building "Roaring Rapids." *(Courtesy of Magic Mountain)*

in the stream moving. Water is propelled by two pumps through the river at speeds of up to thirty miles an hour. Underground wave machines create the turbulence, whirlpools, and crosscurrents to toss the boats, even causing them to spin out.

When "Roaring Rapids" was completed in 1981, eight months after it was begun, all of the native trees were taken from the nursery and moved back to their original locations.

Amusement Parks, Then and Now

Amusement parks haven't always been so big and complicated and computerized. Once

Rafts are not attached to a track at "Roaring Rapids," but move at the whim of the river. Each trip is a different—and wet—experience. *(Courtesy of Magic Mountain)*

they were a simple kind of entertainment.

Many of the early amusement parks in the United States were built by streetcar companies. In the mid-1850s, there were no automobiles, and only very wealthy citizens had their own carriages. The average person walked or rode the streetcars to get where he or she wanted to go.

The streetcars were crowded six days a week. But no one rode them on Sundays. To get some Sunday business, the streetcar owners had to give their customers somewhere to go on their days off. So they built amusement parks at the ends of streetcar lines.

The early amusement parks had swings and slides, pony rides and merry-go-rounds, picnic areas and places to dance. Coney Island, on the Atlantic Ocean near New York City, had sand and surf and a roller coaster as well. The combination of a beach and thrilling rides appealed to vacationers. Soon other towns and cities were building similar parks along bodies of water. Balloon rides and parachute jumps became popular.

Another ride, the Ferris wheel, was named for its inventor, G. W. G. Ferris, an engineer from Galesburg, Illinois. Designed, constructed, and erected for the Chicago World's Fair of 1893, the first Ferris wheel carried over two million people during the fair. It inspired other builders to copy it, and soon the Ferris wheel became a popular ride at parks.

Disneyland—A Theme Park

Walt Disney had been entertaining people for many years with cartoon films and television shows. In 1954 he announced plans to build a 180-acre park in Anaheim, California. He wanted to build a family park where parents and children could have fun together.

On July 17, 1955, he opened Disneyland. It was built on a simple idea: choose several themes, such as fantasy, the future, and adventure, then develop an amusement park around them. Use imagination and keep guests' happiness in mind. A second park, Walt Disney World,

opened near Orlando, Florida, on October 1, 1971.

The theme park—an amusement park with rides, restaurants, and other attractions relating to a particular idea, or theme—has become very popular. Each of the Six Flags parks focuses on the history of settlers who lived in the states surrounding the park. The theme of Opryland, U.S.A., is American music. Many of the attractions at Carowinds in Charlotte, North Carolina, present some aspect of the Old South.

Disneyland Castle *(M. Mareschal)*

A Good Business

Amusement parks are in business to make a profit, and they do. At large, well-run parks, guests stay about seven hours, eat one and a half meals, and buy $1.50 worth of merchandise per visit. Ninety-four percent of the customers will pay a good price to return.

There are about thirty major amusement parks in North America today. There are also large amusement parks in England, Germany, Japan, and many other countries throughout the world.

Smaller parks are also popular. Often a small park is owned by a town or one family. Such a park might consist of one ride attached to a local zoo. Sometimes the attractions are built around a theme such as railroads, fairy tales, or flowers.

All amusement parks, large and small, have one thing in common—dedication to family fun in a clean and safe environment.

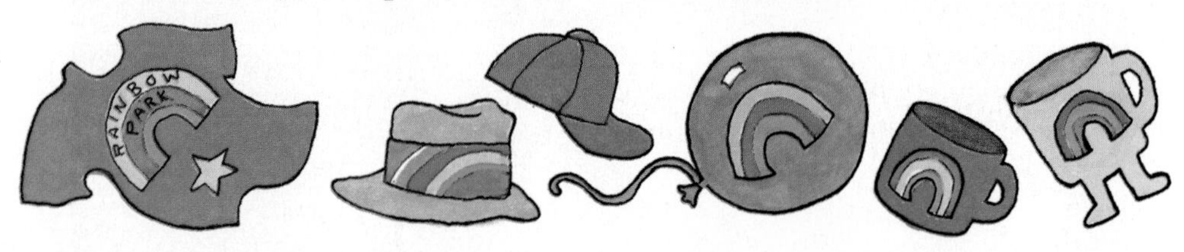

Think About It

1. Why do you think the author began the article the way she did?
2. Why do you think people like to ride scary roller coasters?
3. What is the most important thing to amusement park personnel? Why?
4. How are roller coasters kept in safe working order?
5. How is the building of "Roaring Rapids" an excellent example of conservation?
6. How have amusement parks changed over the years?
7. Invent your own amusement park ride. Give it a name and write a description of it.

Roller Coaster

by DAVID McCORD

Roller coasters have been around for a long time. Here a poet remembers the rides he took when he was young, when roller coasters were simpler and part of every small amusement park and carnival.

These roller-coaster cars, some said,
Are people sitting up in bed.
See? There they sit beyond all hope,
Positioned to roar down the slope.
So down the grade they plunge and then,
As on a wave, climb up again,
Swing sharply round some dreadful bend
Whose precipice ahead will send
Them feetfirst where you'd dare not look!
A dime or two was all it took
In *my* day for that scary run.
I don't say that it wasn't fun:
Just glad it's over with and done.

Well, roller-coaster days are gone
Most places. If you've not been on
One, nothing much that I can say
Will help you understand the way
It's not exactly you who take
The ride on wheels which have no brake:
Your stomach does the traveling,
The rest of you unraveling
Behind it, like a ball of twine
(While spider-legs run up your spine)
That's rolling off a roof with no
One there to catch it down below.

But worst, of course, is each slow climb
To heights you couldn't call sublime,
Where suddenly you round that curve
Precisely as you lose your nerve.

In Portland, Oregon, a park
Stood close to us, and after dark
In summer I could hear the screams
From roller coasting, see the gleams
Of lights cut off by cars that swung
Across them. That's when stomachs hung
In space apart from bodies shot
Straight down the rails. If I had got
To sleep, sometimes I dreamt *my* bed
Was on that roller coaster, led
By other beds ahead, and mine
Unrolling like that ball of twine
Up on the roof, as in my sleep
I gathered speed to make the leap,
And some hot night was broken by
A single yell . . . and I . . . and I . . .
Now if you like this sort of thing,
And come back safe, give me a ring.
But if you *don't* come back, don't bother;
Not to hear at all, I'd rather.

Using Graphs

Personnel at amusement parks want to know which of their rides are the most popular. One way to find out is to keep track of how many people go on these rides every day. These figures can be compared easily when shown in a graph.

There are several kinds of graphs, each giving a different kind of information. Look at the title of the **bar graph** below. What is the graph about? At the left side of the graph are the names of some amusement park rides. The numbers at the bottom tell how many people rode them per day. What does the number 10 stand for? Which ride did the fewest people go on?

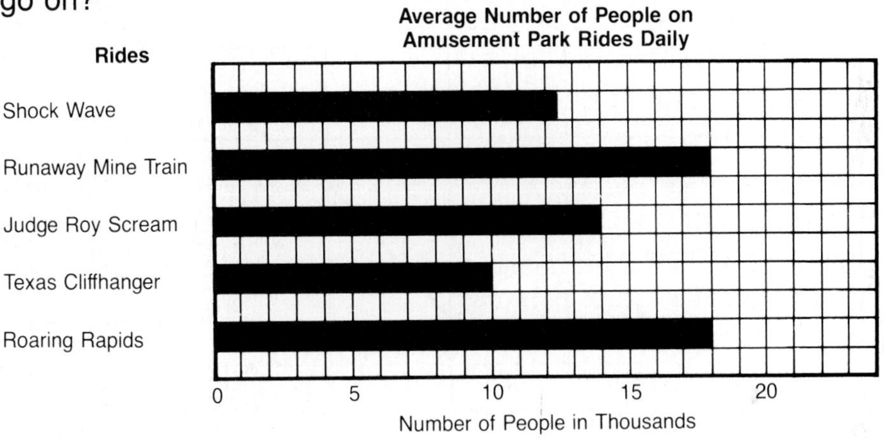

A **circle graph** shows a different kind of information. It shows percentages of a whole. A whole is 100 percent. Look at the circle graph at the right. You can see that the "Texas Cliffhanger" has the fewest people riding it. What percentage of people rode it?

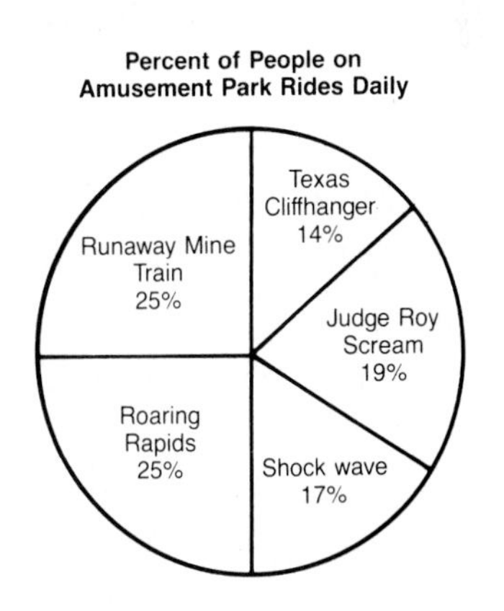

You can look at either the bar graph or the circle graph to find out that the "Runaway Mine Train" and "Roaring Rapids" are the most popular rides. But which graph would you look at to find out how many people rode on these rides? Which graph quickly shows you that these two rides accounted for half the riders at the amusement park?

Another way of showing information is a **line graph.** The line graph below shows the changes in the numbers of people on "Shock Wave" on different days of the week. Study the graph and answer the questions below it.

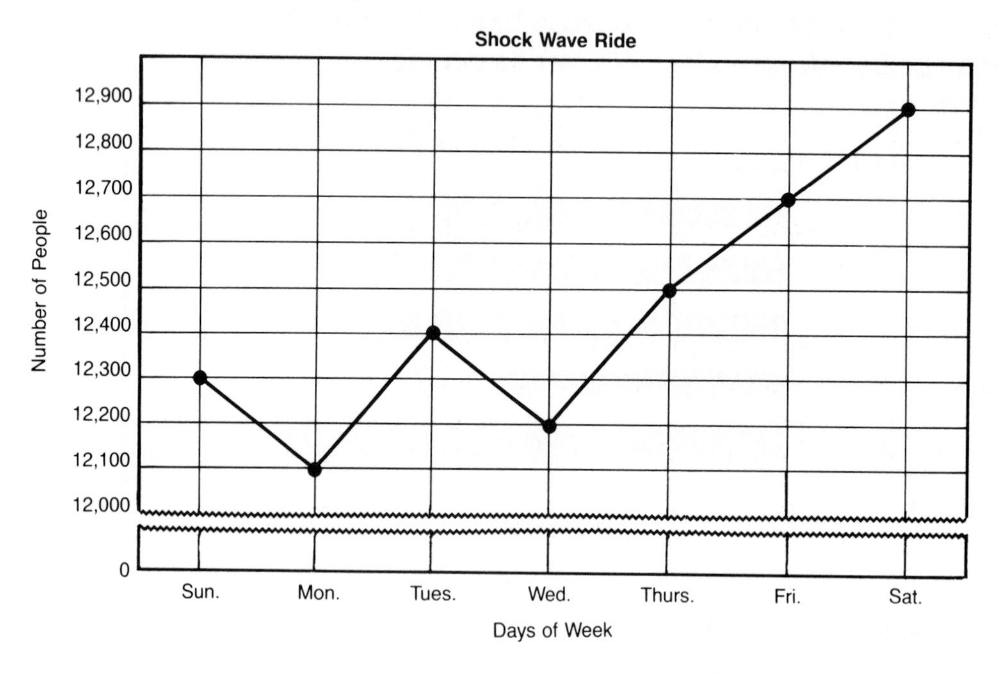

1. How many people rode "Shock Wave" on Tuesday?
2. How many more people rode it on Thursday than on Sunday?
3. What is the most popular day for the ride?
4. How many people rode on that day?
5. What is the least popular day for the ride?
6. How many people rode on that day?

LEARN NEW WORDS

1. The **astrologer** studied the stars and predicted what might happen in the future.
2. The king would soon **decree** that the prisoners be released.
3. She was to **inherit** her father's wealth when he died.
4. The minister was considered very **sage** because she could solve many problems.
5. The boy rode his beautiful **steed** without a saddle.
6. In only three steps, the teacher **strode** across the room.
7. As **successor** to the throne, the prince needed to learn how to rule from the present king.

GET SET TO READ

What kinds of things do people argue about? What are some ways an argument can be resolved?

Read this story to find out how a father plans to make his two sons stop arguing.

the Great Persian Horse Race

by RUTH HUME

Once upon a time there lived a wealthy Pasha of Persia. His kingdom had lots of trees and water and green grass—and only a little sand. He had happy subjects and so many jewels that it took seven jewel barns to hold them all. The Pasha had only two problems in life: his twin sons, Ali and Wali.

Ali and Wali cared for nothing but horses. Each prince owned a magnificent stallion, the finest and fastest horses in all of Araby. They had flowing white manes, golden hoofs, and tails that flashed by like silver comets when they rode at full speed in the royal hunt.

But which horse was faster? Ali and Wali quarreled endlessly about this. The older they grew, the more they argued. The more they argued, the more they annoyed their father. Finally, the Pasha could stand it no longer, and he summoned the entire court.

"I am about to make a speech!" he roared. "I decree the following: In three days time, a race between these two white horses will take place down the main road of the kingdom. The owner of the winning horse will receive a golden cup lined with my rarest rubies, diamonds, and pearls. And on the cup these words will be inscribed: *To the greatest and fastest horse in the entire universe!*"

The boys were delighted. Each prince was sure his horse would win, and each could already picture his noble

steed contentedly munching oats from the great golden cup. They bowed to their sage father and turned to leave, so they could at once begin preparing their horses.

"Wait," shouted the Pasha. "There's more! There's a *second* prize. I decree that the *loser* of the race," the Pasha went on, "will be declared my legal successor when I am gone and will inherit the entire kingdom, including all the jewels in the seven royal jewel barns. He will become Pasha in my place!"

Well! *That* changed things a bit! Naturally each prince wanted his horse to be declared the fastest in the universe. But if it meant giving up inheriting the entire kingdom to his brother? Suddenly it seemed to Ali and Wali that maybe it wouldn't be so bad to own the *second* fastest horse in the kingdom.

On the day of the great race the sky was clear, the breeze cool, and the entire population of the kingdom was gathered to watch the great stallions flash by.

But what did they see? The noble steeds were being walked by their royal masters as though they were tired old farm horses. Every few hundred feet Ali would unsaddle his horse and tie him to a tree to rest. Then Wali would get off *his* horse to let him graze. At evening both horses were returned to the stables.

"My horse has a sore foot," said Ali. "He can't run."

"My horse is hot and tired," said Wali. "He can't make it to the finish line."

And that's how it went. Every day a new excuse turned up, until finally the Pasha of Persia grew purple with rage.

"Summon the Royal Council!" he howled one morning. "Send for all my advisors! Call the court astrologer!" And while these sage persons puzzled, the Pasha himself strode up and down plucking at his beard and pulling his hair.

In the corner of the great assembly room stood a round little man named Snip. He was the Pasha's barber, and he looked very nervous. "Sire," he said at last, bowing his way by the court astrologer and to the Pasha's side. "Please, Sire—"

"Don't bother me, Snip!" roared the Pasha as he strode up and down. "Can't you see I'm extremely busy plucking at my beard and pulling my hair?"

"Yes, Sire!" said Snip. "And that's what worries me! You're going to make yourself bald! Now if I might make just a little suggestion—" And he stood on the tip of his toes and whispered a few words into the Pasha's ear. The purple color in the Pasha's face faded to a gentle red. "Huh? What—? You mean—?"

"Exactly, Sire," murmured Snip.

"Summon my sons!" bellowed the Pasha in a voice that could be heard across the kingdom.

Ali and Wali were brought before their father. The Pasha pointed a long finger at them and roared two words. Just two.

Ali and Wali looked at each other in amazement, thought for a moment, then turned and rushed out of the palace and back to their horses. And in a moment the two mighty steeds were tearing down the road and streaking toward the finish line like great forks of silver lightning.

Thus ended the great race.

But how did Snip do it? Can you figure out the two-word message the Pasha gave his sons? If not, see the answer on the next page.

The Pasha said, "Exchange horses!"

Snip had reminded his master that it was the horse and not the rider who would be winner of the race. Since each prince wanted his own horse to *lose* the race, each one rode his brother's horse as fast and well as he could, to make it win.

And that's exactly what happened!

Oh, by the way, which brother crossed the finish line first and thus became successor to the Pasha? Well, it doesn't really matter, because no one in the kindgom could tell the difference between Ali and Wali anyway!

Think About It

1. What did Ali and Wali quarrel over?
2. What plan did the Pasha have for ending the quarrel?
3. Explain why neither Ali nor Wali wanted to win the race.
4. Which person unexpectedly gave the Pasha the wisest advice?
5. How did the Pasha get Ali and Wali to race each other?
6. Write your own story about a contest. Tell what the contest involves, who is in it, and what the outcome is.

LEARN NEW WORDS

1. The Mississippi River **coincides** with the western boundary of the state of Illinois.
2. Sometimes two baseball players will **collide** when they both try to catch a fly ball.
3. I closed my eyes so that I wouldn't see the **collision** of the two cars.
4. Even though a **deception** can be funny, few people really enjoy being tricked.
5. The **diversion** of traffic to another street was due to a freight car collision.
6. The dam **diverted** the flow of water away from the town.
7. It's easier to touch your toes when you **flex** your knees.

GET SET TO READ

What are some examples of the force of gravity? Why is gravity important to us?

Read this article to learn how gravity can perform some amazing tricks on you.

BET YOU CAN'T!

Science Impossibilities to Fool You

by VICKI COBB and KATHY DARLING

Bet you can't read these tricks without trying at least one. They look s-o-o-o easy, you won't be able to resist. But anyone who tries is in for a truly humbling experience because there is no way to win. Each challenge is designed to trick you into trying something impossible.

Actually these impossible odds were stacked at the beginning of time by nature. It took some of the greatest minds in the history of the world to figure out what was happening. Galileo, Newton, and a number of others saw beyond the limits of human senses and experiences. They reasoned and experimented and figured out why some things just won't work. Now you can take advantage of their discoveries. Take a chance. Even if the odds are impossible, you're bound to have a good time.

The Artful Use of Gravity

Gravity is the biggest downer of all time. True? Yes. But, surprise! Gravity can pull sideways or even up. The sun is pulling on the earth in a direction that is anything but down.

Gravity is the force of attraction between two masses. When gravity is the only force operating, it draws the smaller mass to the larger one. The reason we think of gravity as a downer is that the most familiar example is

the force of attraction between the giant earth and our bodies.

One way gravity exerts its force is very curious. All the weight of an object seems to be concentrated at a single center point. If an object has a supporting base, its "center of gravity" must be located directly over the base, or the object will tip over. When an object has a regular shape, like the earth, it is easy to locate the center of gravity. It coincides with the geometric center. A seesaw is balanced at its geometric center, its center of gravity.

But an irregularly shaped object, like the human body, does not have a center of gravity that necessarily coincides with the geometric center. In fact, the center of gravity can be moved around. Skiing, for example, is one sport where an athlete is constantly making adjustments by shifting his or her center of gravity to maintain balance. This section of the article will show how you move your center of gravity around. That's where the fun comes in. The artful use of gravity can throw you totally off balance.

Up Against the Wall

BET YOU CAN'T PICK UP A DOLLAR BILL THAT'S RIGHT IN FRONT OF YOU!

The Setup: Stand with your heels against a wall and your feet together. Place a dollar bill on the floor about a foot in front of your feet. Now try to pick up the dollar without moving your feet or bending your knees.

The Fix: That dollar is as safe as if it were in the bank. You can't pick it up. Here's why. When you stand straight against the wall, your center of gravity is over your feet (your support base), as it should be. When you bend forward, you move your center of gravity forward. In order to keep your balance, you must move your feet forward, too. This maintains the base under the center of gravity needed for stability. Since the rules of this trick don't allow you to

move your feet, you're dollarless. And if you persist in trying to pick it up, you'll fall flat on your face!

While you are standing there with your back to the wall, here are some more wasted efforts.

BET YOU CAN'T JUMP!

The Setup: Keep your heels, hips, and shoulders against the wall. Without leaning forward, try to jump. What's the matter? Are your feet stuck to the floor?

BET YOU CAN'T LIFT YOUR FEET OFF THE FLOOR!

The Setup: Turn your right side to the wall. Put your right foot and cheek against the wall. Now try to lift your left foot off the floor.

The Fix: Both of these stunts require you to shift your center of gravity away from your support base. The first can't be done without falling over, and the second can't be done without moving the wall. The body maintains balance with little adjustments so automatic that we never think about them.

Glued to Your Chair?

BET YOU CAN'T GET UP FROM A CHAIR!

The Setup: All you have to do is get up from a chair. Sit in a straight-backed armless chair. Keep your back against the back of the chair and put your feet flat on the floor. Fold your arms across your chest. Now, keeping your feet flat and your back straight, try to stand up.

The Fix: The key to this trick is gravity. In the sitting position, the center of gravity is at the base of your spine. By trying to stand up with your back straight, you prevent the center of gravity from moving to a position above the feet, which are your support base. Human thigh muscles simply aren't strong enough to make up for the balance problems during the getting-up period. So you remain glued to your chair.

On Your Toes

BET YOU CAN'T STAND ON YOUR TIPTOES!

The Setup: Stand facing the edge of an open door. Your nose and stomach should just touch it. Place your feet on either side of the door, slightly forward of the edge. Now try to rise onto your tiptoes.

The Fix: You'll be caught flat-footed on this one. The reason you can't do this trick is because it moves your base of support out from under your center of gravity. In order to stand on your toes, you must transfer the center of gravity forward. To transfer the center forward, you must lean over. The door prevents you from doing this.

Forces of Deception

Forces can be as invisible as gravity or pressure. But regardless of whether it is in the form of a push, pull, or collision, force can be made to work for you instead of against you.

When forces collide head on, if they are equal and in opposite directions, they cancel each other out and nothing happens. Having two equal teams in a tug-of-war, for example, will often result in a stalemate. But unequal forces coming from different directions *can* affect an object. That's the secret of most martial arts. The angle of attack throws an opponent off balance when it comes from an unexpected direction.

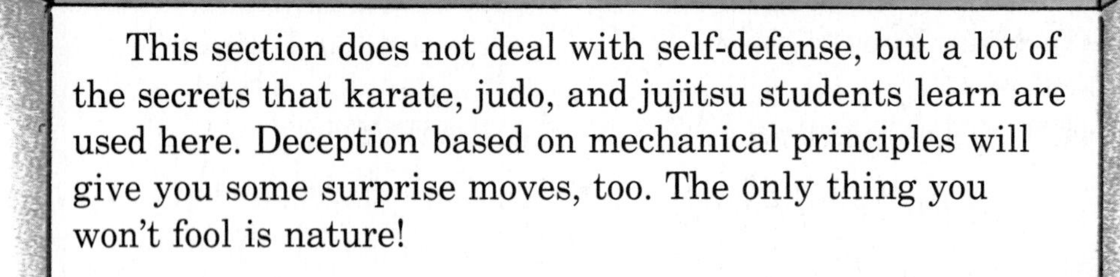

This section does not deal with self-defense, but a lot of the secrets that karate, judo, and jujitsu students learn are used here. Deception based on mechanical principles will give you some surprise moves, too. The only thing you won't fool is nature!

No Pushover

BET YOU CAN'T BE PUSHED BACKWARD!

The Setup: Hold a broomstick horizontally in front of you. Extend your arms with your hands gripping the stick about the same distance apart as your shoulders. Challenge someone to try to push you backward. He or she must grasp the middle of the stick and push using a steady, forward pressure (no sudden thrusts).

The Fix: It's impossible to move you a single inch backward. The secret defense is force diversion, whereby you change the direction of your opponent's force. To do this, flex your elbows out like wings and push slightly upward to counter any pressure. The force that is supposed to knock you backward is diverted into your flexed arms and upward.

Possible Pitfall: This trick depends on timing, so you may need to practice it to make your moves at just the right moment.

While you have the broomstick and a friend, try this one, too.

BET YOU CAN'T BE THROWN OFF BALANCE!

The Setup: Hold the broomstick horizontally again, this time with your thumbs up, about six inches on either side of the center of the stick. Have your friend hold the ends of the stick and try to knock you off balance.

The Fix: When your opponent pushes forward, you push the broomstick upward. The force of the push will be diverted away from any direction that could knock you off balance. It doesn't matter whether your hands are on the center of the stick or the ends. The force diversion still works.

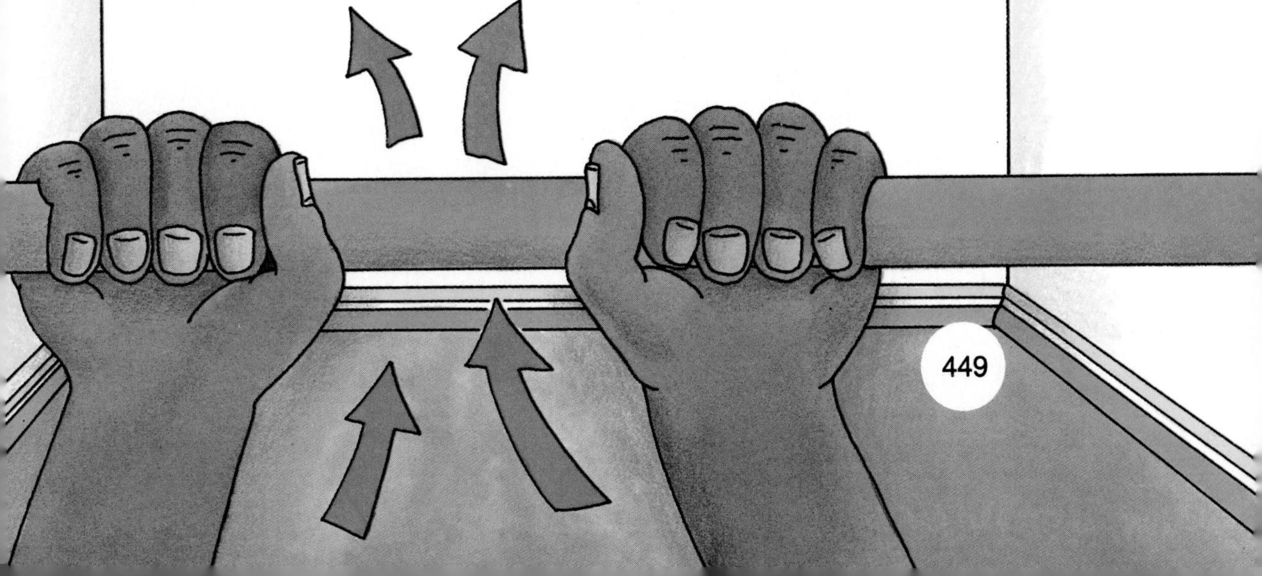

An Untearable Situation

BET YOU CAN'T RIP A TISSUE!

The Setup: You will need a paper tissue, a cardboard tube from a roll of paper towels, a rubber band, table salt or sand, and a broomstick. Stretch the tissue across the end of the paper towel tube. Fasten it in place with the rubber band. Pour three inches of salt into the tube. Now hold the tube in one hand and jam a broomstick into the salt. Try to push hard enough to rip the tissue.

The Fix: The tissue is thin and the broomstick is strong, but you won't be able to rip that tissue! The force you put on the stick is not all going straight down the tube toward the tissue. There are many tiny spaces between the salt crystals. When you jam the stick into the salt, the crystals collide, sending the force in every direction. The salt takes some of the force and divides the rest so that it is diverted to all the surfaces of the tube. Only a tiny fraction of the original force reaches the tissue. The human body is not a strong enough powerhouse to deliver the force needed to send the stick through the tissue.

For centuries, bags of sand were used to stop speeding bullets in a dramatic use of this marvel of nature.

A Piercing Moment

BET YOU CAN'T POP A BALLOON WITH A PIN!

The Setup: Blow up and tie a balloon. Put a small piece of cellophane tape on it. Now try to pop the balloon by sticking a pin through the tape.

The Fix: The balloon is unpoppable! Air leaks out, but it won't explode with a bang. The rubber of the balloon skin and the tape react differently to the stress created by the escaping air. The balloon skin is weak and rips when the air pushes against the edges of the hole. The tape is a stronger material and can resist the force of the escaping air.

An unpoppable balloon is a good party stunt, but can you see how this principle is used to make blowout-proof tires?

A Raw Deal

BET YOU CAN'T BE FOOLED BY A HARD-BOILED EGG!

The Setup: You are the expert egg sorter in this trick. You will need a raw egg and a hard-boiled one. Without cracking either, you can identify the hard-boiled one just by spinning the eggs.

The Fix: Hard-boiled eggs spin faster and longer than raw eggs. A hard-boiled egg is a solid. It spins easily. A raw egg contains a liquid. Liquid requires more force than a solid to set it in motion. When you spin a raw egg, the liquid on the inside does not move as rapidly as the solid shell. This creates a drag between the inside of the shell and the surface of the liquid, which slows down and eventually stops the movement of the egg.

Think About It

1. What is gravity?
2. What is meant by the center of gravity?
3. Choose one trick and explain how gravity makes it work.
4. What is the secret of most martial arts?
5. How can a sandbag stop a speeding bullet?
6. Why does a hard-boiled egg spin more easily than a raw one?
7. Try one of the tricks you have just read about on a friend. Then write a paragraph about what happened.

There's a Piece Missing!

by RAYE BUSH

My sister Leslie has always been a nut about jigsaw puzzles. It's good in a way, because you always know what to get her for Christmas or birthdays. She likes the difficult ones, and we all have fun picking them out. Mom keeps an old card table in the attic just for Leslie's puzzles. When a new puzzle arrives, the table is brought down and set up in the family room. It stays there until the puzzle has been completed and admired for a few days, then it goes back to the attic. At least that's the way it always was until last Christmas. Of course she got a new puzzle, and I don't think any of us will ever feel quite the same about jigsaw puzzles again.

Mom bought the puzzle at a dime store. It showed a picture of a village in Spain that sloped down to the sea. There was a small harbor with fishing boats and brilliant sunlight and velvet shadow. It was a cluttered, colorful picture, and we all agreed that it would be very difficult. Leslie loved it and got to work on it right after we'd had breakfast.

Leslie always starts with the border and then continues from there. I help her by laying out all the border pieces in another place, and so on. The lid of the box is propped up where it can be seen by everyone and referred to regularly. That evening Leslie got all the border done before bedtime and was very pleased.

The next day, as soon as her chores were done, Leslie was back at the puzzle. I was in the kitchen helping Mom with the dishes when I heard my sister say, "That's funny!"

"What's funny, Les?" I called out.

"Come and look, Kim."

I put down the dish towel and went to the family room. Leslie was staring at the puzzle and then at the picture on the box.

"Look at this, Kim. Tell me what you see."

I looked at the puzzle. Leslie had almost completed the lower right-hand corner. It showed a few small houses and the beginnings of a street. The figure of a man could be seen in the shadows.

"Yeah. So what?" I asked.

"Well, look at the picture on the box. Do you see a man in that corner?"

I looked hard at the box and saw that Leslie was right. The man was not in the picture.

"That's strange," I said.

Leslie called Mom to take a look, and she saw the same thing.

"It probably just means they had more than one picture, and they put the wrong one on the box," said Mom. "But it means you may find other parts different, too."

"That'll be kind of fun," said Leslie. "It will be more challenging."

Leslie went back to work on the puzzle, and I went off to read. She got quite a bit more done on the puzzle that night and went to bed unwillingly.

The next day I was up in my room when I heard her let out a yell.

"Mom, Kim, come here quickly! I don't believe this!"

We rushed to the family room.

"Look! Look at it! Do you see it, or am I going crazy?"

We looked at the puzzle. I heard Mom give a start of surprise. There were now two men in the picture. The first one, the one we had seen the day before, had moved and was at the top of the completed street and about to enter a building. The second man was at the bottom of the street peering around. The two men were dressed quite differently and were easy to tell apart. The first man wore a light blue shirt and white slacks and had blond hair. The second man was dressed like a fisherman and had a cap.

"Mom, what does it mean?" I had a funny feeling.

"I don't know, honey. It's the strangest thing I have ever seen. Let's see what Dad thinks when he gets home."

"I'm going to try to get some more done," said Leslie. "Maybe there will be more people in the picture."

When Dad came home, we told him about the puzzle. He looked at it, but he could offer

only the same theory as Mom—two different pictures. We left the puzzle unwillingly and went to supper.

After supper Leslie had to run some errands so it was about two hours before she returned to the family room. We were all in the living room when Leslie burst in on us.

"You had better come and look at it! You'll never believe me!"

We all trooped into the family room. About four more inches of the puzzle had been completed; and as we looked, we realized that the two men had moved again. The blond man was now about two streets away. He was running, and it looked as if he were heading for the harbor. The fisherman was at the top of the first street, and he had something in his hand. Although the figures were small, we could tell that it was a weapon of some kind.

All I could think to say was, *"Wow!"*

"Then I'm not crazy," said Leslie. "Do you all see it?"

"I see it," said Dad, "but I'm not sure I believe it."

"It looks as if the second man is chasing the first man," Mom added.

"That's just what I think!" Leslie said excitedly. "That second man has a gun or a knife. It's funny that they don't move when I'm here, only when I'm out of the room. I went up to the kitchen to get some milk, and when I came back they'd moved. I have a feeling that I should hurry and finish the puzzle so the first man can escape."

"Or get caught." We all looked at Dad in surprise.

"But, Dad," I said, "that second man has a gun!"

"Come on, everybody," Leslie urged. "Don't just stand there; help me with the puzzle."

We all started to search for pieces, and by bedtime half of the mysterious puzzle was completed. Of course, the two men didn't move; they remained frozen in the picture. Leslie complained loudly about being sent to bed and swore she'd never sleep, but Mom and Dad wouldn't listen to her. I didn't think I'd sleep, either, but I did. I was startled to hear the ringing of my alarm clock, and my immediate thought was the puzzle. I encountered Leslie on the landing, and without a word we sprinted to the family room.

The two men had moved once again. The blond man was approaching the harbor. The second man was running across a rooftop. He was still some distance behind the first man but was getting closer. A ray of sunlight glinted on the weapon in his hand, and we could now see clearly that it was a knife.

"Oh, Kim!" Leslie was terribly upset. "How can I do my chores and leave this?"

I started to say something about Mom never letting her neglect her chores to do a jigsaw puzzle and then suddenly stopped. "Les, look!" I pointed to the harbor in the left-hand corner of the puzzle. Among the fishing boats was a modern, brand-new motorboat. We rushed to look at the box. There wasn't a motorboat in the picture.

"That's his way of escape!" cried Leslie. "He's heading for that boat, Kim. I've *got* to finish this puzzle. They move when I'm not here. There is no way of

knowing how far that second man will get while I'm gone!"

"Les, you could remove the piece with the second man on it until you can work on the puzzle tonight."

"I've thought of that, but I have a funny feeling it won't work. I think if I try to remove him he'll show up somewhere else and maybe even closer to the first man." My sister was dead serious.

"Then all you can do is leave it and do your chores. You'll be able to finish it tonight."

That evening we discovered that the men had moved again. The first man had reached the harbor; the second man was about two streets away. We both felt that the important thing to do was to finish the harbor so that the first man could make his escape. We worked after supper until bedtime, and we had the harbor complete except for one piece. Mom and Dad joined us, and the whole family tried fitting every blue piece that was left. Leslie was frantic.

"It's missing! We've tried every piece at least twice. Oh, what are we going to do? There is a piece missing!"

"Honey, we all tried. The piece is probably here; we've just overlooked it. Let's go to bed, and we'll start again first thing in the morning." Mom put her arm around Leslie, who was almost in tears. There was really nothing else to do. We all went to bed.

First thing next morning we discovered that, as we had expected, the two men had moved again. The blond man was now on board the motorboat, while the other man was only one street away fom the harbor. The piece that was missing was the strip of water at the entrance to the harbor, so the boat was obviously trapped until the piece was found. Leslie said she definitely wasn't worried about the men moving while she was there but we *had* to locate the missing piece before we left the puzzle again. We exhausted a fruitless two hours looking. It was nowhere to be found. Leslie was really in tears by now.

Mom came down to see how we were doing, and when she

saw the state Leslie was in, she got very upset.

"This is just silly, girls. I don't know what's going on here, but I want to see it finished. You still can't find that piece?"

"No, Mom!" Leslie wailed.

"All right. I'll go down to the store and buy another puzzle just like this one, and we'll get the missing piece from that. Will that be better?"

Leslie was joyful, "Oh, Mom, what a great idea! Will you please hurry? Kim and I will stay here to make sure no one moves."

We both settled down to await Mom's return. We had finished all the rest of the puzzle by the time she got back. It looked great except for that one hole.

Mom looked glum. "I'm sorry, girls, but they didn't have another one. In fact, they acted as if they had never had *this* one. They said I must have bought it at another store."

"This is the craziest thing that ever happened to me," I said. "What do we do now?"

Leslie rushed to the cupboard where we keep our games and started pulling out boxes. "I've got an idea!" she said excitedly. "I have loads of puzzles that have pictures with water in them. Maybe we can find one that will fit."

I looked doubtful. "I don't know, Les. I don't think it will work. It's the same feeling you had that taking out a piece wouldn't work."

Just then the phone rang, and Mom had to leave to answer it. Leslie and I were arguing about a piece from another puzzle when Mom called to us.

"Kim, Leslie, please come here for a moment. It's Grandma calling long distance. She wants to say hello. Hurry up!"

We had no choice; we had to leave the puzzle. We were gone from the family room for only five minutes at the most, but when we got back, our worst fears had been realized. The fisherman had reached the harbor. The boat was still locked in by that blank space.

"Search on the floor!" yelled Leslie.

We both fell to our knees and began to search, then realized at the same moment that we were not watching the puzzle. We jumped up and peered at it. Everything looked the same. Then Leslie grabbed my arm.

"Look at the man in the boat."

I looked. "He's waving."

"He's waving at us."

"What's he trying to tell us?"

"He can't move again with us looking," said Leslie. "Turn your back for just a moment."

We both turned our backs. Leslie counted to three, then we turned back quickly, and, sure enough, the man had changed position. Now he was pointing upward.

"What does he mean?" I couldn't understand it.

"He means the sky. He means to look in the sky."

"But we went through all those pieces, Leslie, and none of them fit."

"We overlooked it, or we missed it. I don't know. I just know it's in the sky. Come on, help me."

We began taking out the sky pieces and refitting them, one at a time, into the blank in the ocean. Just as I was beginning to suspect that we had all gone crazy, my sister let out a cry.

"Kim, I've found it! This is it! Look, look, this is it!"

She was right. The piece fit as smoothly as silk. The harbor was complete.

"I don't understand it. We tried all those pieces before," I protested.

"Oh, who cares! It fits. That man knew we were trying to

help him all along. Now we have to leave so he can get away. Come on."

She grabbed my arm again and yanked me upstairs. We waited, very impatiently, for about fifteen minutes; then we went back down, taking Mom with us. We hadn't waited quite long enough. The boat with the blond man was gone, and the fisherman stood on the edge of the wharf shaking his fist at us!

Leslie's face grew pale, and she drew back from the puzzle. I couldn't take my eyes off her. Slowly the color came back, and she started to smile.

"Look, Kim. It's all right. He just faded away."

I looked at the puzzle. It was a pretty, colorful picture of a Spanish village, with one piece missing from the sky, and that was all.

It will be Leslie's birthday in a few months. I *was* going to buy her a jigsaw puzzle. Maybe I'll get her some cologne.

La Calle (The Street)

by OCTAVIO PAZ

A long and silent street.
I walk in blackness and I stumble and fall
and rise, and I walk blind, my feet
stepping on silent stones and dry leaves.
Someone behind me also stepping on stones, leaves:
if I slow down, he slows;
if I run, he runs. I turn: nobody.
Everything dark and doorless.
Turning and turning among these corners
which lead forever to the street
where nobody waits for, nobody follows me,
where I pursue a man who stumbles
and rises and says when he sees me: nobody.

La Calle (The Street)

Es una calle larga y silenciosa.
Ando en tinieblas y tropiezo y caigo
y me levanto y piso con pies ciegos
las piedras mudas y las hojas secas
y alguien detrás de mí también las pisa:
si me detengo, se detiene;
si corro, corre. Vuelvo el rostro: nadie.
Todo está oscuro y sin salida,
y doy vueltas y vueltas en esquinas
que dan siempre a la calle
donde nadie me espera ni me sigue,
donde yo sigo a un hombre que tropieza
y se levanta y dice al verme: nadie.

READ ON!

Man from the Sky by Avi. This is a suspenseful adventure story involving a girl, a boy, and a mysterious man who parachutes from an airplane with a bag full of stolen money.

The Fledgling by Jane Langton. Read this unusual fantasy about a shy young girl who learns how to fly from an old goose. Her two land-bound cousins try to protect her from the dangers in the sky.

My Trip to Alpha I by Alfred Slote. This futuristic story explains a special method of interplanetary travel. Jack's voyage introduces him to this new way of traveling and eventually gives him the clue to a mystery.

A Young Person's Guide to Ballet by Noel Streatfeild. This action-packed book gives a lot of information about ballet by following the three-year training of two children, Anna and Peter. It includes diagrams of ballet positions as well as many photos.

Escape! The Life of Harry Houdini by Florence Meiman White. Many old photographs illustrate this interesting biography of the world's greatest escape artist.

The Dollhouse Murders by Betty Ren Wright. Dolls come alive in this intriguing story, and they tell a twelve-year-old girl about an unsolved murder that happened long ago.

UNIT 6

At Great Risk

LEARN NEW WORDS

1. The water was calmer in the **cove** than in the ocean beyond.
2. The spider **scuttled** across the windowsill.
3. I asked **skeptically**, "Do you really know how to drive?"
4. He bent his head **sullenly**, silent but angry that he had been scolded.
5. A clear, hot day can always **tempt** me to go swimming.
6. He tried **wheedling** his mother into letting him stay up late.
7. She looked **wistfully** at the new bike; she was tempted to buy it.

GET SET TO READ

In this story, the main character feels that he can't do anything well. How could this cause problems for someone? How does having confidence help people?

Read this story to find out how Craig gets help in dealing with his problems.

Sea Gardens

by LAURENCE YEP

Craig Chin has just moved with his parents from San Francisco's Chinatown to a small town farther south in California. He at first misses the city and has trouble making friends in his new school. He also feels like a failure in sports, especially basketball, because he can't make any teams. His father had been a star basketball player in high school—the first Chinese player to make the All-City team—so Craig feels he has really disappointed his father. Then one day, Craig meets a distant relative everyone calls Uncle. Uncle, in his seventies, lives alone at the edge of town near a cove. He seems to like Craig and invites him to come swimming.

That Saturday Uncle was already down on the beach. He looked thin and bony as he sat with his jacket draped around his shoulders. One lonely sea gull wheeled about, crying over the calm waters of the cove.

With my towel tucked under my arm I went down to the beach. The tide was really low today. The beach was a lot bigger, and I could see a lot of the reef.

Uncle had a small crowbar in his hand. It was tied to his wrist by a thong. I watched as Uncle slipped the end of the crowbar between the shell and the tan flesh of an abalone.

"You went diving for abalone?" I asked.

"I walk through my gardens and I find this one."

I looked around the cove, but it looked especially empty and lifeless now. Even the lonely gull was off to some other place.

"What gardens?" I asked skeptically.

Uncle smiled as if it were his secret. "I thought you were one smart boy. Can't you see them?"

He slipped the thong of the crowbar from his wrist and dropped it into a basket.

"No, I can't." Sullenly, I folded my arms across my chest.

"You think maybe you see, but you don't. Not really." He nodded his head firmly. "You gotta look at the world. Really look."

"Like you?" I was beginning to feel impatient with Uncle.

"No. I only do it in a small, small way. But if you can make your mind listen to your eyes, really listen, what wonders you see." Uncle looked out at his cove wistfully.

"This is one special place here. This is the edge of the world. This is where the magic can happen." Uncle searched my face, looking for some sign of comprehension, but I could only look at him in confusion. Uncle smiled to himself sadly. He pretended to become stern. "Well, do you want to swim or talk, boy?"

"Let's swim." I was already wearing my swimming trunks underneath my pants, so it didn't take me long to get ready. In the meantime, Uncle had shrugged off his jacket and waded into the water to begin swimming. I stared at him in surprise.

He moved quickly and easily through the water. There was nothing wasted about his motions when he swam. They were pure, simple, graceful.

"Come on." Uncle turned to me from the water. "You just remember one thing. The currents in my cove, they aren't very strong, but even so, don't fight them."

I gave a yelp the moment I waded into the water. The water was so cold that it felt like someone had been chilling it in the refrigerator. I could feel the goose bumps popping out all over my skin, and I began to shake.

Uncle waved one hand from where he was floating. "Come on. You get used to it."

I nodded nervously and kept on walking. The beach sloped downward sharply, and I immediately found myself in the water up to my chest. Then a wave broke against the reef and spray went flying and the sea surged through the narrow opening. The pull of the sudden current wasn't all that strong, but it caught me by surprise so I was knocked off my feet.

I couldn't see. There was only the clouded, stinging salt water all around me. I flailed with my arms, trying to get my feet on something solid, but I couldn't find anything. And then I felt the current begin to draw me away from the beach as it began to flow out toward the sea. I really panicked then, forgetting everything I'd ever been taught. I wanted air. My lungs tried to drag it in, but all they got was salt water. I began to choke.

Then strong hands appeared magically, gripping me on either side. I tried to grab hold of Uncle. Something. Anything, as long as I could hold on to it. Somehow, though, Uncle managed to avoid me. My head broke above the surface. I could see the light for a moment before the salt water, running down my face, made my eyes close. I gasped, coughed, and gasped again, trying to get the film of seawater out of my lungs.

Uncle's strong hands pulled me steadily in toward the beach. Then I could feel firm sand under me. I stumbled. Uncle's hands held me up until I got my balance. I started to stagger toward the beach with Uncle supporting me. Gratefully, I felt the air around my shoulders and then my chest and then my stomach. I stretched my arms out and stumbled out of the surf to fall onto the beach. I lay on my stomach for a moment, coughing and spitting. I could feel the sea tugging at my ankles, as if it were alive and trying to drag me back in.

Then I felt Uncle's shadow as he sat down heavily beside me. "You sure you can swim, boy?" he asked skeptically.

I sat up, beginning to shiver. Uncle covered my shoulders with my towel. "I could have told you. I'm just too clumsy."

Uncle put on his jacket and sat down. "You feel too sorry for yourself. And that's not good."

"Are you crazy?" I started to shiver, so I pulled the towel tighter around my neck.

"You're the crazy one." Uncle flung sand over his legs. "You want to stay on the beach when you can be out in the water."

"Drowning isn't my idea of fun." I wiped some of the water from my face.

Uncle put his hands behind him and leaned back. "Well, maybe if you're scared . . ."

With a corner of my towel I finished drying my face. "Who said I was scared?"

"Me," Uncle said. "I say you're scared."

"Nothing scares me," I said.

Tunelessly, Uncle hummed to himself and tapped his fingers against the sand.

"Well, even if I am," I mumbled, "it's stupid to do something just to prove I'm not scared."

"Yes, no, maybe so. Something good shouldn't scare you." Uncle began to rub his palms together so that the sand sprinkled down. "Maybe I ask you to put your head on a railroad track, and you say no, well, that's different."

"I'm still not going in." I shook my head for emphasis.

"You can walk on the water then?" Uncle smiled.

I liked Uncle when he said that. I mean, Dad would have gone on shouting or wheedling or both, but instead Uncle turned the whole thing into a joke. He seemed to relax then. "You want to go for a walk instead?" He nodded at the beach. "I mean on solid ground?"

"Sure," I said, even though the cove wasn't more than twenty yards wide at any point.

Uncle rose and started across the wet sand toward the cliffs on one side of the cove, and I followed him. When he was by the cliffs, Uncle pointed to the walls above the water at the foot-wide bands of chalky little white bumps. "These are mussels, and those"—he gestured at a blackish band about a foot wide below them—"are barnacles." The bands looked like they were painted on both sides of the cove where the tide would reach it about a yard above its present level. "The water's out or they'd all be open to eat the little things in the water.

"And you see the starfish?" Uncle pointed at the water where there was a bright orange spot just below the surface. "He's waiting now. When the water gets higher, he'll climb back up to the barnacles and mussels." We waded cautiously into the surf. Uncle took my wrist and guided it under the water. I felt the rough surface of the starfish.

Uncle let go of my wrist, and I traced the shape of the starfish and felt the five legs, one of them curled up slightly. My fingers closed round the body of the starfish and I gave a tug; but it felt as if it were part of the cliff wall.

Uncle laughed in delight, like a kid sharing a new toy with someone else. "You want a starfish, you need a crowbar. Once a starfish sits, nobody can pull it up."

I let go of the starfish. "Is this your garden then?" I looked around the cove, feeling disappointed. The bands of mussels and barnacles and the starfish didn't make up a sea garden in my mind.

"This is just the start of my garden." Uncle smiled, both proud and pleased—like someone who knows a secret that you do not. "Too bad you don't want to see more of it."

I looked uncertainly at the cove. "You mean I have to swim?"

"Out there." He pointed to the reef that was exposed at low tide.

He was one shameless old man to tempt me that way and he knew it. I almost refused again, but I have to admit I was curious about that garden.

"Okay. I'll try just once more," I grumbled.

"We'll stay in the shallow end. Then, if you feel good, we can go out." Uncle walked farther into the water and half turned around as he took off his

jacket. I whipped the towel off my shoulders and threw it high up on the beach. Uncle threw his jacket beside it. I waded into the sea until I was waist deep. I kept waiting for Uncle to shout instructions at me the way Dad would have, but he didn't.

I took a deep breath. Then another good one. Holding my arms ahead of me, I bent forward and kicked off from the sand. There was that shock for a moment of letting go of the land, and then I was floating. The cold water didn't feel so bad this time. I twisted my head to the side and breathed in the air and then slid over, floating on my back, letting the sun warm my face and skin.

Uncle began swimming in the water toward me, and then his body was floating alongside of me. He didn't shout anything at me or tell me how to do things better; he just warned me, "Careful. Don't go out too far."

So we stayed floating on our backs for a few minutes.

"Do you want to swim out to the reef?" I asked finally.

"Oh-kay." Uncle grinned. He started to move his arms. A glittering shower raised around his head as he swam out toward the rock reef. I followed him much more slowly and clumsily. Once Uncle was at the reef, he stretched out his arms and clung to a large boulder, hoisting himself up. He perched on the boulder with all the ease of a sea gull, as if he had done this thousands of times. I suppose he had, if you thought about all the years he had spent in the cove.

Aware of Uncle watching me, I kept on churning toward the reef. I thought he might have some instructions for improvement by now. But still he didn't say anything.

Instead, he only reached out one hand. I clasped it and Uncle almost pulled me up out of the water to sit beside him—I mean, as if he were as rooted as a starfish to that boulder.

"Shhh. Listen." Uncle swept his hand along, palm down to the sea, in a short, sharp gesture for quiet.

At first, though, my main concern was getting a better grip on that big rock, but then as I sat there, I could feel the rhythm of the sea surging against the rocky reef that protected the cove, trying to make the opening in the reef bigger. The sea wasn't pounding so much as steadily pushing, as if it knew it had all the time in the world and could be patient. But after sitting there for a while, I almost felt like the reef was living and I could feel its heart beating.

"We'll start up there, boy." Uncle pointed toward the top of the reef.

"What about the big waves?"

Uncle shook his head. "I don't think there will be any more. And if there are, the reef will protect us." He patted a rock affectionately. Then he turned and began climbing. I followed him more cautiously the three feet or so to the top of the reef. I took one look at that big empty sea beyond the reef, and then I turned my head back in toward the cove.

Uncle waved his hand to indicate both sides of the reef. "When the sea goes out, all around here—maybe in little cracks, maybe on ledges—there are pools left. And the rocks, maybe they protect the pools so the big strong waves"—Uncle pantomimed a crashing wave stopped short—"the waves can't reach the pools. Then all kinds of things can grow." He spoke slowly and proudly, as if he were just about to pry up the lid to a treasure chest.

At that moment, to my right —from a crevice I thought would be too small for anything to live in—a bright blue-and-purple crab scuttled out. It was only a few inches across. It paused when it saw us and lifted its claws, ready to defend itself.

Uncle wiggled a finger above its head just out of the reach of its claws. The crab scuttled back into its crevice. "The brave, bold hero," Uncle said with a laugh. "Maybe when he goes home, he tells a lot of tales about fighting us." Carefully Uncle stood up then. He held out his hand, and I took it for support as I got slowly to my feet.

"Now do what I do." Confidently, Uncle turned his back to the sea and began to edge sideways along the top of the reef.

Uncle made it look real easy, but I found myself spreading my arms for better balance and I began to wish the rocks wouldn't vibrate. It was like walking on the back of some sleeping snake that might wake up and shake me off at any moment.

Uncle stopped where two rectangular slabs of rock leaned their tips against one another. One rock faced toward the sea, the other faced toward the cove. He waited for me. I looked down between the rocks. There was a shallow depression on the giant boulder on which the two slabs rested. I caught my breath. The stone looked gray-black when it was wet, and the sea water was almost clear here; and in the daylight, the colors seemed even brighter. There were anemones of all colors—animals shaped like flowers, whose thin petals moved with a life of their own in the still water. Uncle leaned forward, supporting himself against the slabs. His hand barely stirred the surface of the pool as his finger brushed the petals of a red anemone. In the wink of an eye, the anemone had closed up, looking like a fat, bumpy doughnut. The other anemones

closed up too. Uncle removed his hand from the pool. We waited for a little while until one by one they opened once again. They were all kinds of bright colors—orange, red, yellow, solid colors that would make any artist ache inside to be able to use.

Uncle paused where a flat slab of rock leaned against the top of the reef. He pointed inside. "Can you see it?"

I looked in at the shadows. It looked like a big ball of spines within the water under the slab. "What is it?"

"A sea urchin," Uncle explained. "It came up into the high tide pools."

Even as we watched, the sea urchin retreated farther into the shadows by moving its needle-like spines.

"You know all the pools around here. Well, some of them are big. Some of them are small. And every pool is cut off from the other. Maybe the pools are this far apart." Uncle held his hands an inch from each other. "But the pools, they might as well be miles and miles apart because the animal in one pool won't know about an animal in another pool. You take an animal around here and it would probably think its own pool is the whole world, and it doesn't know there are pools and pools all around it." Uncle sounded awed by the magic and vastness of what he owned.

"I never dreamed there was so much to see," I said.

Uncle leaned forward and pretended to peer at something. "You have to learn how to pay attention to things." He added, "But first you have to like yourself." He gave a tug to his trunks and sat down. "People who don't like themselves, they spend all

their time looking at their faults. They don't have time to look at the world."

"What's there to like about myself?" I asked sullenly. I sat down and leaned my chest against my thighs. "I'm lousy at swimming. I'm lousy at basketball. I'm lousy at making friends. I'm not like anything Dad wants."

Uncle raised one eyebrow. "Is that all you think your father wants? Play games all the time?"

"I just wish," I said wistfully, "that I could be as good as my dad."

Uncle sighed and shook his head. "You try too hard to be your father's son." He seemed dissatisfied with what he had said—as if he didn't have enough English to explain all his thoughts to me and he knew I didn't know enough Chinese if we used that language. Uncle folded his legs into a lotus position as if he wanted to become more comfortable before he stretched his arm out toward me. "It's not good if you do everything just like your father. Everyone is different. That's what makes them special." Uncle waved his hand grandly to include the entire reef. "You think it good if all the animals look the same, hah?"

"I have to keep on trying." I shrugged my shoulders, annoyed with Uncle for being so insistent.

There was a long silence while we both listened to the ocean beating against his reef.

I leaned back to look up at the broad sweep of sky overhead. Somehow, sitting on the reef, I felt like the world was a much bigger place than it seemed when I was standing on solid ground. And so much of what I knew when I was on the land didn't seem as certain anymore. I couldn't help hunching my shoulders a little.

Uncle must have been observing me. "Back to the beach, boy. Look at you. You're shivering."

"Not at the cold. It's—"

"No arguments. This reef's not a good place when the tide rises. Come on." Uncle slipped off the rocks into the water.

When we were back on the beach again, I began to shiver for real. A strong wind had begun to sweep in from the sea, so that it was a lot colder than when we had first swum out to the reef. I got my towel from where I had thrown it on the beach and came back toward Uncle, rubbing at my arms and back briskly.

Uncle did not bother to towel himself. He had rolled around in the sand until he had a thin film covering him. Then he had put on his jacket and sprawled out on the beach to soak up what sun there was.

I looked at him. "Does anyone visit you here?"

"Oh, the older ones in my family, they used to visit." Uncle grasped a handful of sand. "But maybe they're too old now. Maybe they don't like to drive the long way from the city. And the younger ones, they don't remember. They forget about the fun they have swimming here. Even some I teach how to swim." He flung the sand into the air and watched the wind scatter it along the beach. "They prefer the tame water in those concrete ponds in their own back yards. They turn their faces from the sea and the things I show them." He added, "Even your father."

"Did you take my father diving for abalone here?"

"Sure," Uncle said.

"When can I go?" I asked him.

Uncle scratched his cheek for a moment as if he were feeling uncomfortable. "I have to give you real special training to go diving. Not everyone can dive."

"Then when can we start?" I asked impatiently.

"You don't even swim so good. You swim better. Then we can begin your training." Uncle

slapped his hands at an imaginary surface. "You still fight the water too much. You must use the sea and you must let it use you."

"But how can I learn to swim better so I can be trained?" I rubbed the back of my neck in annoyance. "You never tell me what to do."

Uncle blinked his eyes, puzzled. "You learn from inside you." He tapped at his heart. "Not from outside. And not from some old man's big mouth."

"So when do you think I'll be ready?"

Uncle folded his arms across his chest and leaned forward so that his forearms rested on top of his drawn-up knees. "You have to be comfortable in the water. I can't say."

So maybe his cove wasn't a perfect place. It was still special. For all of his quirks, Uncle still managed to make me feel like a real person. "I wish I could stay here."

Uncle was so surprised that he couldn't completely hide his pleasure. "Well, you can't. But you can come here next Saturday."

Think About It

1. How did Craig feel about himself at the beginning of the story?
2. What happened when Craig first tried to swim out to the reef?
3. What made Craig try swimming out to the reef again?
4. Describe what Craig and Uncle found in the tide pools.
5. What advice did Uncle give Craig about liking himself?
6. Why did Craig ask Uncle to teach him how to dive for abalone?
7. Select one or two sentences from the story that tell the theme of the story. Write about why you picked those sentences.

LEARN NEW WORDS

1. She had to **acquire** the skills necessary for the job.
2. I found little useful information **amid** the many pages of trivia.
3. The little boy watched **forlornly** as his toy boat sank in the middle of the pond.
4. The king and queen demanded **loyalty** from their subjects.
5. Her **suitor** brought her flowers and swore his loyalty to her.
6. She swam **vigorously** to get away from the torrent of a nearby waterfall.

GET SET TO READ

What does wisdom mean to you? How does a person become wise?

Read this legend to find out what Mapuri, who wants to be wise, finds out about wisdom.

THE HUNTER WHO WANTED AIR

An Amerindian legend
retold by ALEX WHITNEY

Some Amerindians live amid the thick rain forests of South America. Most of their legends, like this one, stress loyalty, bravery, and honesty—qualities that have always been important to their way of life.

The first time Mapuri the hunter noticed Tafeela, she was weaving a basket under a shelter of thatched grass. So enchanted was he by her grace and beauty that he immediately strode into the nearby hut of her father Okono and asked for permission to marry Tafeela.

"I shall let Tafeela decide for herself whether or not she will marry you," said Okono, as he went to the doorway and summoned his daughter.

When Tafeela entered the hut, Okono explained the reason for Mapuri's presence. Tafeela looked hard at her suitor. Then she stood on tiptoe and whispered in her father's ear.

"Tafeela thinks you are good-looking," Okono told Mapuri, "but she says she will only marry someone who has wisdom. You are known to be an expert hunter and a skilled fisherman, but—" Okono hesitated, a little embarrassed, "I doubt if anyone would call you wise."

"Then I shall become wise at once!" Mapuri said airily.

"And just how do you plan to acquire wisdom?" Okono wanted to know.

"Very simply," declared Mapuri. "I have heard that Mankato, chieftain of the tribe that lives upriver by the waterfall, is great in wisdom. I shall go to him. When he has taught me all that he knows, I shall return and marry Tafeela!"

And so, Tafeela's suitor went off merrily whistling an imitation of the honeybird's song.

Early the following morning Mapuri ran to the river and leaped into his *corial,* the dugout canoe he had carved from a tree trunk. Then he paddled vigorously upstream until he heard the thunderous roar of the waterfall.

When he had pulled his canoe onto a sandy cove, he hastened toward a group of isolated beehive-shaped huts set back from the riverbank. Amid the excited barking of dogs, he exchanged greetings with a group of villagers. He told them he had come to see Mankato.

Mapuri was led to a large hut, roofed with pale-yellow palm straws that swept down to the ground. Seated cross-legged in the entrance was an old man with a magnificent head of graying hair.

Mapuri stood before him and came to the point at once: "Mankato, I wish to learn how to be wise."

The old chieftain's eyes twinkled from behind half-closed lids. "Before one can acquire wisdom, one must truly desire it," he said.

"I desire it more than anything else at the moment!" cried Mapuri.

"Then you shall have your first lesson," said Mankato, rising slowly to his feet. "Come, let us walk to the river."

When the pair arrived at the river bank, Mankato told Mapuri to kneel in the shallow water. But as soon as Mapuri had done so, Mankato firmly pushed the young man's head underwater. He held it there for a moment or two.

Choking and spluttering, Mapuri raised his head out of the river. Then he drew in great gulps of air.

"What did you think about while your head was underwater?" asked Mankato, seemingly unaware of his would-be pupil's distress.

"Air!" wheezed Mapuri.

"What!" exclaimed Mankato. "Did you not think of your skill in the hunt?"

"No!" gasped Mapuri. "All I could think of was air!"

"Did you not think of your nets brimming with fish?" persisted Mankato.

"No," said Mapuri, "I thought only of air!"

"When you want wisdom as much as you wanted air, then shall you become wise," said Mankato. And without a backward glance at Mapuri, the old man walked away.

The long shadows of early evening lay on the river when Mapuri returned to his village. As he walked wearily past Okono's hut, Tafeela came out from the doorway.

"Did you learn how to be wise, Mapuri?" she asked.

Mapuri hung his head and looked forlornly at his toes. "Alas, Tafeela, I have learned only one thing," he said. "Air is more important to me than wisdom."

Tafeela's eyes sparkled beneath her fringe of glossy black hair. "In that case," she said, "I shall accept your offer of marriage."

Mapuri could hardly believe his ears. "*Kiriwani!* Impossible!" he cried. "Surely you must realize that many, many moons and many, many suns will come and go before I will be able to claim wisdom!"

Tafeela laughed softly. "That may be true, but you possess another quality more valuable than all the game in our forest, more priceless than all the fish in our river: honesty. And honesty, Mapuri, is the first step on the path to wisdom," said Tafeela.

Think About It

1. Why did Mapuri wish to become wise?
2. How did Mapuri think he could become wise?
3. What did Mankato demonstrate to Mapuri?
4. What did Mapuri find out about wisdom?
5. Why did Tafeela decide to marry Mapuri?
6. Write a paragraph describing the kind of person Mapuri is and why you think there is a legend about him.

LEARN NEW WORDS

1. His hands were dry and **calloused** from years of hard work.
2. She was **capable** of doing all the work by herself, but she wheedled the others into helping her.
3. They explored the western **frontier**, where people had never been before.
4. The heroes and **heroines** who built our nation will remain immortal in the pages of our history.
5. The **lush** green grass grew tall in the rich soil.
6. The **productive** farmland gave the pioneer family a plentiful crop.
7. The **prospector** panned for gold in the stream.
8. We needed a set of rules and **regulations** for our new business.
9. Our garden **yielded** many kinds of flowers as well as vegetables.

GET SET TO READ

What do you know about the pioneers who traveled to the West? What do you think their lives were like?

Read this article to find out what life was like on the frontier.

HIDDEN HEROINES:

WOMEN OF THE WEST

by ELAINE LANDAU

After the American Revolution, settlers of the eastern states slowly began to look westward. During the late 1700s and early 1800s, many pioneers headed for the rich lands lying directly beyond the Appalachian Mountains.

Most of these pioneers journeyed in wagons or carts pulled by a horse or a mule. Some brought cows for milk as well as to haul belongings. Poorer settlers set off on foot, taking only what they could carry.

The vast wilderness made their journey hard. The settlers hacked their way over steep, narrow mountain ridges. They swam across icy streams and traveled down swiftly moving rivers on rafts. Thousands reached the rich farmlands of Kentucky, Tennessee, Ohio, and Illinois, where they set up frontier settlements. By 1830, the first big wave of western migration had pushed the frontier across the Mississippi River, into the grassy plains beyond.

Meanwhile, explorers, missionaries, traders, and fur trappers told of lush pastures and valleys lying past the Rocky Mountains. Their stories excited many who were eager to set out for new lands and new adventures. By the 1840s, more people began the long journey westward.

The frontier really boomed in 1848 with exciting news that thrilled the nation and echoed around the globe: gold had been discovered in California! Thousands of people from all over the world flocked west hoping to find wealth. And a number of women were among those who sought their fortunes digging for the precious ore.

A miners' camp was full of rough language and actions. In those days, it was not considered a proper place for a woman. So if a female prospector wanted to join a camp, she had to disguise herself as a man. But many women were unwilling to do this. Instead, they camped out near their claims with other women miners or by themselves. This way, too, they could better guard their claims.

As time passed, profitable claims became scarce. Even the rich veins of ore were quickly drained when tapped, and yielded less and less gold. The average miner worked long hours and made only about three dollars a day. Expenses were extremely high, since food and other supplies had to be brought in from the East. Some people hauled clean water many miles and sold it to the miners for as much as fifty dollars a barrel. A single can of peaches might cost as much as twenty dollars.

Although thousands of people headed for the mining regions, others believed that the new territory between the early

Women miners stayed at camps like this one.

frontier settlements and California might be turned into productive farmland. They hoped to make a good living from the crops the land yielded. Many thousands of prospectors who failed to find gold or who never reached the gold fields joined the settlers in Nebraska, Utah, and the Dakotas. Some went north to Washington and Oregon.

Women were active in settling these new areas. Many widowed and single women who hadn't caught "gold fever" were excited about having farms of their own. Some worked extra hours and saved a part of their earnings for travel expenses. Others formed groups, pooled their few dollars, and headed west. A few women were able to find work as cooks with the wagon trains going west.

A wagon train usually consisted of twenty or more wagons. Because space in the wagons was limited, the settlers could bring few belongings with them. Often a cherished rocking chair had to be left behind. Most wagons only had room for such important items as salt, flour, seeds, and bedding. The entire family slept on a large feather mattress. Cooking utensils and other housewares were sometimes hung from the horses' saddles.

Before the journey began, the heads of families met with the wagon master, who was familiar with the route. They drew up regulations to govern the group and protect themselves. They also drew up regulations to divide chores.

Both female and male family heads signed up to join the wagon trains. The women shared all tasks equally with the men. They did guard duty, patrolling the camp armed with rifles to ward off animals. They scouted ahead in search of water and to check the trails. And they helped supervise the general progress of the train.

Wagon trains usually left in the spring, before heavy snows could block the mountain passes. But the journey westward was still long and dangerous. Thunderous cloudbursts often flooded the trails. After pushing their wagons through mud and over

Westward-bound pioneers pause for a moment.

rocks, the pioneers still had to swim sizeable streams, dragging their horses and wagons across.

Women family heads were responsible for themselves and their families. When a wagon broke, they repaired it themselves. Often, if a horse died, a woman would hitch herself up to a wagon to keep going.

Their hands became rough and calloused from driving the teams and doing the repairs. At times, they had to endure hailstorms that tore the canvas tops of their wagons. On other days, they traveled under a scorching sun that burned the leather of their boots. And there was always the danger of disease that might spread if not caught in time.

Many died—women, men, children. But most made it to the new frontier.

After arriving on their new land, the families immediately set to work to build homes. This was not an easy task because the land was often bleak and sometimes treeless. Those who chose to settle the grassy plains had no lumber to build a log cabin or even a wooden frame for a house.

Instead, these settlers built soddies—homes of dirt and soil. First they plowed up furrows of sod which they molded into foot-long blocks. They piled the rows of sod blocks on each other to form walls. Then they covered the one-room structure with a thatched roof.

A sod house was warm in the winter and cool in the summer, but families living in them were never really comfortable. Dirt crumbled from the walls, falling on their food and beds. Snakes and gophers often dug tunnels through the walls and floors. And rats and mice lived in the thatch.

Frontier women made everything their families needed. Most began work at daybreak and did not rest until late evening. They cooked, spun cloth and made clothing, raised children, and tried to keep their dirt homes clean. With calloused hands they cleared and plowed fields, tended and harvested crops, milked the cows, raised hogs, rode and trained horses, and did just about every chore on the farm.

These capable women not only worked, they also made most of their own tools. To make pitchforks, they attached handles to deer antlers. Many of the women learned to use a knife well enough to carve spoons, forks, and bowls out of animal bones. They fashioned cups and

Most pioneer families, such as these freed slaves, lived in soddies.

containers out of vegetable gourds and animal horns.

Pioneer women had to be capable because they were often on their own. Even married women found themselves alone much of the time. Twice a year, many of the men traveled far to marketing centers to sell the family's crops. This enabled them to get a good price for their produce. But it also kept them away from their families for as long as four months at a time.

Men also went on long hunting expeditions to provide their families with meat and furs for the winter. Still others left their wives to care for the homestead, while they went off in search of more productive farmland.

Many men never returned. Some died fighting Indians whose lands they had invaded. During the 1840s the Plains Indians allowed the pioneers to pass through their hunting grounds. At times, the Indians even guided them, helping them at difficult river crossings. Some tribes supplied the wagon trains with vegetables and buffalo meat in exchange for things the Indians wanted.

However, in the late 1850s and early 1860s, white farmers began to establish homesteads on Indian lands. To get the Indians to leave, the farmers paid them cash for their land. But money meant nothing to the Indians, who didn't realize that if they accepted these slips of paper, they would have to give up their land.

The Indians believed that the land and everything on it should be used fairly by all. They felt that soil, streams, and trees were too precious to be sold. But many pioneers believed any piece of property could be bought with enough money. When they no longer allowed the Indians to hunt in the lush forests or fish in the streams they had "bought," fierce fighting broke out.

Although most of the fighting was done by men, both Indian and pioneer women suffered greatly. Many lost their husbands and sons in battle. Many women were killed. The fighting lasted for many years.

Meanwhile, women saw to it that the homesteads ran smoothly. They handled any emergency that arose. Most learned to shoot a rifle soon after arriving in the West. Alone so much of the time, they had to protect themselves, their children, and their homes against thieves and wild animals.

Despite severe hardships, many pioneer women survived and even prospered on the prairies and in the forests and mountains of the West. It was their early heroic struggle that gave a heritage of strength, independence, and courage to those who came after.

This woman has just killed a coyote that had been raiding pioneer homesteads.

Think About It

1. Why did so many people travel west in the 1800s?
2. Describe conditions of life on the frontier.
3. What kind of work did pioneer women do?
4. Why did even a married woman have to be capable of doing everything herself?
5. Why did the pioneers and the Indians fight each other?
6. Why do you think this article is called "Hidden Heroines"?
7. Pretend you are a pioneer. Write a journal entry describing your day.

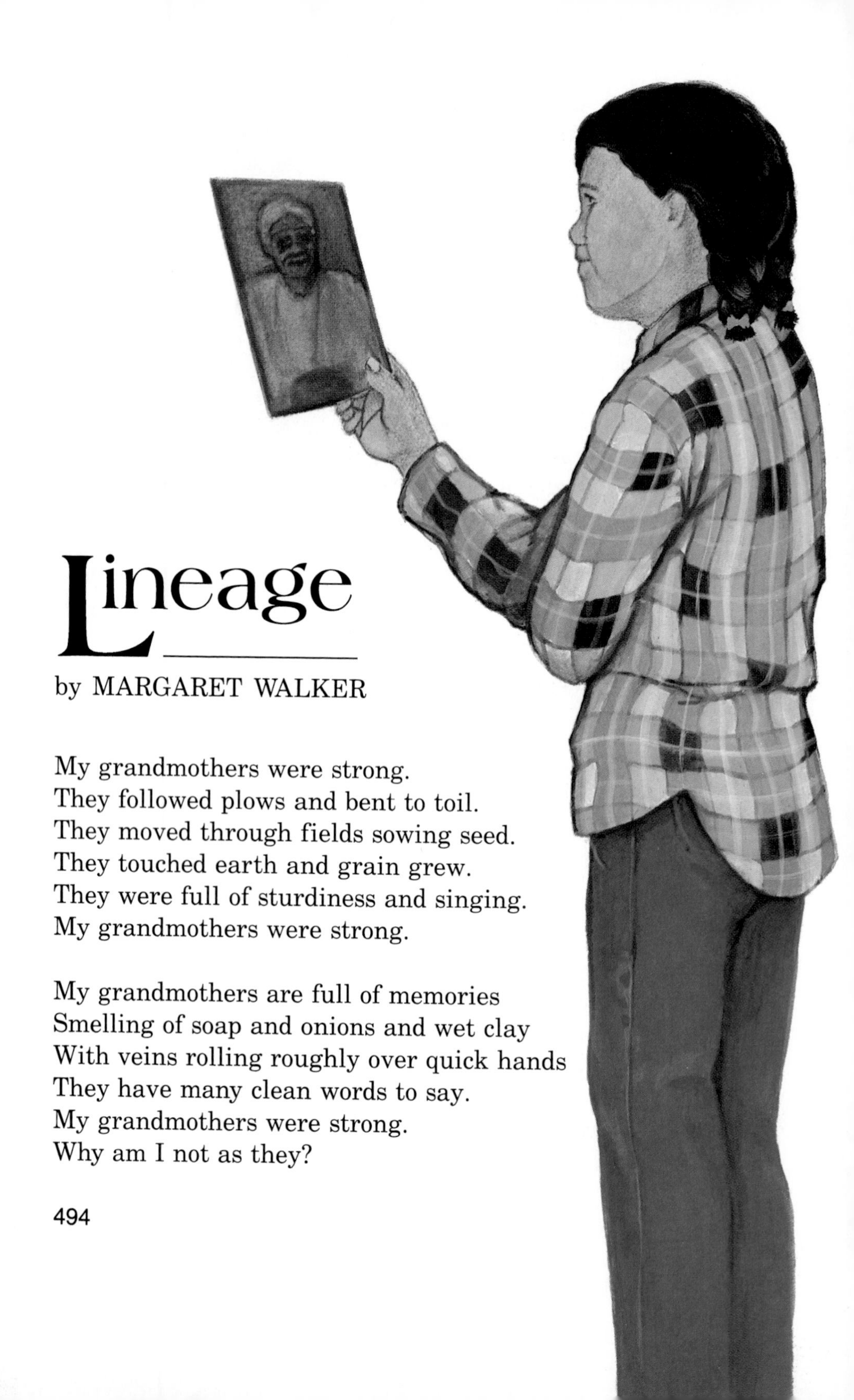

Lineage

by MARGARET WALKER

My grandmothers were strong.
They followed plows and bent to toil.
They moved through fields sowing seed.
They touched earth and grain grew.
They were full of sturdiness and singing.
My grandmothers were strong.

My grandmothers are full of memories
Smelling of soap and onions and wet clay
With veins rolling roughly over quick hands
They have many clean words to say.
My grandmothers were strong.
Why am I not as they?

LEARN NEW WORDS

1. She cried out in **anguish** after she fell from the horse.
2. I didn't have time for a **decent** breakfast, so I was hungry by midmorning.
3. He showed his **gratitude** for the family's hospitality by buying them a present.
4. Even though she failed at first, she had enough **grit** to try again.
5. He reacted with great **indignation** to her obnoxious remarks.
6. With a nod, she **mutely** agreed to join us.
7. He shrugged his shoulders **noncommittally**; he was clearly not going to take sides.
8. The road ran **parallel** to the line of trees.
9. A horse is definitely **superior** to a mule in one way: it is a faster runner.

GET SET TO READ

When you say someone has courage, what does that mean? How does a person become courageous?

Read this story to find out why Larnie decides she must go on even though she is afraid.

Courage Isn't Something You're Born With

by IRENE BENNETT BROWN

It is 1875. Larnie Moran has moved with her mother and father from the city of Leavenworth, Kansas, to a small farm on the vast prairie. One of Larnie's many chores on the new farm is to take care of the milk cow, Bessie.

One morning when Larnie goes to the stream to bring Bessie back, the cow is gone. Bessie has apparently pulled up her stake during the night and wandered off. But the Morans must have that milk cow because Larnie's sickly mother is about to have a baby who will need the cow's milk. Larnie quickly rides out on the family mule, Sunflower, to look for Bessie. She arrives just in time to see Bessie disappear into a large herd of cattle on the trail to Wichita.

Running to catch up with the herd, the mule trips and falls, bringing Larnie down with her. When Larnie wakes up, she sees a young boy running off with her mule. She catches up to him later as the boy is gently soaking the mule's lame foot in the river. But still the boy won't let Larnie get near her mule. The boy's name is Buzzard. He wants to be a cowboy, and he needs the mule to catch up with the cattle herd—the same herd Larnie is after.

Neither Larnie nor Buzzard will give in to the other, and eventually, when it gets dark, both of them fall asleep. The next morning, however, Larnie wakes up first, quietly gets Sunflower, and rides off toward Wichita, leaving behind Buzzard, who is still sleeping.

There was no sound to keep Larnie awake as she traveled, save the soft plodding of her mule's hooves in the dust of the trail, and that was not enough. Her head bobbed drowsily. Would she ever catch up with the herd?

An entire day had passed since she had first learned that Bessie was missing. She wondered why Papa hadn't come to help her in all that time. She could envision Papa, though, telling her, "If you just won't be a scary chicken running for cover at every little thing that happens to you, you can get Bessie by yourself. Courage isn't something you're born with. You learn it. You learn it by facing head-on whatever it is that has you quivering in your boots."

Suddenly, catching sight of movement off the trail on her left, Larnie was wide awake. She saw a grayish-white blur in the grass some twenty yards away. A dog? No, it wasn't a dog; the animal loping along parallel to her was larger than a dog. Its movements were too wildlike for a dog.

A shiver of fear raced along Larnie's spine when another animal, similar to the first but darker in color, appeared from nowhere to join the first. Wolves!

Larnie was unable to take her eyes off them. She was sure the wolves were as long as she was tall. They were frightfully lean and so hungry-looking, and they loped patiently along beside her in the grass at the edge of the cattle trail.

Above the hammering in her chest Larnie could hear her father's voice. She remembered that he had said, when they first bought the farm, that wolves were getting to be a big problem for Kansas farmers with stock. Since so many buffalo had been killed for their hides, there was little left for wild wolves to prey on except horses and cattle. And people? Larnie wondered. Was that why the shaggy creatures hovered there, never stopping or turning aside for long? Did they want her, or was it Sunflower that they were after?

"Wolves like easy prey," she remembered Papa saying, "sick creatures, the old and slow, or the very young." Easy prey. Mixed feelings of guilt and horror began to grow inside Larnie. She lifted the floppy edge of her bonnet and turned for a long look over her shoulder, back across the open prairie. She hoped to see nothing. A soft cry escaped her when she noticed the small figure jogging steadily along in her trail: Buzzard.

Not that she was surprised to see him. Because she had held Sunflower to a walk due to the mule's bad leg, she worried that Buzzard might catch up to her. It was possible he had awakened and set out after her as soon as she left the river behind.

Unwillingly, Larnie admitted to herself that Buzzard had shown kindness to Sunflower. He could have gone on, ridden the lame mule into the ground, if he had chosen. On foot, Buzzard would be easy prey for the wolves.

Yet, Buzzard wanted her mule in the worst way! He would stop at nothing to get it. He couldn't care a whit if she never caught up to the herd and got her cow back. Obviously, she would be foolish to help him.

She must, though. He was a human being. There ought to be two of them, she and Buzzard united against the wolves, should the animals attack. Larnie reined Sunflower about and went back, toward Buzzard.

Her heart beat faster when she realized that the wolves were watching her. They stopped, then turned back with her, keeping pace off to the side. Larnie shuddered and murmured a small prayer, "Keep away, wolves. Stay over there where you are, please."

When she was close enough for him to hear, she called out softly, "Buzzard, wolves. Look." She pointed to the brutes slinking through the grass. "I think we will have a better chance together."

Buzzard nodded. Larnie saw that a dead jackrabbit bobbed from his belt. If they had to, perhaps they could let the wolves have the rabbit, although she hoped they could cook and eat it themselves. She would like an end to this constant gnawing in her middle.

Larnie dismounted. "You ride a while," she told Buzzard with a sigh. His face, under the dirt, looked pale and tired. "You're not to try to take my mule," she added in a firm whisper. "But I will share her. We can take turns, one riding, the other walking, as long as Sunflower limps, and until we reach the cattle herd. I don't have to do this. I probably shouldn't. I'm only slowing myself down from getting my cow. Do you understand? Will you be fair?"

Buzzard nodded mutely, too out of breath to speak aloud. His eyes told Larnie little, except that maybe he was as scared of the wolves as she was.

A long while later, Larnie broke the tense silence. "Do you think they are going to attack us?" she asked Buzzard. For the first time in perhaps a half hour she turned her glance from the loping wolves to the boy astride her mule. He looked more rested now. Color was coming back to his grubby cheeks. He shrugged noncommittally. "Don't know. As long as we stay bunched together, you and me and the mule, and keep moving, maybe not."

"That's what I thought," Larnie said. After a moment she added, "It's strange. You and I aren't exactly friends, but we do need each other."

When they came to Cowskin Creek, they found it steep-banked and nearly empty. Buzzard, and Larnie leading Sunflower, waded into the sluggish brown water and halted on the far bank. "Let's build a fire, cook the rabbit, and give Sunflower a chance to graze," Larnie said wearily.

While Buzzard built the fire and cleaned the rabbit, Larnie stood in the shade of a straggly hackberry shrub with a hand above her eyes to block the dazzle of the afternoon sun so she could look for the wolves. "I don't think the wolves crossed the river," she called to Buzzard after a moment. "I can't see them anywhere. Do you think they'll be coming after us?"

Buzzard grunted, "Reckon we'll see 'em again after I've had me a good dinner. Those wolves know I'm not good eatin' with my ribs stickin' to my backbone."

Larnie smiled in spite of her fear. Her mouth began to water as the rabbit browned and filled the air with a delicious smell.

"I still have two dried apple slices for dessert," she said hopefully, "if—"

"You can have some of my rabbit," Buzzard growled. "You did me a good turn."

"I wonder," Larnie said later, as they ate the blackened rabbit meat while squatting by the fire,

"if wolves are afraid of fire in the daytime. I still haven't seen any sign of them."

Buzzard, busy eating, didn't answer.

Larnie was hungry for talk and, still curious about the boy, she said, "Buzzard, did you run away from home? Does your family know where you are?"

For a long time Buzzard sat mutely, looking at his grimy feet, and then finally directed his answer to them. "My pa has a no-account farm down in Indian Territory. There was him, Ma, and eighteen of us young 'uns. Half of us went hungry every meal. I wanted better—got me the notion of bein' a cowboy. After Pa—after Pa—" Larnie watched, astonished, as a look of terrible hurt came over Buzzard's face. He fell silent, and she knew she mustn't ask him any more now.

Larnie traced a finger in the dust before finally saying, "I used to live in the city—in Leavenworth, Kansas. I miss it so much, my friends and all." Her throat filled up, and it was a moment before she could go on. "You couldn't picture how wonderful it was in Leavenworth," she told Buzzard.

Buzzard did not look very interested. He suddenly got to his feet and stomped out the small fire. "Take another turn ridin'."

Larnie climbed on Sunflower and jiggled the reins to be off.

"The wolves are following again," Buzzard stated later. Larnie looked and spotted the wolves loping just as before to the left of them. "Don't they ever give up?" she cried in anguish.

Ahead of them Larnie could see a gray-green stretch of prairie covered all over with strange small brown mounds of earth, and she temporarily forgot the wolves. "Look! What are they?" she said, pointing to the tiny buff-colored creatures that were staring back at them from atop many of the mounds.

"A prairie-dog town, and a big one!" Buzzard laughed. "Look at that!"

"They're cute," Larnie agreed, delighted. "I think they are barking at us—listen . . . " The shrill barking coming from the watchful prairie dogs

crouching at the entrances to their burrows did sound very much like the barking of dogs. Larnie laughed.

The wolves, whom they had forgotten about, were suddenly there. Larnie watched, frozen in anguish, as they lunged every which way in violent motion through the prairie-dog town. Most of the prairie dogs had disappeared down their burrows, but some were not so fortunate, and the small screams of animal terror tore at Larnie's heart. "Get up!" she yelled at Sunflower. "Go!" She rode away fast and did not look back.

Later, Larnie let Buzzard catch up. She turned Sunflower over for his turn at riding. Walking alongside, she swallowed against the lump in her throat and asked, "Do you think, now that the wolves aren't so hungry, that they will still follow us?"

Buzzard shrugged again noncommittally. Finally he said, "Poor little prairie dogs. But that's the way of it. Every creature's got to eat, and we can thank those little fellows."

They did not see the wolves again. It was late in the afternoon when Buzzard asked Larnie how long she had been away from home. Larnie looked at the sky. "Two days," she answered through a dry throat, hardly able to believe it was true.

"You ought to go back," Buzzard grunted. "You got nothin' left to eat. There's no sign of that herd now. Looks like you aren't goin' to catch up with it. Why don't you go back home?"

Larnie's answer came from the very depths of her being. "I would like to do that more than anything else in the world. But I can't. Not without my cow." She shook her head and her eyes grew blurry. "I thought my papa would catch up with me and help me get Bessie. Something must have happened to keep him from coming to look for me. Or," she sighed, "he is leaving it to me to find Bessie by myself. That's been Papa's way, ever since we bought our farm."

Buzzard threw Larnie a superior look. "Well, sure. A man's got a man's work to do. He can't go botherin' himself about a milk cow."

Larnie looked to see if Buzzard actually meant the foolish thing he had just said. When she saw that he did, she could hardly bring herself to reply. But in a moment she said generously, "I do hope you get to be a cowboy. About Bessie, you don't understand, I guess. She isn't simply a cow. Bessie is the only thing that can keep my mama's baby alive, once it is born. If that isn't important, I don't know what is!" Beginning to feel really angry now, Larnie asked, "Why do you think I am here? Miles from anyplace, starved enough to eat my own arm, scared sick of wolves, and—and you and everything!"

Buzzard looked at Larnie in surprise, a weak smile playing around his mouth. "So maybe you got a little grit in you," he said. "Or maybe you're just stupid."

Larnie halted in her tracks. "That does it! Give me my mule, right now. I'm riding!" She shook with indignation. Buzzard grinned slightly as he turned Sunflower over to her, but Larnie detected an unwillingness in his movements. Was he still planning to steal her mule?

For the next few hours they did not speak. When the haystack appeared ahead and eastward of them, pink and mauve ribbons of sunset streaked the sky in the west.

"Somebody's cut and dried wild prairie hay," Larnie heard Buzzard say from behind her. "Farmer's home place is yonder, likely. I reckon I'll stay the night in that haystack."

"I will, too, I suppose." Larnie said, turning Sunflower toward the haystack. Larnie watched Buzzard make himself a nest in the fragrant golden needles, and then she urged Sunflower around to the other side. "What if there are snakes in this hay?" she called to Buzzard as she dismounted.

There was a moment of silence; then Buzzard grunted, "Just tell 'em to move over."

Larnie glared in Buzzard's direction, carefully examined the hay for herself in the half-light and, feeling uneasy, made ready to spend the night. She tied Sunflower's reins about her wrist and lay thankfully back in the hay. After coming this far, she told herself, she was picking up some grit, and not all on the outside. If Buzzard tried to take the mule from her during the night, she'd fight.

In spite of feeling tired, Larnie could not fall asleep. She lay listening to the night sounds: the cooing of turtledoves, the faraway yelp and howl of a coyote or wolf, the close-by rustlings in the haystack.

Sleep came at last. In a beautiful, vivid dream, strong arms lifted Larnie and carried her to her own soft bed. "Thank you, Papa," she murmured as he tucked her in. She smiled happily.

Next morning, Larnie awakened slowly. Her first thought was that she had become used to the haystack to the point where it seemed actually comfortable. She stirred lazily, her eyes closed, and sniffed the delicious smell of side meat and cornmeal mush cooking. Food cooking? It wasn't a dream, then. Papa had brought her home in the night. Larnie snuggled deeper into her quilt; in another minute she would get up.

"Lucas! John. Come eat. I'll fetch something to the girl."

Larnie shot straight up in bed. Her eyes snapped open; her breathing nearly stopped. She did not know the voice she had just heard. Throwing aside the quilt, she scrambled from the bed to her feet, and stared, wild-eyed. She whirled in a circle, looking at the whitewashed mud walls, the greased-paper window, the crude furniture which was like the furniture at home. But she was not home.

"Stars in Goshen!" the same voice exclaimed behind her, and then there was a loud clatter of dishes on the floor.

Larnie swung around and faced a darkly tanned little prune-faced woman in a faded blue gingham dress. She stared at Larnie as if she were a ghost. A plate of food she had been holding had crashed in a mess on the floor. "I've seen all!" she cried, and clapped a wrinkled brown hand over her mouth.

"Where am I?" Larnie got out. "What's happened?" Seeing her dress on a chair by the bed, Larnie snatched it and pulled it over her head.

The woman shook her head. "It's a miracle. You're on your

feet, standin' up!" A smile warmed her lined face. "Why, your little brother told us the doctor said when the disease hit you, you'd be crippled for life. And look at this!"

"I don't know what this is all about," Larnie protested.

"Of course you know," the woman laughed, with a wave of her hand. "You and your little brother, both of you orphans, were on your way to your uncle's in Wichita."

Larnie gaped, tried to break in, but the woman persisted. "You were tryin' to get there before this rare disease hit you that your doctor's been warnin' you about. Like a bolt of lightning, along about sunset last evening, the disease struck you, your little brother told us. Poor little thing, you. He said you had no control over your legs at all."

Larnie stumbled to the chair and dropped into it. He had done it. Buzzard was somehow behind this awful nightmare. Why? To take off with her mule! "Where is my little brother?" she asked, her face hot, as anger replaced her earlier shock.

"Stars in Goshen, the boy was off by first light this morning, hardly gave me time to fix him a decent breakfast. He said he'd find your uncle and come back with a wagon to get you. I told the little fellow he'd best bring the Wichita doc back with him, too. But, look now." She pointed as Larnie stood up and walked toward her.

"I think I know what—" Larnie began, but the woman interrupted, taking her hand.

"You come on out here to the table, so I can show my boys." She led Larnie into a large main room. Two blond young giants, wearing the rough, patched clothes of prairie farmers, sat at a table in the center of the room. They looked at Larnie in surprise. "Luke, John, would you look? Little girl's not crippled at all this morning."

"I can explain," Larnie tried again. "I'm not crippled and I never was. The boy who told you that just did it to steal my mule."

The men, one hardly more than a boy and handsome, the other lantern-jawed and serious, still looked puzzled. But they began to eat their food again as fast as their forks could lift. The older brother gestured for Larnie to join them at the table. "We're the Hillyers—Ma, Luke, and me. Welcome."

She went, hesitated by an empty chair, then quickly sat down. "My name is Larned Moran. I live southwest of here with my papa and mama on a farm." Larnie closed her eyes, feeling dizzy, and then she looked again at the men's plates. Fried cornmeal mush, fried side meat with gravy, honey and biscuits. Chicken a la king served on rose china back in Leavenworth had never looked this good.

Larnie swallowed and gripped both sides of her chair. A few dried apples and some burned rabbit had not been enough to keep her satisfied for two days.

Her glance fastened on the woman filling the plate, and her hand trembled as she reached for it. Never before in her life had she been so aware of the marvelous textures and flavors of food. The meal seemed superior to anything she had ever had before. She closed her eyes and chewed steadily, gradually easing the aching hole that was her stomach.

Abruptly, it came to Larnie that Ma Hillyer was still talking. "My John found you. Your mule had come snuffling around our door. When John went to catch it, the mule ran from him to the haystack, where he found you, asleep. Your little brother woke up just as John came. Right off he told John you were lame and begged him not to wake you."

Somehow Sunflower's reins had come loose from her wrist. Maybe she had picked them loose in her sleep, and it had resulted in all this, Larnie thought. That Buzzard! He had had the nerve to get a decent night's sleep in a bed before taking off with her mule, after telling his whopping lie. No doubt he had lost some of that nerve before he'd had a chance to eat a really good breakfast. He deserved to be hungry!

When she had finished eating her own meal, Larnie told

the Hillyers the truth—about following the herd to recover her cow Bessie and about Buzzard.

The Hillyers listened, concern, amusement, and shock taking turns in their expressions. "The scamp," Ma Hillyer kept saying with indignation, "the little scamp!"

John looked at Larnie thoughtfully a moment. "I've heard tell of settlers' milk cows being taken into wild beef herds by mistake," he said, stroking his long jaw. "Those folks figured they had no choice but to go without milk. And hope that someday they could buy another cow—it bein' almost impossible to find their cow in a herd of so many."

Larnie nodded, gnawing at her lip. "I know. But I have to have my cow." Then in a quiet voice, Larnie explained why a milk cow was necessary at her home.

Ma Hillyer rocked back in her chair, shaking her gray head. "I wish I was a neighbor to your mama. We womenfolk need each other so in times like this. But the prairie is big. We're scattered miles and miles apart." Her eyes sparkled with tears. "You do have to have a milk cow, honey. I know about this kind of thing. A young teacher back home lost her babe to starvation because she had no milk."

Something tightened in Larnie's chest, and then she saw Ma Hillyer's face brighten. "We'll lend you a horse," the woman announced, "so you can get to that herd faster and get your cow. The trail is straight west of here, a mile."

"She'd best give up and go on home," the older son, John, persisted. "The prairie is no place for a little girl alone. Someday this'll all be peaceful farm country, but that's not the way of it now."

His mother waved him to be silent. "Pay no mind to John," she said. "Go on after your cow, honey. Wouldn't be the first time one of us womenfolk did a thing that couldn't be done. The little bay, Kate," she told her sons, "saddle Kate. On her way home Larnie can leave Kate."

Aglow with gratitude, Larnie found it hard to speak. "Thank you," she said finally, with a direct look into Ma Hillyer's eyes. "I'm going to tell my mama and papa how good you have been to me, when I see them. Thank you for the horse, the bed, breakfast. I was nearly starved. I ate too much. I'm sorry."

"Hush." Ma Hillyer laughed. "We got plenty. We don't know any strangers. There aren't many that come to our door, but those that do are friends. Don't recollect a young girl ever comin' by, though, 'crippled' or otherwise." She looked worried. "What I'd like to do is send my boys to do your errand for you."

Larnie drew her shoulders up. "It's all right." She pulled on her bonnet and tied it under her chin. "I've come this far. The loan of your horse will make things easier."

"That worthless little scamp can't be too far ahead of you, on your mule," Ma Hillyer said with a confidential smile. "You won't have any trouble catchin' up to him on Kate. You give the rascal a thumpin' for tricking us, will you?"

Larnie smiled. "I'll be happy to."

Outside, Luke was throwing a saddle on a sturdy red-brown mare. Larnie stroked the mare's beautiful long face for a moment. "We'll get along fine, won't we, Kate?" she said softly. The mare's ears twitched.

Luke helped her mount. John, standing aside, grunted, "I still say you ought to go on back home," he said, grinning slightly. "But go on after your cow. I hope you get her. Be careful, though."

Ma Hillyer said nothing, but she looked up at Larnie and reached out to pat the girl's knee. Tears welled up in the little woman's eyes, and she scurried back into the sod house.

Larnie's chin trembled in gratitude. "Tell her good-by for me. Thank you again. Good-by."

Larnie does catch up with Buzzard again and has more trouble keeping him from stealing her mule. Read Skitterbrain *by Irene Bennett Brown to find out about the other people Larnie meets as she single-mindedly goes after her runaway milk cow.*

Think About It

1. Why did both Larnie and Buzzard need the mule?
2. Do you think Larnie was foolish to go back for Buzzard when she saw the wolves? Why or why not?
3. How did Buzzard get away with the mule the second time?
4. Why didn't Larnie give up her search for Bessie and go home?
5. In what ways did Ma Hillyer help Larnie?
6. Do you think Larnie ever finds her cow? Write a paragraph giving some reasons for your answer.

LEARN NEW WORDS

1. We inquired about the **barrier** across the road that prevented cars from passing.
2. The mountain **crags** appeared tall and sharp in the distance.
3. A **crescent** smile was painted on the clown's face.
4. They were all **enthusiastic** about their vacation abroad.
5. He grew very thin because of his **meager** diet.
6. A small amount of food was enough to **sustain** them until they could find more.
7. The dog took playful **swipes** at the boy with his paw.
8. You can't stand a cone on its **tapering** end.

GET SET TO READ

Why is following directions important? Name some situations in which paying attention to directions is essential.

Read this story to find out how following directions becomes a matter of life or death to the people of an Inuit village.

The Long Hungry Night

by E. C. FOSTER and SLIM WILLIAMS

Long ago, Nukruk Agorek lived with his family in a small Inuit village. Inuits call wolves "the singing ones," and Nukruk Agorek's name means "The-Friend-of-the-Singing-One." He came to have this name because of his unusual friendship with a young wolf called Agorek.

The story opens at the beginning of the long, sunless winter. The fish have slowly disappeared from the local waters. The whales, seals, and walruses who fed on the fish also have left the area. The villagers grow hungry as there is less and less food for them. Agorek's wolf pack also grows hungry. One day Nukruk Agorek and his village can no longer hear the wolves singing in the distance.

The villagers call a meeting to decide what to do. The oldest member of the village, Ancient Grandmother, addresses the council. She tells them of another harbor far away where they can find food. She remembers when her people went there for food when there was none at home. Ancient Grandmother describes this hidden harbor opening on a different sea.

"A different sea?" a villager considered this slowly.

"How can such a thing be?" another villager asked. "The sea is the sea. Always the same. It is there, below the igloos. How would we find a different sea?"

"Leave the shore," Ancient Grandmother told them. "Leave the shore and go across the tundra."

The villagers crowded around her, hopeful again, interrupting each other with eager

questions. "How far?" "How many sleeps?" Is it open tundra all the way?"

"But, Ancient Grandmother." Nukruk Agorek was finally able to work in his question. "How can we find the sea if we go inland across the tundra?"

"The harbor I speak of opens on another sea, beyond the mountains. Hills shelter the beach, and the harbor is deep and broad. You will find many fish there, I believe, and bear and walrus on the ice."

"My father used to tell of a very bad winter and of traveling a great distance for food," Nukruk Agorek's father, Areega Angun, remembered.

"I, too, have heard such tales," an old man said. "And they are true. The place was very far away, but the people found much food. I never knew where the place was. I was still a child not long out from under my mother's parka. Ancient Grandmother was quite young."

"It is at least a chance," Areega Angun said after a time of silence while the villagers considered the possibilities. "In how many sleeps might we reach this different sea?"

"Five sleeps, I should think," Ancient Grandmother told him.

"Tell us how we must go, Ancient Lady, and we will be on our way," a villager said.

"Leave the sea where the shore curves out above the village, and go straight ahead—two long sleeps, I think; maybe a little longer—until you reach a broad frozen river. Then go upstream. The sleds will move easily over the smooth frozen river. In one long sleep the river should lead you through the first low ridge of hills and onto higher ground. Go on until high frozen falls block the river. Then turn aside. Across the high ground you will see higher crags and bluffs, hard to climb.

"Look for twin peaks, steep and high." Ancient Grandmother held up her hands and brought her fingertips together before her face. "Between them is open passageway, and hidden beyond lies the harbor and the sea."

Hurriedly the villagers made their plans. Half of the men were to go, half were to stay behind with the women and the children, to help bring in the meager daily haul of fish to keep the village from starvation.

Two hunters drove two of the dog teams, and Areega Angun himself drove the third.

Nukruk Agorek wanted to go, and he believed his father really wanted him to go along. But Areega Angun shook his head.

"You are needed here," he said. "Your uncle will need all the help you can give him at the fishing holes until we return."

So Nukruk Agorek stayed behind. He worked hard with his uncle and the other villagers who were left. Nukruk Agorek didn't mind working. What was hard was the waiting.

In two sleeps the teams ran across the crusted snow. Hope strengthened each one's endurance. They stopped just short of exhaustion for both men and dogs and set up snow-block igloos carefully, so they could use them again on the way home.

Before the third sleep they had traveled some distance up the frozen river. Before the fourth they had turned aside below the frozen falls and started toward the mountains. Against the deep dullness of the black sky, the ragged crag tops shone in the light of the swelling crescent moon.

The men halted the dog teams and looked up at the unbroken rock wall stretching before them. It sloped back and very high directly ahead, and jaggedly down a little to each side in the distance.

"I see no peaks," said one of the hunters.

"No passage through," the other frowned.

"It may be the peaks are not so high, nor the passage so plain as Ancient Grandmother sees them with the eyes of her memory."

"Neither were the falls so high as Ancient Grandmother described them," someone said.

They went in as close as they could to the high barrier of rock rising before them. They searched far, walking toward the right, where the moon rises. But they saw no peaks, nor any passage through. So they turned back and searched far to the left, toward the horizon where the moon sets. But by the faint light of the crescent moon they found neither peaks nor passage, nor any foothold to climb the steep bluffs.

The snow swept in and made them turn. Feeling their way along the base of the cliffs, hungry, exhausted, disappointed almost to the point of hopelessness, the hunters stumbled blindly back to the igloo.

The wind whistled across the mountains, bringing with it a smell of the sea. While some of the men unhitched the dog teams, Areega Angun stood still and listened to the screaming gusts.

"What do you hear?" asked one of the hunters.

"Listen, and tell me," Areega Angun answered.

One after another, they stopped and listened. Down the whistling wind, time and again, another sound came from across the cliffs. As the whistle of a wind gust died down, a rising note, high and clear, lingered faintly.

One man herded the dogs into the igloo entrance and hushed them. The others waited, scarcely breathing. Then they all heard it, unmistakably; a triumphant, rising trill. The call of the-singing-ones!

"Wolves!" someone said.

"They sing from the other side of the cliffs," said another.

"The-singing-ones have long been gone from the hunting range behind our village," someone else observed.

"This may be a strange pack. They may always have lived beyond the mountain barrier," another argued.

"That may be," Areega Angun agreed. "But if it is Agorek's pack—and it is true they no longer sing from the tundra near our village—if it is Agorek's pack, they have found the pass to the far side of the cliffs. Let us try calling them."

The next time the wolf song came to them on the wind, Areega Angun sang out an answering call. But the wind was strong, and the cliffs were high. So his call was probably carried away, back toward the frozen river.

One after another the members of the group called, but there were no answers. Finally they crawled into the igloo to rest.

When they woke from that sleep, the wind had quieted. Again they heard the wolf songs from many places. Even far out across the tundra toward the horizon where the moon rose, it seemed, on the near side of the mountains. But nothing to lead them, and never an answer to their tries at calling.

"If Nukruk Agorek were here, he would know if Agorek were singing. He would know if these singing ones are Agorek's pack," one of the men said.

"It is true I considered taking him," Areega Angun answered. "I think now that we must bring Nukruk Agorek here."

So two hunters hitched the strongest dogs to one sled and started back to the village, a long journey of four sleeps.

The ones who stayed went on searching for the peaks and the pass leading to the sea. Most of their meager food supply was gone. What little had remained had been sent with the two hunters to sustain them on the journey back to the village. So half of the men looked for food, while the others continued the search. They managed to bring in enough rabbit and ptarmigan to keep them all alive, but barely.

The two hunters were warmly welcomed back to the village. The women were glad to have news of their menfolk, although it could hardly be called good news.

Nukruk Agorek could scarcely believe his good fortune when the hunters said they had come to take him back with them.

Ancient Grandmother was questioned again about the twin peaks. She insisted they were there. She even took a stick and drew a picture in the snow. Two steep sloping cones, one a little smaller than the other, with a low V-shaped place between them.

"The highest point along the cliffs looks like that, a little," one of the hunters said.

"But there is only one high point, and no passageway. At least none we've been able to find," the other added.

"Go back and look again," Ancient Grandmother instructed them. "There are two peaks. And a pass between."

Nukruk Agorek loved skimming over the snow behind the dogs. He hoped the-singing-ones were Agorek's family; in his excitement he forgot he was hungry, forgot even to feel tired.

Even before they reached the igloo at the base of the mountain, they could hear the wolf song. But very faint and far away.

Later, with his father and the other men, Nukruk Agorek helped search along the base of the rugged cliffs, skirting the tumbled boulders, climbing up over them, searching down between them, always seeking that passage to the sea. And always, he listened.

Sometimes they heard nothing but the wind. Sometimes it seemed the wolf songs echoed all around them in the distance.

But never once was the boy able to recognize that special sound, that special tone, that was Agorek's.

The group no longer looked for the peaks. There simply were no peaks. At least not twin peaks. They sought only a way

to the sea. And always, Nukruk Agorek listened for the wolf songs. He was so eager to hear Agorek's voice that he was unwilling to go back to the igloo when the tired men needed rest.

"Do you think this can be the right place, Father?" he asked Areega Angun again. "Ancient Grandmother says there are *two* peaks."

"The cliffs are irregular and rugged, you can see," Areega Angun answered. "She might mean any two rises, not necessarily that highest point before us."

"But there's only one that looks right," Nukruk Agorek protested.

Areega Angun shook his head. "It is strange," he said. "We followed her directions, and they led us to this place."

"Yes, we followed as she told us," someone agreed. "We crossed the tundra, went upriver to the falls, and turned."

"But—" another hesitated. "I didn't think the falls were very high."

"Ancient Grandmother said *high* falls." Nukruk Agorek backed up that opinion.

"High falls or low, one peak or two, what does it matter?" a practical hunter cut short the discussion. "What we seek is passage to the sea."

"Oh, yes! Passage to the sea." One hunter lifted his head and drew in a deep breath. "I can smell the sea. It must be right there, just beyond the bluffs. But how do we reach it?"

Areega Angun sighed. "I had hoped the-singing-ones might lead us to the pass. But they do not answer our calls. I think the wind blows away our voices, and they do not hear us. I thought I was right to have Nukruk Agorek come from the village." He smiled forlornly at his son. 'But the-singing-ones still do not answer. We have not heard Agorek's call. It is likely these wolves we hear from across the mountain are a strange pack whose regular range lies there."

Again they went along the base of the cliffs, searching toward the horizon of the rising moon. They set up another igloo when they stopped to sleep. Again and again as they went on, Nukruk Agorek called. He called when the-singing-ones were silent; he tried to answer when the wolf songs came across the mountains on the wind. They couldn't know whether his calls carried across the cliffs or were only blown back behind him.

Another sleep went by. Still they found no passage between the rough rock walls slanting steeply up to the ragged cliff tops and the single cone-shaped high point.

One more time of searching, one more sleep, and the men agreed they would have to give it up and go home, empty-handed, defeated. They were growing weak from hunger.

For Nukruk Agorek the misery was threefold. Besides the hunger and the disappointment of failure, which he shared with the group, he felt grief for his wolf friend. Since the last time he had heard Agorek near the village, he had comforted himself with the belief that the-singing-ones had gone off to a better hunting range. Now he was sure they must have starved.

The wind had died down. For the moment, it was almost calm. The-singing-ones across the mountains were silent. Nukruk Agorek thought he'd try one more time, although he knew it was really useless.

While his song billowed out on the clear night air, his father and the others silently cut snow blocks and set up the last igloo, the same deep dejection in each one's heart. They had ceased their searching.

Silence followed the song. Nobody had anything to say. Then, after a long moment, they heard a thin, clear thread of sound, coming from very far away, up toward the source of the river.

Nukruk Agorek answered and ran toward the sound. The waning half-moon cast its shadow out before him. The next call was unmistakably from across the cliffs. Or, more likely, from above them.

The sleds had not been unpacked. The men hitched up the dogs and followed. It was a long way. The hunger-weakened men, eager but weary, plodded after Nukruk Agorek along the base of the tapering bluffs. To their right, some way below, the course of the river paralleled the line of the bluffs.

The boy was well ahead of the men when he saw his friend. The wolf was above him on the flat top of a rock bluff. Nukruk Agorek had come a long way from the high peak that towered over the igloo. The sloping bluffs were much lower here, only two or three times a boy's height, and not quite so rugged.

Agorek skittered back and forth, but he couldn't seem to find a way down. Nukruk Agorek finally found a snow-packed irregularity in the rock wall, hacked toeholds out of the hard snow, and so was able to climb up to the frantic dancing wolf on top of the bluff. As always, the meeting was joyous, a matter of licks, laughter, playful

swipes, and tumblings in the snow.

"Oh, Agorek!" The boy's eyes sparkled as he regarded the handsome animal. "I'm so glad you heard me! I was afraid I might never see you again!"

Agorek hadn't starved. He wasn't even thin, as he had been the last time Nukruk Agorek had seen him. Now he was lean and vigorous and full-furred. The pale brown of his winter coat glistened in the waning light.

The men were still some distance away when one of the wolf pack called, and Agorek, with a swipe of his tongue across the boy's cheek and an enthusiastic bump that bounced him off his feet, bounded off.

Nukruk Agorek watched him running off in the moonlight,

along the top of the bluffs, back in the direction from which he had come. Then he saw the wolf turn left and disappear down the far side of the rocks.

The far side. The sea side! Nukruk Agorek gulped in a quick surprised breath, and began to look around. To his left, snow and rocks blocked his view. But on the right he could look down across the snow-covered, boulder-strewn land all the way to the river. Ahead, that lower land narrowed as the river curved in toward the cliffs. And there, as far ahead as where Agorek had disappeared, he saw the falls! And they were *high,* as Ancient Grandmother had said. Three times as high as the falls where the men had left the river. The water, frozen into long, parallel threads of solid ice as it fell, flashed like fire as the light of the moon, just above the horizon, touched it.

He turned to call to his father and the others coming near below him. Instead, his eyes popped, and his mouth fell open. There before him were the twin peaks. The second peak couldn't be seen from the lower falls, because it was directly behind the other one. Even when they had searched along the base of the first peak they couldn't see it, because it was smaller and a little lower, and the high bluffs from which the first peak rose cut off their view.

Enthusiastically, he scrambled down the steep wall to where the group waited.

"There *are* twin peaks, just as Ancient Grandmother said! The second one is there, *behind* this one!" He pointed beyond the cliff. "The falls *are* high! They're 'way up there!" He pointed upriver. "And Agorek went down on the other side of the bluffs!"

The words tumbled out, and Nukruk Agorek's listeners, men and dogs, were caught up in his excitement.

"We turned off too soon," one of the men said. "Now I understand. We never got to the high falls."

Areega Angun agreed. "Let us go on to the high falls and turn from there, as Ancient Grandmother directed."

Tired as they were, the men from the starving village went on, Nukruk Agorek leading the way to the falls. Ahead, the long rock ledge, over which the falls dropped, blocked their way. But to the left, the cliffs where the wolf had come from tapered down to the level of the land below the falls, leaving a narrow path around the base of the mountain. Beyond, the way lay open for them to follow a gentle rise back toward the pass between the peaks. For a moment they had to stop and marvel. There before them were the twin peaks, similarly cone-shaped, similarly steep. One a little smaller, a little lower than the other—just as Ancient Grandmother had said.

They hurried up the low slope, dogs barking, men puffing and panting.

Two ranges of low mountains came together at the twin peaks. At their feet, in the angle between the ranges, sloping beaches edged a wide frozen bay. The northern lights shone on the glittering ice. All empty and cold. But while they paused, taking in the scene below them, they heard a seal bark. Someone saw a walrus. Far out they saw a white bear lope across the ice floes.

"There *must* be fish below that ice," a hunter said.

"The Ancient Lady spoke truly," another agreed softly. "Here there must be food to sustain us all for a long time."

"We only had to follow Ancient Grandmother's directions," Areega Angun said. "She told us well. But it is not always easy to listen well, even to what is well told."

Think About It

1. Why did the villagers need to find another harbor?
2. What advice did Ancient Grandmother give?
3. Why did two hunters go back to the village to get Nukruk Agorek?
4. How did following directions become a matter of life or death to the villagers?
5. How did Nukruk Agorek find the passage to the sea?
6. What did the fact that animals were present in the new-found bay mean to the hunters?
7. Write a set of directions for someone in your class to follow.

The Mother's Song

translated from the Inuit
by PETER FREUCHEN

It is so still in the house.
There is a calm in the house;
The snowstorm wails out there,
And the dogs are rolled up with snouts under the tail.
My little boy is sleeping on the ledge,
On his back he lies, breathing through his open mouth.
His little stomach is bulging round—
Is it strange if I start to cry with joy?

LEARN NEW WORDS

1. We went on several **expeditions** to explore the land beyond the high mountains.
2. Both of our candidates won their elections by slight **margins**.
3. The mountain climbers had to use **oxygen** masks to breathe when they reached a certain altitude.
4. She filled her backpack with **provisions** for the journey.
5. The police officer put **restraints** around the thief's arms to control him.
6. The rocks made the river a **treacherous** one to canoe.

GET SET TO READ

Some people have triumphed where others have failed. Why do you think some people can do things others cannot?

Read this article to find out about some superhuman achievements.

SUPERHUMAN Achievements

by SHEP STENEMAN

Olympic Feet

Scarlet fever and pneumonia left four-year-old Wilma Rudolph unable to walk properly. Since she didn't want to let her eighteen brothers and sisters always beat her to the dinner table, she kept on doing the exercises that were supposed to make her stronger.

By the time she was in her teens, she had no trouble walking. In fact, she had developed into a terrific runner. At sixteen, she won a bronze medal at the 1956 Olympics as a member of the United States relay team.

Her greatest performance came at the 1960 Olympics in Rome. She won gold medals by wide margins in the 100-meter and 200-meter races. Then she made up the time her slower teammates had lost in the 400-meter relay and went on to win the race for the United States. In 1960, Wilma Rudolph was the world's fastest woman runner.

Across the Ice

Expeditions have been made to the North Pole by dog sled, airplane, airship, submarine, icebreaker, and snowmobile. But no one had ever made this treacherous journey to the polar region alone.

Japanese explorer Naomi Uemura wanted to be the first. He headed north from Canada's Cape Columbia on March 5, 1978, with a team of dogs and a sled loaded with half a ton of provisions. During his journey he was scheduled to receive five airlifts of food and supplies. After that no provisions would be dropped for him, and he would be entirely on his own.

An attacking polar bear nearly put an end to his expedition only four days after it had begun. Uemura had to hack his way through ice ridges nearly thirty feet tall, with temperatures as low as minus thirty-six degrees Fahrenheit. Later, as temperatures rose, cracks in the ice became a problem. Uemura had to reach for ice blocks he could use as bridges across the open water. On April 29, after fifty-five days and six hundred miles of travel, Naomi Uemura reached the North Pole. He had done what few had done before him—and he had done it alone.

Everest Conquered

Mountaineer Edmund Hillary of New Zealand joined a British expedition in 1953 that was headed for the top of Mount Everest, five and a half miles above sea level.

The British team moved into the Himalayan mountains of Nepal in early April. Tenzing Norgay, the greatest of the native Sherpa guides, joined the team. At one point in the expedition, Norgay saved Hillary's life when some thin ice broke under his weight.

As the climb progressed, the going got rougher and some of the climbers couldn't continue. The cold became fierce, and the air was so thin that the climbers had to wear oxygen masks. Even the leader of the expedition had to turn back. Only Tenzing Norgay and Edmund Hillary were able to keep climbing.

Their oxygen was running low on May 29, but Hillary and Norgay made one last attempt to reach the top. They pulled themselves over a huge boulder and climbed across ridges until there was nowhere else to climb. Finally, at 11:30 A.M. that day, Edmund Hillary and Tenzing Norgay reached their goal—the top of the world.

Barrel of Fun

A few fearless souls had shot rapids below Niagara Falls in barrels, but no one had ever survived going over the falls. That didn't stop Anna Taylor. In 1901 the plucky forty-three-year-old schoolteacher decided to challenge the falls. She had a special barrel built that was weighted on the bottom to keep it from tipping over and cushioned on the inside to prevent injuries.

Anna Taylor climbed into the barrel above the Horseshoe Falls on October 24. The barrel was sealed and then pumped full of air. It was then towed out into the rushing current and set free.

The barrel tumbled through swirling, rock-filled waters and hurtled on toward the falls. Thousands of people held their breaths as they saw the barrel plummet over the edge into the churning water below.

It took fifteen minutes for boaters downstream to catch up with the bobbing barrel. They quickly opened it. Anna Taylor had survived!

Her scalp had been cut, and her back and shoulders ached, but she was still lively enough to wave to the crowd. Later she told them not to try to repeat "the foolish thing I have done."

Channel Challenge

The English Channel is a body of water that stretches between England and France. It is twenty-one miles across at its narrowest point. The channel's treacherous currents and icy waters have challenged long-distance swimmers for more than a hundred years. An Englishman named Matthew Webb made the first cross-channel swim in 1875. By 1926, four other men had accomplished the dangerous feat.

In 1925 an eighteen-year-old New Yorker named Gertrude Ederle tried to make the crossing—and failed. A year later on August 6, 1926, she tried again. She was coated with grease to protect her from the cold water. She plunged into the Channel at 7:09 A.M. to begin her long swim to England.

Ederle was only halfway across when a storm began to rage. Fierce currents and high waves threatened to tire her, but she refused to give up.

The crowd waiting on the English coast began to cheer as they saw Ederle in the distance. People waded out to meet her, and wrapped her in blankets as she stumbled to her feet.

Gertrude Ederle was the first woman to swim the English Channel. She had done it in fourteen hours and thirty-one minutes—nearly two hours quicker than the fastest man had done at the time.

Better the Second Time

Cynthia Nicholas, a nineteen-year-old student from Ontario, Canada, swam the English Channel from Dover, England, to the coast of France in 1977 in just under nine hours. Nicholas had enough energy and stamina to turn around and swim back to England. She was the fifth person—and the first woman—to make the round-trip swim. And she did it in the record time of nineteen hours and fifty-five minutes. That was more than ten hours faster than the previous record.

Escape Artist

Master magician Harry Houdini was one of the greatest escape artists of all time. In 1903 Houdini was handcuffed, bound at the legs, and then locked inside an "escape-proof" jail cell. It took him only twenty minutes to undo the restraints and break out.

In London he accepted a challenge to escape from a special pair of handcuffs that had six "pick-proof" locks. Houdini managed to free himself in one hour and ten minutes.

In 1906 he jumped into a river from a Detroit bridge wearing two pairs of handcuffs, and freed himself while still under water. Six years later he made escapes from straitjackets while dangling upside-down high above the ground. No lock, restraint, or cell ever managed to hold the great Houdini.

Think About It

1. Describe one of these accomplishments that you found the most interesting.
2. What do you think all of these superheroes have in common?
3. Why do you think the author called the achievements in this article "superhuman"?
4. Of the achievements in this article, which do you think is most important and which least important? Why?
5. If you could add another superhuman achievement to this article, what would you add and why?
6. Write a paragraph telling why you think some people want to accomplish things that no one has ever done before.

Expository and Narrative Writing

Expository writing is writing that explains something. Most entries in an encyclopedia and chapters in your science book are examples of expository writing. They explain what things are or how things work. In fact, the lesson you are reading is an example of expository writing.

Narrative writing is writing that tells a story. It presents a series of events with a beginning, a middle, and an end. There are two kinds of narrative writing. One is fiction, a story that an author makes up, such as a novel or a short story. The other is nonfiction, a story based on facts. History and biography are examples of nonfiction narrative writing.

Read the two selections below and answer the questions.

A. Pair skating involves certain moves specifically designed for a man and woman skating together. The most spectacular moves are various *lifts,* in which the man picks up his partner and carries her above his head. Pair skaters perform most moves together. The partners may separate at times and perform individually, but the two must maintain the impression that they are performing as a true team.

B. Kitty and Peter Carruthers have two things in common. Both are champion ice skaters. Both are also adopted. Each was born of different parents. Kitty was adopted by Charles and Maureen Carruthers about two years after Peter was. Both Kitty and Peter were strong and fast at an early age.

The Carruthers family lived near a busy Massachusetts highway, so Mr. Carruthers made the children a small ice rink in the yard to give them a safe place to play. Both children enjoyed skating right away. They began to take skating lessons, and soon they decided to skate seriously. This meant hours of practice every day on a real rink, not their little back yard one. It meant long hours of traveling to take part in competitions. Later on, it meant living away from home to be near a good skating teacher. Kitty and Peter moved to Wilmington, Delaware, to train with Ron Ludington. Their parents remained in Massachusetts because of their jobs.

By 1980, Kitty and Peter came in second in the U.S. championships, making them one of three pairs that went to the 1980 Winter Olympics. Kitty and Peter placed fifth in those Olympic Games. That was their first big world competition. In 1981, they won the U.S. championship. They won again in 1982, 1983, 1984. Then in 1984, they won an Olympic silver medal at Sarajevo, Yugoslavia. Now, the brother and sister have something else in common. They have a place in the record books.

1. What is the difference between the ways the selections present information?
2. What form of writing is selection B? What form is A?
3. What kind of writing would you use to explain how to buy a good pair of ice skates? Why?
4. What kind of writing would you use to tell someone's life story? Why?

Alesia

by ELOISE GREENFIELD and ALESIA REVIS

The Accident

It happened in Washington, D.C., on an evening in August. Nine-year-old Alesia was having a good time. She and her friend, Percy, were racing their bikes, flying down the alley to see which one could go faster. When they reached the street, Percy took a quick look for cars and kept going. Alesia was right behind him.

It wasn't a street that was heavily traveled; only a few cars came through now and then. But a car *was* coming that day, at just that very moment, headed straight toward Alesia. She never saw it. When they got her to Providence Hospital, she was pronounced DOA—dead on arrival.

But Alesia didn't die. She's seventeen now and very much alive. This is her story.

Eloise Greenfield

Wednesday, March 19

This morning I woke up and looked at the clock. It said four-thirty. I said, "Uh-uh! This isn't me!" I rolled on over and went back to sleep. And then I overslept.

I get up at five-thirty on school days, because it takes me kind of a long time to do things. So this morning I had to rush to get dressed and eat and have all my books in the book bag by the time the school bus came at eight o'clock.

Daddy had put my wheelchair out front before he went to work, and the bus driver, Mr. Gordon, put it on the bus for me. Then Mrs. Smith, the bus attendant, came to my door and I held on to her arm and walked to the bus.

I can walk some now, if I hold on to a wall or a piece of furniture or somebody's arm, or if I push my wheelchair. I can even walk a little way without holding on to anything. And I remember when I couldn't do any of those things.

But I don't remember getting hit by that car. I only know what people tell me. My friend, Valerie, said she had been on the bike with me for a while, but I had let her off just before I started to race with Percy. I'm so glad she got off, so that she wasn't hurt, too. And I'm glad the doctors

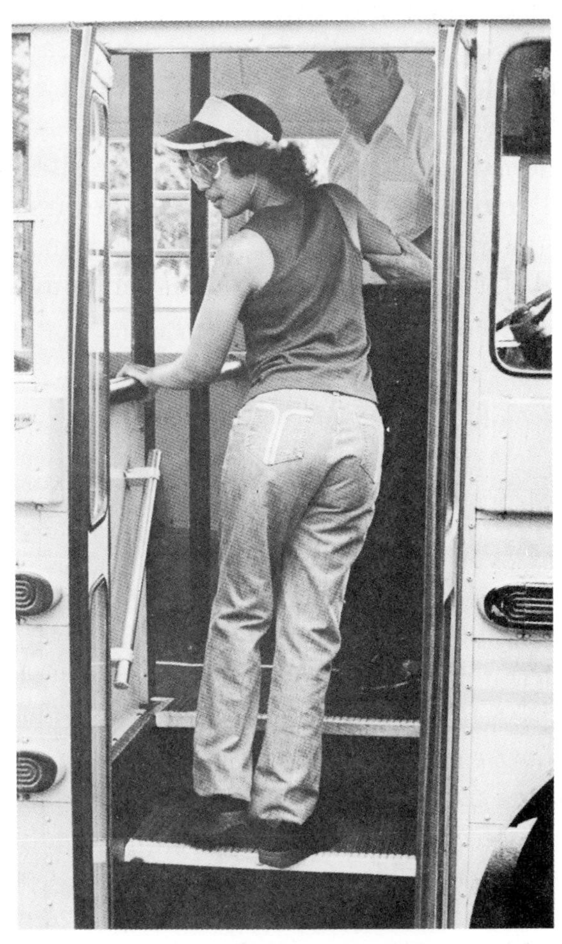

Getting on the bus to go to school isn't easy.

at the hospital didn't give up on me. They kept working on me and then they came out and said to Daddy and Mama, "We've done all we can. It's up to Alesia now."

I was unconscious for five weeks. A lot of people were praying for me, and some of them didn't even know me.

The day I woke up and started to talk, some of the nurses wanted me to surprise Mama. They wanted me to say, "Hi, Mama," when she walked into the room. But Daddy said no; he didn't know if she could stand the shock. So he called her at work and told her the good news. Mama says that after she got off the phone she just said four words—"My child is talking!" And she got out of there and came to the hospital as fast as she could.

I had my tenth birthday party in the hospital, on October 8. I don't remember that, either, but the first time I went back to visit after I got out, something about that hospital smell just struck me. I said, "I remember this smell, yeah, I remember this smell!"

Tuesday, March 25,

Nothing much happened at school today, except work. It's almost time for Easter vacation and I already have homework for over the holidays.

Tomorrow we're supposed to have a party in our Child Study class. That's one of my favorite classes. We're learning all about the unborn baby, and what to do when an infant cries, and how to take care of small children. I like children.

When Mama used to take me grocery shopping in my wheelchair, little children would come up to me and they'd stare and ask a whole lot of questions.

They'd say, "Why are you in that chair?"

I'd say, "Because I can't walk."

"Why can't you walk?"

"Because I got hit by a car."

"Why'd you get hit by a car?"

"Because I rode my bike out in the street."

And then they'd say, "Didn't you know better than to do that?"

I used to get so tickled. But it's not funny when grown folks start staring. You expect it from little children, but not from grown folks. It really gets me when they do it. They could just glance at me and keep on about their business, but they stare so hard, it makes me feel self-conscious.

School can be hard work . . .

Some people move way away from me when they see me in the wheelchair, like they're afraid they might catch my disability. They have disabilities, too—faults and things like that, everybody has them. Mine is just more noticeable, but they don't think about it that way.

A lot of people are nice, though. Everywhere I go, whenever I need help, there's always somebody. One time, Mama took me downtown on the subway, and when we got off, the elevator wasn't working, and there was this long, steep flight of steps we had to go up. A man and a woman came over and helped Mama carry me in the chair all the way up those steps. I don't know what we would have done if they hadn't offered to help.

. . . but it has its lighter moments.

Some people try too hard to help, even when I say I don't need it. Sometimes in a store, I'll be looking at a blouse or something, and somebody will say, "You want me to get that for you?"

I'll say, "No, thank you."

"You want me to push you?"

"No, thank you."

"You want me to . . ."

They just keep asking me, even though I say no. I'm glad when people are nice enough to help me when I need it, but I like to do as many things as I can by myself.

Monday, April 7

Today is Easter Monday. Mama stayed home from work and we went shopping. I need a pair of shoes, the special kind that hook on the brace I wear on my leg. Shopping for brace shoes isn't any fun. They never have any good styles in those shoes. I don't wear my brace too much now, but I used to have to wear it all the time because my left leg was so weak.

I can't wait till I learn to really walk again.

Walking, real walking, is gliding. Just gliding along and not thinking about it. Not having to hold on to anything, or wonder whether your knee is going to give out, or worry about stepping on a rock and losing your balance. Walking fast or slow whenever you want to. And when you want to stop, you just put your foot down and stop, and don't have to think, "Should I stop right here or stop right there?" And you don't need any assistance—not a wheelchair or a crutch or anything or anybody. You just glide.

If anybody asked me what I want most in the whole world, I would say, "To be able to walk again." I daydream about it. I can just see myself walking up the street by myself. Without anyone around me. One time I even went so far as to daydream I was running, and I was just so happy.

Sometimes I start thinking about what I would be doing if I could walk. One day I was coming home from visiting my sister, Alexis, and I thought to myself, "Why aren't you walking?" I got choked up, and when we got home I went to my room and just started crying.

Once when I was feeling really down, I asked Mama how she would feel if I just gave up on everything. Mama said, "If you had given up when you were in the hospital, you wouldn't be here now."

Sunday, April 13

In the evening, Mama and I went outside so I could practice my walking. I have to concentrate on keeping my body straight. And I have to remember to put my foot down the right way. I didn't have on my brace, but I guess I did all right because I didn't fall.

After the accident, when I was learning how to take steps again, I did the same thing a baby does—I crawled first. Ms. Schiller, my physical therapist, taught me to do it. She said it would make my hands and shoulders and knees stronger.

One day I told Mama I wanted to try to walk. I said I thought I could do it, and when Mama asked Ms. Schiller if it would be all right, she said it wouldn't do any harm.

I fell a lot, just like a baby, trying to go from crawling to walking. It was hard on me and hard on Mama, too. She would be holding me, but I was a big girl. I was about twelve, and she couldn't always keep me from falling.

Here I am with my mother and father after church services.

I remember the first time I walked by myself. Alexis was in high school then. She was on the basketball team, and she was going to take me to watch her practice. She went to open the car door for me while I sat in the den; but we were going to be late, so I said to myself, "Let me help her out a little." I decided I would try to walk to the front door.

Nobody else was home, so I had to do it by myself. I was kind of scared, but I wanted to do it, so I pushed up off the arms of my wheelchair and stood up. There wasn't going to be anything for me to hold on to, because if I leaned over to hold the furniture, I would fall. So I put my mind on walking and nothing else, and I just took a step, and another one, and then about three more, and I was at the door of the den. I grabbed the wall and started smiling, I was so happy I'd made it that far.

I stayed there for a minute and got myself together. I was hoping my knee wouldn't give out, so I practiced bending it a little bit, and then I started across the living room. I didn't look in the mirror because I knew it would make me nervous to see myself walking. I looked straight ahead, and I made it to the next wall. Then I had to walk just a few more steps to get to the door—and I did it! I said, "I made it, I made it!"

I looked out to see where Alexis was. She was coming toward the house, and I was glad she was looking down because when she lifted her head to open the door, I was standing there waving at her. She was so surprised. She burst out laughing and gave me a great big hug. She was still smiling when we got to practice, and everyone was asking me, "What's Alexis smiling so much about?" I said, "I walked to the front door all by myself." They all thought it was nice, but I could tell they didn't really understand why we were so happy.

Monday, April 28

I sure can't say that nothing happened at school today. Something *did* happen. I got stuck on the elevator. At first everything was all right. The elevator stopped at the fifth floor to let two teachers off, and Keith and I were going to get off at the seventh, but all of a sudden the elevator stopped between floors. We waited for a minute to see if it would start up again, but it didn't, so we decided to phone for help. Keith made the call; I couldn't reach the phone from my wheelchair. He called the principal's office and told them we were stuck.

It took almost two hours to get us out! If I hadn't had some company, I think I would have been scared, but Keith kept saying funny things. He kept me laughing the whole time.

My brother Allen can make me laugh without even trying hard. He can just say something or do something, and I start cracking up. I don't know how he does that. Allen's younger than I am, but he helps me a lot. He used to go get snacks for me when I couldn't get them for myself. And he would take me outside in the wheelchair and go find my friends to come and talk to me. And when

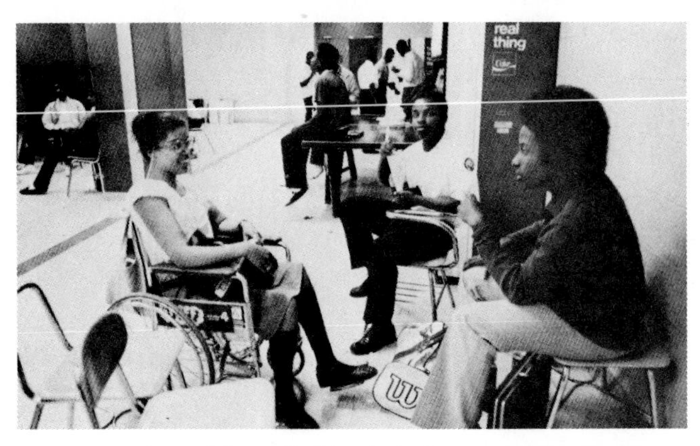

I have fun talking with friends in the recreation room.

I was feeling bad because I wanted to do something I couldn't do, he could almost always make me laugh.

My mouth used to twist a lot to the left whenever I laughed or smiled. I remember one time when I was in the sixth grade I was talking to some of my friends and somebody said something that made me laugh. Tears came to my eyes. I was laughing so hard, and when I tried to say something, my friends started teasing me, laughing at me, because I was talking on the side of my mouth. I stopped laughing and I said, "You shouldn't laugh at that. That's not funny." And they said, "We're sorry."

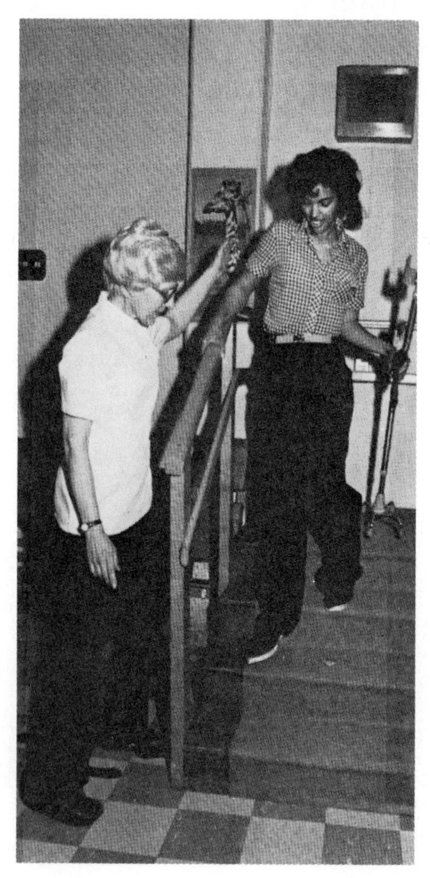

My physical therapist helps me learn to go down steps by myself.

Thursday, May 29

Today I went to see Ms. Schiller, my physical therapist. I had to get my heel cord stretched. That's that cord at the back of your foot that connects your heel to your leg. Mine was tight because I hadn't been to therapy for a while. It was so tight I couldn't put my heel down on the floor. Ms. Schiller pulled it and it hurt so much I felt like crying. But I knew she was trying to help me, so I just stayed pretty much cool. And after she had finished, my heel could touch the floor.

I do exercises every night just before I go to bed. I exercise my arms, and I pull my knee up to my chest ten times, and I cross my right foot over my left and my left foot over my right.

When I was younger, I had to go to the physical therapy room almost every day so Ms. Schiller could help me do all the things I needed to do to improve—sit-ups, rolling on a mat from one end to the other, things like that. I used to love the scooter board. That's a board with four small wheels on it, two in front and two in back. I would lie on my stomach on two scooter boards, because I was kind of tall, and I'd push myself up this ramp, get to the top, turn around, and come flying back down.

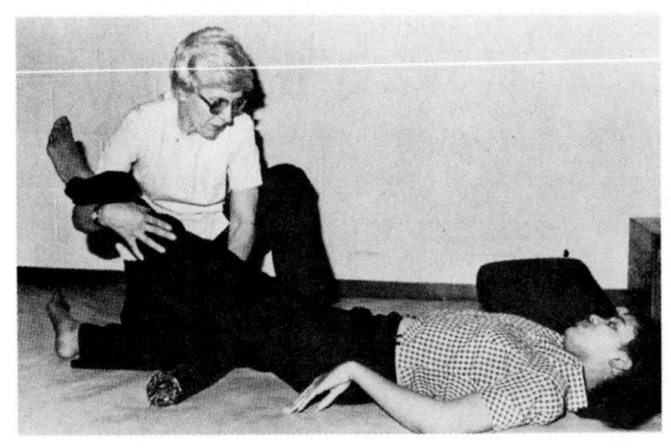

Sometimes therapy hurts, but I have to stretch the muscles in my legs.

Thursday, June 26

Summer is definitely here because I started on my summer job today at the Interstate Commerce Commission. I work in the personnel office. Everybody there is nice. One man is deaf, and he's going to teach me some sign language. I know I won't get bored at work because I have a lot to do. I go on errands, make copies on the copy machine, file charts, and sometimes I answer the phone. When I pick up the phone, I say "Personnel" in a sweet voice.

Wednesday, October 8

Today is my birthday, my eighteenth birthday. At lunch time I was in the activity room, sitting at a table with Thomas, and when I told him it was my birthday, he went out into the middle of the room and said, "Hey y'all, today is Alesia's birthday!" Then he came back to the table and said, "How did you like that?" And in homeroom class, Danny came over and kissed me on the cheek and said, "Happy Birthday!"

This evening, Daddy, Mama, Allen, and Alexis took me out to dinner to celebrate. Then Alexis baked me a cake and everybody sang "Happy Birthday" to me.

I'm a woman now; I'm not a girl anymore. I keep thinking about that. In three years I'll be twenty-one. In less than one year I'll be out of high school. I've just about decided to go to college. If I do, I want to live on campus. I want to get used to being out in the world and see what I can do on my own.

When I was in the accident, after I woke up from the coma and got a little better, I left Providence Hospital and went to the Hospital for Sick Children. I could use my right hand, and I could feed myself, but that was about all I could do on my own. My whole body was so limp that my neck wouldn't even hold my head up. There was this green, collarlike thing on the back of the wheelchair to keep my head from just falling from one side to the other, and Daddy and Mama would turn my head for me so I could look at them when they came to see me.

It helps you to do things when you have people pulling for you. You're pulling for yourself, of course, but then you have other people pulling for you, too. Your family and friends and everybody. You know if you don't try, you let them down. They've gone out of their way trying to please you and everything, and then you just sit there and don't try, it kind of puts them down.

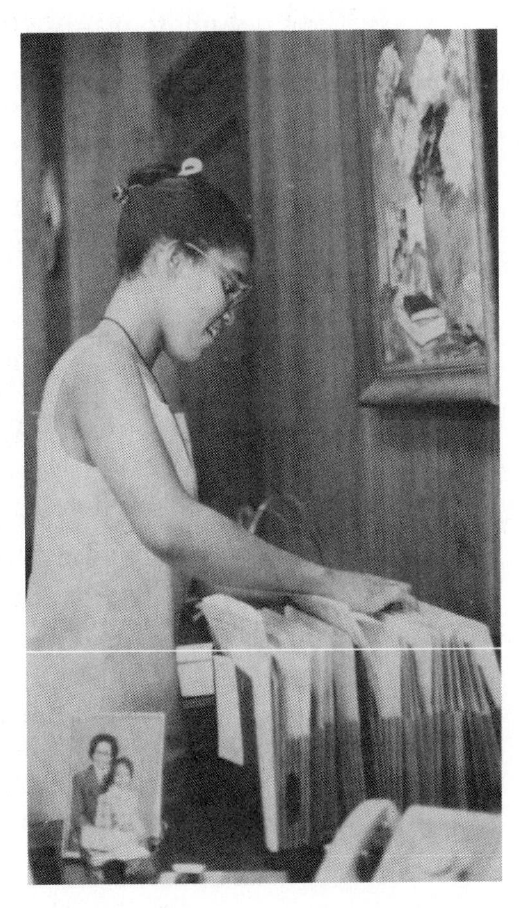

I had a summer job at the Interstate Commerce Commission.

Sometimes I worry about what my future is going to be like. But then, I know that it's going to be all right. When I was in the hospital, unconscious, the doctors told Mama and Daddy that if I lived, I would probably be like a vegetable for the rest of my life. I wouldn't be able to think or care about things or laugh or anything. But it didn't happen that way. I'm not a vegetable; I'm a person. And I'm still here, still living.

READ ON!

Comeback Stars of Pro Sports by Nathan Aaseng. Read about some well-known athletes who beat the odds to make a comeback. Some of them are Jim Plunkett, Virginia Wade, James Silas, and Woody Peoples.

Children of the Wild West by Russell Freedman. Numerous old photographs illustrate this interesting story of what life was like for the children on the Western frontier in the nineteenth century.

Groundhog's Horse by Joyce Rockwood. The horse that belongs to Groundhog, a Cherokee boy, is stolen by a group of Creeks. Groundhog must face the dangers of recovering his horse alone in this exciting adventure story.

The Gift of the Pirate Queen by Patricia Reilly Giff. Grace gets help with her difficulty at school from hearing stories about her Irish ancestor—the courageous pirate queen, Grace O'Malley.

Long Claw: An Arctic Adventure by James Houston. Full of danger and suspense, this story follows an Eskimo brother and sister across the ice in search of food for their family.

Courage, Dana by Susan Beth Pfeffer. Risking her life to save a small child doesn't solve Dana's other problems at school. Read what she learns about another kind of courage.

GLOSSARY

Pronunciation Key

Symbol	Key word	Symbol	Key word
/a/	ham	/o/	fox
/ā/	cane	/ō/	bone
/ä/	father	/ô/	cloth
/är/	star	/ôr/	corn
/ãr/	square	/oi/	oil
/ch/	chair	/ou/	cloud
/e/	bell	/sh/	shoe
/ē/	leaf	/th/	thumb
/ėr/	fern	/TH/	the
/hw/	whale	/u/	duck
/i/	pig	/ū/	cube
/ī/	kite	/ü/	soup
/ir/	beard	/u̇/	put
/ng/	wing	/zh/	usual
		/ə/	*a* in zebra
			e in seven
			i in cabin
			o in wagon
			u in circus

A

a·ban·don (ə ban′ dən), *verb* to desert; to give up. When the mining camp was *abandoned,* it became a ghost town.

a·broad (ə brôd′), *adverb* out of one's country. Jack will be traveling *abroad* in Europe and Asia during summer vacation.

ac·com·pa·ny (ə kum′ pə nē), *verb* **ac·com·pa·nied, ac·com·pa·ny·ing.** to go along with. She was not lonely because her children *accompanied* her on the trip.

ac·cu·rate (ak′ yər it), *adjective* correct; without error. Her costume was *accurate* in every detail.

ac·quire (ə kwīr′), *verb* **ac·quired, ac·quir·ing.** to get; to obtain. By playing tennis every day, Eddy *acquired* a nice tan over the summer.

ac·ti·vate (ak′ tə vāt), *verb* **ac·ti·vat·ed, ac·ti·vat·ing.** to start; to set in motion. The machine is *activated* by pressing a pedal on the floor.

ag·gra·vate (ag′ rə vāt), *verb* **ag·gra·vat·ed, ag·gra·vat·ing. 1.** to make worse. She *aggravated* the injury by playing tennis. **2.** to irritate; to make angry. Your off-key humming is starting to *aggravate* me.

am·a·teur (am′ ə chər *or* am′ ə tər), *noun* one who pursues an art, science, or sport for pleasure rather than pay. Because Sally had sold some pictures, she could not enter the contest for *amateur* photographers.

am·bi·tion (am bish′ ən), *noun* **1.** the desire to attain a goal. Mark had no *ambition* to follow in his dad's footsteps. **2.** the goal that is desired. Susan's *ambition* is to jump two feet farther than she did last year.

a·mid (ə mid′), *preposition* in the middle of. There, *amid* all the weeds in the field, grew a rose.

an·guish (ang′ gwish), *noun* great pain or suffering of mind or body. We understood their *anguish* at losing their home.

an·gu·lar (ang′ gyə lər), *adjective* bony and lean. The tall, thin man with the extremely long arms and legs had an *angular* appearance.

an·tic·i·pate (an tis′ ə pāt), *verb* **an·tic·i·pat·ed, an·tic·i·pat·ing.** to foresee; to expect. We *anticipated* problems that did not occur.

a·pol·o·get·ic (ə pol′ ə jet′ik), *adjective* expressing regret for an offense or fault. Ed was *apologetic* about the cold food because he knew we preferred hot food.

ap·par·ent (ə pãr′ ənt), *adjective* **1.** plain to see. His hunger was *apparent* to us. **2.** seeming. The magician's *apparent* mistake was just a trick. *—adverb* **ap·par·ent·ly.**

ap·pren·tice (ə pren′ tis), *noun* a person who learns a trade by assisting a more experienced worker, often for little or no pay. After two years' hard work under the guidance of an electrician, the *apprentices* became skilled electrical workers.

arc (ärk), *noun* a part of a curved line, especially a part of a circle. The rows of seats formed an *arc* in front of the stage.

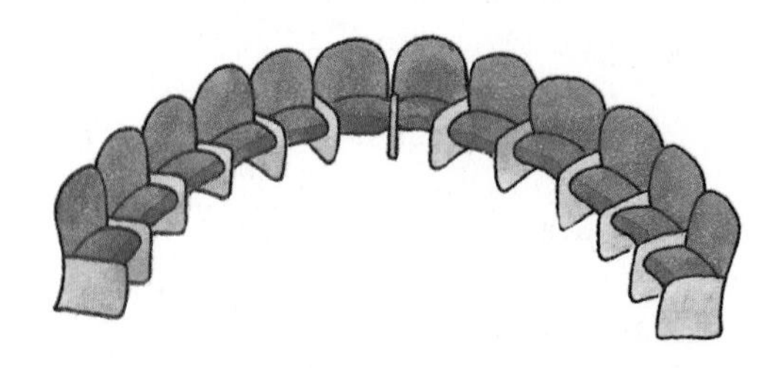

ar·chi·tect (är′ kə tekt), *noun* one who designs buildings and oversees their construction. The *architect* designed a house that is unusually attractive and comfortable.

a·ro·ma (ə rō′ mə), *noun* a pleasant smell. The *aroma* of baking pies makes my mouth water.

as·so·ci·ate (ə sō′ shē āt), *verb* **as·so·ci·at·ed, as·so·ci·at·ing.** to connect different ideas, objects, and people in one's thinking. I always *associate* that actor with Westerns.

a·stound (ə stound'), *verb* to startle; to amaze. Getting a perfect score of 10 is an *astounding* feat in gymnastics.

as·trol·o·ger (ə strol' ə jər), *noun* one who claims to predict the future by studying the positions of the planets and stars. The general would not attack unless his *astrologer* predicted victory.

as·tron·o·mer (ə stron' ə mər), *noun* one who studies the sun, moon, stars, planets, etc. The planet's moon was named by the *astronomer* who discovered it.

au·burn (ô' bərn), *adjective* reddish brown. His hair wasn't really red; it was *auburn.*

au·thor·i·ty (ə thôr' ə tē), *noun, plural* **au·thor·i·ties.** the right and power to order, decide, enforce rules, etc. Although the king has absolute power in his own country, he has no *authority* here.

av·a·lanche (av' ə lanch), *noun* a large mass of ice, snow, earth, etc., that slides down the side of a mountain. The *avalanche* was so large that it blocked the road to the ski resort.

ax·is (ak' sis), *noun, plural* **ax·es** (ak' sēz). an imaginary line through an object around which the object rotates or seems to rotate. A top will always spin better if its weight is spread evenly around its *axis.*

B

bar·ren (băr' ən), *adjective* without vegetation; lifeless. The *barren* moonscape looked like a beautiful but forbidding desert.

bar·ri·cade (băr' ə kād), *verb* **bar·ri·cad·ed, bar·ri·cad·ing.** to close off or block. The huge table was set in front of the door to *barricade* it.

bar·ri·er (băr' ē ər), *noun* something that holds back or stops movement or passage. The moat around the castle was a *barrier* against the enemy.

ba·sis (bā' sis), *noun, plural* **ba·ses** (bā' sēz). foundation; the part on which other parts rest or depend. The *basis* for her poem is an event that took place in her childhood.

beau·ti·fi·ca·tion (bū' tə fə kā' shən), *noun* the act of making beautiful. The *beautification* of the old neighborhood required a great deal of work.

be·tray (bi trā'), *verb* to be disloyal to. Alissa *betrayed* her friend's trust by telling her secret.

soŭp, pŭt; **ch**air; /hw/ **wh**ale; wi**ng; sh**oe; **th**umb; /ᴛʜ/ **the**; /zh/ u**s**ual; /ə/ zebr**a,** sev**e**n, cab**i**n, wag**o**n, circ**u**s

bi·lin·gual (bī ling′ gwəl), *adjective* able to speak and understand two languages well. Pablo, who is *bilingual,* feels equally comfortable talking in Spanish and in English.

C

caf·e·te·ri·a (kaf′ ə tir′ ē ə), *noun* a self-service restaurant or eating place. I usually eat lunch in the school *cafeteria.*

cal·cu·late (kal′ kyə lāt), *verb* **cal·cu·lat·ed, cal·cu·lat·ing.** to figure out; to estimate. Tod studied the road map and *calculated* how far it was to the next town.

cal·i·ber (kal′ ə bər), *noun* degree of worth. By examining the intricate carving, you can see that this sculpture is of a high *caliber.*

cal·loused (kal′ əst), *adjective* having calluses; hardened; toughened. His *calloused* hand was too clumsy to thread any of the small needles.

ca·pa·ble (kā′ pə bəl), *adjective* able; skilled. After years of experience, she is a *capable* sailor. **capable of** having the ability for. She was *capable of* becoming an excellent athlete.

cap·sule (kap′ səl), *noun* **1.** a small container. The medicine comes in *capsules,* in tablets, or in liquid form. **2.** a part of a spacecraft that can be separated from the rest. The spaceship's crew rode in this tiny *capsule.*

ca·reen (kə rēn′), *verb* to swerve sharply. The driverless car *careened* off the road and crashed into a lamppost.

car·pen·try (kär′ pən trē), *noun* the craft of building with wood. A useful skill in *carpentry* is knowing how to use a jigsaw.

cher·ish (chãr′ ish), *verb* to hold dear; to love deeply. He *cherished* the child as if she were his own.

ci·der (sī′ dər), *noun* a drink made from apple juice. We used the apples from our own trees to make *cider* for the party.

co·in·cide (kō′ in sīd′), *verb* **co·in·cid·ed, co·in·cid·ing.** to be in the same place at the same time. The center of the smaller circle *coincides* with the center of the larger one.

col·lide (kə līd′), *verb* **col·lid·ed, col·lid·ing.** to bump together violently; to crash. I *collided* with Janet, and we both dropped our books.

col·li·sion (kə lizh′ ən), *noun* a crash. All the cars involved in the *collision* were badly dented.

co·ma (kō′ mə), *noun* a state of deep unconsciousness caused by injury or disease. Barb has not opened her

h**a**m, c**ā**ne, f**ä**ther, st**är,** squ**ãr**e; b**e**ll, l**ē**af, f**ėr**n; p**i**g, k**ī**te, /ir/ b**ear**d; f**o**x, b**ō**ne, cl**ô**th, c**ô**rn, **oi**l, cl**ou**d; d**u**ck, c**ū**be, eyes or spoken since she went into a *coma.*

co·me·di·an (kə mē′ dē ən), *noun* one who entertains people by making them laugh. The *comedian* made the audience roar with laughter.

com·et (kom′ it), *noun* a mass of material that orbits the sun in a long, oval path, appearing as a bright ball with a cloudy tail. Scientists can often predict when a *comet's* light will be visible from earth.

com·men·tar·y (kom′ ən tãr′ ē), *noun, plural* **com·men·tar·ies.** an explanation; a series of comments. The television news often includes a sports *commentary.*

com·mit·ment (kə mit′ mənt), *noun* a pledge or obligation. The doctor's *commitment* to helping all the patients did not allow her time to rest.

com·mo·tion (kə mō′ shən), *noun* noisy activity; confusion. By the time the police arrived, the *commotion* created by the accident had died down.

com·par·i·son (kəm pãr′ ə sən), *noun* an examination or statement of differences and similarities. The horse is a small animal in *comparison* with the elephant.

com·pas·sion (kəm pash′ ən), *noun* a feeling of sharing the suffering of another, along with a desire to help. The cruel king had no *compassion* for his defeated enemy.

com·pe·ti·tion (kom′ pə tish′ ən), *noun* **1.** a contest; a struggle to win. The swimming *competition* is the first race. **2.** the rivals one struggles against in a contest. The *competition* has won more games than we have.

com·pre·hend (kom′ pri hend′), *verb* to understand. The instructions were so complicated that only an expert could *comprehend* them.

com·pro·mise (kom′ prə mīz), *verb* **com·pro·mised, com·pro·mis·ing.** to settle a disagreement in such a way that each side gives up some of its demands. Rather than spend all day at the zoo, we *compromised* by going to the zoo in the morning and the ball game at night.

con·ceit·ed (kən sē′ tid), *adjective* overly proud of oneself; not modest. There's a difference between being proud of one's achievement and being *conceited* about it.

con·dense (kən dens′), *verb* **con·densed, con·dens·ing.** to put into shortened form. They cut out almost half of our favorite movie when they *condensed* it for television.

con·fi·den·tial (kon′ fə den′ shəl), *adjective* secret; only to be known by a select group. It was supposed to be a *confidential* report, but the newspapers made it known to all.

con·se·quence (kon′ sə kwens), *noun* **1.** an effect or result. The boys had their fun; now they must face the *consequences.* **2.** importance. We didn't think about that incident because it was a matter of no *consequence.*

con·ser·va·tion (kon′ sər vā′ shən), *noun* the careful use and protection of natural resources. Our efforts at *conservation* were successful; we kept the lake from becoming polluted.

con·sist (kən sist′), *verb* to be made up or composed of. A baseball team *consists* of nine different players.

con·sole (kən sōl′), *verb* **con·soled, con·sol·ing.** to comfort in time of grief or disappointment. We praised the winners and *consoled* the losers.

con·spir·a·tor (kən spir′ ə tər), *noun* one who makes secret plans with others. The captured traitor named all of the other *conspirators* to the police.

con·stel·la·tion (kon′ stə lā′ shən), *noun* a group of stars thought to resemble an object, an animal, or a mythological character. The Big Dipper is probably the best-known *constellation* in the sky.

con·sult (kən sult′), *verb* to seek advice from. I *consulted* a banker because I needed information about a loan.

con·ta·gious (kən tā′ jəs), *adjective* easily spread by contact with others; catching. The disease is *contagious,* so the patient was put in a private hospital room.

con·vert (kən vėrt′), *verb* to change in form; to exchange one form for another. She *converted* her dollars to British pounds.

co·or·di·nate (kō ôrd′ ən āt), *verb* **co·or·di·nat·ed, co·or·di·nat·ing.** to work or cause to work together in a common cause. The police and fire departments *coordinated* the teaching of the safety class.

corpse (kôrps), *noun* a dead body, especially a human body. They placed the *corpse* in a coffin.

cos·mic (koz′ mik), *adjective* dealing with the universe as a whole. *Cosmic* travel—travel beyond our solar system—is still far from being a reality.

cove (kōv), *noun* a small, sheltered bay or inlet. The boat raced for the *cove* to find protection from the storm.

crag (krag), *noun* a steep rock that juts out of a cliff or mountain. The climber crept out onto the mountain *crag* to see the view below.

h**a**m, c**ā**ne, f**ä**ther, st**är,** squ**ãr**e; b**e**ll, l**ē**af, f**ėr**n; p**i**g, k**ī**te, /ir/ b**ear**d; f**o**x, b**ō**ne, cl**ô**th, c**ôr**n, **oi**l, cl**ou**d; d**u**ck, c**ū**be,

cra·ter (krā′ tər), *noun* a bowl-shaped dent in the surface of a planet or moon. Years after the war, bomb *craters* could be seen in the field.

cred·it (kred′ it), *verb* to believe or trust. We could hardly *credit* their story because it was so fantastic. **credit with** to think someone has. We *credited* them *with* the ability to think for themselves.

cres·cent (kres′ ənt), *adjective* shaped like the moon as it appears in its first quarter, with curved edges ending in points. We enjoy making *crescent* rolls.

crit·ic (krit′ ik), *noun* a person whose job is to judge and report on the quality of a work of art. While some *critics* liked the play, most did not.

cul·ti·vate (kul′ tə vāt), *verb* **cul·ti·vat·ed, cul·ti·vat·ing.** to prepare and tend soil to grow plants. After they had *cultivated* their fields all summer, they expected a good harvest.

cul·ture (kul′ chər), *noun* the arts, beliefs, customs, etc., created by a certain people at a certain time. The Romans borrowed many ideas and forms of art from Greek *culture.*

D

dal·ly (dal′ ē), *verb* **dal·lied, dal·ly·ing.** to waste time; to dawdle. We *dallied* at the table until the restaurant closed.

de·cent (dē′ sənt), *adjective* **1.** proper; respectable. Cheating is not *decent* behavior. **2.** good enough. We hoped to get a *decent* night's sleep.

de·cep·tion (di sep′ shən), *noun* an act of deceiving or tricking. She caught onto his *deception* and warned everyone not to trust him again.

de·ci·pher (di sī′ fər), *verb* to change from a code to ordinary language. We worked hard to *decipher* the secret message.

de·cree (di krē′), *verb* **de·creed, de·cree·ing.** to make a law or decision by authority. The court *decreed* that no damage had been done.

de·fec·tive (di fek′ tiv), *adjective* faulty; not performing properly. The machine overheated because its fan was *defective.*

den·im (den′ əm), *noun* a heavy cotton cloth often used to make jeans, work clothes, etc. I cut up some old jeans to make patches of *denim.*

de·press (di pres′), *verb* to sadden; to make gloomy. The news of our team's loss *depressed* all of us at school. *—adjective* **de·press·ing.**

de·prive (di prīv′), *verb* **de·prived, de·priv·ing.** to take away from; to keep from having. We were *deprived* of a vacation when the workload became heavy again.

de·ranged (di rānjd′), *adjective* insane; mentally unbalanced. The character went from acting perfectly sane to acting *deranged* in a matter of moments.

des·ti·na·tion (des′ tə nā′ shən), *noun* the place to which a person or thing is going. The train started in Detroit and its *destination* is Chicago.

de·tect (di tekt′), *verb* to discover or notice the existence of something. Did I *detect* a note of anger in his voice?

de·vour (di vour′), *verb* to eat greedily or quickly. The children *devoured* their lunch so they could finish the game.

di·a·logue (dī′ ə lôg), *noun* conversation; in written works, the words spoken by characters. The *dialogue* in this play sounds as natural as everyday conversation.

di·am·e·ter (dī am′ ə tər), *noun* a straight line passing from one side of a circle or sphere through the center to the other side. A basketball hoop has an eighteen-inch *diameter*.

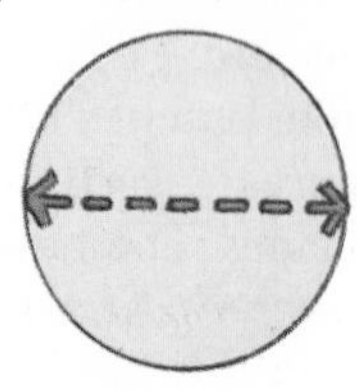

dig·ni·ty (dig′ nə tē), *noun* the condition of being worthy or honorable. Even in his rags, the man had a certain *dignity* about him that had to be admired.

di·min·ish (də min′ ish), *verb* to make or become smaller; to lessen. My huge appetite *diminished* when I saw the high prices on the menu.

dis·grace (dis grās′), *verb* **dis·graced, dis·grac·ing.** to be a cause of shame or dishonor to. We felt they had *disgraced* us with their bad behavior.

dis·in·te·grate (dis in′ te grāt), *verb* **dis·in·te·grat·ed, dis·in·te·grat·ing.** to break up; to fall apart. The paper streamers *disintegrated* in the downpour.

dis·par·ag·ing (dis păr′ ə jing), *adjective* showing a low opinion. She did not like the performance at all and wrote a *disparaging* review.

dis·pute (dis pūt′), *noun* a quarrel or argument. The *dispute* with our neighbors began when their dog began digging holes in our yard.

dis·rupt (dis rupt′), *verb* to throw into confusion or disorder. Our class picnic was *disrupted* by the sudden storm.

dis·solve (di zolv′), *verb* **dis·solved, dis·solv·ing.** to be taken up into a solution. At the bottom of the glass was a spoonful of sugar that had not yet *dissolved*.

dis·tress (dis tres′), *noun* suffering caused by fear, worry, or sickness. Worrying about the lost jewel case caused the man great *distress*.

h**a**m, c**ā**ne, f**ä**ther, st**är,** squ**âr**e; b**e**ll, l**ē**af, f**ėr**n; p**i**g, k**ī**te, /ir/ b**ear**d; f**o**x, b**ō**ne, cl**ô**th, c**ôr**n, **oi**l, cl**ou**d; d**u**ck, c**ū**be,

dis·turb·ance (dis tėr′ bəns), *noun* trouble; something that interrupts, annoys, or causes disorder. Because of *disturbance* from the storm, we couldn't understand the radio broadcast.

di·ver·sion (də vėr′ zhən), *noun* the act of turning something aside or changing its course. The *diversion* of the river brought water to many farms.

di·vert (də vėrt′), *verb* to turn something aside from a path or course. The jet was *diverted* to St. Louis because of the heavy snowstorm.

do·mes·tic (də mes′ tik), *adjective* of the home, household, or family life. Cooking meals is one *domestic* chore I enjoy.

dom·i·nate (dom′ ə nāt), *verb* **dom·i·nat·ed, dom·i·nat·ing.** to control; to have power over. The old elephant *dominated* the herd.

dras·tic (dras′ tik), *adjective* extreme or severe. We knew we had to do something *drastic* to save the pony's life.

drows·y (drou′ zē), *adjective* **drows·i·er, drows·i·est.** sleepy. My eyes kept closing during the lecture because I was *drowsy*.

E

ebb tide (eb′ tīd′), *noun* the tide when it is moving back after reaching its highest point. You can walk on the wet sand along the shore at *ebb tide*.

ec·cen·tric (ek sen′ trik), *adjective* odd; unusual. My *eccentric* uncle has a different hat for every day of the year.

e·con·o·my (i kon′ ə mē), *noun, plural* **e·con·o·mies.** the management of a country's money, goods, and services. Changes in government could lead to improvements in the *economy*.

ed·i·ble (ed′ ə bəl), *adjective* fit to eat. If those mushrooms are not *edible,* they will make you sick.

e·lat·ed (i lā′ tid), *adjective* extremely happy. The parents were *elated* when they learned their boy had been found.

e·lude (i lüd′), *verb* **e·lud·ed, e·lud·ing.** to avoid or escape by cleverness. The base runner could not *elude* the catcher's tag.

em·bod·i·ment (em bod′ ē mənt), *noun* a perfect example. The monster in that movie was the *embodiment* of evil.

em·pha·sis (em′ fə sis), *noun, plural* **em·pha·ses** (em′ fə sēz′). importance. That school places so much *emphasis* on sports that other subjects are neglected.

em·phat·ic (em fat′ ik), *adjective* expressed or performed with force. For an answer, he gave an *emphatic* shake of his head that everyone could see. —*adverb* **em·phat·i·cal·ly.**

en·a·ble (en ā′ bəl), *verb* **en·a·bled, en·a·bling.** to make able; to give the means to do. Television *enabled* us to see the first human step on the moon.

en·gulf (en gulf′), *verb* to make something disappear by surrounding and sweeping over it. After fog *engulfed* our boat, we decided to head back to shore.

en·ter·prise (en′ tər prīz), *noun* an important project or undertaking. That store was the largest business *enterprise* in town.

en·thu·si·as·tic (en thü′ zē as′ tik), *adjective* warmly interested; eager. The audience greeted the well-known performer with *enthusiastic* applause.

en·vi·ron·ment (en vī′ rən mənt), *noun* surroundings and conditions that affect the growth and development of living things. The *environment* of Mars does not permit life to exist there.

e·qua·tor (i kwā′ tər), *noun* an imaginary line around the earth midway between the poles. Temperatures are higher close to the *equator*.

e·rect (i rekt′), *verb* to put up. After the sculpture was built, it was *erected* in front of the post office.

e·rup·tion (i rup′ shən), *noun* a bursting forth. There was an *eruption* of applause when she finished the piece.

es·ca·la·tor (es′ kə lā′ tər), *noun* a moving stairway. When you ride the *escalator* in a large store, you can see the displays on each floor.

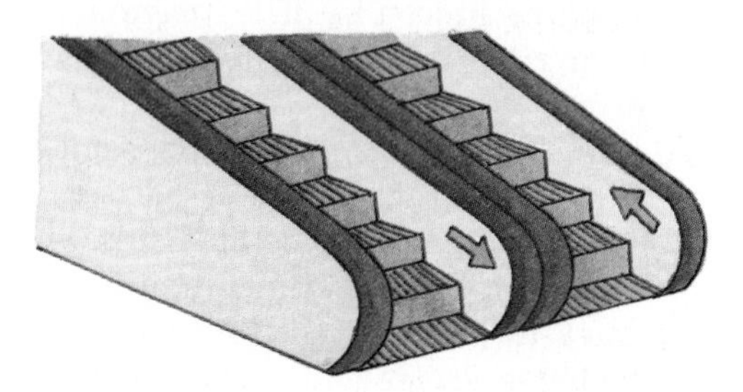

e·vap·o·rate (i vap′ ə rāt′), *verb* **e·vap·o·rat·ed, e·vap·o·rat·ing.** to change to a vapor. The dew *evaporated* in the mid morning sun.

ex·cur·sion (ek skėr′ zhən), *noun* an outing; a brief journey. They went on an all-day *excursion* to the beach.

ex·e·cute (ek′ sə kūt), *verb* **ex·e·cut·ed, ex·e·cut·ing.** to do; to perform. The girl sprang off the board and *executed* the dive perfectly.

ex·ec·u·tive (eg zek′ yə tiv), *noun* one who makes major decisions as to how an organization is run. The most powerful *executives* had a meeting with several employees to discuss plans for a new warehouse.

ex·ert (eg zėrt′), *verb* to put into effect. She *exerted* her influence on the actor and got us free tickets to the play.

ham, cāne, fäther, stär, squãre; bell, lēaf, fėrn; pig, kīte, /ir/ beard; fox, bōne, clôth, côrn, oil, cloud; duck, cūbe,

ex·pe·di·tion (ek′ spə dish′ ən), *noun* a trip made for a definite purpose. I read about the latest scientific *expedition* to the moon.

ex·pose (ek spōz′), *verb* **ex·posed, ex·pos·ing.** to uncover; to lay open to. The plant died because it was left outside and *exposed* to the cold.

ex·tent (ek stent′), *noun* degree; measure. She helped us to the *extent* that she was able to.

ex·ter·mi·na·tion (ek stėr′ mə nā′ shən), *noun* total destruction. The ruthless king ordered the *extermination* of his enemies.

ex·tinc·tion (ek stingk′ shən), *noun* the condition of no longer existing. No one really knows what caused the *extinction* of the dinosaurs.

F

fa·tal (fā′ təl), *adjective* causing death. Two people were killed in the *fatal* accident.

fe·line (fē′ līn), *noun* a cat. Lions, panthers, and tigers are large *felines*.

fes·tive (fes′ tiv), *adjective* joyous; merry. Mr. Brent's laughter is always a sign of a *festive* mood.

flex (fleks), *verb* to bend or cause to bend. When your hand feels stiff, it will help if you *flex* it.

for·lorn (fôr lôrn′), *adjective* wretched or miserable because of neglect. The *forlorn* old farmhouse had been empty for years. —*adverb* **for·lorn·ly.**

fron·tier (frun tir′), *noun* an area within a country that marks the point of furthest settlement. It's hard to believe that a large city like Chicago was once just a small trading post on the American *frontier.*

func·tion (fungk′ shən), *verb* to work; to operate. This car was designed to *function* on land and on water.

G

gang·ster (gang′ stər), *noun* member of an organized group of criminals. The police surrounded the *gangsters* in their hide-out.

gaunt (gônt), *adjective* thin and bony; starved-looking. The clothes of the *gaunt* young man hung loosely on his body.

gen·e·ra·tion (jen′ ə rā′ shən), *noun* a group of people who were born at about the same time, usually in about a thirty-year span. Each *generation* tends to think its music is better than the following generation's.

gen·ius (jē′ nyəs), *noun* **1.** brilliant intelligence. We can thank the *genius* of Edison for the phonograph, the light bulb, and the motion picture. **2.** a person of the highest intelligence. Marie Curie, who made discoveries about radioactivity, was a great scientific *genius.*

ghast·ly (gast′ lē), *adjective* **ghast·li·er, ghast·li·est.** dreadful; terrifying; horrible. The monster in the horror movie was *ghastly.*

grat·i·tude (grat′ ə tüd *or* grat′ ə tūd), *noun* appreciation; thankfulness. We sent flowers to express our *gratitude* for their kindness.

grit (grit), *noun* **1.** tiny bits of sand or stone. The lettuce must be washed carefully to remove dirt and *grit.* **2.** *informal* courage. After the accident, it took a lot of *grit* to continue training as a diver.

H

haugh·ty (hô′ tē), *adjective* **haugh·ti·er, haugh·ti·est.** too proud of oneself and scornful of others. The *haughty* woman refused to speak with anyone but the top manager.

heed (hēd), *verb* to pay attention to. If you don't *heed* your doctor's advice, you will not get well.

her·i·tage (hãr′ ə tij), *noun* something that is passed from one generation to the next. These songs and stories are part of our cultural *heritage.*

her·mit (hėr′ mit), *noun* a person who lives a solitary life apart from others. The *hermit* chased the neighbors off his property.

her·o·ine (hãr′ ō ən), *noun* a woman or girl admired for her bravery or accomplishments. These pioneer women were *heroines* of the old West.

hid·e·ous (hid′ ē əs), *adjective* extremely ugly. For Halloween, Cindy wore a ghost costume and a *hideous* face mask. —*noun* **hid·e·ous·ness.**

hos·pi·tal·i·ty (hos′ pə tal′ ə tē), *noun, plural* **hos·pi·tal·i·ties.** Friendly, generous treatment of visitors. As a sign of *hospitality,* Donald offered all his guests something to eat and drink.

hu·mil·i·ate (hū mil′ ē āt), *verb* **hu·mil·i·at·ed, hu·mil·i·at·ing.** to humble or disgrace. Our team was *humiliated* by a long series of losses.

hur·tle (hėr′ təl), *verb* **hur·tled, hur·tling.** to move or cause to move with violent speed. The runaway horse *hurtled* right into the crowd.

hys·ter·i·cal (hi stãr′ ə kəl), *adjective* excited or frightened beyond control. The children became *hysterical* when they saw the fire trucks in front of their own house.

h**a**m, c**ā**ne, f**ä**ther, st**är,** squ**ãr**e; b**e**ll, l**ē**af, f**ėr**n; p**i**g, k**ī**te, /ir/ b**ear**d; f**o**x, b**ō**ne, cl**ô**th, c**ôr**n, **oi**l, cl**ou**d; d**u**ck, c**ū**be,

I

im·mi·grant (im′ ə grənt), *noun* one who comes to a country to settle there. The Statue of Liberty was the first view of America many *immigrants* had at the end of a long voyage.

im·mor·tal (i môr′ təl), *adjective* **1.** living forever. Is anyone *immortal*? **2.** forever famous or remembered. My favorite author is the *immortal* Mark Twain.

im·pact (im′ pakt), *noun* the action of one body striking against another. Although there wasn't much *impact* when the two cars bumped, our car was quite badly damaged.

im·ply (im plī′), *verb* **im·plied, im·ply·ing.** to suggest; to say indirectly. Ed *implied* the answer without actually saying it.

im·pulse (im′ puls), *noun* a sudden urge. She acted on *impulse* when she leaped onto the stage to speak.

im·pul·sive (im pul′ siv), *adjective* tending to act on a sudden notion rather than after careful thought. Throwing away those perfectly good dishes without thinking about who could use them was an *impulsive* act.

in·con·ven·ient (in′ kən vē′ nyənt), *adjective* bothersome; causing difficulty. It's not *inconvenient* for me to give you a ride because I pass right by your house.

in·dig·na·tion (in′ dig nā′ shən), *noun* anger at something that is bad or unfair. We wrote a letter to express our *indignation* at their carelessness.

in·di·vid·u·al·ly (in′ də vij′ ü ə lē), *adverb* singly; one by one. The police put each witness in a separate room and questioned them *individually*.

in·fin·i·ty (in fin′ ə tē), *noun, plural* **in·fin·i·ties.** a time, space, distance, or quantity that is actually or seemingly endless. Do we see all the stars in the universe, or do they reach out through *infinity*?

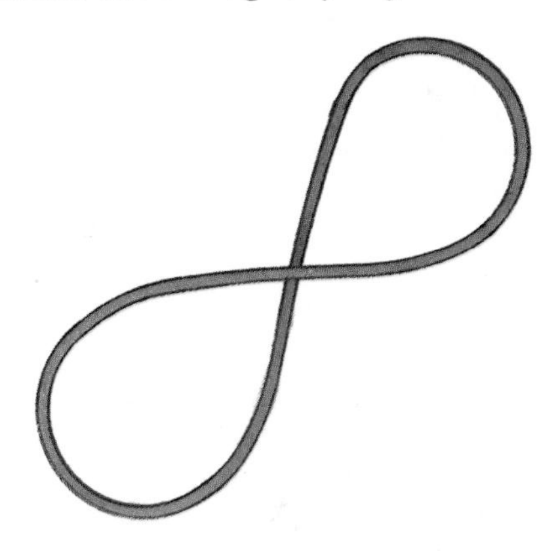

in·gen·ious (in jē′ nyəs), *adjective* clever; creative; original. This *ingenious* invention can slice vegetables or chop nuts in no time at all.

in·ge·nu·i·ty (in′ jə nü′ ə tē *or* in′ jə nū′ ə tē), *noun* inventive skill; cleverness. It took great *ingenuity* to get the machine running again.

in·grat·i·tude (in grat′ ə tüd *or* in grat′ ə tūd), *noun* a lack of thankfulness. Because of Ed's *ingratitude,* they vowed never to help him again.

in·her·it (in hãr′ it), *verb* to receive someone's property after that person dies. When Betty's grandfather died, she *inherited* his paintings.

in·quire (in kwīr′), *verb* **in·quired, in·quir·ing.** to ask. Did you *inquire* about the best way to get to George's house?

in·quis·i·tive (in kwiz′ ə tiv), *adjective* wanting to learn. The *inquisitive* girl always had interesting questions to ask. —*adverb* **in·quis·i·tive·ly.**

in·scrip·tion (in skrip′ shən), *noun* words or letters written, carved, or engraved on a surface. The *inscription* on the trophy had my name misspelled.

in·sight (in′ sīt′), *noun* the ability to understand the true nature of something. Years of experience gave Mike *insight* into the workings of City Hall.

in·tel·li·gent (in tel′ ə jənt), *adjective* capable of learning; smart. Some people believe that dolphins are extremely *intelligent* animals.

in·tense (in tens′), *adjective* very deep, strong, or concentrated. I have an *intense* fear of drowning.

in·ter·sec·tion (in′ tər sek′ shən), *noun* a corner where two or more roads cross. The car should have stopped at the *intersection.*

ir·re·sist·i·ble (ir′ i zis′ tə bəl), *adjective* too strong to be resisted; overpowering. The *irresistible* aroma of baking bread drew me to the kitchen.

i·so·late (ī′ sə lāt), *verb* **i·so·lat·ed, i·so·lat·ing.** to separate and set apart from a group or a whole. Because he had mumps, we had to *isolate* Willie from the other campers.

L

la·ment (lə ment′), *verb* to express sorrow over; to mourn. The entire nation *lamented* its lost leader. —*noun* a sorrowful song or poem. The poet wrote a beautiful *lament* to express her grief at her friend's death.

launch (lônch), *verb* to set into motion with force. The large rockets used to *launch* the spaceship fall off when their fuel is used up.

li·a·ble (lī′ ə bəl), *adjective* unpleasantly likely. Because of her fear of heights, she's *liable* to fall if she climbs too high.

lit·er·al (lit′ ər əl), *adjective* reflecting the exact meaning of a word or group of words. It's funny to think of the *literal* meaning of the phrase "raining cats and dogs."

lob (lob), *verb* **lobbed, lob·bing.** to throw or hit an object in a high arc. I *lobbed* the rock over the high fence and into the lake.

loy·al·ty (loi′ əl tē), *noun, plural* **loy·al·ties.** faithfulness. She would never criticize her family because her *loyalty* to them is so strong.

lush (lush), *adjective* forming a thick, plentiful growth. The rains turned the dry little bushes into *lush* greenery.

lux·u·ri·ous (lug zhůr′ ē əs *or* luk shůr′ ē əs), *adjective* very comfortable and, often, costly. The expensive home was filled with beautiful furniture and *luxurious* carpets.

M

make·shift (māk′ shift′), *adjective* serving as a temporary substitute. We kept dry in a *makeshift* tent made of blankets and rope.

mal·func·tion (mal′ fungk′ shən), *verb* to work improperly or not at all. The accident happened because the brakes *malfunctioned.*

ma·li·cious (mə lish′ əs), *adjective* spiteful. He hurt several people with his *malicious* lies. *—adverb* **ma·li·cious·ly.**

man·u·al (man′ ū əl), *adjective* used by or done with the hands. I have an electric drill and a *manual* drill.

mar·gin (mär′ jən), *noun* a quantity or degree of advantage. She won the first race by just one point and the second race by a wide *margin.*

mas·quer·ade (mas′ kə rād′), *noun* a disguise; a costume. I went to a party where everyone dressed in a clown *masquerade.*

ma·ture (mə chůr′, mə tůr′, *or* mə tyůr′), *verb* **ma·tured, ma·tur·ing.** to reach full mental, physical, or emotional development. It is not good for a child to *mature* too quickly. *—adjective* fully developed. This tree won't bear fruit until it is *mature.*

mea·ger (mē′ gər), *adjective* lacking in quantity; poor. We could earn only a *meager* living at that job.

mech·a·nize (mek′ ə nīz), *verb* **mech·a·nized, mech·a·niz·ing.** to equip with machinery. They *mechanized* the factory and doubled their production. *—adjective* **mech·a·nized.**

mer·chan·dise (mėr′ chən dīz *or* mėr′ chən dīs), *noun* goods sold or bought. Because the *merchandise* was damaged, he sold it for half price.

meth·od (meth′ əd), *noun* a regular way of doing something. My sister washes the car one way, but I prefer to use a different *method.*

mi·grate (mī′ grāt), *verb* **mi·grat·ed, mi·grat·ing.** to move regularly to a different place at a certain time of year. Butterflies, like birds, *migrate* south for the winter.

min·er·al (min′ ər əl), *noun* any natural substance that is not an animal or plant. Salt, gold, quartz, iron, and uranium are all *minerals.*

mock (mok), *verb* to make fun of, often by mimicking. They *mocked* George for wearing big rubber boots when it was hardly even raining.

mod·er·ate (mod′ ər it), *adjective* kept within reasonable bounds; not extreme. The island's *moderate* weather draws tourists all year long.

mod·ule (moj′ ül *or* mod′ ül), *noun* any of the self-contained parts of a spacecraft, each of which is used for a particular job within the mission. The command *module* orbited the moon while waiting for the landing *module* to return.

mol·ten (mōlt′ ən), *adjective* melted. The *molten* steel glowed red in the blast furnace.

mo·nop·o·lize (mə nop′ ə līz), *verb* **mo·nop·o·lized, mo·nop·o·liz·ing.** to have complete control over or use of. She *monopolized* the television, not letting us watch any of our programs.

mo·not·o·nous (mə not′ ən əs), *adjective* always the same; never changing; dull. Because the chore was so *monotonous,* no one in the family wanted to do it. —*adverb* **mo·not·o·nous·ly.**

mourn·er (môr′ nər), *noun* one who grieves, especially over a death. Many of the *mourners* cried as they gathered beside their friend's grave.

mute (mūt), *adjective* silent; not spoken. His *mute* answer was a simple nod of his head. —*adverb* **mute·ly.**

N

non·com·mit·tal (non′ kə mit′ əl), *adjective* not indicating how one feels or what one thinks or plans to do. When we asked them to the party, their answer was *noncommittal.* —*adverb* **non·com·mit·tal·ly.**

O

ob·nox·ious (əb nok′ shəs), *adjective* extremely unpleasant or disagreeable. The *obnoxious* child bullied all the other children constantly.

ham, cāne, fäther, stär, squãre; bell, lēaf, fėrn; pig, kīte, /ir/ beard; fox, bōne, clôth, côrn, oil, cloud; duck, cūbe,

ob·sta·cle (ob′ stə kəl), *noun* something that stands in the way of accomplishing a purpose. We couldn't drive any further because there was an *obstacle* on the road.

o·ver·whelm (ō′ vər hwelm′), *verb* to overpower; to completely overcome. The beauty of the sunrise *overwhelmed* us so that no one said a word.

ox·y·gen (ok′ sə jən), *noun* one of the elements; a colorless, odorless, tasteless gas. There was not enough *oxygen* in the tiny room, so I felt faint.

P

pac·i·fy (pas′ ə fī), *verb* **pac·i·fied, pac·i·fy·ing.** to make quiet and peaceful. The crying baby was *pacified* only when her father picked her up.

pains·tak·ing (pānz′ tā′ king), *adjective* done with great care; thorough. Her prize-winning report was the result of *painstaking* preparation. *—adverb* **pains·tak·ing·ly.**

par·al·lel (păr′ ə lel), *adjective* lying in the same plane but not touching at any point. Railroad tracks are like two *parallel* lines that never cross. *—adverb* in a parallel course. The new highway runs *parallel* to the old road.

par·lor (pär′ lər), *noun* a room in a house used to entertain visitors. Our guests sat in the *parlor* and talked while we prepared dinner.

pas·sion (pash′ ən), *noun* **1.** a powerful or strong feeling. Love and hate are *passions.* **2.** a very strong liking for something. My aunt has a *passion* for all types of music.

pat·ter (pat′ ər), *noun* rapid speech. Bob's a great comedian whose *patter* keeps the audience roaring.

pause (pôz), *verb* **paused, paus·ing.** to wait a moment before continuing an action. We will *pause* here for a rest. *—noun* a moment of waiting. There was a short *pause* while the speaker drank some water.

per·ish (păr′ ish), *verb* to die, especially in a violent way. We found the bodies of many cattle that had *perished* in the flood.

per·pet·u·al (pər pech′ ü əl), *adjective* lasting or seeming to last forever. The waves beating onto the shore seemed to be in *perpetual* motion.

per·son·nel (pėr′ sə nel′), *noun* the entire body of people working for a company or organization. The *personnel* of the company were sorry to hear that the owner had died.

per·suade (pər swād′), *verb* **per·suad·ed, per·suad·ing.** to convince; to win over to one's way of thinking. Although Jean was hesitant, I *persuaded* her to join our group.

so**ü**p, p**u̇**t; **ch**air; /hw/ **wh**ale; wi**ng; sh**oe; **th**umb; /ᴛʜ/ **th**e; /zh/ u**s**ual; /ə/ zebr**a,** sev**e**n, cab**i**n, wag**o**n, circ**u**s

pet·ri·fy (pet′ rə fī), *verb* **pet·ri·fied, pet·ri·fy·ing.** to stun or paralyze with fear. We were *petrified* when we saw the huge animal charging toward us.

phan·tom (fan′ təm), *noun* a ghost or something like a ghost. Even as we stared, the *phantom* disappeared into thin air.

phase (fāz), *noun* a stage of development or growth. Things went well in the first *phase* of the experiment but not in the second *phase.*

pir·ou·ette (pir′ ü et′), *verb* **pir·ou·et·ted, pir·ou·et·ting.** in dancing, a full turn of the body on the toes or the ball of the foot. The ballet dancer *pirouetted* across the stage.

plan·ta·tion (plan tā′ shən), *noun* a large farm tended by many workers, who often live there. Crops such as cotton, sugar cane, and rubber are often grown on *plantations.*

po·di·um (pō′ dē əm), *noun* a raised platform upon which a speaker, orchestra leader, etc., stands. The principal called the graduates to the *podium* to accept their diplomas.

po·ten·tial (pə ten′ shəl), *noun* a possibility for future growth or accomplishment. William has the *potential* to be a great musician, but he must practice much more.

pre·cise (pri sīs′), *adjective* exact. The storekeeper had no change, so we had to give him the *precise* amount. —*adverb* **pre·cise·ly.**

pre·scrip·tion (pri skrip′ shən), *noun* a written instruction from a doctor telling what treatment or medicine a patient should receive. The doctor gave me a much stronger *prescription* for my new eyeglasses.

pre·vi·ous (prē′ vē əs), *adjective* coming before something else; earlier. Our *previous* teacher was very different from the one we have now.

pri·mar·y (prī′ mār′ ē), *adjective* first in order of importance. The rescuers' *primary* goal was to save the people.

prin·ci·ple (prin′ sə pəl), *noun* a basic truth or law. The *principle* of gravity was explained by Isaac Newton.

probe (prōb), *noun* a device that is sent or put into a place to gather information. The *probe* could not find any signs of life on the bottom of the lake. —*verb* **probed, prob·ing.** to search for information. He *probed* the skies with his telescope.

pro·duc·tive (prə duk′ tiv), *adjective* producing or capable of producing large amounts of something. Our garden was so *productive* this summer that we had too many vegetables.

pro·fu·sion (prə fū′ zhən), *noun* a great quantity. The *profusion* of dishes and silverware covered the entire table.

pro·hib·it (prō hib′ it), *verb* to forbid by law or rule. I can't leave the car here because parking is *prohibited* in this area.

pro·ject (prə jekt′), *verb* to send out with force. He *projected* his voice throughout the theater.

pro·pel (prə pel′), *verb* **pro·pelled, pro·pel·ling.** to cause to move. The rockets are *propelled* by two large liquid-oxygen thruster engines.

pro·por·tion (prə pôr′ shən), *noun* the size of one thing compared with that of another. The garage in this drawing is too big in *proportion* to the house.

pros·pec·tor (pros′ pek tər), *noun* one who searches an area for gold or other minerals. The *prospector* took his pick and shovel and went out to search for gold.

pro·vi·sions (prə vizh′ ənz), *plural noun* stocks of food and other necessary supplies. We had enough *provisions* to last through the winter.

R

ral·ly (ral′ ē), *verb* **ral·lied, ral·ly·ing.** to regain strength; to make a comeback. We *rallied* too late and lost the game by one point.

re·al·is·tic (rē′ ə lis′ tik), *adjective* resembling real people or things; lifelike. His paintings are so *realistic* they look like photographs. —*adverb* **re·al·is·ti·cal·ly.**

realm (relm), *noun* kingdom. The king traveled about his *realm* in disguise.

reck·less (rek′ lis), *adjective* without caution; careless. Running into the busy street was a *reckless* thing to do.

rec·og·ni·tion (rek′ əg nish′ ən), *noun* credit or attention for one's accomplishments. I was a fan of hers before she won national *recognition.*

re·en·try (rē en′ trē), *noun, plural* **re·en·tries.** the act of entering again. We awaited the spacecraft's *reentry* into the earth's atmosphere.

ref·u·gee (ref′ yə jē′ *or* ref′ yə jē′), *noun* a person who leaves a country to find safety in another country. Frightened *refugees* poured across the border before the battle began.

soüp, püt; **ch**air; /hw/ **wh**ale; wi**ng; sh**oe; **th**umb; /ᴛʜ/ **th**e; /zh/ u**s**ual; /ə/ zebr**a,** sev**e**n, cab**i**n, wag**o**n, circ**u**s

reg·u·la·tion (reg′ yə lā′ shən), *noun* a law or rule by which something is controlled or directed. You must obey the new traffic *regulations.*

re·in·force (re′ in fôrs′), *verb* **re·in·forced, re·in·forc·ing.** to strengthen with extra support. Dina *reinforced* the glued boards by hammering in some nails.

ren·o·vate (ren′ ə vāt), *verb* **ren·o·vat·ed, ren·o·vat·ing.** to renew; to repair. We *renovated* the old train station and made it into a museum.

re·press (ri pres′), *verb* to hold back; to restrain. I tried to *repress* my yawns throughout his entire speech.

res·ig·na·tion (rez′ ig nā′ shən), *noun* an announcement of one's decision to quit. Mr. Kwan submitted his *resignation* to his boss because he had found a better job.

re·solve (ri zolv′), *verb* **re·solved, re·solv·ing.** to make a firm decision. I *resolved* never to eat there again.

re·sound (ri zound′), *verb* **1.** to sound loudly. Music *resounded* from the speakers. **2.** to be filled with sound. The canyon *resounded* with the cannon's roar.

re·straint (ri strānt′), *noun* something that holds back. If you walk your dog in one of the city parks, you must use a leash as a *restraint.*

re·tire·ment (ri tīr′ mənt), *noun* the act of giving up one's work or career. Since their *retirement,* my parents have finally had time to travel.

re·venge (ri venj′), *noun* an act of getting even or paying back for a wrong. The boy wanted *revenge* for the destruction of his home.

rid·i·cule (rid′ ə kūl), *verb* **rid·i·culed, rid·i·cul·ing.** to make fun of; to laugh at. Some people *ridicule* what they don't understand.

round·a·bout (round′ ə bout′), *adjective* not direct. Her *roundabout* route took twice as long to travel.

row·dy (rou′ dē), *adjective* **row·di·er, row·di·est.** noisy and disorderly. When that large group of people arrived, the quiet party became *rowdy.*

ruth·less (rüth′ lis), *adjective* cruel, merciless. He was kind and generous to his friends but *ruthless* to his enemies.

S

sa·cred (sā′ krid), *adjective* holy. In many religions, there are books or places that are considered *sacred.*

sage (sāj), *adjective* **sag·er, sag·est.** wise; learned. The *sage* judge always chose punishments that were neither too harsh nor too lenient.

scut·tle (skut′ əl), *verb* **scut·tled, scut·tling.** to move with quick little steps. A thousand ants *scuttled* over the sidewalk and into the street.

ser·e·nade (sâr′ ə nād′), *noun* a piece of music performed in honor of someone, especially a sweetheart. The hero in the play sang a *serenade* to his loved one.

sheen (shēn), *noun* shininess; gloss. When I'm sick, my hair loses its *sheen* and becomes dull.

skep·ti·cal (skep′ tə kəl), *adjective* doubting; inclined to disbelieve. Rather than believe the salesman, I was *skeptical* about his claims. — *adverb* **skep·ti·cal·ly.**

slug·gish (slug′ ish), *adjective* slow-moving. The usually *sluggish* stream flowed quickly after the rainstorm.

smirk (smėrk), *verb* to smile in an unpleasant, self-satisfied way. Wendy *smirked* when she discovered she was the only one who could give the answer.

sol·i·tar·y (sol′ ə târ′ ē), *adjective* single; lone. In the middle of the island grew a *solitary* tree.

som·ber (som′ bər), *adjective* gloomy; without joy. I never laugh or smile when I'm in a *somber* mood.

so·phis·ti·cat·ed (sə fis′ tə kā tid), *adjective* having acquired worldly knowledge or refinement. The *sophisticated* couple would eat at only the most elegant restaurants.

spe·cies (spē′ shēz), *noun, plural* **spe·cies.** a group of animals or plants that are of the same kind and able to breed with one another. There are many different *species* of dogs.

spec·trum (spek′ trəm), *noun, plural* **spec·tra** *or* **spec·trums.** the bands of color seen when white light, especially light from the sun, is broken up into parts, as in a rainbow or by a prism. A rainbow shows all the colors of the *spectrum.*

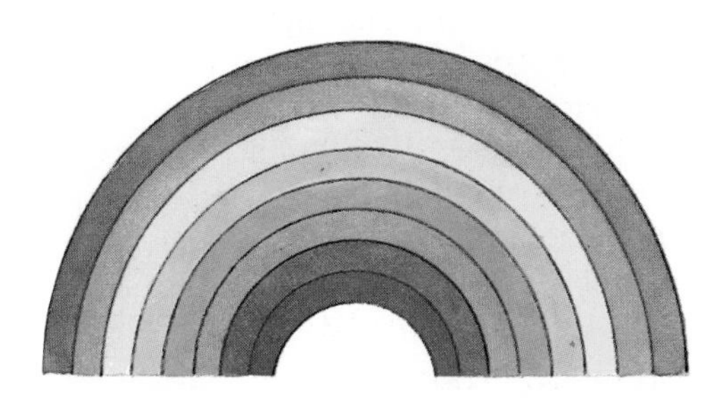

sprint (sprint), *verb* to run at top speed, especially for a short distance. We were able to catch the bus because we *sprinted* to the bus stop.

sta·bil·i·ty (stə bil′ ə tē), *noun, plural* **sta·bil·i·ties.** steadiness; security. The braces on the ladder give it extra *stability.*

stam·i·na (stam′ ə nə), *noun* the ability to resist fatigue; endurance. Shelly can run long distances because she has a lot of *stamina.*

stam·mer (stam′ ər), *verb* to speak in an unsure manner, as from fear or embarrassment. My voice shook so badly that I could barely *stammer* an apology.

sta·ple (stā′ pəl), *adjective* used or needed constantly. Rice is a *staple* part of the diet of about half the people in the world today.

star·tling (stärt′ ling), *adjective* shocking; astonishing. We awoke to the *startling* news that we had not won after all.

steed (stēd), *noun* a riding horse. Each guard rode a beautiful white *steed.*

stride (strīd), *verb* **strode, strid·ing.** to walk with long steps. It took the tall boy very little time to *stride* across the room.

suc·ces·sion (sək sesh′ ən), *noun* the act or process of following in order or sequence. There was a *succession* of small storms before the tornado hit.

suc·ces·sor (sək ses′ ər), *noun* one who follows another in an office or position. Last year's winner will introduce his *successor* this year.

suit·or (sü′ tər), *noun* a man who is courting a woman. To win her favor, her *suitor* sends flowers every day.

sul·len (sul′ ən), *adjective* silent and angry. The *sullen* child ruined her own birthday party by refusing to join in the fun. *—adverb* **sul·len·ly.**

su·perb (sü pėrb′), *adjective* excellent; of superior quality. The ballet last night was *superb,* but tonight it will be even better. *—adverb* **su·perb·ly.**

su·pe·ri·or (sə pir′ ē ər), *adjective* high or higher in quality or ability. Her work was *superior* to that of all the others.

surge (sėrj), *verb* **surged, surg·ing.** to move with increasing power. When the enemy's lines broke, our army *surged* past and overtook them.

sus·tain (sə stān′), *verb* to feed or support; to keep alive. Crops from this land can *sustain* a whole family.

swipe (swīp), *noun* a heavy, sweeping blow. I made three *swipes* at the ball before I actually hit it.

sym·pho·ny (sim′ fə nē), *noun, plural* **sym·pho·nies.** a complex musical work written for many instruments. The *symphony* for full orchestra was so beautiful it sent chills up my spine.

T

ta·per (tā′ pər), *verb* to make or become gradually thinner toward one end. This candle *tapers* to a point.

taut (tôt), *adjective* pulled very tight. The fishing line was so *taut* that I thought I had hooked a whale.

tech·nol·o·gy (tek nol′ ə jē), *noun, plural* **tech·nol·o·gies.** the use of scientific knowledge in industry. Advances in *technology* have created many new kinds of jobs.

tempt (tempt), *verb* to try to persuade a person to do something unwise by making it seem attractive. The idea of having time to myself *tempts* me to skip hockey practice today.

ten·ta·cle (ten′ tə kəl), *noun* one of the thin, flexible parts that extend from the body of an octopus, jellyfish, or other animal. The octopus's *tentacles* were wrapped so tightly around the rock that the diver could not pry them loose.

ter·ror·ize (tãr′ ə rīz), *verb* **ter·ror·ized, ter·ror·iz·ing.** to cause intense, overpowering fear. The hijackers *terrorized* the plane's passengers when they pulled out guns.

terse (tėrs), *adjective* brief and to the point. In some situations, a *terse* "no" can be much kinder than a "maybe."—*adverb* **terse·ly.**

trans·fer (tran sfėr′ *or* tran′ sfėr′), *verb* **trans·ferred, trans·fer·ring.** to move or shift from one person, place, or thing to another. My left arm got tired, so I *transferred* the load to my right arm.

tran·som (tran′ səm), *noun* a small window above a door that can be opened for fresh air. Since our key would not open the door, I had to climb through the *transom.*

treach·er·ous (trech′ ər əs), *adjective* not to be trusted; dangerous. We didn't dare cross the *treacherous* bridge.

triv·i·a (triv′ ē ə), *plural noun* things of little importance. He couldn't remember the important facts because his mind was so full of *trivia.*

tur·bu·lence (tėr′ byə ləns), *noun* violent disturbance. The air *turbulence* was so bad that the pilot flew to another city to land.

U

ul·ti·mate·ly (ul′ tə mit lē), *adverb* eventually; in the end. *Ultimately* the cat got hungry and climbed down on its own.

un·re·li·a·ble (un′ ri lī′ ə bəl), *adjective* unpredictable; not to be depended on. I'm afraid to drive long distances because my car is *unreliable.*

un·ruf·fled (un ruf′ əld), *adjective* calm. The pilot was *unruffled* and confident in spite of the serious storm.

ur·gent (ėr′ jənt), *adjective* needing immediate action or attention. Because of the accident, there is an *urgent* need for blood donors.

u·ten·sil (ū ten′ səl), *noun* any instrument or container used for a practical purpose. I put the forks in with all the other eating *utensils*.

V

vain (vān), *adjective* unsuccessful. We made a *vain* attempt to catch the bus and then decided to take a taxi. **in vain** unsuccessfully. The puppy tried *in vain* to get out of the box.

veg·e·ta·tion (vej′ ə tā′ shən), *noun* plants; plant life. We found it difficult to hike through the dense *vegetation*.

venge·ance (ven′ jəns), *noun* revenge; punishment for wrongdoing. The navy wanted swift *vengeance* against the pirate ship.

ver·ti·cal (vėr′ tə kəl), *adjective* upright; straight up and down. Raise the ladder to a *vertical* position.

vic·tim (vik′ təm), *noun* one who is harmed by another or by an accident or illness. The thief was easily identified by two of his *victims*.

vig·or·ous (vig′ ər əs), *adjective* strong and lively; full of energy. After a *vigorous* workout, I like to sit quietly. —*adverb* **vig·or·ous·ly.**

vis·u·al·ize (vizh′ ü ə līz), *verb* **vis·u·al·ized, vis·u·al·iz·ing.** to form a picture in the mind. I can't *visualize* Dad as a little boy.

viv·id (viv′ id), *adjective* bright and distinct; intense. This artist paints in *vivid* blues that remind me of a bright autumn sky.

W

whee·dle (hwē′ dəl), *verb* **whee·dled, whee·dling.** to try to persuade or to get by pleading or flattery. By using every possible argument, Andy *wheedled* a promise out of him.

wist·ful (wist′ fəl), *adjective* full of yearning or longing. The book is a collection of *wistful* memories of his childhood. —*adverb* **wist·ful·ly.**

Y

yield (yēld), *verb* to produce. This farm *yields* the best crops in the area.